SAY WORD!

CRITICAL PERFORMANCES

Presenting key texts by contemporary theater and performance artists along
with illuminating commentary by leading critics

Series Editors: Una Chaudhuri and Robert Vorlicky
Founding Editors: Lynda Hart and Paul Heritage

Say Word!

Voices from Hip Hop Theater

An Anthology Edited and with an Introduction by Daniel Banks

The University of Michigan Press   ANN ARBOR

For Oni, goddess of word and love

This book may not be reproduced, in whole or in part,
including illustrations, in any form (beyond that copying
permitted by Sections 107 and 108 of the U.S. Copyright
Law and except by reviewers for the public press), without
written permission from the publisher.

Published in the United States of America by
The University of Michigan Press
Manufactured in the United States of America
∞ Printed on acid-free paper

2014   2013   2012   2011   4   3   2   1

*A CIP catalog record for this book is available from the British
Library.*

Library of Congress Cataloging-in-Publication Data

Say word! : voices from hip hop theater : an anthology /
   edited and with an introduction by Daniel Banks.
      p.   cm. — (Critical performances)
   Includes bibliographical references.
   ISBN 978-0-472-07132-6 (cloth : alk. paper) — ISBN
978-0-472-05132-8 (pbk. : alk. paper)
      1. American drama—African American authors.
   2. Experimental drama, American.   I. Banks, Daniel,
1965–
PS628.N4S29   2011
812'.6080896073—dc22   2011000476

Preface: In the Cipher

Hip Hop is a community-based culture and practice. So, as this book is intended for a wide readership, shout out to the artists, activists, scholars, Hip Hop heads, curious allies, producers, directors, actors, students, educators, poets, peacemakers . . . and everyone else. Welcome!

There are many Hip Hops. For this project to look and feel like Hip Hop, multiple voices need to be heard. I am most comfortable in the cipher—the community of artists who stand in a circle and riff, rap, dance, jam, groove, bop, sway, sing, pop, lock, break, and lose themselves in the collective act of creation. True, in a cipher, each member steps forward for a moment to flaunt her talents. But then that individual steps back into the collective circle to support each successive person doing the same. And, in many ciphers, when a person steps forward, he is not alone—participants meet each other in the middle to battle, dialogue, and trade rhymes or dance moves. So, in a cipher, a person never really stands out on her or his own taking credit for the whole thing.

I see my role here like that of a DJ, sampling and remixing the words and ideas of other community members, scholars, and practitioners, back-spinning historical data, extending certain philosophical breakbeats, and beatmatching narrative rhythms. As many of us have been building and growing this form together, we have encountered some of the same experiences. Hopefully this narrative will make the reader want to get up and grab the Hip Hop Theater mic.

I lived in Europe from 1988 to 1992 while Hip Hop music was attaining crossover popularity in the United States. When I returned, I was on the back end of the commercial Hip Hop music tsunami. Like many people, I thought of Hip Hop solely as a music genre. Although familiar with Hip Hop—I was in high school in Boston when "Rapper's Delight" dropped, and I grew up with the disco and funk references sampled in much of Hip Hop music—it was not how I personally identified. Jazz and R&B were my quotable quotes and I supported myself singing this music in Paris and other cities. So I was a little surprised when in 2002 Kamilah Forbes, Artistic Director of the New York City Hip-Hop Theater Festival, called me and asked if any of the shows I had recently directed would be available that year for the Festival. I said something like, "What shows? I don't direct Hip Hop Theater"; and she said, "Yes you do," and cited several pieces.

Was I, in fact, directing Hip Hop Theater, and was I part of this movement? I am part of a generation of artists born under the sign of Hip Hop. My peers, colleagues, and I had a shared collection of cultural influences: we had our artistic juices jump-started when we encountered ntozake shange's choreopoem *for colored girls who have considered suicide when the rainbow is enuf;* we read Imamu Amiri Baraka's plays and waxed poetic about the virtues of all of Lorraine Hansberry's work, not just *A Raisin in the Sun;* we wondered at Marita Bonner's *The Purple Flower* and worshipped the kaleidoscopic nature of Adrienne Kennedy's writing; at one point or other we practically lived at the Nuyorican Poets Café; we could all quote at least a few lines from Pedro Pietri's *Puerto Rican Obituary;* we swooned at poets Sonia, and Nikki, and June, and Audre, and Gwendolyn, and Maya—and dared to call them by first name as if they were some distant older cousin or aunt; we attended Danny Hoch's, Sarah Jones's, and John Leguizamo's shows; and many of us had been taught, mentored, or inspired by Laurie Carlos, Robbie McCauley, Jessica Hagedorn, Sekou Sundiata, Jawole Willa Jo Zollar, Woody King, Rhodessa Jones, Baraka Sele, and other artists who explored and pushed the relationship between form and function in contemporary performance.

Some of us could quote Tupac or Biggie lyrics; some of us could quote Lauryn Hill or Erykah Badu lyrics; we all knew who Gil Scott-Heron was and that the Last Poets rapped long before Sugarhill Gang. We had all seen *Breakin'* and other early Hip Hop movies. The list of this shared archive spread out in front of me like a previously hidden landscape and I had the powerful realization that it was indeed something I belonged to, although I had not realized it. The obstacle to "belonging" had been in believing the music industry hype that Hip Hop was solely a genre of music and not the cultural context of my generation and the confluence of these shared influences.

Over the next several years, I worked closely with the Hip-Hop Theater

Festival, organizing panels and programming and directing several readings, including a workshop of Chadwick Boseman's play *Deep Azure* in the D.C. Festival. At the time I was teaching at the Tisch School of the Arts, so I brought as much of this work onto the New York University campus as possible, inviting students, faculty, and community members from all different fields to come together with a common pursuit—to explore the intersections of art and activism in Hip Hop culture.

Crucial to the early development of Hip Hop Theater as a genre was Project 2050. Developed in 2000 by Roberta Uno at New WORLD Theater, University of Massachusetts, Amherst, this visionary, ten-day summer program for teens drew its name from the year that, at the time, sociologists predicted the majority/minority demographics in the United States would shift in favor of people of color. (The *New York Times* more recently projected that the year will be 2042.) Young people from the local area had an opportunity to explore their own thoughts about society through "future aesthetics," drawing on a Hip Hop Theater framework that incorporated critical and artistic training. Project 2050—of which I was fortunate to be a part in 2001 and 2002—brought together educators from New York and other parts of the country, creating a network of artists and activists in Hip Hop Theater.

In 2004, I began teaching both academic and performance-based courses in Hip Hop Theater at NYU. And thus was born the Hip Hop Theatre Initiative, whose purpose is (1) to integrate theater training with the performance elements and politics of the activist culture of Hip Hop and (2) to train performers to lead arts workshops and facilitate dialogue about the social issues pertaining to Hip Hop. My approach was always as a facilitator/curator, bringing in Hip Hop Theater pioneers as guest teachers. Since then, with the participation of students and other artists, we have led workshops in Ghana, South Africa, Mexico, Italy, Hungary, Israel, Palestine, Azerbaijan, and across the United States. In each setting, the dual focus has been on artistic creation and leadership training, making sure there are youth co-leading and people in place to carry on the work after we leave.

We were not the first to take this kind of program abroad—many Hip Hop artists have worked internationally. Since 2001, Emcee Toni Blackman, dubbed the "Hip-Hop Ambassador" by the U.S. State Department, has traveled to such countries as Senegal, Ghana, Ivory Coast, Swaziland, Botswana, South Africa, Indonesia, Thailand, Taiwan, and the Philippines to give workshops in emceeing, freestyle, and spoken word. Many other artists are now traveling abroad—in 2009, both Universes and Will Power traveled to several countries in Africa. We have all experienced how urgently people around the world desire a new form of theater that connects to the popular and resistant youth culture of Hip Hop.

On a panel at the Hip-Hop Theater Festival in 2002, Philadelphia-based choreographer Rennie Harris, a pioneer of Hip Hop dance theater, said something to the effect of, "I didn't become Hip Hop; Hip Hop happened to me." I took this statement to mean that, as the movement was named and borders were drawn, many of us found ourselves living squarely on that previously unidentified land mass. Back-spin and repeated beat: there are many Hip Hops—geographically, aesthetically, representationally, and politically. Of the many Hip Hops, each one is real and important to the individual who holds her or his version dear. As in any culture, not each member of the culture connects in the same way—but there is, nevertheless, a personal and mysterious connection. My Hip Hop is one that unites people around the globe under the banner of creative collaboration, using all its performance elements as a common vocabulary to share our stories with each other and with our audiences.

Say Word! offers a broad cross-section of stories about the members of Hip Hop culture, their struggles, their art, their lives, their loves, and their communities. I have a direct connection to many of the pieces in this collection, in some cases having directed readings, workshops, or productions. I admire all of the writers for their crafts/wo/manship, vision, and rigorous understanding of how to meld Hip Hop and theater into a genre that can speak to a wide audience. I have seen it happen. I have seen Will Power turn to an elderly European American couple in the front row of the audience for his virtuosic piece *The Gathering* and lovingly reassure them that he was going to look after them and explain things they did not understand. And he did. How could any audience member *not* fall in love with Hip Hop Theater?

Hip Hop Theater has allowed me to find my voice and to work in a genre to which I can bring my multiple selves and multiple theatrical languages, while it offers the inclusive theater utopia for which many performing artists long. My students often tell me that they find themselves in these plays. I wish the same for you.

Acknowledgments

It took more than a village . . . First and foremost, many thanks to Una Chaudhuri and Robert Vorlicky. This book was their brainchild. And also the good people at University of Michigan Press—LeAnn Fields and her crew, Rebecca Mostov, Catherine Cassel, and Scott Ham. I am deeply appreciative. To the students, faculty, and staff in the Department of Undergraduate Drama at the Tisch School of the Arts who helped develop this work, especially Kevin Kuhlke, Awam Amkpa, the *Re/Rites* crew, the Hip Hop Theatre Lab, 5P (Wade Allain-Marcus, Utkarsh Ambudkar, Archie Ekong, Tristan Fuge, Eboni Hogan, Danielle Levanas, Brittany Manor, and Prentice Onayemi), and NYU-in-Ghana. You set this off. Richard Schechner and Paul Carter Harrison for their continued mentorship. Special mention to my art fam and partners in this work: Rha Goddess, Baraka Sele, Abu-Jamal "A.J." Muhammad, Kathy Ervin—you kept love and spirit aloft. Kamilah Forbes, Clyde Valentin, Danny Hoch, and the rest of the HHTF team—your work inspires. Thank you for that first phone call!

To other friends and colleagues fighting the fight not represented in this book—I am constantly inspired and lifted by your energy, talent, and commitment. This collection is a testament to your collaboration and support: Baba Israel, Marc Bamuthi Joseph, Chinaka Hodge, Toni Blackman, Kwikstep and Rockafella, Steve Sapp and Mildred Ruiz, Angela Kariotis, DJ Center, Jerry Gant, Talvin Wilks, Kim Euell, Ella Turenne . . . the list goes on and on. A shout-out to the other folks at NYU without whom this book would not have been possible—Martha Diaz, Marcella Runnell Hall, Richard Chavolla, Allen McFarlane, and the Center for Multicultural Education and Programs. To Adam, Maxinne, and Janine—for always having my back, and to my family for their love and encouragement. Also to Black Theatre Network and Black Theatre Association/ATHE for long supporting this work.

To those who paved the way and have left their love with us—Marvin Simms, Sekou Sundiata, Dr. Barbara Ann Teer, Oni Faida Lampley, Floyd Gaffney, Handy Withers Jr., Esiaba Irobi, and my grandparents. I stand on your shoulders.

My deep gratitude to all the writers and artists for contributing their important work to this collection.

Contents

Introduction: Hip Hop Theater's Ethic of Inclusion

To declare one's own identity is to write the world into existence.
—Éduoard Glissant, *Caribbean Discourse*

The term *Hip Hop Theater* first appeared in the early 1990s when London-based dancer/poet/Emcee Jonzi D used it to describe a blended performance style.[1] Trained in both modern dance at London Contemporary Dance School as well as in Hip Hop dance as a youth growing up in East London, Jonzi D fused the full range of his art practices and did not compartmentalize them, as the traditional dance and theater worlds demanded he do at the time. In the United States, journalist and performer Holly Bass wrote an article for *American Theatre* magazine in 1999, "Blowing Up the Set: What Happens When the Pulse of Hip-Hop Shakes Up the Traditional Stage?" in which she detailed the presence of Hip Hop Theater at that year's National Black Theatre Festival in Winston-Salem, North Carolina. The following year, playwright/actor Eisa Davis published an article for *The Source* magazine, "Hip Hop Theatre: The New Underground." In it, she introduced the performance ensemble Universes and discussed other emerging Hip Hop Theater artists, including Rickerby Hinds, Danny Hoch, Will Power, Sarah Jones, Kamilah Forbes, and Psalmayene 24, most of the same artists featured in Bass's piece. These articles sounded a clarion call for a new form of theater in the United States that was youth driven and proposed a unique alchemy of Hip Hop aesthetics and sociopolitical content.

---

1. A note about spelling: Hip Hop is a global culture, and for many heads, including myself, it is also a nation, one that transcends the geography of birth and embodies its own utopic ideal. I therefore consider Hip Hop to be a proper noun. There are many possible spellings of Hip Hop. While other groups and organizations may choose to spell it with caps, no caps, a hyphen, no hyphen, or as one word, I take my cues from Universal Zulu Nation (the first Hip Hop organization), and from KRS-One's Temple of Hip Hop, both of which have unequivocally situated Hip Hop culture as activist and committed to peace (discussed at greater length in this introduction).

In the summer of 2000, two separate and notable Hip Hop Theater festivals took place, sharing some of the above performers. Jennifer Nelson, Producing Artistic Director of the African Continuum Theatre in Washington, DC, produced the Hip Hop Theater Fest, a continuation of work she began to support and nurture in 1997. Nelson's festival took place at the Kennedy Center and brought audience members that were unfamiliar with Hip Hop and Hip Hop Theater together with audiences that had previously never been to the Kennedy Center. This appeal to multiple constituencies would become a signature of much of the Hip Hop Theater produced by institutional theaters. Later that summer at PS 122 in New York's East Village, Hoch premiered the first New York City Hip Hop Theater Festival (HHTF). And in 2002, Rickerby Hinds (author of *Dreamscape* in this collection) produced the Cali IE (Inland Empire) Hip Hop Theater Festival (a.k.a. Cali Fest) in Riverside, California. Both HHTF and Cali Fest would become the most enduring presenters of the genre in the United States, growing into annual happenings. HHTF would eventually include year-round events in New York with additional festivals in DC, the Bay Area, and Chicago.

Both Hoch and Hinds founded their festivals as ongoing public platform for artists working at the intersection of theater and Hip Hop, most of whom did not have the support of well-funded, institutional U.S. theaters. Hoch describes the mission of HHTF as theater "by, about, and for the hip-hop generations," an intentional sampling of W. E. B. Du Bois's 1926 "Advice to the Krigwa Players Little Theatre" that a "Negro" theater was "About us . . . By us . . . For us . . . Near us . . ." (Du Bois 1926, 134). For several years, Hip Hop Theater pioneer, performer, and playwright Will Power stated that his vision of Hip Hop Theater incorporated one or more of the performance elements of Hip Hop culture in production—that is, DJing, Emceeing, Dance, Writing (aerosol art), and Human Beatboxing. More recently, he has begun to expand that definition to "theater artists exploring their relationship to hip-hop." This definition focuses, as Power says, on "content, form, or content and form" (Power 2008).

At its origin, Hip Hop Theater was born out of this struggle to own both content and form and, in that way, owes a direct debt to the activist and resistant culture of Hip Hop. One of the challenges in discussing Hip Hop is that it is often misunderstood as only a music genre. It is much more—Hip Hop is a global, multiethnic, grassroots youth culture committed to social justice and self-expression through specific modes of performance. Rap is an important part of Hip Hop culture as a form of counterhegemonic art, and there are many thoughtful, conscious artists using the mode of rap to communicate progressive social messages. The music and poetry of these artists unite people by questioning some of the very circumstances that have led other, primarily commercially minded, artists to use rap to express themselves in ways that promote violence, sexism, and material culture (values found in most forms of pop music and in U.S. and global cultures, at large). One of Hip Hop's many contradictions is that some of these very same commercial artists have foundations and use the profits from this nonprogressive work to give back to their communities in significant ways. However, rap, in any form, serves as important cultural critique—both in terms of content and in viewing its ascent inside a larger context of global capitalism. It is an appreciation of Hip Hop as culture and critique that this book engages.

HOW IT CAME TO BE: THE BRONX, THE WEST AND SOUTH BRONX

The Bronx is often cited as the epicenter of the explosion of youth energy that has come to be known as Hip Hop.[2] But, as artist and activist Rha Goddess says, "Lightning can strike many places at the same time." In the 1970s in many urban centers across the country, marginalized youth of color and their allies turned to rap, dance, DJing, aerosol art, and other forms of self-expression to protest the reduction of social services and the bleak post–Civil Rights landscape that met their generation.

From 1973 to 1977, reports Hip Hop historian Jeff Chang, 30,000 fires were set by slumlords in the South Bronx in order to collect insurance money. Here the notorious practices of "redlining" and "planned shrinkage" reduced firefighting services and garbage collection, shutting hospitals and schools, causing widespread unemployment and igniting gang violence.[3] This landscape is captured by Grandmaster Flash and the Furious Five's epic 1982 track "The Message" and is also visible in early Hip Hop films *Style Wars* (1982) and *Wild Style* (1983). Trapped in such an environment, youth in this area had to provide for themselves and be agents of their own freedoms and self-expression.

In response to cuts in municipal services and activities, DJs such as Kool Herc, Grandmaster Flash, Grand Wizard Theodore, and Afrika Bambaataa

---

2. The politics and aesthetics of this movement, especially the West and South Bronx narrative, have been well historicized and theorized by Hip Hop scholars. See, especially, the writings of Raquel Cepeda, Jeff Chang, William Jelani Cobb, Chuck D, Michael Eric Dyson, Juan Flores, Kyra Gaunt, Nelson George, Robin D. G. Kelley, Bakari Kitwana, Mark Anthony Neal, Raquel Z. Rivera, Tricia Rose, Joseph Schloss, and Cristina Véran.

3. "Redlining" is a practice of creating discriminatory cost structures in or denying services to certain urban areas, including, for example, insurance, loans/banking, real estate, health care, and other opportunities that further isolate already poor and/or marginalized groups—see Wallace 1988; Kelley 1997; George 1998.

held parties in parks, schools, and basketball courts. These community gatherings provided outlets of fun and entertainment that had, at their core, friendly competition, improvisation, and self-determination; as such, they also embodied practices that would become central to the culture. Each of these DJs contributed to the innovation of the form and the development of the movement as a performative, sociopolitical culture whose aesthetics helped members to "write themselves into existence" in a city that, by all accounts, did not much want to hear about, know about, or see them.

With the founding in 1973 of the Universal Zulu Nation, Bambaataa, a former Black Spade gang member, created a space where young men and women known as the Zulu Kings and Queens could "battle," using their creative skills and imagination rather than lethal weapons. Since then, committed artist-activists have opened Zulu Nation chapters around the world, spreading Hip Hop's message of peace and collaboration. The works presented in this book demonstrate how a theatrical movement has grown out of the politics and aesthetics of Hip Hop.

As described by Bambaataa, Hip Hop culture is about inclusion:

> Hip Hop means the whole culture of the movement . . . when you talk about rap . . . Rap is part of the hip hop culture . . . The emceeing . . . The djaying is part of the hip hop culture. The dressing, the languages are all part of the hip hop culture. The break dancing, the b-boys, b-girls . . . how you act, walk, look, talk are all part of hip hop culture. . . and the music is colorless. Hip Hop music is made from Black, brown, yellow, red, white . . . whatever music that gives you that grunt . . . that funk, that groove, or that beat . . . It's all part of hip hop. (qtd. in Davey D 1996)

Hip Hop also recognizes the ability—as well as the frequent necessity for its members—to hold seeming contradictions in the same space. Hip Hop heads know that multiple truths can coexist harmoniously and do not need to be "resolved." Hip Hop playwright and theater producer Claudia Alick explains, "If you are Hip Hop, you have the ability to belong or exist in several different places at once and be many different things at the same time . . . and structure and content, they mirror each other" (qtd. in Banks 2008). To listen to a DJ set carefully or watch a b-boy's or b-girl's moves is to see all these elements at play—the body and technology in synch, in contrary motion, one nation, as it were, "under a groove." Hip Hop is competitive and loving; spiritual and material; loud in-your-face and poetic and deep; contemporary, cutting-edge, up-to-the-minute, and connected to the ancestor-elder-predecessor artist-warriors from which we came.

Legendary Emcee and activist KRS-One, the founder of the Temple of

Hip Hop, adds, "Hiphoppas are judged by the *content of their character* and skill, not by the color of their skin, their choice of religion, or social status. Since the early days of our cultural existence, our moral pillars have been peace, love, unity, and happiness" (KRS-One 2003, 181). Known as "the Teacher" in Hip Hop circles, KRS-One has, in what he calls the "Refinitions," added on to the four "original" elements of Hip Hop, plus the oft-called fifth element, Human Beatboxing. His additions include Street Knowledge, Street Fashion, Street Language, and Street Entrepreneurialism. Today Hip Hop Theater and Hip Hop Pedagogy are also often cited by members as further cornerstones to the culture.

KRS-One's manifesto, sampling Martin Luther King, reflects Hip Hop's connection to a history of antiracism and social justice work and how its aesthetics engage this history. This is the Hip Hop that signed a Declaration of Peace at the United Nations on May 16, 2001, organized by the Temple of Hip Hop (KRS-One 2003, 203). This Hip Hop also holds action and education summits around the globe, works with youth for empowerment and community development, stages protests against misogynistic lyrics, and holds dialogues about fatherhood and workshops to end domestic violence against women. Indeed, as Eden Jeffries, a Hip Hop activist and documentarian points out echoing the above point about seeming contradictions, "Hip Hop is unique for its ability to allow competition and inclusivity to coexist—and it's this that fosters its progression and constant reinventing of itself" (Jeffries 2008). Hip Hop is a big poetry, dance, music, rhythm, loud, silent, protest, peacemaking, political, jack your body, swing, jazz, funk, rock, rap, beatboxing, DJing, graffing, meditational, Zen, Kemetic, Judeo-Muslim-Christian, Hindu, Buddhist, Black, White, Caribbean, Latina, Latino, Asian, Indigenous, male, female, transgender cacophony that, wherever you see it, is about the present moment. Whether it is spinning on your back or head or rapping the vote, Hip Hop is immediate, necessary, always changing, and consistent in its struggle for recognition, respect, and inclusion.

SOMETHING FROM SOMETHING

Theorists and heads alike often say of Hip Hop that it is "something from nothing." While this phrase may be accurate from the perspective of financial capital, what it does not take into account is the deep level of cultural capital and knowledge that forms the basis of Hip Hop. For example, Grandmaster Flash, who attended a technical high school, flipped his skills as an electrician and used them to invent styles of DJing that have transformed the way the world listens to music. Writers in the Bronx employed multiple literacies in memorizing train and patrol schedules and routes; displayed rigorous, almost military devotion in practicing their skills (as do all Hip Hop artists); and relied on team-building and strategic-planning skills to reach a global audience. DJs invented whole systems of spinning and remixing vinyl, while tapping into the electricity of a municipality that provided little recreation and radically reduced social services.

Another one of Hip Hop's revolutionary practices is versioning and re-naming—taking ownership of a deprivileged situation through an act of self-determination, as well as the ongoing creation of Hip Hop vernacular. KRS-One's reframing of "the elements" as "Refinitions" acknowledges the multiple institutions of knowledge and cultural production that Hip Hop validates and out of which it self-defines. In so doing, he challenged the institutionalization of the elements (a very Hip Hop thing to do), especially as they were co-opted by commercial interests, and simultaneously created his own resistant speech-act by inventing a new term. Even *KRS-One* as an appellation was a recuperation of the name *Krishna* with which residents of the New York City men's shelter where he lived taunted him because of his interest in the *Bhagavad Gita* and Hare Krishna. He flipped this act of aggression and began tagging *KRS* and, later, the anagram *KRS-One*. These innovations should be considered as forms of cultural capital that need to be enumerated and validated so that Hip Hop is not obscured in the history books as a brief, accidental moment in U.S. or world history.

Hip Hop is, rather, "something from something." There was never "nothing" there. However, by removing material resources in places like the Bronx, those in power created conditions (through "redlining" and "planned shrinkage") such that young people would internalize this myth of nothingness, making them feel marginalized and criminalized in the context of a more affluent, usually European American, public sphere. Clearly Hip Hop has won a partial victory over the colonial circumstances out of which it grew by becoming mainstream on a global level—yet corporations continue to appropriate its performance forms for capital gain, while perpetuating such oppressive ideologies as misogyny, violence, and homophobia. Hip Hop was and is *something*—and to grapple with it seriously reveals the overlapping ethnic, cultural, and geographic influences in today's world, as well as the ways in which racism, classism, and sexism continue to serve as systemic tools of oppression by the media. Hip Hop culture struggles against the basic tenets of the marketplace as embodied by much of popular music and, specifically, the rap music industry with which many people associate the name Hip Hop. It is like a two-headed snake, one head trying to free itself from the other, which has been hypnotized by a larger force.

HIP HOP'S INTERCULTURALITY

Hip Hop has its origins in many cultures. In the early days, the Bronx pioneers of Hip Hop were from African American, Puerto Rican, Cuban, Dominican, Jamaican, and Bajan parentage, with European American allies (such as Rick Rubin, Henry Chalfant, Martha Cooper, Ruza "Kool Lady" Blue, and Malcolm McClaren) involved in helping to make some of the art forms commercially profitable.[4] Yet despite this cultural and ethnic plurality—clearly visible in photos from back in the day and early Hip Hop films—Hip Hop is often marketed as solely an outgrowth of African American culture.

In terms of understanding the full cultural history of Hip Hop in the United States, it is useful to consider the questions: Why is it so important for the record industry to put forth Hip Hop as a "Black" form, especially while the founders and leaders of the culture assert otherwise? Why does the record industry market hypermasculine and/or hypersexualized images of African heritage male and female rappers to large, but separate, audience bases of inner-city youth of color and privileged European heritage suburban youth? The way that the record industry employs and exploits the majority of recording artists (with the exception of the small percentage that do succeed commercially) is economically identical to the post-emancipation industry of sharecropping, creating a system of indebtedness where the artist does not own his or her own work and must repay ever increasing debts against a promise of future work. This is one way in which the industry is able to insert content that may not represent the creative intent of the artist (KRS-One 2003; Hurt 2006).

Even within Hip Hop culture, participants, theorists, and artists often struggle to explain Hip Hop's origins and ethnic affiliations. These notions of "belonging" exist on the interstices of colonial and postcolonial history and how this history has impacted the groups that gave birth to Hip Hop. This is evident, for example, when considering the control that language exerts in the United States as to how African Americans, Caribbean Americans, and Latinas and Latinos of African heritage identify (or are given the option to self-identify) and the competition and division created between and among people who share geographical origins.

---

4. See Fricke and Ahearn 2002; Chang 2006; and Farris Thompson in Perkins 1996. Nelson George writes, "I'd argue that without white entrepreneurial involvement hip hop culture wouldn't have survived its first half decade on vinyl.... Scores of white stepmothers and fathers adopted the baby as their own and many have shown more loyalty to the child than more celebrated black parental figures" (1998, 57). There were also a few European American and mixed heritage heads from early days—specifically in Writing and B-boying.

In *The New H.N.I.C.: The Death of Civil Rights and the Reign of Hip Hop*, Todd Boyd writes that Hip Hop is an "outgrowth" of "Black nationalist sentiment" (2003, 17). On the next page, Boyd explains, echoing Bambaataa's statement above, "Hip hop transcends the boundaries of culture, race, and history, while being uniquely informed by all three" (18). These are not necessarily contradictory statements. The former statement pertains to the culture's place in a lineage of revolutionary praxis, while the latter describes affiliation and cultural influence. Boyd's statements reveal the complexity of the social fabric in the Bronx and how these groups influenced—and continue to influence—each other.

Similarly, Afrika Bambaataa states, in Nelson George's legendary *Source* interview with him, Kool DJ Herc, and Grandmaster Flash, "Now one thing people must know, that when we say Black we mean all our Puerto Rican or Dominican brothers. Wherever the Hip Hop was and the Blacks was, the Latinos and Puerto Ricans was too" (qtd. in Forman and Neal 2004, 50; also discussed in George 1998, 57). The youth of the South and West Bronx developed the performance forms of Hip Hop with and against each other—such as the various historical waves of breaking and the contributions in style and form that different ethnic groups brought to the dance.[5] The function of Hip Hop was similar for these groups living in close proximity and rocking it side by side. As Hip Hop pioneer Grandmaster Caz of the Cold Crush Brothers explains, "Hip Hop came from desperation. It came from people's desperate need for an outlet" (in Chalfant 2006). The physical and geographical journey to the Bronx was, indeed, different for each group; but the expressive and spiritual responses to its oppressive environment reveal significant points of cultural connectedness.

As Hip Hop head and activist Tamara Davidson explains, "The reason why Hip Hop is so inclusive and plural is because African culture is prevalent in so many cultures. We all have ancestors in Africa, thus Hip Hop really speaks to so many cultures. So it's not a contradiction to say that the core ethos comes from African aesthetics, because I think this fact leads to the plurality of Hip Hop" (Davidson 2008). Indeed, it is a seeming contradiction that Hip Hop heads live with—on the one hand, Hip Hop is a culture with its performative roots in African and other pan-indigenous practices and ways of knowing. However, the culture is not exclusively populated by

---

5. Juan Flores (2000) and Raquel Z. Rivera (2003) discuss the "African retentions" in Puerto Rican culture as a result of both the cultural and ethnic mixings that colonialism set into motion, and the proximity of Nuyoricans and African Americans living side by side in the Bronx. Their work is also seminal in documenting the contribution of Latinas and Latinos in the arts and development of early Hip Hop culture.

people of African heritage, even though deeply rooted in the creative and philosophical contributions of people of African heritage from different cultures and locations. And, today, Hip Hop is a dominant presence globally, especially among young people asserting their independence and desire for a return to community-based interactions and social justice.

IN THE BEGINNING WAS THE WORD

Until lions have their own historians, tales of hunting will glorify the hunter.
    —Akan proverb

Hip Hop is an intricate interweaving of related aesthetics. Even in the development of the form, the elements evolved as overlapping circles of creativity: the Emcee grew out of the DJ's need to have more freedom behind the 1s and 2s; B-boys and B-girls began to break in relation to the DJ's technical and compositional innovations of extending the break-beat; Writing, already in existence, extended the public art and performance of outdoor parties to beyond the confines of a park or lot.

In addition, Hip Hop has a fervent connection to "the word." Common vernacular expressions include "Word!" "Word is bond," "Word up," "Say word," and a repeated sentence coda of "You know what I'm saying," compressed into one syllable. These phrases remind the speaker and the listener of the power of "the word," the importance of being understood and recognized, and the contractual relationship between listener and speaker. Indeed, the opening line of *Goddess City*, the first play in this anthology, is, "in the beginning there was . . . word" and the last line is "WORD." In Hip Hop Theater, the spoken word is often foregrounded, blended with these other equally significant elements.

Paul Carter Harrison revolutionized African American dramatic theory by identifying the power of the word as the central and core connection to an intricate system of African and African-derived aesthetics. Harrison writes, "In the West African nation of Mali, the Dogon people's version of the Word is Nommo, which is understood to be the creative force that gives form to all things" (Harrison in Harrison, Walker, and Edwards 2002, 316). Nommo is a concept that many Hip Hop Theater practitioners were raised on artistically—Marc Bamuthi Joseph and Anthony "Made" Hamilton both cite Nommo in *Total Chaos* (Chang 2006), and it infuses the interactive relationship between performer and listener.

This attention to Nommo and the word also indicates a spiritual connection for many Hip Hop Theater practitioners and an acknowledgment of the African retentions of Hip Hop. Harrison continues in his description,

"When Nommo force is properly activated, man demonstrates a capacity to manipulate the forces of nature. . . .While the community of the dead—the ancestors—may be activated for this purpose, the problems of life fall upon the living" (Harrison 1972, 3). Hip Hop has adopted certain African-derived ritual practices, such as call-and-response and pouring libations for the ancestors, learned from respected elders and mentors. This ethos reveals, as Harrison writes, "an understanding that 'community is the social force'" (3), and marks Hip Hop as a return to community-based practice.

Spoken Word, as poetry and as theatrical text, is another important practice within Hip Hop that reveals a similar connection to cultural memory. Marc Bamuthi Joseph widely toured a tour de force dance/performance/poetry piece entitled *Word Becomes Flesh*, while Pulitzer Prize–winning, Hip Hop generation playwright Suzan-Lori Parks instructs, "Words are spells in our mouths" (1995, 11). KRS-One advises readers of his inspirational book *Ruminations*, "Learn how to speak, and then learn the power of speech." Like Harrison, he discusses the "metaphysical meaning" and power of words and explains, "Your liberation and life success may be directly related to your knowledge of [the language a person uses]" (KRS-One 2003, 64–65). Hip Hop is dominated by the spiritual and revolutionary belief that we make our own world through the performativity of our words and thoughts.

This is, in fact, a refrain of the millennial generations—from the passionate embrace of Don Miguel Ruiz's book *The Four Agreements* (1997), based on Toltec life philosophy (whose first agreement is "Be impeccable with your word"), to the runaway success of the film *The Secret*.[6] These generations born under the sign of Hip Hop, in the context of a world system that seems less and less concerned with the welfare of people, have turned their attention to the belief that there is power left to us, in our ability to transform our circumstances through our thought and speech. In this worldview, the Word's power is that it creates Being, which, in this case, might be considered the process of coming back into being from the margins—the lions writing their own history. The wordsmiths of Hip Hop reveal a history where the Word is crucial to the self-definition and perpetuation of the culture. In fact, each of the performance elements of Hip Hop, like the Word, alters the world and reality of the artist.

---

6. *The Secret* is an Australian-produced film and book, endorsed by Oprah Winfrey, in which a team of scientists, ministers, philosophers, and inspirational speakers instruct the viewer in the "law of attraction," i.e., how an individual can influence his own destiny and attract to himself the life he desires (Byrne 2006).

THE RITUAL ELEMENT OF HIP HOP THEATER

The storyteller is crucial to the construction of such a culture. In parts of West Africa, such as Mali and Senegal, the storyteller is often called *Griot* (male) or *Griotte* (female) or *Djeli* in Mande.[7] In the Mande language, *Djeliya* is the word that, like the English term *Orature*, refers to a performance style that includes storytelling, riddles, proverbs, call-and-response, song, dance, and gestures. The *Djeli* is the agent of this ritual activity, a living archive who carries the culture of a people. The *Djeli,* as described by poet and per-former Wanita Woodgett, is, thus, "the glue of a community" whose roles include "teacher, historian, genealogist, musician, composer, spokesperson, adviser, praise-singer, diplomat, interpreter, ceremony-participant, and war-rior." The *Djeli* "serv[es] as a bridge between the generations" and "passes morals, values, practices, and history from one generation to the next" (Woodgett 2005, 1–2).

These roles are significant in considering the intersections of Hip Hop and theater, especially in thinking about the overlapping functions of the Emcee in Hip Hop and the actor in Hip Hop Theater. As contemporary *Djelis,* the Emcee and the actor are also the "glue" that can bind people to-gether; or unbind, when manipulated by forces external to the community. The Word in Hip Hop and Hip Hop Theater is more than an instrument of storytelling—as described above, it is an agent of world-making. The Emcee and the actor are the physical representatives of this power.

Hip Hop Theater, like each of the elements of Hip Hop, is a space for members of Hip Hop culture to take control of their own stories, carving out a place at the table in the history of U.S. theater. As in Clifford Geertz's no-tion that ritual is a story that people tell themselves about themselves (2000, 448), it is where we legitimize our voices, our audiences, and our unique cul-tural ways of telling stories important to these audiences. Thus, like any cul-ture's ritual theater, Hip Hop Theater is where members from within the culture come for reassurance, to find the values of the culture reiterated, to hear the history retold, and to locate ourselves inside of our own cultural frame. It is not just about information. Equally important is the cultural mind-set and logic. In terms of form, a Hip Hop head will, most likely, feel at home in a poetic, nonlinear, fragmented narrative with multiple ethnicities represented on the stage and multiple languages spoken. And the storytelling would almost certainly need to be interdisciplinary—indeed, any narrative

---

7. *Griot* is often assumed to be French-derived but may, in fact, come from the Portuguese *criar,* or be related to various African languages (Hale 1998, 358).

about Hip Hop that does not draw on the culture's multiple forms of creative expression would seem strangely un–Hip Hop.

In terms of function, for someone within the culture, Hip Hop Theater, like Hip Hop, is both a ritual of resistance and of self-determination. For those audience members from the outside, Hip Hop Theater gives a glimpse into these inner workings—the culture's stories, core values, and ways of thinking and knowing. This is how any culturally specific theater functions, such as Noh theater, performances of the Hindu epic *The Mahabharatha*, or Yiddish, Gaelic, and indigenous theater forms. These performances provide a cultural negotiation through expressive means for people both inside and outside of the work's cultural context. I propose, therefore, that Hip Hop Theater is the ritual theater of Hip Hop culture.

PREDECESSORS

Hip Hoppers who see themselves as part of an artistic and cultural movement know their histories. Hip Hop Theater did not just appear—it is the inevitable product of intersectional histories, in this case, artistic and cultural. As discussed above, Hip Hop inherited *Djeliya*/Orature as a method of sustenance and sustainability from its ancestral cultures. In addition, Hip Hop, spoken word, and Hip Hop Theater all owe a debt to the art and politics of a host of artistic foremothers and fathers who paved the way. For instance, quick, rhythmic speaking clearly did not begin with Hip Hop's version of rap—it can be found in many world cultures: *Djeliya,* Kabuki theater, R&B, and preexisting Western poetic and theatrical forms, such as opera recitative, Gilbert and Sullivan patter songs, and the lyrics of Tom Lehrer, as well as the practice of auctioneering (not without its own historical resonance).

The tradition of Jamaican toasting and dub music incorporated the patter of U.S. radio DJs from the 1950s and may have found its way back to the United States via Caribbean immigrants and their children, who themselves became the first DJs and Emcees of Hip Hop culture (Hebdige 1987). The intensity and lyricism of the sung-spoken, rhythmic storytelling of the *Djelis* of Mali and Senegal feel like a not-so-distant relation to rap and spoken word. These epic tales and praise songs resound with the same urgency and import that rap represents to its generations of listeners.

Soul legend James Brown is frequently identified as one of the first rappers. Other early influences oft-cited in Hip Hop scholarship include Linton Kwesi Johnson, H. Rap Brown, Malcolm X, Muhammad Ali, Eddie Jefferson, Jon Hendricks, preachers, bluesmen and blueswomen, such as Muddy Waters, Bessie Smith, and Ma Rainey, and poets of the late 1960s and early 1970s

(Baker 1991). The Last Poets (David Nelson, Gylan Kain, and Abiodun Oye-wole) helped ignite "rhythm and poetry" as a sociopolitical form of cultural performance, a precursor to some Hip Hop Theater. The group was born on the anniversary of Malcolm X's birthday, May 19, 1968, in Marcus Garvey Park and dropped their first album *Last Poets* in 1970. They have frequently been referenced as the predecessors to rap groups such as Public Enemy.

Gil Scott-Heron—whose first album *Small Talk at 125th and Lenox* also appeared in 1970—similarly mixed political poetry over music and a beat. The Last Poets and Scott-Heron added soul and funk to their soundtracks, and the meter of the poetry and its dramatic effect became deeply imbricated with the music (for example, the dialogue with the drumming at the end of Scott-Heron's "Whitey on the Moon"). The Watts Prophets from Los Angeles formed in 1967 and, similarly, recorded protest poetry, sometimes with musical accompaniment—their third album was titled *Rappin' Black in a White World* (1971). In addition, the Watts Prophets are cited as a major influence in rap and Hip Hop poetry (Powell 1991; Ankeny 2008; Sapp in Burnham 2005; Decker 1993). Other poets that have deeply influenced (and, in many cases, taught) Hip Hop and Hip Hop Theater generation performers include Amiri Baraka, Sonia Sanchez, Nikki Giovanni, Audre Lorde, June Jordan, Pedro Pietri, Gwendolyn Brooks, Louis Reyes Rivera, Sekou Sundiata . . . and the list goes on.

In the 1970s, writers experimented with new forms that combined multiple elements of performance, resulting in a re-fusing of what had been separated by social realism. The Black Arts Movement produced a wealth of nonlinear poetic and political drama. The choreopoem, a term coined in relation to ntozake shange's *for colored girls who have considered suicide when the rainbow is enuf* (1974)—a collection of poems staged as an ensemble, total theater piece with an emphasis on physicality and embodiment—became its own genre. *Sister Son/ji* (1969) by Sonia Sanchez, a poetic one-act that preceded *for colored girls*, paved the way for this type of performance; and others carried it on, such as the group Thought Music (founded by Laurie Carlos, Robbie McCauley, and Jessica Hagedorn in the 1980s) in their piece *Teenytown* (1988) and other groundbreaking work. McCauley's *Sally's Rape* soon followed in 1989, and today it is not unusual for artists to reintegrate in their plays the multiple essential components of live theater—text, music, and movement—such as Talvin Wilks (*Tod the Boy Tod*, 1990), Carl Hancock Rux (*Geneva Cottrell, Waiting for the Dog to Die*, 1991, and *Who 'Dat Who Killed Better Days Jones*, 1993), Sharon Bridgforth (*Con/flama*, 2000), Daniel Alexander Jones (*Phoenix Fabrik*, 2002), and Universes (*Slanguage*, 2001 and *Eyewitness Blues*, 2005). What these pieces have in common are poetic diction, often nonlinear sequencing, and a focus on the personal narratives of disenfranchised peoples.

There were also clear predecessors to Hip Hop Theater on Broadway. Melvin van Peebles's *Ain't Supposed to Die a Natural Death* (1971) was a spoken word, jazz, gospel, R&B, soul portrait of Harlem street life; Micki Grant's *Don't Bother Me I Can't Cope* (1972) used poetry and song to express the life struggles of young African Americans. Shange's *for colored girls* (1975) and Luis Valdez's *Zoot Suit* (which premiered in 1978 at the Mark Taper Forum in Los Angeles before transferring to Broadway in 1979) influenced several generations of theater artists through both their form and content. Many Hip Hop Theater practitioners owe a historical stylistic debt to Douglas Turner Ward's Negro Ensemble Co. (founded in 1967) and Dr. Barbara Ann Teer's National Black Theatre (1968). Dr. Teer saw her actors as "activators" and "liberators" who created community-driven, socially relevant art (Thomas in Harrison, Walker, and Edwards 2002, 361; Benston 2000). While she began her research in 1968, her building finally opened in Harlem in 1990, and the company still exists today, after her death in 2008, training new generations of performer/educator/activists under the name the Institute of Action Arts. At the New Federal Theatre, Woody King began in 1970 producing theater that focused on the "African American experience," supporting a wide variety of ethnic and cultural writing, including many of the pieces and genres discussed above (New Federal Theatre 2004).

These are just some of the New York companies. Theaters across the nation—such as Jennifer Nelson's work in DC, John O'Neal's Junebug Productions in New Orleans, and Rhodessa Jones and Idris Ackamoor's Cultural Odyssey in San Francisco—have long experimented with performance styles that draw on elements of ritual married with political content. Some of these groups are nationally known, while some have existed mainly in communities—church groups, community centers, schools, dance theater, or even young (and not so young) people creating a vehicle on their own to have their stories told and acknowledged—and have not been on the radar of institutional U.S. theater. As Marc Bamuthi Joseph writes in his inspiring essay "(Yet Another) Letter to a Young Poet," "Everyone is in your cipher" (in Chang 2006, 13). People have been ciphering for as long as they could form a circle—it is the collective consciousness of the community, a way in which we "see" and "know" each other. It is also a way people maintain the well-being of their community. It is how non-ego-driven art is made and where skills are practiced and emotional release is encouraged in a safe environment. Are all these theaters predecessors to, or current practitioners of, Hip Hop Theater? I would suggest that all forms of political and/or culturally specific theater are, in some way, in dialogue with each other—for, in a country that encourages assimilation, to be culturally specific is an act of resistance. The history of these institutions does not exist hierarchically, but horizontally, in a discursive plane of the simultaneous resistance to dominant power and the celebration of survival. All the works listed above exist on a continuum of aesthetics and politics that are inextricable.

Early Hip Hop Theater pieces in the United States or pieces that were influential and groundbreaking to the genre include Dael Orlandersmith's one-woman, spoken-word dramas, *Beauty's Daughter* (1995), *Monster* (1996), and *The Gimmick* (1998); Danny Hoch's solo performances *Some People* (1994) and *Jails, Hospitals, and Hip Hop* (1998); Sarah Jones's *Surface Transit* (1998) and *Bridge and Tunnel* (2004, produced by Meryl Streep off- and on Broadway); Hip Hop Theatre Junction's *Rhyme Deferred* (1998); and Will Power's one-man, multicharacter, neighborhood-oriented shows, *The Gathering* (2001) and *Flow* (2003). Original members of the Rock Steady Crew, calling themselves The Rhythm Technicians, performed what is often billed as the first Hip Hop Theater musical. *So, What Happens Now?* (1991) played at PS 122 in New York City to high acclaim and was followed by *Jam on the Groove* (1995) at the Minetta Lane Theater. Playwright Robert Alexander's work in the middle and late 1990s is cited as a bridge between first- and second-generation Hip Hop–influenced plays. Alexander has mentored writers such as Claudia Alick and young writers in the Bay Area and is coeditor of an anthology of Hip Hop Theater, *Playz from the Boom Box Galaxy* (2009) with Kim Euell, a dramaturg and another important ally to Hip Hop Theater practitioners.[8]

There are Broadway shows that were either Hip Hop Theater or have a shared aesthetic and audience draw. *Bring in 'da Noise, Bring in 'da Funk* (1995) was a history of the African American experience told through tap dance that began off-Broadway at the Public Theater and then transferred to Broadway for a successful run of almost three years. It was choreographed by Hip Hop gen'er Savion Glover with poetry text by reg e gaines, a godfather to Hip Hop Theater and generous mentor to a generation of poets and artists. *Def Poetry Jam on Broadway* (2002) was clearly Hip Hop, but garnered much debate in "theater" circles as to whether it was theater. To me, this is a moot point, when considering the young audiences it attracted who had the opportunity to listen to their own stories being told in a Broadway theater through a familiar and empowering vernacular.

John Leguizamo's solo shows *Mambo Mouth* (1991), *Spic-O-Rama* (1992),

---

8. Alexander and Euell's book was released as this anthology was going to print.

and *Freak* (1998) attracted young audiences of color to Broadway shows in great numbers. And, in *Drowning Crow* (2004), Regina Taylor's intricate adaptation of *The Seagull*, the theatrical experiments of Constantine Trip (aka C-Trip, the character formerly known as Treplev in Anton Chekhov's original) were in an interdisciplinary rapped form that can only be described as Hip Hop Theater. In addition to its content, the play starred several actor-rappers, including Anthony Mackie, best known for his work in the film *8 Mile* (2002) and *Up Against the Wind* (2001), a theatrical ode to Tupac Shakur by Michael Develle Winn.

Other pioneers who have moved and innovated the form include Marc Bamuthi Joseph, Aya de Leon, Baba Israel, Hanifah Walidah, Dan Wolf, Tommy Shepherd, Psalmayene 24, Angela Kariotis, Nilaja Sun, Piper Anderson, and Vanessa Hidary; the companies Hip Hop Theatre Junction, Felonious, Progress Theatre, Universes; the numerous playwrights and performers in this anthology, as well as Eisa Davis, Christina Anderson, Claudia Alick, Zell Miller III, and many more. Performance poets such as Toni Blackman, Dennis Kim, Chinaka Hodge, Willie Perdomo, reg e gaines, Jessica Care Moore, Liza Jessie Peterson, and Pandora Scooter have helped theater artists think through the nature of this work and in building the genre.

Dance companies also experiment with form and content, integrating poetry and DJing, and choreographers have collaborated with more narrative theater artists. Such groups include Rennie Harris's Puremovement, Olive Dance Co., and Kwikstep and Rockafella's Full Circle Productions. DJs have worked hard to make this genre complete—Reborn, Center, Excess, Spooky, Mohammed Bilal, and Tendaji Lathan, among many others. International artists who have made an impact in the United States and with whom the Hip-Hop Theater Festival and other institutions have collaborated include Jonzi D, Benji Reid, and Kwesi Johnson (all from the UK, working with dance/movement and experimenting with form and storytelling techniques), Storm (France/Germany), Made in 'Da Shade (Netherlands), and Godessa (performance poetry from South Africa). This is an embarrassingly incomplete list that could go on for pages and I beg the indulgence of the many important artists whose names do not appear here. I only start it to give the reader a sense of how quickly Hip Hop Theater—as a movement, as a practice, as a genre, and as a marketing tool—has spread in the past ten years.

SO WHAT *IS* THIS THING CALLED HIP HOP THEATER?

Today, there are Hip Hop Theater courses being taught on college campuses across the country; Hip Hop Theater camps; Hip Hop Theater festivals, whether commercially produced or university-sponsored; grants, panels, and conferences all dedicated to Hip Hop Theater. It is a salient moment to consider, "What is Hip Hop bringing to theater?" Here are some possible answers, as well as subsequent questions. After reading the plays in this book, I hope you, the reader, will add to this discussion.

Hip Hop brings to U.S. theater the voice of today. While clearly building on the past, Hip Hop Theater represents the creative energy as well as the political and social concerns of young people.

Hip Hop Theater is "avant-garde"—it creates new forms that work against the mainstream or dominant forms of theater and that utilize and advance technology in the process. Yet while Hip Hop Theater's resistance is against mainstream theatrical forms, Hip Hop reflects popular culture, making Hip Hop Theater unique as both avant-garde and "popular."

As such, Hip Hop Theater also embodies and introduces an important dialogue about theater and class. On the one hand, its appeal to young audiences outside the mainstream suggests how elitist traditional theater is; yet Hip Hop Theater also risks elitism on several levels. Many of the best-known practitioners are college-educated professional artists with theater backgrounds and so-called formal education and theater training. However, as described above, there is also Hip Hop Theater happening in neighborhoods and communities across the country—but does this work receive the designation "theater," or is the term being used only in certain contexts, venues, and states of professional development? Much of Hip Hop Theater is still "popular," a designation that depends on where a given show is performed, how produced and marketed, and how expensive the tickets are. Nevertheless, an increasing number of Hip Hop Theater productions cross over to commercial realms that may not feel inviting to some Hip Hop Theater audiences. Many practitioners, as well as producing organizations, are working to bridge this divide.

Although conceptually Hip Hop Theater is not that new (every generation has its own version of resistant theater), it is unique in the ways it blends particular elements of popular culture and theater; the incredible variety this synergy produces; and how this form reflects the diversity of Hip Hop and of the United States as a whole. Hip Hop Theater tells the stories of folks whose faces are not usually seen consistently or in great number on "mainstream," institutional theater stages (or in mainstream theater audiences, with some notable exceptions).

Hip Hop Theater has progressed rapidly in its relatively short lifetime and there is no shortage of artists working in or around this form. Many theaters and producers have had an important hand in supporting the growth of this genre.[9] *American Theatre* magazine, the publication of Theatre Communications Group, has also been a key proponent of the form—in 2004 senior editor Randy Gener ran a five-feature series focusing on Hip Hop Theater, its practitioners, and the politics of production within the U.S. theater landscape. This series put in-depth, firsthand accounts of Hip Hop Theater into the hands of artistic and managing directors of well-funded institutional theaters, as well as subscribers and other arts professionals in the United States and abroad. Yet Hip Hop Theater also faces key challenges as it becomes better known and mainstream theaters become more and more curious about its power to attract different demographic groups to their institutions. One crucial issue is the need for better criticism. Hip Hop Theater needs reviewers and critics who have the background to assess it based on its own aesthetic principles and logic, instead of a more traditionally Eurocentric lens or one that primarily values realism. Serious Hip Hop Theater criticism requires an appreciation of the cultural and aesthetic logic of the form and an ability to help translate these complexities for a wider audience.

Another challenge that Hip Hop Theater faces as it enters the mainstream is the danger of commodification, as echoed in KRS-One's statement: "Sometime around 1990, Hiphop the culture became Hiphop the product" (KRS-One 2003, 198). Hip Hop Theater faces the same dilemma that Hip Hop does, as its founding artists are getting older, having families, and trying to make a full-time living off their work in this form. How do we keep the "authenticity" of Hip Hop Theater *and* have a relationship with the market that, by nature, has a history of mass marketing and diluting cultural production? This challenge leads to the question, "Who defines Hip Hop Theater?" Is it a term that is more useful to presenters and producers than to artists? Does anyone "own" the designation? Who has the right to be the arbiter of what is Hip Hop Theater and what is not? What happens when people from outside of the culture create stories that have very little to do with Hip Hop—or, even worse, reveal their prejudices about Hip Hop and Hip Hoppers—and mass-market a commercial show with suspect val-

---

9. These include the Public Theater (New York), Harlem Stage, New Jersey Performing Arts Center, New York Theatre Workshop, the Marc Taper Forum (Los Angeles), Berkeley Rep, Oregon Shakespeare Festival, PS 122 (New York), Under the Radar, Centerstage (New York), Actors Theater of Louisville (Kentucky), Children's Theatre of Minneapolis, New WORLD Theater (Massachusetts), La Jolla Playhouse, Oregon Shakespeare Festival, Theatre Royal Stratford East (United Kingdom), Contact Theatre (Manchester, UK), and quite a few others that have supported artists and projects, both on the commercial and the community side.

ues and artistry? Is it Hip Hop Theater if it is near and for the people, but not by? Is Hip Hop Theater destined to go the route of Hip Hop music, in terms of its commercialization and deracination of intent and core cultural values?

Some prominent practitioners such as Universes and Zakiyyah Alexander eschew the label *Hip Hop Theater*. My students often express ambivalence over the name, simultaneously asserting, "We love Hip Hop Theater" while resisting being "defined" by a brand. Is the label *Hip Hop Theater* necessary? Is the form, itself, only a fad, as was repeatedly said about Hip Hop music? What happens when Hip Hop Theater allies itself with commercial institutions—what will become of the genre when their interest fades (or if they begin to lose subscribers)?

The practitioners of Hip Hop Theater have been asking themselves these questions for a decade—and continue to do so. We don't all necessarily agree. Nor do we need to. Unsurprisingly, we sometimes seem to disagree with ourselves in the same sentence and we change our minds over time. Nevertheless, we keep making the work, trying to reach new audiences, and bringing our communities into the theater. We work to renew the engagement between people and art, having art reflect the lives of society at large, across all lines of culture, class, and color.

What distinguishes Hip Hop Theater more and more is this engagement with community. Rarely does a Hip Hop Theater artist only perform at night. During the day she is giving workshops with youth and community members; he is doing his own pamphleting on the streets of inner-city neighborhoods or downtown to try to attract young people into the theater; they are facilitating community dialogues about the issues raised by the work, or the state of Hip Hop, or the negative reputation that Hip Hop has garnered—thanks to the music industry—as violent, misogynistic, and overly identified with greed or capitalism. Hip Hop Theater practitioners and artists are working intergenerationally to promote healing in communities. We are attempting to document a community's history, challenges, needs, stories, and cultural resources. We are facilitating youth creating their own work, using their own voices, skills, and obsessions as source material—serving as conduits for us all to "write ourselves into existence."

Hip Hop theater addresses ethnicity, class, culture, gender, sexuality, and generation—it is a theater of the issues that confront not just young people, but the whole world. This anthology includes plays such as *Goddess City* that, through poetry, dare to dream of a better world for people in general and women in particular. There are pieces such as *Dreamscape* and *Deep/Azure* that depict their protagonists' relationship to power structures, most notably the police; plays that depict the impact of Hip Hop on the lives of its adherents, such as *Welcome To Arroyo's, In Case You Forget*, and *Blurring Shine;* and works such as *You Wanna Piece of Me?* and *Low* that, through innovations in storytelling, employ verse, rhythm, and/or DJing to mix and re-mix the lives and narratives of young people and reveal the challenges of growing up in the age of Hip Hop. As with everything Hip Hop, these descriptions are not exclusive of each other—each piece belongs to several of these categories. More information about the plays, productions, and authors can be found on the website http://www.press.umich.edu/special/hiphop/. Also on the website is an additional work, *From Tel Aviv to Ramallah,* a full-length beatbox performance piece that looks at the role Hip Hop culture serves among young people in a conflict zone.

Those of us who work in Hip Hop Theater have seen the genre's effectiveness in uniting people and promoting understanding between and among cultural groups. It is the theater the world desperately needs at this particular moment in history as we contemplate the sustainability of the planet and the future of capitalism as a viable economic structure. Hip Hop Theater is the theater of now.

PART I

Spoken Word Theater

The plays in this book are divided into three parts: "Spoken Word Theater," "Hip Hop Theater Plays," and "Solo Performance." There is a particular ethic in Hip Hop culture that language creates reality. Therefore, in certain modes of creative expression, language is often heightened and poetic, as found in the practice of rapping, as well as spoken word slams. The authors in this first part of the book take spoken word to another level by creating full-length performance pieces out of their attention to poetic language.

In *Goddess City* (1998), a choreopoem for three women by Abiola Abrams and Antoy Grant, the protagonists are fallen goddesses. They are forced back to earth to remember who they are and re-member their traumatized, disconnected, and dislocated senses of self. Practitioners of Hip Hop Theater are cognizant of the debt owed to the works and artists that have preceded them. *Goddess City* is close kin to ntozake shange's *for colored girls who have considered suicide when the rainbow is enuf*. It is an intricate weaving of cultural references, songs, children's games, and women's struggles. It is episodic in form and, in early drafts, these scenes were called "peaces"—a clear language play that also speaks to the authors' intentions. The play epitomizes intertextuality, drawing on multiple sources and giving direct credit to the original authors of the texts that are sampled. Like many Hip Hop Theater plays, the work incorporates practices and rituals specific to Hip Hop culture, such as call-and-response and shout-outs (giving credit to the band). The final scene is a triumphant ritual of rebirth, indicating how Hip Hop can be a source of positive transformation.

Dreamscape (2004) by Rickerby Hinds also embodies a ritual—in this case, a ritual of death and transition. During the course of the piece based on actual events, nineteen-year-old Myeisha Mills succumbs to the police bullets that kill her in a mistaken shooting. As each bullet enters her body, Myeisha recalls a moment in her short life that relates to the invaded body part. She reassembles her mutilated body across and through her life experiences in what might be considered a ritual of reincorporation, pulling the shattered fragments of life and body back together again into a whole entity—her self. Myeisha takes control of her death by recontexualizing these experiences; she finds freedom in this process of reliving and reclaiming her past. Like the women in *Goddess City,* Myeisha performs childhood songs, games, and re/membered fragments of cultural wealth. She, herself, is an archive—not only of her own experience, but of her culture's.

Playwright Hinds casts the onstage DJ as the coroner who attempts to wrest control of Myeisha's body from her. This struggle makes her dance, also resignifying the role of the DJ as a kind of boatman over the river Styx. However, he is more than villain—like the early DJs in the Sedgwick Avenue days in the Bronx who gave hope and a renewed sense of community and vitality in their block parties, it is in response to the DJ's/coroner's "cuts" that Myeisha finds her strength and asserts her significance. Her final line is "You know me," a challenge to the audience to see beyond her as statistic. *Dreamscape,* through its language and dramatic structure, epitomizes the integrated kind of performance that Hip Hop Theater proposes, as it illustrates the multilayered act of translation in which the director and cast must engage to represent, accurately and with the audience as witness, this young woman's life and culture.

In *Deep Azure* (2005), Chadwick Boseman also delivers a story based on actual police violence against a young person. The play is written in verse and has garnered frequent comparisons to Shakespeare (in fact, an early workshop of the play in 2004 was performed at the Folger Shakespeare Library in Washington, DC). In addition to the heightened language of the verse, Boseman invents language, reformatting words, tenses, and grammar to evoke the real-life circumstances depicted in the play. The character Deep is referred to as a "prince," and his murder has epic stature. The story is viewed through the eyes of his "widowed dame," Azure, the girlfriend he leaves behind. During their relationship, Azure struggled with an eating disorder. In mourning Deep's death, she grapples with the relationship between loss and lack, and begins to heal herself. As in any epic, the protagonists battle internal and external forces to keep their culture and their people alive. While some of the language may appear poetic or hyperreal on the page, in performance much of its cadence and diction will feel familiar to a Hip Hop audience, as the play samples vernacular speech as well as fundamental Hip Hop texts. The play can certainly be appreciated for its virtuosic use of language and for the devastating story, without an understanding of these interpolated texts and motifs. However, to recognize the full complexity of Boseman's writing requires knowledge of the archive of sources on which it "signifies," in much the same way that critical editions dissect Shakespeare's writing.

Moreover, what the saturated and far-reaching diction of *Deep Azure* accomplishes, with its layered references to Kemet (ancient Egypt), mystic Judaism, and Christian iconography, is to begin to suggest that maybe the writing is not so much a hybrid of Shakespeare and Hip Hop, but that Shakespeare's texts themselves exist in a continuum of communal storytelling. In other words, *Deep Azure* feels not so much like a Western classic that has been flipped but, rather, like a world classic through which the reader/viewer may be able to understand more clearly Western classics. Thus this play provides a crucial heuristic for thinking about Hip Hop Theater texts, in that the chronology of influences may not be a vertical one. Hip Hop, with its clear echoes and evidence of cultural memory, suggests instead a Möbius-like history of the world, and a play like *Deep Azure* reveals how critical it is to avoid constructing a linear historical narrative around the aesthetics of the genre.

a collaboration by Abiola Abrams and Antoy Grant

goddess city

GODDESS CITY: "LINER NOTES":
SCRIPT KEY: The format of this script is unique. Because of the interactive call and response and overlapping verse, we formatted our original script using a key of underlining, italics and bold print to indicate which character is speaking. We have chosen to publish the play using this original notation. The Goddess of Fever's lines are *italicized*, The Goddess of Nerve's lines are **bold print** and The Goddess of Truth's lines are <u>underlined</u>. Character lines are centered. Script notes are justified to the left, in brackets [...]. Lines throughout may be spoken, sung, or rapped. The title of each piece is announced or projected as a part of the performance.

goddess of fever [italics]
goddess of nerve [bold]
<u>goddess of truth [underline]</u>

◆

WORD
VOICEOVER: Setting: Goddess City

[An instrument sounds and the silent procession begins. Goddess Tribe enters first, consisting of the Goddess City band, DJ, percussionists and background singer-dancers. The audience hears the Goddesses before they see them.]

VOICEOVER: once upon a rhyme, eye 3 opens to reveal the city of goddess, eden's sister, where purple heavens are reflected in indigo waterfalls and nature's dancing flowers drink from the river's dew at sunrise.

book of goddess—chapter 1—in the beginning there was...word

[Dressed in goddess regalia, Nerve, Fever, and Truth enter, freezing on each syllable with contagious jazz movements.]

WORD

3x:	au	**da**	*ci*	ty
2x:	gau	*da*	ci	**ty**
2x:	*god*	dess	**ci**	*ty*
	god	**dess**	*tribe*	
		tribe		
		tribe		
		tribe		

OATH

setting: we are in goddess city, with goddess tribe.
beauty and decadence, comfort and natural pleasures prevail.

greetings!

daughters & suns, here ye
there is no need to fear we
hold your hands like this & repeat after me:

"i acknowledge/ that i am now/ in the space/ between infinity and reality/
and i agree/ to participate /in this journey/when i am called/
i am now ready to receive / goddess city
i am now ready to receive / goddess city"

we thank you.

let /there/ be/ dark!

[Blackout.]

please enjoy our offering

MY TRUE LOVE
[Love song with rap, spoken word, and dance. The Goddesses of Nerve, Fever, and Truth sing words of praise to themselves.]

every time i see your reflection
the mirror of you is an exception
i take a moment to look, deep into my soul
and tell you, you're more beautiful than egypt's gold
in the morning, afternoon, and even midnight too
i long for the feel of you.
your sensuality beckons me
to places i will soon reveal

my love, you're beautiful from head to toe. you taught me everything i know.
helped me appreciate me more. knowing you this well has made me whole.

your soft full lips, your smooth dark skin
the way that your body is glistening
luscious love curves and contoured back
perfect belly button makes my mind one track
thick trees meet sweet peaches
nectar from your river straight to goddess city reaches
tasting the fruit from your summer's vine
rich with the flavor of blackberry wine

my love, you're beautiful from head to toe. you taught me everything i know.
helped me appreciate me more. knowing you this well has made me whole.

you're so beautiful can't you see
what your love is doing to me
wish everyday was eternity
holding you close how's suppose to be
love supreme me and me living in a state of ecstasy
look in the mirror and i see my true love looking back at me
love yourself that's the key
see, no mystery
that's how a goddess be
that's how a goddess be
that's how a goddess be...

GODDESS ANTHEM
[Funk music. The Goddesses swirl ritualistically.]

3X: *you are entering goddess city*
you are entering the realm of goddess city, *goddess city,* goddess city

population: infinity
goddess city limits: the imagination
unit of currency: ultra-pride

we are mothballs in the soup of the status quo
we are mothballs in the soup of the status quo
we are mothballs in the soup of the status quo

english and ebonics will be spoken simultaneously
there will be no translator

auntie earth was swirling through chaos, then
head goddess in charge looked down & said,
"this is not good."

so, we have just been selected

3. goddess of truth to reflect your life
b. goddess of fever to inspire your very being
& 1. goddess of nerve to put your fears on hold

our mission: to give a voice to the voiceless by sharing stories of the soul
here's the catch... the council has decreed that once we've landed on your
planet
1. we shall be born of wife and man without knowledge of our powers
because
b. we will not remember that we are goddesses
3. *experiencing day-to-life life exactly as you do*
that is, until our need to rise forces us to realize our birthright

goddesses
in the image of isis, *psyche*, **ameratsu**
goddesses
indistinguishable from any mortal woman.

you are now able to move about our thoughts freely

oh and, by the way, if we fail this mission the earth will be destroyed

if you're nappy & you know it give a snap
if you're nappy & you know it give a snap
if you're nappy & you know it & you feel it's time you show it
if you're nappy & you know it give a snap

GENOSISTER

[Percussionist beats and tribal dance.]

i want to tell you why we are going

do you know where you're from? *do you know?*

krik krak. krik krik krak
this story begins on the water planet a few centuries back.
we left goddess city to vacation on earth.
spending moons and wombs, knowing its inhabitants.
we were home three millennia when the first holocaust shackled our
descendents.

"do you know where you're from? do you know?"

the masters of earth clan craved free labor,
so they visited my mother, africa

[Ululation]

they said, mother, introduce us to your suns with big arms who build the
huts
and your mahogany daughters who unpuzzle crops.
and they trapped, kidnapped, purchased them from their brothers, and set
sail.
going from island to isla to isle throughout the so-called west indies and
southern american continent. for the slaves-in-training it was time for
seasoning.

countries spent spring stacked in the space of a twin bed's feces.
the leftovers were shipped to the newest version of the old world.
a king and a queen kissed the ocean's frozen floor; "overboard!"

did you hear the one about the igbo? him walk back to africa like jesus on the
water

one, two, three **jump** or do time on slave row.
heartbreak killed a village as the cemetery sailed on.
when the graveships docked, more lives vanished.
but, a few men with big arms who build the huts
and mahogany women who unpuzzle crops
survived by refusing to die,
becoming the diaspora of earthtribe.
we go to earth to heal these wounds.

TRANSCITY

[Religious sounding chimes. The Goddesses, as actors and as characters, chant, dance and give homage to their actual earthly matrilineal line. They stand, legs together, arms overhead forming a trident (Ψ) to salute the ancestors. In the script, homage is given to the ancestors of writers Abiola Abrams and Antoy Grant, who played the original Goddess of Nerve and Goddess of Fever. However, performers should feel free to insert their own parentage.]

goddess sighting; we enter the temple haven

begin the rescue mission to birth
choose your kindred wisely
this is the sacrament of the memory inhibitor.

[The Goddesses each begin with a soft chant that gains momentum:]

auntie earth we come to thee, goddess city trinity

[Nerve forms the sign of the trident with arms above her head:]

**child of norma abrams, beryl abrams, & evadney hosannah of guyana
with the nerve of lena horne, goddess of performance**

auntie earth we come to thee, goddess city trinity

[Fever forms the sign of the trident:]

*child of dazrene grant & therephene dunn of jamaica
with the fever of dorothy dandridge, goddess of arts*

auntie earth we come to thee, goddess city trinity

[Truth forms the sign of the trident:]

child of (truth's mother's name & truth's grandmother's name) of (name of truth's country of birth)
with the truth of dr. maya angelou, goddess of word

hail to the gatekeeper
in the name of ancestors past,
in the name of ancestors present
in the name of ancestors to come
bricks in the bridge to goddess city
before we were, you were
before you were, there was word.
voices screaming to be heard.
artists speaking for our lives

goddessness is a state of mind.

[As the Goddesses travel their words begin slowly and then race at the speed of light.]

spiraling   backwards   faster speed   light   ultimate   sight mind   spirit

chasing   physical   properties   pre-charted   dimensions

erasing   thought   pattern from celestial   planes

chasing lowered   frequency   slower vibrations   mind spirit   flowing

down   down   down   water water ice ice flash

light light   colder slower   solid flesh mesh   rounded shapes   unknown paths chosen

enlighten   higher awareness

spirithood   encasement   physical   presence   presence present.

[The Goddesses breathe a sigh of relief at their safe transport.]

oooh

[Nerve, Fever, & Truth begin a chant and a drum beat fades into sounds, music and voices from birth to approximately ten years old—baby crying, baptism music, first steps, ice cream truck, parents' voices and children playing.]

ooh she walle walle

[Their chant becomes a childhood song and as the transition to childhood is complete, Nerve, Fever, & Truth emerge as children in a world that is a hybrid of Goddess City and urban America.]

ooh she walle walle, ooh, she bang bang
ooh she walle walle, ooh, she bang bang
bang   bang   bang   bang
we're he-ere!

NEW GIRL ORDER

[Block party.]

somewhere on earth 3 lil girls are playing

that's the way uh huh uh huh i like it uh huh uh huh
that's the way uh huh uh huh i like it uh huh uh huh
fever is my first name / uh huh uh huh
dancing is my game / uh huh uh huh
audacity is my birth sign / uh huh uh huh
& boys are on my mind

twist, twist,
my name is truth & i'm doing the twist
no body else can do it like this
i can twist it to the west, twist it to the east
twist it like my mama use dax hair grease

oh shake, shake, shake; shake, shake, shake
shake your boodie, shake your boodie
my name is nerve /watch me sing/ you mess with me/ i'll do my thing,
my sign is fly & that's all right/ cause nerve means i'm dyn-o-mite

ooh, she think she bad
correction i know i'm bad
ooh, she think she fine
fine enough to blow your mind
ooh, she think she cool
cool as a goddess
lovely as a queen
pretty as a princess
smooth as vaseline

we look like charlie's angels!
but you ain't got no hair

AM I PRETTY

am i pretty?
am i pretty?
am i pretty?

ain't your momma pretty?
she got meatballs in her titties
she got scrambled eggs between her legs
ain't your momma pretty?

how will i know i'm pretty?
will i just wake up on the first day of school, and look in the mirror and see it.

will pretty be there looking back at me
and will i go running into momma's room and say   look momma i'm
pretty!?

will i be one of those girls who will never be pretty?
then i will have to get my hair pressed real pretty by miss headley
so i can shake it like my father is white

shake it like my father is white

will i only know i'm pretty if someone tells me i'm pretty
or will i know it too when i'm all by myself?

am i only pretty on easter sunday when I have my new dress on at church
when everyone is nice so lightning don't strike them for all the sins they
committed?

ring around the rosy, my family's feeling cozy
gunshots, gunshots we all fall down

will i have to wait to meet an older boy that all the girls like, who tells me
he thinks I'm pretty. then will i be able to really see it?

like thelma! **no like tudi** *what about buckwheat's sister?* ***ill she's ug-lee***

she real black, got nappy hair, a broad nose & thick lips
and from what some people say, that's not pretty!

i heard ms. feder, she's my favorite teacher, tell my best friend that she was
pretty too, but how can she be pretty if i'm pretty, we don't even look the
same.

am i pretty?

LISTEN

[Nerve, Her friend Rickita, and her little sister Tia.]

What we was devising wasn't some movie shit, but a real live stick-up bit.
Casin' the joint: Flashlights. Guns. The whole nine. And the plan was all
mine. Right next door to Rickita, lives that rich stuck-up bitch Ayo. Ayo's
daddy run the numbers, the whole school knows. Fake-ass green eyes, Ayo
always tellin lies. Like we a bunch o'AIDS babies. And Tia Tia crack-eater.
Your mama had rabies! So we bustin in her crib, my whole dang crew: Me,
Rickita, my little sister Tia, ain't nothin we can't do. Get this, they call us
The Robbin Hos! So fools know what's up. I put my baby sister down just
to shut her up. We bonded ourselves to each other in blood by opening our
fingers up. I know that sounds like some bugged out mess, it just means we
got our back. You know, we down for whatever. And junk like that. So I laid
out our sorority & we each got a part. I'm the brains of the op & Rickita is
the heart. Tia going to wait at Ayo's back door. If somebody's comin, she'll
tap on the floor. Ayo's grandps'll be the only one home and pops can't even
get outta bed alone. If we get busted, Rickita gonna start to sing, "Is anybody listening?" Just like they did in Wildboy's video sting. Two weeks ago,
the Robbin Hos tried to make friends with Ayo. So no one would suspect us

for the robbery, yo. We walked right over and sat at her table, bitch ain't even speak. Bust how Miss Fuss looked straight through us. Still, we almost changed our minds the weekend she went away, but it turned out to be so fly we ain't even have to pick the locks. Her moms keeps Ayo's spare keys in these fake looking plastic rocks. Yo, I gotta admit, her bedroom is banging. I never seen so much clothes before. I'm going straight for the closets. I know what I'm looking for. Those green suede Gucci boots she was sporting at the show when she knocked my sister Tia down in the cold, wet snow. We'll teach her a lesson though.

Ok. Here we go. It's on. Ssssssssh. There ain't no money in that couch. Damn what was that noise? Tia? Rickita? Oh man, that must be the grandfather. I'm a just wave the gun so he'll crawl back upstairs. Shit I thought she said he couldn't walk. Maybe we should just go out the front. Is that a cane? Oh shit, Gucci boots. Bitch, you supposed to upstate. Shit. She comin.

[Gunshots.]

Tia? Shit. Tia, you forgot the code. Rickita! Rickita give her mouth to mouth or something; Is anybody listening? Didn't you take first aid? Is anybody listening? Call an ambulance! Is anybody listening?!

[All three assume positions of slumber, and softly begin to repeat "am I pretty." This repeated question alternates with the sounds of their lives from childhood to young adulthood. Their voices become older signifying a transformation into adolescence.]

> i don't think i'm pretty.
> **_do you think i'm pretty?_**

BOOK OF NERVE—SCENE 2
[Nerve pumps herself up for an audition.]

> do you have the nerve?
> The center of my energy is power
> yes I am the woman of every hour
> go 'head, dare me & i'll do it
> but you dis me, kid, you blew it
> nerve says the words that you fear to hear
> swam back to guyana cause my granny lives there
> follow da leader & the leader is me
> wild chile african style with bravery
> whoop! here i is. bam! it's my world
> kneel down at my gown like the boss miss ross
> sam is not my uncle & jemima ain't my aunt
> i'm like a goddess in that way

AUDITION RENDITION

[Nerve is auditioned by Fever and Truth who represent Casting Directors. Scripted lines and improv.]

hi, my name is nerve

that's funny, can you turn around please?

[Nerve spins.]

wow, nerve, do you think that you can lose 40 pounds in a week?
and can you straighten your hair? forget it. you're too dark for this commercial. *next!*

[Blackout. Spotlight on Nerve, who reacts by becoming the grotesque representation of what she thinks the auditioners see, replete with old Hollywood minstrel persona and routine.]

**ya ta ta ta ta ta. da ta ta ta ta ta. ya ta ta ta ta ta ta-ah
mo biscuits, suh?**

BEAUTY SHOP

hair i am
at the beauty shop ?!?!
what are we gonna do today?

today i can honestly say i don't know what to do with my hair.
i've changed my hair so many times to fit what they say is in—low hair,
short hair, medium length hair, shoulder length hair, long hair. nappy hair,
peasy hair, kinky hair, natural hair.

can i touch your hair?

*bantu knots, china bumps, one big afro, two smaller afro puffs, one big afro
puff on top and even locks, could somebody hand me the beeswax?*

your hair reminds me of africa.
or is it the '70s?

**texturized, relaxed, permed, jerri-curled, wave nouveau,
single processed, double processed, over processed**

you cut your hair!

no it all fell out!!

low fade, finger waves, wedges, shags, mushrooms, and bobs

why don't you let it grow long?
i did!
beehives, braids, spritz curls, french rolls, ponytails, fake buns to real ones

is that her hair *or is it a weave?*
curly weaves, straight weaves, wet & wavy weaves, bone straight weaves to
yak weaves and any combination of all these, weaves. hair pieces, synthetic
wigs, human hair wigs.

who does she think she is?

highlights, lowlights, sun streaked. dark brown, medium brown, light brown,
sandy brown, auburn and honey blonde. black, blue black, burgundy, rooster
red, bright orange.

she must be jamaican!

wash and set, blow-dried, pressing combed, curling ironed.

keep it short!
keep it long!
keep it straight!
keep it natural!
just do what you gonna do!

forget it, i'm gonna just lose those 40 or 50 pounds, shave my head and get
me a wig.

CONSTITUTION
[Reggae-rock.]
2X: *one day, i'm gonna have my say*
i'm gonna slay dem dragons and a make dem pay.

i'm gonna dance to the rhythm, *dance-dance to the rhythm* of the music
that is my life, &
i will **eat meat** & *wear a weave* in a dark cafe in brooklyn where
dreadlocked patrons have agreed to have a monopoly on righteous hipness
and i will not apologize.

while wearing dubious tattoos over my multi-pierced body
i will address my friends in politically incorrect terms that will seize your
sagging skin load
as your bad hip flips through my script mode & no, moral majority, i will not
apologize.

because the dilly yo is this; if i be me, i will contradict;
cause while my *baggy jeans are saggin* on the rhyming scene
i'll be a *smilin tearin stylin* model pageant queen & i will not apologize.

2X: *one day, i'm gonna have my say*
gonna slay dem dragons and a make dem pay.

it will be *hip to hop to hippety hop* to music peppered with crime the world
gave us

& though i am no moschino ho, nor am i a versace hottie,
i will close my eyes and bop to a boombox beat
that will make bob dole c. delores in his tucker

and i will take responsibility,
yes i will take responsibility,
yes i'll take responsibility
for sanctioning b-b-b-b-bullets with my cd collection,
but i will not,
i cannot,
apology will never be an option.

convention told me that my nostrils were so wide...

how wide girl?

so wide that you could drive a train through 'em.
the better to scare you with, my dear

that train speeding through my wide nose
& over my chocolate skin and bushy hair will pass you byyy.......
one day

MAD POET
[Angry nationalists.]
what you mean, y'all don't know who I am? i'm the mad poet!!!
you're the only person who has the courage to speak out
tell them why you're mad poet
no justice!: **no peace**   no justice!: **no peace**
you fit the description.   *you fit the description.*   you fit the description.
of a negro who's gonnna be in trouble
you in the back with the black shirt on   you on the side; yeah don't try to
hide
there's nothing you can do   *it's not up to you*
you fit the description
strolling through saks to pick up a few things
had some bags in your hand, from a day of shopping
salesperson clocking you

the manager's eyes lock on you
they all wanna see what you're gonna do
you get tired of them being up in your grill
so you put the stuff back y'all know the drill
two doors down mall security cuffs ya
snatch away your bags and proceeds to ruff ya up up up stairs you go
searching you, g, from head to toe and you ask yourself why?
cause you fit the description
black, 4'9"–5'9" small to medium build, shoppin in expensive ass store

driving in your brand new expensive car *chillin*
music turned up head boppin from the *rhythm*
out with your girl just enjoyin your *evenin*
you hear sirens soundin 5-o's howlin
officer what did i do wrong?
license and registration?
45 minutes detained
evenin all rearranged
here he comes and you ask why?
cause "you fit the description"
black, 5'2"–6'2" medium to heavy build, committing a d-wb in a upn—
break it down

driving while black <u>in you people's neighborhood</u>
headin home late one night after a long, long day
you notice someone following you
you guess they're going your way
you slow down your steps to see if they go by
they slow down their steps and stay right behind
you start walking faster now there's no one around
their pace seems to quicken in a more quieter sound
so you say lemme turn down a street that I know they won't go
and usually more people flow
all of a sudden you feel them grab you on your back
and throw you up against the wall
face smashed to the bricks
<u>**bam, smash, slam, wack**</u>
*some sadistic version of a <u>**dadadadada batman**</u> and robin flick*
they say "gimme your wallet and then i'ma kill you"
you toss over your wallet
*then pull out your gun, <u>**shoot, shoot, shoot**</u>*

and that's that
that black body falls to the ground
and you ask yourself why—cause you fit the description
you fit the description
you fit the description
of somebody who's
<u>gonna be in trouble</u>

[Fever & Truth soothe Nerve and try to remember the original mission which is now only a deeply buried remnant. They find inner strength through outward earthly role models that empower Nerve.]

3X: <u>GENESIS OF DIVAS DOING EARTH'S SPOKEN SONGS</u>
<u>alice walker</u>
wizard
<u>amina baraka</u>
ia
<u>lorraine hansberry</u>
trailblazer
nikki giovanni
<u>**lyricister**</u>
sonia sanchez
revolutionary
hattie mcdaniels
<u>realist</u>

BOOK OF TRUTH—VOLUME 3

[Truth pumps herself up for an audition.]
<u>you can't handle the truth.</u>
<u>sincerity.</u>
<u>you're getting what you're seeing</u>
<u>a gospel feeling absolute being</u>
<u>unaltered, untouched, clean & pure</u>
<u>integrity, principles & virtues galore,</u>
<u>for i am not an imitation of life</u>
<u>the deal with me? realness is right</u>
<u>reflect, contemplate, meditate</u>
<u>on the cult of honest personhood</u>
<u>a mystery corrector</u>
<u>a human lie detector</u>
<u>my serum solves the world's ills</u>
<u>then my diligence pays your moral bills</u>

don't get it? you will, cause hey
i'm like a goddess in that way

AUDITION MANIA

[Shakespearian actress Truth is auditioned by Fever and Nerve who represent Casting Directors. Scripted lines and improv.]

Hi, my name is truth

o.k. truth, go ahead

life is but a walking shadow, a poor player that struts
& frets his hour upon the stage...

stop. Truth, let's hear the next line, less urban this time

it is a tale told by an idiot full of sound and fury signifying...

*we're still getting that ghetto thing. Clearly, you are just not right for
Shakespeare, but tomorrow, we're auditioning for an urban rap group. You do
rap, don't you? Thank you.* **Next!**

[Blackout. Spotlight on Truth, who reacts by becoming the grotesque representation that the auditioners seem to see, replete with minstrel routine.]

getting jiggy with it; jigga jigga jigga jigga boo!

BLACKER BERRY!

[Announcer. Nerve introduces rap battle.]

**you are watching gtv
television for the ghetto
who will be the next queen of rap-n-soul?
It's the battle of the century,
first up, dust off your x-hats! Blacker berry is here to drop serious
knowledge...
Blacker berry!**

[Truth takes center stage as her alter ego, singer and spoken word poet Blacker Berry.]

Wave your hands together from side to side like this
oh onkh and onkh and onkh and onkh

i am black
black black black black black
pure black love is where i'm livin at
you never see me wearing whitey's labels
even though i did a nike spot on cable
spiritual folks know that black folks rule

but whitey don't teach you that in school
i am malcolm before he went to mecca
the man makes you act like a ho rump shaker
vegetarian nubian blacker berry
teaching more science than the dictionary
incense and candles make me natural and strong
exposing conspiracies through my song

thank you, thank you

BOU-SHE
[Bourgeois, wealthy unemployed prep school drama majors.]
i'm sick of all these rappers & singers.
It seems like if you have an album out you can wiggle your way
into feature films, tv, and now even broadway.

It does not matter that they can't read the script,
or they garnish their sentences all the way through with "you know what
i'm saying."

"you know what i'm saying."

No it's rougher "you know what i'm saying" with the face

*that's sick! With all the really talented actors out there that for years have
studied voice, acting, dance, and even martial arts. Look, I broke my nail in
class.*

And then after graduation moving to ny where they have the best shops but
manhattan is so crowded you end up having to live in brooklyn or queens.

brooklyn? ewww. *you live in brooklyn?*

anyway it's so far from barney's and bergdorf's.

don't get me wrong, i'm happy for all my brothers and sisters that are working...

brothers & sisters? I thought you were an only child.

*I mean like in the ethnic sense; but what about me, i can't sing, so an r&b
album is out of the question unless it's on the milli vanilli tip.*

But look at me, with my porcelain cocoa skin and curly hair,
do i look like I could play a hard-core gangsta rapper?

*I've decided if i don't make it in the next year and i'm sure I will,
& since my mom's from jamaica...*

jamaica? <u>You're from jamaica?</u>

No, not me, my mother.
Anyway, i've decided i'm going to record a reggae rap album

<u>sorta like the next patra but with fashion sense?</u>

I don't want to do this but this is where this business has brought me. If all i've
done to prepare myself as an actress isn't enough, i'll give dem what dem want
and den some.

<u>Can we be in it?</u>
Sure

[Nerve, Fever, and Truth sing and dance dancehall reggae style.]

<u>dem what dem want and den some.</u>
<u>give dem what dem want and den some.</u>

KILLA KILLA BEE
[Announcer. Fever introduces rap battle.]
next up on gtv's battle for queen of rap-n-soul:
watch your backs folks, she's strapped, but that ain't nothing, we all strapped,
blap, blap, blap.........it's the hard core gangster,
killa killa bee

[Nerve as her alter ego Killa Killa Bee takes center stage.]
Bop ya head like this.
i said bop ya head like this. Ha ha bullets flying through the air
bzzz blood spattered everywhere

wicky, wicky, wicky what would you do if i pulled a gun
turn tail like a punk and begin to run
wiggedy-what would you do if i pulled a knife
act like a beeyotch and give up your life
what would you do if I snatched your heart
you bizet to jet before i start
w-w-w why're you sweatin me   peepin out the jeep.
ha ha i'm   rollin deep
i am the pimp and the ho   so niggas here we go
cause the killa killa bee rocks every show:
sipping cognac and 40 ounce style
me and cleopatra sippin forties on the nile

got all the spices
combined them together
yes more flavor
than you could ever endeavor
ever uphold
it's a scientific fact
i was born to wear gold!!!
yes, yes y'all
yeah, yeah
peace

LIL HO
[Announcer. Truth introduces rap battle.]

next up on ghetto television, we have she of the ill tatas, lil ho & the battle
rap y'all better hold on to your man cause she comin on the stage to
penetrate you.
she the latest artist from that hot, young producer y'all know him, scruff
daddy.
lil ho

[Fever as her alter ego rapper Lil Ho takes the stage.]
what's up to all my peoples in the projects, section 8 y'all
i wanna dedicate this to my friend who had got shot.
[Fever pauses for a brief moment of grief.]
jerk your meat to the beat
jerk your meat to the beat

phone sex is something that your man & i share
he knows what to say to take me there
the sound of his voice and his vocal vibrations
leads me into a session of masturbation
the words from his lips i'm anticipating
and forces me into pulsing sensations
the juices run down my inner thighs
i wish you were here to stick him deep inside
of this lil ho who needs him so bad
i want you to spank my thick round ass
and tell me i'm a bad girl on punishment damn!

i'm the lil ho with the sexy plan, player hater's you know where i stand
jerk your meat to the beat

[Competing alter egos go for the gold in an overlapping rap battle.]
how many times must you figure/that you got to pull the trigger/before you get to be a real.....

<u>blacker berry is here, with a spiritual plan,</u>
<u>spiritual black power is where i stand.</u>
<u>onkh and onkh, and onkh and onkh</u>

[Blacker Berry turns upstage and drops a prayer mat.]
Yo, blacker berry, that ain't even east, yo
<u>keep it real, y'all</u>
keep it real
yeah, keep it real

[The rapper-singers become the women from Bou-she.]
give dem what dem want & den some
give dem what dem want & den some
that was so cool!
omigosh that was such a good show
<u>now did your broker say buy or sell?</u>
i think he said sell
[Whispered:] <u>*out*</u>

[Nerve & Fever soothe Truth and try to remember their original mission, which is now only deeply buried remnants, by roll calling their earthly role models that empower Truth.]
3X: <u>*G.O.D.D.E.S.S*</u>
gloria naylor
<u>storyteller</u>
iyanla vansant
<u>humanist</u>
susan taylor
<u>guide</u>
zora neale hurston
<u>*teacher*</u>
toni cade bambara
<u>*preacher*</u>
angela bassett
<u>*thespian*</u>

<u>BOOK OF FEVER—EPISODE 4</u>
[Fever pumps herself up for an audition.]
i give you fever
i am so incredibly hot

feel my island fire inspire to your head's curly top
my vernacular is spectacular.
my talent? overwhelming.
mission impossible? i'm the one for the job
cinnamon brown diva down female james bond
i'm all up in your face
my weapon is mental mace
my sexy love potion will cause quite a commotion
believe that!
i'm like a goddess in that way

AUDITION 69

[Fever is auditioned by Truth and Nerve who represent Casting Directors. Scripted lines and improv.]

hi, my name is fever.

fever, have you ever thought about bigger breast implants?

I don't have breast implants these are all mine.

mmm, show us what you would do in a lesbian, inter-racial sex scene? never mind. next!

[Blackout. Spotlight on Fever, who reacts by becoming the grotesque representation of what the auditioners seem to see, replete with minstrel routine.]

hey mammy... got milk?

COME WITH ME

[The women become erotic sirens with sexual stripper movements.]

they only think they want sex.
if i gave them what they're really asking for, they wouldn't be able to handle it

[Rhythm and blues song begins.]

come with me to that place where you want to be
come with me. come with me come with me.

i waited such a long, long time
can't get you outta my mind
from the very first time i saw you
been dreaming bout making you mine
i think in all my life
i never seen one so fine
you make my body quiver
with just the thought of you & i

2x: <u>come with me, to that place where you wanna be</u>
<u>come with me, come with me, come with me—</u>

when you were away from home
i'd pick up the telephone just to hear your sexy message
then hang up before the tone
i just had to let you know
had to let my feelings show
mm-mm you drivin' me crazy, baby
& you don't even know
you want it, you got it
can you handle it

2x: <u>come with me, to that place where you wanna be</u>
<u>come with me, come with me, come with me—</u>

tonight is the night
for me to teach you wrong from right
to make my fantasies realities
do everything that i desire
i'm more than you imagined
and better than all your weak little dreams
do 6" boots excite you? you've been bad
& now i'm gonna make you scream
we are gonna make you scream
you want it, you got it. but, can you handle it?

<u>CASTRATION</u>

shame hugs me. the blonde woman tears and the man's eyes spy a slaughtered
pig.
"my god"
<u>"where did you come from?"</u>

and because i forget to exhale when i answer "here" they say,

<u>"here as in here?"</u>
"well, where are your people from?"

and i describe a mosquito-infested island down south.
nurse james & doctor smit go blank when my story sings of africa's ancestors,
we don't know where from
and the dutchman backs out of the infirmary without even a "please pardon
me."

i am in kindergarten, smart-n-cute. nana picks me & nisi up from school.
we are
odds-evens-say shoot-ing
with warm rain when,
we happen upon a new kind of game.
we are blindfolded, hands molded together.

momie & tantie pin me & nisi in hot, itchy grass.
private parts displayed in the mangrove's dry protective shade,
and we see the blunt bone blade that nana's grandma made.
aunt tayma is playing her flute.

our collective scream sours senti's coconut milk at the family's festival feast.

then i am 17 & my would-be-first traces a keloid to my hiding place,
then kenya spencer hides his face. there have been none since.

nana says that if i hadn't been cleansed i'd be having babies
instead of going to college.

anyway people here go to surgeons all the time
to have their noses cut apart or the fat scooped out of their legs.
i only had my clitoris cut off. why are they judging me?

GONE
[Hip-Hop Supremes.]

gone.
rock-a-bye baby on the rooftop,
when the wind blows, the cradle will rock, when the bough breaks

ooh wee, he was a hipster. he wore his gray _adidas_ with burgundy lees just
like
run & 'em said. walked into that high school cafeteria in a way that made
me sing:
mama said there'd be players like this, there'd be players like this my
mama said
mama said mama said

and as he sat, i stood & pledged my allegiance to the pagan god of triple
fat geese.

something in the way he took my hand let me know i was chosen
& we hooked up, coupled, copulated, did the do, as they say.

then the ivy league letter and the dead bunny came on the same day
& there was no way to make it work. teen mama? much drama.
my family doesn't play that. in one minute.
"can i come in you."
<u>"yeah baby go 'head."</u>

pregnant. the ivy league letter and the dead bunny came on the same day.
the proverbial fork in the road splitting right through the heart of my kid.
i chose the road on the right. seven splitting forks later i sit childless,
asking why i am fertile & why it's so easy to count backward
<u>10, 9, 8, 7, 6, 5, 4, 3, 2, 1</u>

and wake up free while sisters in less stylish ghettos sit surrounded.
i walk by them on my way to school refusing to be a slave to a child
rather than a college when i know too well on a school night he whispers,
"can i come in you?"

and i let him. i let him spray & shoot one fell swoop, my body a dream
catcher that brings with the promise of a new life the seeming end of
mine.
i hear him whisper & i answer 7 times
<u>*"you keeping it?"*</u>
we flush egg/sperm cocktails. same guy/different faces. same whisper/
different voices. the promise of planned parenthood—they won't tell your
parents.
"next."
vacationing at the best clinics in the city.
<u>*mama said mama said*</u>

mama said this one will break the habit.
he came in me, now the son-of-a-gun won't come with me, says he can't
stomach it. wishes me luck this morning as i sob into the phone
while my kid sister makes note of how not to be.
<u>*mama, mama said*</u>.

<u>GROCERIES</u>

plastic?
paper.
<u>thank you.</u>
<u>*groceries...*</u>

<u>*"you over-estimated the groceries you could carry"*</u> *you figure, as long as the
bags hold out, you can leave a couple at your front door and come back for*

them. so you figure, so you leave two bags, jog up 3 long flights of stairs, and
kick your dorm room open with your sneakered foot. you mean to put your
stuff in the kitchenette and run back down for the tampons, cat food, and way,
way, way too many rice cakes. thanks to oprah & janet it's still in to be thin. so

"*you over-estimated the groceries you could carry*" that glass bottle of
apple juice did it every time. you stick the yogurt in the freezer then you
hear his voice.
smooth, like a wannabe sunday night dj
"*yo, don't worry #6, i got it.*"
and suddenly your room number is your name and because
"*you over-estimated the groceries you could carry,*" you run downstairs to
find
bigger, luna's captain-of-the-football-team-boyfriend
stuffing fallen boxes of oatmeal and, uh-uh, tampons into your grocery
bags.
"no *i* got it, bigger" you bellow, angry at yourself for always being so paranoid.
"*damn shorty, you must be having a hard-ass day?*"
you nod as bigger swings your bags easily up past the second floor all the
way to the 3rd
you gotta admit, sure does make things simpler having a guy around.
"thanks bigger, so what do i owe you?"
you say, standing between your door & luna's and you take your bags...

nowhere. bigger pushes your tampons and rice cakes and apple juice
through you and shoves you into your safe space, owning it.
"**bigger what the hell're you doing?!?**"
"*shut the fuck up*"
you can't get past his blade. your cat screams because the football player
with a runny nose wrenches your head backwards and slams your door
closed with your nose.
your warm blood paints your face.
fist/ after fist/ after fist/ after fist/ pounds/ in/ to/ your/ uterus.
"*stop weeping, bitch.*"
which death will you choose?
your head hits the floor and a serrated knife snatches the skin on your
throat.
then in a moment that seems sickly seinfeld, bigger can't hold the knife *and*
get your jeans-n-panties down over your wide hips. he orders you to
"*take them off. slowly. Slowly, yeah like that.*"

"no! bigger don't do this. please don't do this."
your legs and hands do what he says because his dagger splits your tongue.
#32 smashes the spit out of you, stomps your thighs open & then
bangs something molded and ugly into your flesh
on the crimson crochet mat his girlfriend gave you for kwanzaa.
you over-estimated the groceries you could carry,
and now you're carrying much more as bigger's dry thrusting holds your
limp
body prisoner with all of the charisma that is a knife and *my mind won't
die.*

[Nerve & Truth soothe Fever and try to remember their original mission
which is now only a deeply buried remnant. They find inner strength
through outward earthly role models that empower Fever.]

3X: *G O D D E S S*

gwendolyn brooks

bard

ntozake shange

motivator

billie holiday

messenger

audre lorde

activist

phyllis wheatley

survivor

josephine baker

artiste

BOOK OF REVELATIONS—CHAPTER 5

slip, slip, fall, collapse into the abyss of ...

unbirth

[Chaos, fervor, & frenzy.]

"can anybody feel me?"

purple foggy madness is choking me

"does anybody know me?"

is this light in my mind violet or violent?

how thin is the line?

"sister, sister help me"

where is the barrier between fuchsia and screaming cats

"sister, sister, know me."

free me from this melody
i want to trust

"sister, sister love me"

i want to trust.
somebody, take me.

take my life. take my pain.

universe take my pain
i exist in vain
somebody take this pain
i surrender
universe take my pain
5x: universe take my pain

<u>RE-MEMORY</u>

no more auditions
i am re-membering our mission
<u>what is this that i begin to know?</u>
we bring into being our own show?

we 3 have been selected to find the celebrated city within earth's chaotic life

the council has ruled that once we've landed on your planet
we will not remember that we are goddesses

<u>and we will be born without knowledge of our powers & will experience</u>
<u>life much as you do until our need to rise becomes so great that we realize</u>
<u>our birthright</u>

<u>*our mission: to give a voice to the voiceless by sharing stories of the soul*</u>

one fever, <u>one truth,</u> **one nerve,**

<u>*one goddess,*</u>

<u>*one person,*</u>

<u>*emerge*</u>

INITIATION
[Ceremony.]

welcome to INITIATION.......   goddess city on earth
the soles of our ebony feet greet each other \ not a shuffle to be heard
what becomes a goddess most & who becomes a goddess?
"she, summoned of the winds."
present. who gives me?
we do. "how do you emerge?"
with goddess courage

[Fever & Truth initiate Nerve.]

the pain that i have survived in this lifetime is but an illusion.
my power is more than this.
i embrace my mirror and adore her, finally finding kisses that have never
been lost.
let your nerve break the conspiracy of silence.
then say yes, this is when and where i enter. tell me...

what becomes a goddess most & who becomes a goddess?
"she, summoned of the fires."
present. who gives me?
we do. "how do you emerge?"
with goddess love

[Nerve & Truth initiate Fever.]

fever is the center of the sun. my rays warm souls, making many into one.
beating my own sacred drum, i come to avenge the hottentot venus.
is this what is feared? this me invisible to wolf-whistlers.
our spirit seeks the same, so let us spin the yarn again.

what becomes a goddess most & who becomes a goddess?
"she, summoned of the soil."
present. who gives me?
we do. "how do you emerge?"
with goddess virtue

[Nerve & Fever initiate Truth.]

i come in truth.
what am i?
my kaleidoscope dances in the moods of my skin. and the colors of my soul.
name me goddess.
the stage is our altar. today, we write ourselves free.
so that an ocean of slaves can swim home in our veins.

auntie earth we are complete
ready to save you from defeat
with goddess tribe by our side

we'll rise to the skies to claim the ultimate prize

because goddessness *is a state of mind!*

[Goddesses of Nerve & Fever & Truth are reborn and ascend into Goddesshood.]

P...O...*E*...*M*...

[The Goddesses re-emerge for an ENCORE walking the stage like a runway as they are each introduced. First up, Nerve, with Truth's help, introduces the Goddess of Fever.]

'scuse me while I goddess trip:
strutting into your consciousness,
hair is optional,
permeating all you thought was real
giving you the day sweats, she is the goddess of fever.

[Fever, with Nerve's help, introduces the Goddess of Truth.]

'scuse me while I goddess trip:
keeping you grounded
in a permanent state of earthliness,
reflecting to you,
peace, justice, and the goddess way, she is the goddess of truth.

[Truth, with Fever's help, introduces the Goddess of Nerve.]

'scuse me while I goddess trip:
big brave nappy pride
to strangle your limited mind
into submission,
goddess of nerve entering the deepest recesses of your delinquent
imagination.

'scuse us while we goddess trip

[Goddesses introduce band-members for their featured solos.]

soothing with savage beats
key soldier, **the bass head,** *the beatkeeper,* and the keeper of the beats.
our band, goddess tribe

& of course, you
daughters and suns daring to express your divinity

you are now goddess tribe
helping us discover the power of love with no apology.

welcome to goddess city
a curly twisted braided wrapped up fro

barefoot midsummer's night colored girls
having too much fun to consider suicide
chile please
ever again

may the audacity of goddess city be with you.

WORD.

[BLACKOUT]

by Rickerby Hinds

Dreamscape: A Play Based on True Events

CHARACTERS:
MYEISHA MILLS: 19, Female, African American
THE DJ: Coroner, Officer Garland, 911 Dispatcher, Toni

The autopsy table and the DJ setup should be set up in a way that allows Myeisha to lay "on" the turntables as if it was the autopsy table and for the DJ to "operate" on her through his/her cutting and scratching of the various recordings.

All other characters in the play should manifest themselves through the DJ. The DJ can also be played by a Beatboxer. DJ or Beatboxer can be male or female.

OFFICER GARLAND should be a combination of the DJ manifesting his voices and MYEISHA speaking on top of it as OFFICER GARLAND.

Words in brackets are suggested, not spoken.

The dancing should be the physical representation of the effect of each shot on Myeisha's body. The "Twelve Mortal Moves" should reflect the cumulative effect of the gun shots. It should also explore different hip hop dance styles.

◆

Prologue

Otis Redding's "White Christmas" gently disquiets the darkness. Chalk outlines of MYEISHA MILLS materialize. Lights rise to reveal MYEISHA rising from an autopsy table/DJ setup. She dances the "Twelve Mortal Moves" as the music is spasmodically disrupted by twelve distortions—these are gun shots—each one finds its target in MYEISHA's body, transforming her movement into a dazzling life-death-dance. She lands in the front seat of her aunt's Nissan Sentra, closes her eyes for a moment then awakens with a jolt.

MYEISHA: *(Frightened.)* Ever have one of those dreams
  Where nothing comes out when you [try to] scream?
  (Commanding herself:)
  Scream
  Screeam!

(Tries to scream but only a series of sampled "Hollas and Scream" are heard.)

See what I mean?

One of those dreams

Christmas was three days ago
Jingle Bells and ho, ho, ho

Just so you know
This ain't gon be one of them feel-good shows
Just so you know

So
Christmas was three days ago
Jingle Bells and "ho-oh, ho-oh, ho-oh" (*as in* somebody saying ho-oh)
Today's December 28th
Third day of Kwanzaa
Ujima
"To build and maintain our community together
And to make our brothers' and sisters' problems our problems
And to solve them together"

I know you didn't know
I didn't know till uncle Darnell told me so during one of his "black-outs"
Oh no, not that kind-a blackout
That's just what we call it when uncle D has one of his moments
And is compelled to bust you out cause of your lack of blackness
You'll see what I mean

It's Ujima though

(Proudly.) Umoja, Kujichagulia, Ujima

So

Me, Shy and my cousin Toni dying to get our party on
Rollin to L. A. though
Tired of Club Metro
Oh
For those of you who don't know me
See, I was born and raised in the I-E
That's the Inland Empire, the I-E
Sixty miles east of the City of Angels

So me, Shy and my cousin Toni dying to get our party on
Rollin to L. A. though
Tired of Club Metro
Four dance floors of Hip Hop, Reggae, *(her least favorite)* Rock en Español
and Retro
So
The Sentra starts to rattle and pull to the right
Ah man, I cannot believe we got a flat in the middle of the night
Not tonight
(At audience:) Okay, let's just let me get the facts folks
What is the deal with automobiles and [my] Black folks
Fo real
And the fact that your spare is always flat, folks
Fo real
And do not get me started on a working jack, folks

[my] Black folks

So I wind up in a fix at the Spirit of 76 that sits on Central'n Brockton
Gat in my lap case I get rocked-on
Waiting for Shy and Toni to get back with the Triple-A card
One in the morning sittin in my aunt Gwen's ride
I can't leave aunt Gwen's Sentra sittin on Central
If it gets stolen scratched towed or broken into
Soon as I see her I'm-a be the one get broken in two
Aunt Gwen gon kill me
Well, maybe not kill

But I sho ain't gon be rollin the Sentra no more
Feel

Ever have one of those dreams
Where nothing comes out when you [try to] scream
Tap

So I'm sitting in the Sentra on Central sensing something
soundin like rappin like tappin
Like...

(Singin with DJ:) "Who's that peepin in my window
Sha-pow nobody now"[1]

Tap

I hear the tappin again
Oh cool it's Toni
Let me let you in, girl where you been? I'm lonely
Got me sittin at this station in the middle of the night
One in the morning losing patience
Something just ain't right

Tap
(To audience:) Now before you trip
Let me go on and admit that...
I'm strapped

Yeah, that's right
I'm strapped

(Slowly starting to rhyme.) With my gat at Central'n Brockt-on
Thirty-Eight in my lap case I get rocked-on

Yo that's nice

(Spittin with skillz this time:) So I'm strapped with my gat at Central'n
Brockt-on
Thirty-Eight in my lap case I get rocked-on
Late at night in my lap there it sat
there I sat
there it sat

---

1. Gipp, Cameron, Patrick Brown, Raymon Murray, Rico Wade, Robert Barnett, Thomas Burton, and Willie Knighton. 1995. "Cell Therapy" on *Soul Food*. Performed by Goodie Mob: LaFace/Heritage.

there I sat
there it sat
there I sat
Took a nap
Rat-ta-tat-tat-tat
Tap

Tap

Tap

I put the gat in my lap cause I was a little terrified
Ta-ta-ta-tappin on the window cousin Toni outside
So I say "hold on cuz, let me let you in"
But 'fore I can
Here comes that damn dream again

(Tries to open door but can't move.)

First I can't holla
Now I can't even move

Tryin to open the door but I can't even move
Can't take this much more cause I can't even move
Feel like a prisoner of war and I can't even move
Can't move can't move can't move can't move
First I can't holla, now I can't even move
(To self:) If you're dreamin Myeisha, girl wake up now fool!

(She sees TONI walking away from car.)

Who you callin' this late on a pay phone
You better come on so we can get on and head on
Home
Toni, where are you goin to?
Where the heck you been?
I'm opening the door least I'm tryin to
Let me let you in
I know you're ready to go home girl, I'm dying to
We'll just explain it all to aunt Gwen
You can just explain it all to aunt Gwen
I'll just explain it all to aunt Gwen

We ain't fixin no flat tonight forget that
Aunt Gwen's just gonna have to "get Black"

We ain't fixin no flat tonight forget that
Aunt Gwen's just gonna have to "get Black."

(Public Enemy's "911 Is a Joke" drops. TONI picks up the pay phone and dials 911. DJ is DISPATCHER. MYEISHA is TONI.)

DISPATCHER: 9-1-1.

TONI: Yes uh, could you guys come down to uhm, Central and Brockton to the 76 gas station because there's a uhm, my cousin's in a car and she has a gun on her, but she's passed out. We can't get in the car cause it's locked.

DISPATCHER: Okay, who's inside the car?

TONI: Uh, my cousin.

DISPATCHER: And she has a gun with her?

TONI: Yes. It's sitting in her lap and uh, she's passed out.

DISPATCHER: She's passed out?

TONI: She's passed out.

DISPATCHER: She has been drinking?

TONI: I don't know. We just came—

DISPATCHER: Do you think she shot herself?

TONI: Yeah, she has a flat. I don't know.

DISPATCHER: Okay. What kind of car is she in?

TONI: It's a Nissan Sentra.

DISPATCHER: Hold on. What color?

TONI: White.

DISPATCHER: Is she in a passenger or...

TONI: She was drive... she was driving. Cause we came to fix, she had a flat tire. We came to help her fix it and uhm, and we just found her like this.

DISPATCHER: Okay so she's in the car by herself.

TONI: By herself.

DISPATCHER: Have you tried to bang on the doors?

TONI: Yeah, we banged on the window and everything. She's passed out. We cannot get her to wake up. The music is loud, so we can't do nothing.

DISPATCHER: Okay. I'm gonna keep you on the phone until the officers are on their way. Okay?

OFFICER GARLAND: On December 28, 1998, I was working the graveyard shift when I received a call from RPD Dispatch at approximately Oh-One-fifty-five hours assigning me to proceed to the point of origin of a 911 call which was Baines 76 Unocal gas station, located at 6575 Brockton Avenue in the City of Riverside. The call conveyed that there was an unresponsive female locked in a white Nissan Sentra with a visible firearm on her lap.

MYEISHA: *(Rapping:) So I'm strapped with my gat at Central'n Brockt-on*
Thirty-Eight in my lap case I get rocked-on

OFFICER GARLAND: At approximately zero-two-hundred hours, I arrived on the scene and spoke with two females standing by the pay phone on the north side of the gas station's premises. The two females advised me that the female in the locked vehicle was a family member, that she appeared to be unconscious, and that she had a loaded firearm on her lap. I saw that the two females were very upset.

DISPATCHER: She been—I'm sorry—has she been drinking today?

TONI: I don't, I don't know! That's what I'm telling you. I don't know. She had a flat tire and she called the house. So we're coming back to give her the Triple-A card—

DISPATCHER: Uh-huh.

TONI: ...so she can get the tire fixed. But this is how we found her. So we don't know.

DISPATCHER: You don't know what's going on.

TONI: Uh-uh.

OFFICER GARLAND: Based on their demeanor and the occupant's non-responsiveness to her family members, I believed that the vehicle's occupant was necessarily in some sort of medical distress especially because her family members did not know what was wrong with her.

DISPATCHER: How long ago did she, did you talk to her?

TONI: Uhm, I didn't talk to her. My aunt did.

DISPATCHER: How long ago was that?

TONI: That was like 20 or 30 minutes ago.
Can you guys, can you guys send an ambulance with you?

DISPATCHER: Yeah.

TONI: Okay.

DISPATCHER: Yeah, since we don't actually know what's wrong with her—

TONI: Uh-huh?

DISPATCHER: And... the gun, you can just see the gun?

TONI: Yes. It's in her lap.

DISPATCHER: It's sitting in her lap?

TONI: Uh-huh.

DISPATCHER: Okay. And she's the only one in the vehicle?

TONI: Yes. *(Pause.)*

DISPATCHER: What is her name?

MYEISHA: My name is Myeisha
Y'all know us E-shas: Myeisha, Moesha, Aisha, La'Resha, La'Creesha, Ta'Nesha, Tyisha

We the E-shas we the first cousins to the Aw-nas

You know the Aw-nas: LaJuana, Tiana, Shawana, Juwanna, Tawanna.

DISPATCHER: How old is she?

TONI: Uhm, she's 19.

DISPATCHER: Nineteen years old?

TONI: Uh-huh.

DISPATCHER: Okay. And the car is just parked in the, in a parking lot?

TONI: Yeah, at the gas station.

DISPATCHER: And when she called you twenty minutes ago she did, said she was alone?

TONI: Uh, I don't know.

DISPATCHER: Oh she never did...

TONI: Cause my aunt talked to her so I don't—

DISPATCHER: Okay.

TONI: —I don't know.

OFFICER GARLAND: As I finished speaking with the two witnesses, Officer Hobart arrived on the scene. I informed Officer Hobart that the vehicle's occupant was apparently unconscious and had a gun. Because the occupant had a gun, I knew that we would have to secure the area and make it safe for emergency medical personnel to render any aid the occupant required.

TONI: How far is the uhm, police station from here?

DISPATCHER: Well they're just, they're in the city just driving around—

TONI: Oh.

DISPATCHER: —But they're on their way there.

OFFICER GARLAND: Officer Hobart and I approached the vehicle with our guns drawn and pointed downward.

TONI: Oh.

DISPATCHER: They don't sit at a police station, waiting...

TONI: Okay, here... I see one police officer. They found the, uh, the car right now. There's a police car right now.

OFFICER GARLAND: Officer Hobart approached along the passenger's side rear door as I approached along the driver's side door. From my position behind the driver's side rear door, I could see that the occupant's gun was on her lap pointed toward the driver's door.

DISPATCHER: Okay. If they're coming—

TONI: In the drive—

OFFICER GARLAND: The gun's magazine was in place and the weapon was readily accessible.

DISPATCHER: They're coming toward you?

OFFICER GARLAND: After Officer Hobart and I verified the occupant had a gun...

TONI: Yes.

OFFICER GARLAND: I held that position until backup arrived.

DISPATCHER: Why don't you go talk to em?

TONI: Okay, thank you.

MYEISHA: Soon's I hear the cops' sirens the first thing pop in my mind
"Man I wish I was a white girl" or at least a little lighter than I'm
Not white in the "I can flip my hair" and "I got blue eyes" kind-a way
But in the "Officer, can you help me out" kind-a way
In the "Young lady are you okay? You look distressed" kind-a way
In the "Are you okay, you need a ride? You look lost" kind-a way
But not today
Tonight my name's Myeisha... and I am Black... might-a had a little to drink
Those are just the facts

But even still with all that I figure I should still be alright
I mean if Toni couldn't hear me I must be asleep, right
And if I'm sleepin I'm dreamin so it must be deep, right
And if I'm sleep and it's deep—then the police'll wake me up, right
Show a little care, help me find a spare, even help jack me up, right
(Pointing out writing on Police Unit:) To Protect and to Serve
Written in black and white
Right?

OFFICER GARLAND: I observed that the occupant appeared to be in dire
medical distress and in need of immediate medical assistance. I observed
that the occupant's mouth was slightly open, her eyes were closed, her
breathing appeared shallow, her lips were quivering, her body was shaking,
and a white substance was accumulating around the sides of her mouth.
Based on my prior experience with persons overdosing on drugs, I believed Mills was experiencing many symptoms which were consistent with
a drug overdose. Believing that time was of the essence, I thought we
should use the quickest means available to remove the gun from her presence so that medical personnel could render the necessary aid.
I would attempt to break the window and retrieve the gun. *(MYEISHA
interrupts OFFICER GARLAND.)*

MYEISHA: *So I'm strapped with my gat at Central'n Brockt-on*
Thirty-Eight in my lap case I get rocked-on

OFFICER GARLAND: After verifying all the officers were in position, I performed a silent three count and then broke the window on my first attempt using the A-S-P baton. I then dropped the baton and leaned to tuck
my body into the front window and grab the occupant's gun. As I reached

in to retrieve the weapon, I heard a "boom" which I believed to be a gun
shot go off toward my right ear.

MYEISHA: *(Rapping:) So I'm strapped with my gat at Central'n Brockt-on*
Thirty-Eight in my lap case I get rocked-on

OFFICER GARLAND: Once I was inside the vehicle, I could no longer see
the weapon

I thought that the occupant had grabbed her weapon and shot me

Once inside the vehicle I heard a boom which I believed to be a gun blast

Once inside the vehicle I heard a boom which I believed to be a gun blast

Once inside the vehicle I heard—

MYEISHA: *(Singing:) Happy birthday to you*
Happy birthday to you
Happy birthday dear officer
Happy birthday to you[2]

(About OFFICER GARLAND on floor of the Sentra:)
Officer Garland, the one on the floor
It's his birthday today he's turning 24

(Singing Stevie Wonder's "Happy Birthday":)
Happy birthday to ya
Happy birthday to ya
Happy birthday
Happy birthday to ya
Happy birthday to ya
Happy birthday
Happy birth—[3]

You see the problem with this version
Nobody knows how to end the thing

Happy birthday
Happy birthday to ya...

Yo wait
December twenty-eight
That would make the officer a Capricorn

Capricorns are supposed to be
Practical and prudent

---

2. Orem, Preston Ware, and Mrs. R.R. Forman. 1935. "Happy Birthday to You": Warner Chappell.
3. Wonder, Stevie. 1980. "Happy Birthday" on *Hotter Than July*. Performed by Stevie Wonder: Motown.

Ambitious and disciplined
Careful and patient
Humorous and reserved
Pessimistic and fatalistic

December 28th
That makes officer Garland a Kwanzaa baby
Ujima baby
[Not really] Well, maybe

December twenty-eight 1998
Means Y-2-K's only a year away
You heard of Y-2-K
You ain't heard of Y-2-K?
Okay
They say one second after twelve next New Year's Eve
After they drop the ball on New York
right
Things are gonna go bananas, fo real

[They] say all the computers in the world are gonna lose their "megabites"
Like even banks and stuff are gonna lose grip on their cash

Of course nobody I know is so naive to believe
That some ATM's are gonna go crazy and start spittin out twenties
(Still not convinced)
I ain't sayin I believe and I ain't sayin I don't
But... you know... me, Toni and Shy got the ATM on University and Main
staked out
We just gon be in the vicinity case cash starts to spit out
Think I won't?

But a thousand years
That's crazy to even try to think
A thousand years of time
If we're lucky we get like seventy-nine
That's like a blink
Like a wink

But at least I get to be one of the very few
In the history of the world to go from the old millennium to the new
Out of everybody in history to ever live

I get to be one of the ones who gets to go through from millennium one to
millennium two
(At audience:)
You too
Know what I'm gonna do
I'm gonna make the millennium that's next
My best
I'm-a make M-two tha bomb
Might even make me an M-two resolution
Start me an M-two revolution

December 28 Y-2-K in a year
Makes officer Garland a Capricorn over there
(DJ drops "What's Your Sign" cut. MYEISHA gets audience hype.)

Let's see what other signs we got in the house tonight
(To audience:) Say what's your sign!?
Say what's your sign!?

Do the Pisces run this motha for ya?

Do the Aries run this motha for ya?

Do the Libras run this motha for ya?

Do the Taurus run this motha for ya?

December 28th Y-2-K in a year
Makes officer Garland a Capricorn over there

OFFICER GARLAND: Once inside the vehicle I heard a boom which I believed to be a gun blast. I immediately fell backwards onto the pavement,
injuring my legs and wrists. I saw the occupant rise forward in her seat.
While still thinking that I had been shot and believing that the occupant
was attempting to shoot me again I began firing into the driver's side door
of the vehicle.

MYEISHA: *(Convincing herself.)* I mean if Toni couldn't hear me I must be
sleep, right?

OFFICER GARLAND: I began firing into the driver's side door of the vehicle

MYEISHA: And if I'm sleep and I'm dreamin it must be deep, right?

OFFICER GARLAND: I began firing into the driver's side...

MYEISHA: And if I'm deep asleep the police'll just wake me up, right?

OFFICER GARLAND: I began firing into the driver...

MYEISHA: Help me find a spare, even help jack me up, right?

OFFICER GARLAND: I began firing

MYEISHA: Right?

OFFICER GARLAND: I began firing

MYEISHA: Right?

OFFICER GARLAND: I began firing

MYEISHA: Right?

OFFICER GARLAND: I began firing

MYEISHA: Right? *(Beat.)*

Ever have one of those dreams

Where nothing comes out when you scream? *(She tries to scream. Nothing comes out.)*

(DJ samples a series of "ones" which mix into the music for MYEISHA's routine in next scene)

1

(MYEISHA is working on dance routine. As the CORONER "cuts up" the following, its effects are manifested in her dance.)

CORONER: The entrance to gunshot number one is located on the right upper arm.

This is a typical distant gunshot wound entrance. The course of the projectile is through the skin and soft tissue of the right arm, and perforating and fracturing the right humerus.

This is a serious, however, non-fatal gunshot wound to the right arm, fracturing the right humerus.

MYEISHA: Did he/she say humorous I think he/she said humorous

(DJ samples a series "humorous.")

That's funny

What's no joke is the fact that me, Shy and Toni

Been workin on our routine, you know, for when we hit the scene

(Mildly defensive.) Yeah, that's right, we them girls, you know the ones

Get you out on the dance floor thinkin you gon have you some fun

Thinkin you gon get your freak on... your grind on... maybe even get you some

But as soon as we get you on the floor you realize you gets none

We bust out the routine we came here to do

Now we ain't tryin to be mean, it's just how we do what we do

So you end up standing there bobbin your head wondering if you're gonna get some attention... create a little tension

So when we see it in your face we give you a little taste, know what I mean

What you don't realize is that it's all built into the routine
Did I mention
*(DJ samples: Shai's "Shy," Tony Toni Tone's "Tony, Toni, Tone Has Done It
Again" and Another Bad Creation's "Iesha." MYEISHA become TONY, SHY,
and then MYEISHA again on cue with the DJ's samples.)*
Like I said
We ain't mean, that's just how we play
We're Tony, Shy, Myeisha
We're three tha hard way!

So anyway, we workin on a new routine the old one's gettin tired
Bout time for it to be retired
So... *(Dances. Stops in the middle of humerus move.)*
See the dilemma?
This is where we're supposed to hit this *(Tries "humerus" move again.)*
It's cool an all
Me myself personally
I think we should be doing more of Aaliyah's moves
Girl is bad... and so smooth
She's got that thing, you know
She should do some more movies or something, you know
I bet you she's gonna really blow up in a couple years or so

But I get the feeling she might wanna give the slip to R. Kelly
Maybe it's just me but he gives me the [willies] *(Does "he gives me the
willies" shake.)*
Anyway, check out what we got so far on the routine down
Then you'll see why a fractured humerus is not such a funny bone
*(MYEISHA dances routine, but can't hit the "humerus move." She notices that
the CORONER cuts the record every time she gets to that move. She battles
CORONER with the "humerus move" for control of the turntables, MYEISHA
wins this battle. MYEISHA then dances the routine, struggling through the
"humerus" part. Frustrated, she makes her way back to the front seat of the
Nissan Sentra where she finishes the routine.)*

2

*(DJ samples a series of "Twos." MYEISHA dances the "fractured jaw move" as
the CORONER "cuts up" the following:)*
CORONER: The entrance to gunshot number two is located on the left pos-
    terior upper neck.
This is a typical distant gunshot wound entrance.

The course of the projectile is through the skin and soft tissue of the left upper neck, and coursing through the mandible and exiting the right side of the jaw.

The mandible is extensively fractured and there is some fragmentation of the teeth.

The exit to gunshot wound number two is on the right side of the jaw.

This is a very serious, however, not rapidly fatal gunshot wound, fracturing the jaw.

MYEISHA: I heard that

Dreams about losing your teeth symbolize the loss of childhood innocence. These dreams often occur at times of transition from one life stage to the next and can be a message that an important milestone is occurring and urging you to face the inevitable.

You know what I'm gonna miss
Graham's Mission Bar-B-Que
Downtown on Main street
Robert be puttin his foot in his Q
Both feet
Oh, don't worry, that's a good thing, it's the same as sayin mmm-mmuh!
That Q's slammin

Beef tips
Cole Slaw
Mac and Cheese
Chicken
That's what I'm a be missin

Pork ribs
Potato salad
Bar-B-Que beans
Greens
Yams
Peach Cobbler

I got something that needs to be said though
So, what's the deal with our Bar-B-Que folks and their bread
Y'all heard what I said
The bread
The bread
If you can call it that

It's the same no matter where you're at
You can be at Graham's, Bobby Ray's in San Berdoo, Louisiana Fish in Mo-Val or M&M's in L.A.
Your meal's gonna come out the same way
Greens gonna be hooked, Mac and Cheese... pleeeease
Baked beans gon be lip-smackin
And the Que's gonna be slammin
But sittin on top of your order, off to the side
I guarantee there's gonna be some paper-thin, no flavor it-ain't-even-Roman-Meal white bread

You heard what I said
White bread
I'm tellin you it's gonna be white
White bread
But if you accidently luck out and get some wheat bread
Don't be lookin for no wheat grains, wheat smell, wheat germ or wheat taste
Nothin like that found in this bread
This wheat bread is gonna be wheat only because that's what the bag said

What's really sad is that since the rest of the meal's so good
We forget about the bread white or wheat
And when it's time to sop up that last bit of Q sauce out of the corners of that take-out Styrofoam container that you can't reach with your plastic fork
That paper-thin, flavorless, you-wish-it was-Roman-Meal-bread gets it done

That's what I'm-a be missin
Bar-B-Que
Fake wheat bread
And

Kissin

Listen

Kissin

Okay
Wesley Snipes in Sugar Hill or Denzel in Crimson Tide
Okay

Denzel in Hurricane or Wesley Snipes in White Men Can't Jump
Okay
Wesley Snipes in Murder at 1600 or Denzel in Devil In A Blue Dress
Okay
Denzel in Glory or Wesley Snipes in Blade
Okay
Wesley Snipes in Blade II or Denzel in The Preacher's Wife
Okay
Denzel in Malcolm X or Wesley Snipes in Jungle Fever
Okay
Wesley Snipes in Blade III or Denzel in Training Day
Okay
Denzel in Mo' Betta Blues or Wesley in Mo' Betta Blues

I heard that dreams about losing your teeth symbolize the loss of child-
hood innocence
These dreams often occur at times of transition from one life stage to the
next.
*(MYEISHA dances, but can't hit the "fractured jaw move." She notices that the
CORONER cuts the record every time she gets to that move. She battles CORO-
NER with the "fractured jaw move" for control of the turntables trying to stop
him/her from cutting the record then letting it play. MYEISHA wins this battle.)*

3
*(DJ samples a series of "threes." MYEISHA dances the "right shoulder move" as
the CORONER "cuts up" the following.)*
CORONER: The entrance to gunshot number three is located on the right
posterior shoulder on the right upper back.
The course of the projectile is through the right posterior shoulder and
through the wall of the back.
This is a nonfatal distant gunshot wound to the back.

MYEISHA: I was always a tomboy
People used to say I must be gay cause I dressed this way
Baggy jeans, sneakers and my shirt hangin loose this way
Always a tomboy and if you don't like it you can kiss this... this way

Looked good playin the field
And still had sex appeal

Played some basketball, but softball was my game
Got my pitch up to 65 my last year at Riverside High

even got a little fame
It's true
Got my picture in the Black Voice News paper page B-2

My best pitch was the Quick-an-Split
Had batters singin the blues
See-ya!
Loved the sound of my pitch in the catcher's mitt when it hit the sweet
spot
It's like, like
(Omit following line if MYEISHA can pop gum or tongue:)
like poppin gum inside your mouth hittin that perfect pop

It sounded good,
Felt good
And I look good
Okay, let me stop
I did look good though
(On the pitcher's mound MYEISHA strikes her left hand with her right as if wearing baseball glove. Blows a bubble, winds up and pitches. We hear the pop. It's the gum/it's the ball in glove.)
I'm thinkin bout walkin on at Cal State, or U.C.R., RCC, Valley or Cal Poly
I messed up and didn't get my applications in on time
(She pitches. Pops gum. Self-congratulatory.)
Tomboy
Shoot, I could-a been a cheerleader if I wanted to
Homeboy
(Cheerleader style:) My name's My-e-sha
I am the best
Come get with me
Forget the rest......
My name's My-e-sha
You know my name
Wanna get with me
Step up your game
(MYEISHA dances, but can't hit the "right shoulder move." She notices that the CORONER cuts the record every time she gets to that move. She battles CORONER with the "right shoulder move" for control of the turntables trying to stop him/her from cutting the record then letting it play. MYEISHA wins this battle.)

4
(DJ samples a series of "Fours." MYEISHA dances the "scalp move" as the CORONER "cuts up" the following:)

CORONER: The entrance to gunshot wound number four is on the left posterior side of the head.

This is a typical distant gunshot wound entrance.

The course of the projectile is through the scalp and exiting the right posterior side of the scalp. The projectile does not enter or fracture the cranium, and the course is only through the scalp.

The exit on the right posterior scalp is a half inch irregular stellate hole without abrasion.

This is a non-fatal distant gunshot wound perforating the scalp only.

MYEISHA: Hold up...!
(DJ samples "wait a minute, let me put some...")
I know he/she did not just say only through the scalp
I know he/she did not just say only talkin bout my scalp!
He/she must not realize that the only place my hair grows is on that scalp

You know what
I'm not even gonna get into the whole Black women and their hair conversation right now
Not with a coroner anyhow
(Reluctant beat.) All I'm gon say is Sarah Breedlove
A.k.a. Madam CJ Walker
A.k.a. first self-made American woman millionaire
Built on Black hair care
(To CORONER:) You hear! *(Beat.)*
Hot iron burns on your forehead, scars your neck
Highlights, low-lights, frostin, tintin
Sleepin sittin up so your new style don't get wrecked
Kitchen sink perms
Combing through them naps
Baby hair pumpin
Getting your dandruff scratched

Now I know some of my sistas you'all gone natural and I ain't hatin
All I'm sayin is you don't wanna go there unless you are aware of the hair
(Sample: LL's "Around The Way Girl." About CORONER's comment.)
Only through the scalp

Lemme give you Mr./Ms. Coroner some advice when addressing a Black woman's hair
The only time you wanna let only come out your mouth is if you're sayin

If only I could get my flip to flip as good as yours
If only I could get my goddess braids to rock as good as yours
If only I could get my wrap to drop as good as yours
If only I could get my micro braids to hold as good as yours
If only I could get my streaks to blend as good as yours
If only I could get my bob to hold as good as yours
If only I could get my Farrah Fawcett Feather to layer as good as yours
If only I could get my quick weave to blend as good as yours

Only through the scalp

And since I'm handing out advice
Let me give the men a little slice
You know me
I'm-a be nice
Brothas should already be aware of this fact
But if you ain't a brotha and you like your coffee black
Here's a little insight to help you with your mack

Do not touch the hair
Permed, relaxed, crimped, slicked, braided, dreaded or fro
Please
Just let the hair go

Do not grab the hair
Do not stroke the hair
Do not caress the hair
Do not clutch the hair
Do not fondle the hair
Do not fiddle with the hair
Do not twiddle with the hair
Do not absentmindedly twirl the hair or swirl the hair or curl the hair
Do not pensively seize the hair
Do not passionately grip the hair
Do not attempt to run your fingers through the hair
Do not kiss the hair
Do not lick the hair

Just

Did I make it clear
Hands off the hair

But if you care to get near the hair then be aware of when hair's just been
done
When sista's just come from Ebony Crest, Shear Elegance or Miss Ellison
Make it very clear that you see the hair you feel the hair
And if allowed to
you would stroke the hair
you would caress the hair
you would clutch the hair
you would grab the hair
you would fondle fiddle twiddle and twirl the hair

I know it's not fair
But hey, hair's not fair
So if you really care
Do not touch the hair

And, oh yeah, when you see a sista goin like this
(Patting hair.)
Don't be fazed
Ain't nothin wrong with her, she's only scratchin her scalp through her
braids
(Facetiously—about the Coroner:)
I know he/she did not say only through the scalp

Only through the scalp.

(MYEISHA dances, but can't hit the "scalp move." She notices that the CORO-NER cuts the record every time she gets to that move. She battles CORONER with the "scalp move" for control of the turntables trying to stop him/her from cutting the record then letting it play. MYEISHA wins this battle.)

5
(DJ samples a series of "Fives." MYEISHA dances the "lower back move" as the CORONER "cuts up" the following:)
CORONER: The entrance to gunshot number five is located on the central
lower back.
The course of the projectile is through the skin and soft tissue of the left
lower back and exiting the left anterior lateral hip.
This is a non-fatal gunshot wound to the left lower back.

MYEISHA: I was in a video
Nah, fo real
I was in a video
I was in this video
It was even on TV
Okay, so it was just like on channel 23
Exclusively local to the IE

Okay see, this emcee from Mo-Val got signed by Inland Empire Records
Local label, think his name was MC D-Lo
And they about to release his first single and they bout to shoot the video

So me Shy and Toni are at Club Metro lettin ourselves go
This kid sees us, says he's shootin a video
Sees us doin our old routine
Not even the new one you just seen
Says he's lookin for some females to represent for the IE
So naturally, you know... Toni, Shy and me
(In the kid's voice:) "You guys heard of Inland Empire Records, right?"
No...
But we still show up for the shoot
Shoot, we just down to get our groove on
They were for real, had a director, a crew an everything
So on "action" we did our thing
Okay, so you probably won't recognize us, you know
I thought they were serious
But when I saw the video all they showed was the angle on the gluteus
I'm mean I like my posterior, but I like my face too

I think they showed it once on B-E-T Un-cut
But in the final cut you don't-see-me
Least not from any angle where you could see me
All they showed was what me, Shy and Toni called the "ho shot"
All bottom no top

Okay, so this is how I-E Records shot me (Giving audience the B-E-T Uncut–angle on the posterior shot. Smirk on her face turns to disappointment to anger to sadness.)

(MYEISHA dances, but can't hit the "lower back move." She notices that the CORONER cuts the record every time she gets to that move. She battles CORONER with the "lower back move" for control of the turntables trying to stop him/her from cutting the record then letting it play. MYEISHA wins this battle.)

6

*(DJ samples a series of "sixes." MYEISHA dances "fractured femur move" as
the CORONER "cuts up" the following:)*

CORONER: The entrance to gunshot wound number six is located on the
left thigh. The course of the projectile is through the skin and soft tissue of
the left thigh, perforating, fracturing and fragmenting the left femur.
This is a non-fatal, however, serious gunshot wound to the left thigh, fracturing the left femur.

MYEISHA: My cousin died once, well, almost died
No, not Toni, my cousin Freddie
Well he kind-a died

Okay, so if you know me and you know I gots sports skills
When it came to Freddie, sports kills
He's un-cordinated like-a-mug I mean like-a-mug
So when I heard he broke his leg I was like
Yeah
And?
Of course he broke his leg, it's Fred, that's what he does

You know how you got that one cousin who always gets hurt
You could be playin tag, hide and seek, jump rope or diggin in the dirt
(Makes a "we made that game up" face.)
You know you played diggin in the dirt
No matter what though
Guaranteed ... Freddie was gonna get hurt
Dropped a brick on his head ... that was funny
That one bled
Broke his left arm twice
Broke his right arm once
Ankles always sprained
Usually the left, but the right one too
Always something caught in his eyes, even thought he wore glasses
Over a hundred stitches, no lie
Had to sleep on the bottom bunk cause he would fall out the bed
That was Fred

So then he gets hurt and starts cryin
We're like like, "Shhh, come on man, you act like you dyin or something"
Thing was
If one of our aunties heard Freddie's boo-hoo our game was through

Toni used to get so mad at him she didn't know what to do
(As TONI in the moment)
Damn Fred, shut up!
You act like a little girl
Long as there was no blood flow though
Freddie was usually good to go

So
They take him to Kaiser—
Oh wait, <u>let me break down</u> the break
This fool goes out to Devil's Canyon out by Cal State
Rollin on a Mo-ped, a Mo-ped
That's a motorcycle that you pedal
So full speed ahead goes Fred
Crashes the Mo-ped

They take him to Kaiser Fontana
Soon's I find out I am on my way to the hospital
To have some fun
Get my bag on

When I get there he's like
"They just wanna keep me overnight then I'm-a go home"
Next day I'm learning about Fat Embolism Syndrome
And Freddie's not at home

He's in a coma
It was induced
That's how it was introduced

Doctors explained it this way

Fat embolism syndrome is a symptom complex of acute respiratory failure
after long-bone fractures. It is thought to be caused by deposition of embolic fat within the pulmonary capillaries, resulting in a capillary leak
within the lung. The source of the embolic fat appears to be marrow fat.

Freddie broke his Femur
The fat was headed to his lungs
Got stuck in his throat

So he's put into an induced coma for two weeks
Cause he was too weak to breathe or speak
Two weeks

Too weak to even eat
Like he was dead
In a hospital bed
They said
Told us it was good for him to hear familiar voices
So I showed up just about every day
Aunt Dee moved in to Kaiser Permanente
Permanently

My Aunt Dee, Freddie's mom, had always been the auntie with faith
You know, the religious aunt who made sure you prayed in you car fore a
long ride
Or dropped a "stay on the Lord's side" if she thought you were starting to
backslide

Aunt Dee moved *into* the I-C-U
I do not kid you

Prayin my cousin back to this side
Sayin
"This coma ain't nothing but a comma in my son's life story"

After sixteen days Freddie woke up in a haze
First thing he says is
"Cuz, I went to New York City"
And I'm thinkin,
"Not pretty
Shame
The Fat Emboli got his brain
How sad"
And he's gettin mad
Cause nobody's believin his New York City dream
Starts to scream about the weather, what he ate, where he went, cash he
spent

Talkin bout he was
[Sample: "Uptown Baby Uptown Baby"]
Talkin bout he was in
[Sample: "Where Brooklyn At?"]
Talkin bout he was in
[Sample: "Strong Island"]
Talkin bout he was in

[Sample: "South Bronx, the South-South Bronx"]
Talkin bout he was in
[Sample: "The Bridge"]
(DJ goes into a serious "South Bronx/The Bridge" mix.)
I'm like, fool, you were right here in
Fontana baby Fontana baby
With yo mama baby yo mama baby
Freddie didn't think that was too funny

Anyways who knows
Maybe Freddie did go to the city

I sure hope Aunt Dee has some of her prayer power left over for me
(Beat)
I ain't never been to New York

(MYEISHA dances, hits the "fractured femur move." She notices that the CORONER cuts the record every time she gets to that move. She battles CORONER with the "fractured femur move" for control of the turntables trying to stop him/her from cutting the record then letting it play. MYEISHA wins this battle.)

7

(MYEISHA remains frozen in position from last scene while DJ samples a series of "sevens." MYEISHA dances "lower back move" as the CORONER "cuts up" the following:)

CORONER: The entrance of gunshot number 7 is located on the right middle back.

The course of the projectile is through the subcutaneous tissue of the right central back. The bullet did not enter the chest.

(She enters the tattoo spot with TONI. Note: when JESUS is italicized it is said in Spanish; when it's not, it is said in English)

MYEISHA: "Toni, you sure bout this spot?"
Yeah girl, this is where I got mine done and you know mine's hot
Ain't nobody in here but Mesicans
I know, but you know how good they can draw
(To Jesus:)
So what's up... *Jesus*?
Yeah, I'm here for a tat
My cousin tells me you got skills
You got a problem with that

My lower back
Nefertiti
Queen
Black
Of course you don't know er, she's not from *La Raza*

Here, Toni, where's the one you drew
(Shows Jesus TONI's Nefertiti drawing)
My cousin got skills, huh?
Wha'd'ya mean *un poquito*

You told me forty not sixty-five
Let's go
What?
(To Toni:) That's all I got
Let me get twenty-five
I'll pay you back

I know I ain't got no job
You don't have to bust me out in front of our Lord and Savior
Just do me this favor I'll get you back
Just like I got yo back last month
Don't front

Nah, this is the last time I'm-a use that [favor]
Almost time for you to slip again anyway
You lucky I'm your cousin

Okay, okay I'm lucky too
(TONI hands her the money)
Aw'rite Jesus let's see what you can do
(Positions herself in tattoo chair)
Hold up, wait
Is it gonna hurt?

Do pigs like dirt, that's funny Messiah
But fo real though

Tiny pieces of fire tappin your skin
But then—
Numb, that'll work

Aw'rite

Begin

Ahhh!
Man, that's so hot it feels cold

I knew that
Just seein if you were following proper hygienic procedures up in here

She was powerful, beautiful and smart like me
Her name means "The beautiful woman has come"
I'm here!

Same way Mesicans get to name themselves Jesus

I'm puttin her there cause only kings get to see the queen
Know what I mean

Trust me, it'll be the last time you see her

Two hours?!

You must not know who I am
I don't cry
Toni, this fool just asked me if anybody every broke my heart
(Emotionless)
Yeah, it hurts
But it's getting numb though

I told uncle Darnell I was thinkin bout gettin a tattoo
I can be just like you
He says,
(Imitating uncle DARNELL) "First of all ain't nobody gon see it dark as you
are
Second, a tattoo ain't nothin but a scar
You can get a scar if you want
From me
For free
The pain'll be the same
Just won't take as long"
Then he starts going into his black-rant

"You would-a never made it as no slave"
It'll be a hundred degrees ... IE heat
And if I forget and say "Man, it is hot"
You would-a never made it as no slave

"This ain't nothin but dry heat
Down South they got that humid heat
plus massa wasn't givin you much to eat"

I get me some new tennis shoes
"You would-a never made it as a slave
They didn't even have shoes
You'd just be steppin with your bare feet on the hard concrete"

He always tried to throw in some lame hip hop to prove he was cool
Even when I did something right, like help him move our couch
"You would-a never made it as a slave"
Now why?
"Don't you know that once you let em know how hard you could work
That's how hard you would work"
So I dropped the couch

I can't even believe he took it to the ancestors
But that's my uncle D
You know how the old folks be

(MYEISHA dances, hits the "lower back move." She notices that the CORO-NER cuts the record every time she gets to that move. She battles CORONER with the "lower back move" for control of the turntables trying to stop him/her from cutting the record then letting it play. MYEISHA wins this battle.)

8

(DJ samples a series of "eights." MYEISHA dances "lower back move"as the CORONER "cuts up" the following:)

CORONER: The entrance to gunshot number eight is located on the right
lower back.
The course of the projectile is through the skin and soft tissue of the right
lower back and perforating and fracturing the third lumbar vertebra.

MYEISHA: Check it out
(Showing lower back.) Can you see it?
It's a "C" curve in the lower back
Believe it or not I was happy bout that

After the X-rays they were like the diagnosis is Scoliosis
I was like *(smelling breath in hand)* Na-ah
No, not halitosis
Scoliosis
I was like, I didn't think so

Because it was a "C" curve in the lower back, right here
You couldn't see the brace that they tried to make me wear for two years
You should see the brace they tried to make me wear for a whole two years
Eight grade was cool
But not in high school

Like I said I was glad it was in my lower back
I just looked a little whack
Especially in jeans
Had a pair of Gloria Vanderbilts that I loved

The only good thing... one day Ricky gets the bright idea to smack me in the back
So he goes *(swinging)* whack!
And then ... *(hurt hand face)* Oh crap!
That's what he gets

If I had done my exercises, they say
I wouldn't-a had to wear the brace 23 hours a day
I just got to take it off for P-E
Supposed to wear it for two years, humph
After the 8th grade I was done
I wasn't bout to show up in high school with a brace
Two whole years before I was endowed with second base

My biggest worry though was back pain at 50
That ... was my biggest worry
(MYEISHA dances, hits the "lower back move." She notices that the CORONER cuts the record every time she gets to that move. She battles CORONER with the "lower back move" for control of the turntables trying to stop him/her from cutting the record then letting it play. MYEISHA wins this battle.)

9
(DJ samples a series of "Nines." MYEISHA dances "left breast move" as the CORONER "cuts up" the following:)
CORONER: The entrance to gunshot number nine is through the left breast. The wound is located five inches to the left of the anterior midline and fourteen inches down from the top of the head. This is a typical distant gunshot wound entrance.
The course of the projectile is through the soft tissue of the left breast, through the anterior chest wall and exiting below the right breast.
The exit to gunshot wound six is located below the right breast.
This is a non-fatal gunshot wound perforating the left breast.

MYEISHA: If you know me you know I wasn't
 One of the early bloomers like my cousin
 Til I was like sixteen it seemed like "A" was gonna be the only letter on my
 bra ever
 Clever Ricky and his friends got to callin me "Manchester"
 Wanna know what I called their sorry behinds
 Never mind
 But then I turned sixteen
 And bam

 I mean boom!

 I mean pow!
 I mean wow!
 I got mine
 See *(Chest pop)*
 Second base all in yo face

 Now it wasn't like I was easy... or fast or loose
 But that don't mean I didn't let loose when I let loose
 I guess if I wanted to I could tell you that I'm a virgin
 But that wouldn't be the honest version
 Waited til I was sixteen though

 I didn't know if we were even doin it right
 No lights
 Dontrey kept talkin bout how the time was right
 How he was the last of his boys in line
 How that wasn't right
 Thing was, Dontrey was foine
 And once we did it we did it all night long *(Curtis Blow style)* till the
 break-a-dawn
 Well, at least that's Dontrey's version
 But let's just say that dawn came with a quickness—can I get a witness...
 That night   ʻ
 But
 It was still alright
 It was still alright

 (Back in the moment) Mouth was slightly open...
 eyes were closed...
 breathing shallow...
 lips quivering...
 body shaking.

Dontrey liked my lips he dug my hips,
but yes, he loved my chest
Confessed my chest was the best
Good guess
He was a breast man
And at sixteen, like I said, I had the best
man
Forget the rest, come caress
Why settle for less
man

Just stop right there
Do not touch the hair

At sixteen stopped wondering found out for sure
At seventeen stopped accepting and started wanting more
At eighteen declared myself a woman, grown... mature
At nineteen awaiting 20... knockin on heaven's door
Awaiting twenty
A weight in twenty
I wait for twenty

At sixteen stopped wondering found out for sure
At seventeen stopped accepting and started wanting more
At eighteen declared myself a woman, grown... mature
At nineteen awaiting 20... knockin on heaven's door

At twenty a teenager no more... grown
I'm gon learn to moan
At twenty a teenager no more... grown
I'm gon learn to moan
But sounds like twenty's getting out of reach
And I'm running out of time
Half-a-dozen on one hand six on the other, figure of speech
And I'm running out of rhyme
Seems like a crime
To waste all that I bring to the table
So why don't we agree to make this tale a fable
Let's agree to make this a fable
Seems like a crime
To waste all that I bring to the table
So why don't we agree to make this tale a fable

(Rapping:) Once upon a time in the Inland Empire
There lived a young girl wanted to spit fire
There lived a young girl wanted to spit fire
There lived a young girl—

Why don't we agree to make this tale a fable
Then if you're able, if you can
If it's not too much to ask

When they finish singing your happy 19th birthday before you make your wish and blow
Put a candle on your cake for me to add to the glow
Close your eyes and wish that what you're seeing ain't nothin but a dream-fable
And I'm gonna wake up nineteen at your birthday table
Close your eyes and wish that what you're seeing ain't nothin but a dream-fable
And I'm gonna wake up nineteen at your birthday table

Put another candle on to add to the glow

Now make your wish and blow

OFFICER GARLAND: Miller's mouth was slightly open, her eyes were closed, her breathing appeared shallow, her lips were quivering, her body was shaking, and a white substance was accumulating around the sides of her mouth.

MYEISHA: At nineteen...
  "Knockin on heaven's door."

(MYEISHA dances, hits the "left breast move." She notices that the CORONER cuts the record every time she gets to that move. She battles CORONER with the "left breast move" for control of the turntables trying to stop him/her from cutting the record then letting it play. MYEISHA wins this battle.)

10
(DJ samples series of "tens." MYEISHA does the "upper left forehead" move.)
CORONER: The entrance to gunshot number ten is located on the left upper forehead. This is a typical distant gunshot wound entrance.
  The course of the projectile is through the skin of the forehead, entering the cranium through the left frontal bone, through the left and right frontal lobes of the brain, through the right orbit perforating and rupturing the right ocular globe and exiting the right orbit.

The direction of the projectile is back-to-front, left-to-right and downward 45 degrees.

This is a fatal distant gunshot wound to the head.

(MYEISHA battles CORONER for control of the turntables trying to stop him/her from cutting the record then letting it play. The CORONER wins this battle.)

11

(DJ samples series of "elevens." MYEISHA does the "left ear move.")

CORONER: The entrance of gunshot wound number eleven is above and behind the left ear on the left side of the head. This is a typical distant gunshot wound entrance.

The course of the projectile is through the scalp, entering the cranium through the left occipital bone, perforating the left cerebellum, perforating the pons of the brain stem and penetrating into the anterior base of the cranium.

This is a fatal distant gunshot wound to the head.

MYEISHA: *(Holds headphones to left ear, as if in recording studio.)*
One-to-the-chest
One-to-the-arm
One-to-the-leg
One-to-the-neck

One-to-the-dome
One-to-the-dome
One-to-the-dome

One-to-the-back
One-to-the back
One-to-the-back
One-to-the-back
One-to-the-back

I bet you ain't seen no female MC who's been shot as many times as me
Not since *Supersonic* has a female MC from the west put it down with the best
You know, one of the J's from JJ Fad lives in the IE
For a minute I was thinkin of rappin in Pig Latin
But that ain't hap'nin
This is the key right here
It's been a year since they shot Biggie

Since Tupac was killed it's been two
It just makes sense that this should happen to me now
I gotta live
I'll be the first female MC ever
Too clever
Before me MCs only been shot a couple times
And lived
I got a dozen and I'll still be spittin rhymes
You can't stop me this is my time to shine

(A red bandana/blood begins to ooze from MYEISHA's headphones/ear. She stops rappin and tries to push bandana/blood back into her ear. When she realizes she can't push it back in, she pulls out the bandana and ties it around her head TUPAC style—she becomes him.)

One-to-the-chest
One-to-the-arm
One-to-the-leg
One-to-the-neck

One-to-the-dome
One-to-the-dome
(MYEISHA re-ties the bandana BIGGIE style—she becomes him)
One-to-the-dome
One-to-the-back
One-to-the back
One-to-the-back
One-to-the-back
One-to-the-back

(MYEISHA battles CORONER for control of the turntables trying to stop him/her from cutting the record then letting it play. The CORONER wins this battle.)

12

(DJ samples series of "twelves." MYEISHA does the "right central back" move.)
CORONER: The entrance to gunshot number twelve is located on the right
central back. This is a typical distant gunshot wound entrance.
The direction of the projectile is back-to-front, left-to-right and slightly
upward three degrees.
This is a fatal distant gunshot wound to the chest perforating the right
lung.
(DJ mixes Kanye's "Breathe In Breathe Out")

MYEISHA: *(To Audience)*
Aw'rite, you ready?
Go! *(She inhales, holds her nose, holds her breath.)*

DJ: The average person can hold their breath for sixty to ninety seconds
The lungs take in oxygen enriched air first and gets rid of carbon dioxide second
The average person breathes in and out 15 to 25 times every 60 seconds
Breath enters through the nose and mouth first, pharynx and larynx second
(MYEISHA exhales)
There are two phases to the process of breathing
Inspiration happens first
Expiration happens second

(MYEISHA inspires and expires 25 times. Breaths should be taken meditatively, gradually slowing, then coming to stop.)
INSPIRATION: creativity
EXPIRATION: release
INSPIRATION: insight
EXPIRATION: conclusion
INSPIRATION: inventiveness
EXPIRATION: completion
INSPIRATION: ingenuity
EXPIRATION: closure
INSPIRATION: imagination
EXPIRATION: exhalation

INSPIRATION: revelation
EXPIRATION: cessation
INSPIRATION: stimulation
EXPIRATION: departure
INSPIRATION: arousal
EXPIRATION: eradication
INSPIRATION: muse
EXPIRATION: expelled
INSPIRATION: motivation
EXPIRATION: termination

INSPIRATION: vision
EXPIRATION: discontinuance
INSPIRATION: illumination

EXPIRATION: extinction
INSPIRATION: elevation
EXPIRATION: execution
INSPIRATION: enthusiasm
EXPIRATION: closure
INSPIRATION: invigoration
EXPIRATION: obliteration

INSPIRATION: enthusiasm
EXPIRATION: collapse
INSPIRATION: excitement
EXPIRATION: finale
INSPIRATION: fervor
EXPIRATION: finish
INSPIRATION: elation
EXPIRATION: termination
INSPIRATION: vivification
EXPIRATION: death

INSPIRATION: awakening
EXPIRATION: passing
INSPIRATION: uplift
EXPIRATION: exit
INSPIRATION: rapture
EXPIRATION: deceased
INSPIRATION: alpha
EXPIRATION: omega
INSPIRATION: beginning

MYEISHA: *(Rushing to get to bed. In one breath.)*
Now I lay me down to sleep
I pray the Lord my soul to keep
If I should die before I wake
I pray the Lord my soul to take
Bless mommy and daddy, Shy, Freddie, Aunt Dee and my cousin Toni
This is Myeisha

You know me.
(MYEISHA stops breathing.
The CORONER wins the battle, "celebrates" by mixing the following while
MYEISHA dances the 12 mortal moves to Otis Redding's "White Christmas.")

CORONER: Right lung weighed 270 grams
  Left lung weighed 325 grams
  Liver weighed 975 grams
  Spleen weighed 100 grams
  Kidneys weighed 100 grams each
  Brain weighed 1,025 grams
  Heart weighed 275 grams and was smooth and glistening…
(MYEISHA finishes her dance then quickly climbs into bed—the autopsy table—"she goes to sleep.")

End

by Chadwick Boseman

Deep Azure

SETTING: CAPITAL CITY

CHARACTERS:

AZURE: African American. Age 21. She graduated from Mecca University last May. Deep's girlfriend. An anorexic-bulimic. She also plays the personified eating disorder. ALTER.

TONE: African American. Age 23. Deep's right-hand man. He was in the reserves before he came to Mecca University. Graduated last May.

DEEP: Is dead at the outset of the play, killed seven days prior by a policeman. He was scheduled to graduate this May.

ROSHAD: Deep and Tone's friend. Once a philosophy major at Mecca, he dropped out of Mecca during his junior year because he's more intrigued by the activist and party life outside of school. Now he's a deejay and a left-handed priest.

STREET KNOWLEDGE: The Duo angelic chorus. Invisible. Twin Lovers. Individually, she is STREET KNOWLEDGE OF GOOD (SK GOOD), and he is STREET KNOWLEDGE OF EVIL (SK EVIL). They are angelic messengers that exist on a higher frequency of light. They transform into many different characters through the play. They are able to send word, song and idea to the other characters. It is important to remember that *SK Evil* is the knowledge of evil. He is not limited to evil. Likewise, Street Knowledge of Good is the knowledge of good. She is not limited to good.

JOYCE SMITH: Deep's Mother. *Played by Street Knowledge of Good.*

OFFICER SMITH: The officer who murders Deep. *Played by Street Knowledge of Evil.*

NOTES FROM THE PLAYWRIGHT:

—This play is generally done with six actors.

—The transformations of Street Knowledge of Good and Evil are intended to occur through the use of popping and locking movements.

—Despite the musicality of the language, the lines should be spoken in a conversational tone, not rapped; except in those places where the author has indicated that the character *(raps)*. Likewise, actors should also not employ affected voices that are commonly viewed as Shakespearean or classical. The heightened performance of this text should flow organically from the depth of the characters' circumstances, intentions and desires.

◆

ACT ONE

Prologue:
(Street Knowledge of Good and Evil, the angelic chorus, goddess and god respectively, are joined as one body, their limbs reminiscent of the many arms of Ganesh.)

STREET KNOWLEDGE: Let us lie a lie more true than truth.
STREET KNOWLEDGE OF EVIL: Label us myth.
   Fact not fitting facts found in real life's riffs to a 't'.
SK GOOD *(together; sings)*: I speak not what is…
SK EVIL *(together)*: I speak not what is…
SK GOOD *(sings)*: … but what has been and could be
SK: Let us…
SK GOOD *(sings)*: …lie to you and bridge the gap 'tween fact and fiction, and while this our tale spins, know no contradiction.
SK: Let us…

SK EVIL:…unwind the lines of a verse with moments prepared, lyrics rehearsed. Call it not play, though events be false.

SK: Let us…

SK GOOD *(sings)*:…Ciphers to this great accompt, suspend your thoughts.

SK GOOD *(together; sings)*: Break your rhyme and reason and latch to our lines.

SK EVIL *(together)*: Break your rhyme and reason and latch to our lines. *(SK EVIL and SK GOOD break away from one another. They begin to create the characters on the stage.)*

SK GOOD: Measure the tears of the not-quite-widowed dame of our Prince, nick-named Deep for the depth of his thought and charity,
   but Christened Joshua, minister of verity,
   held high in the hearts of student and teacher, thug and preacher alike.
   Leaving behind 'Zure, his girl friend, Tone, his main man and Roshad, his right rod,
   this Prince left us dense, and flew home to God too soon.
   Too soon by judgment of the bullshit way he was whacked.

SK: Yes whacked.

SK GOOD: By that I mean murdered and banged by the common senselessness of a neighborhood gang.

SK EVIL: To what set and name falls the blame of this heinous deed?
   Witnesses saw no Bloods, 'cept blood the prince did bleed.
   And though that boy was of blue, he showed no signs of Crip.
   But hear this lie, more true than truth from my very lips.
   T'was an officer of "peace" that waged war on our warrior of light.
   How this brutality came to a fatality one night, that is the question.
   What had he done? Possession?
   No gun. No boat. No bud. No crack. No transgression.

SK: None.

SK GOOD: Blameless.

SK EVIL: Though not the tale told by the Po-po that tailed Deep back from Zure's house, cross three counties,
   claiming he fit the description, busting slugs outside of his jurisdiction.
   But hold.
   Fuck my words. Peep it first.
   Make seeing believing and believing our goal.

SK GOOD: The after-birth of death unfolds.

SK GOOD *(together; sings)*: Let's sling a slang for all sights and seasons in our song, and may our unsettled souls know what star's gone wrong.

SK EVIL *(together)*: Let's sling a slang for all sights and seasons in our song, and may our unsettled souls know what star's gone wrong.

Scene One:

(Early Black. Inside the house, Azure sits at the kitchen table struggling over a bowl of Life cereal. Tone sits in the living room watching the TV. The essential furniture inside the house besides the kitchen table is the couch, under which Azure hides her scale, and a visible toilet, representing the bathroom. The television and the mirror are also essential to the world but can be played through the actor's points of focus. Outside the house, picket signs reading, "NO JUSTICE, NO PEACE," from the day's protest lean against the porch and steps, where Roshad sits, flipping open a pocket knife repetitively. Street Knowledge of Good pop-locks/ morphs into an anchor-woman while Street Knowledge of Evil morphs into an on-site reporter.)

ROSHAD *(whispers, overlaps)*: NO JUSTICE, NO PEACE, NO CROOKED POLICE.
NO JUSTICE, NO PEACE, NO CROOKED POLICE.
NO JUSTICE NO PEACE NO CROOKED POLICE. *(Continues.)*

SK GOOD *(overlaps)*: In the News. Students from Mecca University joined other community activist organizations in front of the courthouse to protest what they are calling the brutal slaying of Joshua Smith.

ROSHAD: *(Building in feeling. His rant overlaps the news cast.)*
THE PEOPLE UNITED WILL NEVER BE DEFEATED.
THE PEOPLE UNITED WILL NEVER BE DEFEATED.
THE PEOPLE UNITED WILL NEVER BE DEFEATED.
WHAT DO WE WANT? JUSTICE.
WHEN DO WE WANT IT? NOW.
WHAT DO WE WANT? JUSTICE. WHEN DO WE WANT IT? NOW.

STREET KNOWLEDGE OF GOOD *(overlaps)*: Smith, a MECCA University student, was killed after an altercation with K.G. County officer Lawrence Smith, no relation, last Thursday. Officer Smith has stated that he was defending himself in a dangerous situation. The students of Mecca and other community activists are hopeful that the grand jury proceedings scheduled for tomorrow will result in an indictment of Officer Smith.

(Unable to stomach any more food, Azure puts the spoon down and slides the bowl away from her.)

ROSHAD *(overlaps)*: WHAT DO WE WANT? JUSTICE.
WHEN DO WE WANT IT? NOW.
WHAT DO WE WANT? JUSTICE.
WHEN DO WE WANT IT? NOW.

ONE, TWO, THREE, FOUR,
CROOKED COPS GET OFF THE FORCE.
FIVE, SIX, SEVEN, EIGHT,
WE DON'T WANT NO COPS THAT HATE.

STREET KNOWLEDGE OF EVIL: What was originally planned as a candle-light vigil and a small observance of silence for the life of Joshua Smith at the flagpole of Mecca University's campus turned into a passionate speak-out and eventually a march from the campus to the courthouse down-town. At the courthouse, the students proceeded to march around the building seven times, chanting slogans of change, demanding that the building live up to its name.

(*Tone cuts off the television. Azure lies down on the couch. Street Knowledge morphs back into their original appearance.*)
ROSHAD: WHAT DO WE WANT? NOW.
  WHAT DO WE WANT? NOW.
  WHAT DO WE WANT? WHAT DO WE WANT? WHAT DO WE WANT? NOW.
  NO JUSTICE. NOW. NO JUSTICE. NOW.
  NO JUSTICE, NO JUSTICE, NO JUSTICE, NOW.
(*Hearing Roshad's rant outside, Tone rises from his seat beside Azure and peeks his head outside to check on Roshad.*)
TONE: Break your spell. You are zoned.
ROSHAD: What up, Tone? You startled me.
TONE: What up, Shad? Why you lampin' alone?
ROSHAD: My brother, Tone, didn't even know it was night.
  Nor did I notice the day's light.
TONE: Early black still. You aight?
ROSHAD: The temper within affects the sight.
TONE: Break your spell I said.
ROSHAD: Juice for your blues. Sit a spell. (*Roshad offers him a bottle covered in a bag.*)
TONE: Shouldn't drink before work, but I might as well. (*Tone takes a swig. Roshad gives his last lick to an expertly rolled blunt and puts it up to his lips.*)
TONE: Sip that ale with this el, you'll be straight enough to sail away.
ROSHAD: El. What a funny way to pray.
TONE: What laughs at it?
ROSHAD: El. It's a name for god in Hebrew.
  But God is lettin' everybody down these days, 'cluding you.
  Fuck Him. Pass the blues.

(Tone passes the brew back to 'Shad, who downs a big gulp.)

TONE: Fuck Him you fuck yourself in the same way.

ROSHAD: Nigga you're just saying what Deep would say.

TONE: Pure and true.

ROSHAD: Slide your jib, spit from the heart and do not take it slow,
for at this point I do not know if there is an El that cares to spy on the
movements of man. It seems his all seeing eye was jacked by B'el,
who hears our silent swears and grants us an evil share.

TONE: Chill, son. The gods do listen.

ROSHAD: If they do, so what? That they did on the night when our main
man was slain, and then what? What good were his eyes and ears if they
produce no action here? Show me the reel to real of what you feel. Are we
not human, nigga?

TONE: We are gods but shall die as men. But I'll descend to your blas-
phemies for a spell. Tis an off-time jive.

ROSHAD: Aight. Spit on.

TONE: Off-time indeed that deed. Were I God, I would've taken a million
other men before Joshua Smith.

ROSHAD: Say word.

TONE: Were I God, and did drive-by with semi, and shot with un-specific
aim into a crowd of peoples a whole round of slugs, I couldn't have taken
one more innocent than my beloved from the oldest of old to the tiny baby
hugged. Tis an off-time jive.

ROSHAD: Amen. Fuck Him.

TONE: But if the gods don't listen, Deep was one who believed, so do not
grieve so far.

(Tone enters a flashback.)

DEEP *(excited)*: Yo, a drug treatment center, a center for the homeless! I'm
trying to build with you, yo.

TONE: I have no science that's sound for your ears.

DEEP: You don't think it's possible?

TONE: I'd rather spit on this not, less the doubt from my mouth foil your plot.
I'll put no such crime on my tongue as keeping the home out of house, en-
forcing the chains on brothers' feet, and withholding justice from its rightful seat.
I will not say that change is impossible, but that you seek is more than
colossal.

DEEP: With God all things are possible.

TONE: And there is the rub of our biggest debate of late.

DEEP: So your unbelief in the Creator makes you the debater?

TONE: That there is one I have no question. That He makes men new overnight, that's where my doubt lies.

DEEP: Then your doubt lies sho 'nuff, and here lies tough proof. Man was created in one day, that day being the sixth, and the whole world formed in a week's tick. Even the twinkling of an eye's not quick for God's magic.

TONE: Fine. You are fixed. And now you fancy to fix all flaws that man has caused. A drug treatment center? A center for the homeless? That's a lot on one plate. Don't let your eyes make your stomach ache.

DEEP: My eye is as big as my soul.

My soul is a sea seen from beach.

I'm just telling you a long-range reach.

TONE: Next thing you know you'll be soapboxing the streets. *(Tone holds his hand out over Deep's like he's healing him. Mocking:)* "The Spirit of the Lord is upon him…The Lord has anointed Him to preach good tidings to the poor."

DEEP: Careful how you play in the pulpit. Many have been drafted for the office they once laughed at.

TONE: So you're serious about this Seminary shift?

DEEP: I think that's the place where I can use all my gifts.

TONE: Berserk.

DEEP: If my change blows your mind, then perhaps the signs divine that were shown to me will spark your belief.

One night, not long ago, I was awakened from sleep's flow by a wind,

but no window was open.

Blinded by a light, but no lamp glowed in the night.

And that wind did enter the gates of my mouth and nostrils

to make me breathe a new breath.

And that glow made windows of my eyes so that I saw past this world's guise,

making me see my own face in front of me.

In this vision, I saw who I am purposed to be.

And that clarity that hit made perfect sense,

since the Creator would have instructions for His creation.

Since this realization, I accept that I am dumb at God's math.

As the saying goes, 'tell Yah your plans if you want Him to laugh.'

What you say is berserk is God's work.

TONE: I know your word as bond, but this sound is libel.

DEEP: All that you've heard from my lips is Bible.

You are known for wearing your boots, but God has proven he can make fools of the wise.

(*The flashback ends.*)

ROSHAD: 'Zure still inside?

  I'm not sure if her staying here is wise.

TONE: She's stayed here before mad times.

ROSHAD: But no time as mad as this. The illness she deals with
  is magnified the more by her trauma.

  I don't know if we're equipped to deal with her drama.

TONE: She's hardly spoken a line in this widowed stage.

ROSHAD: Let us play our rightful parts,

  not taking deeds too big for our hearts.

TONE: Here she feels closer to Deep.

  If Deep is in your heart, know that she is in his.

  By loving each other, he continues to live.

ROSHAD: Pure and true.

TONE: Let's leave this lamp and go peep how she fares,
  and if the not-quite widowed weeps, let us lighten the air. (*Roshad and
  Tone enter the house.*) Sh. She is sound.

ROSHAD: Surround sound.

TONE: The snore of a tired soul. She should be old with all she's been
  through in a week.

ROSHAD: A biased investigation to say the least.

  Crooked ass cops.

TONE: Not all but some.

ROSHAD: The ones that ain't crooked stay wise and play dumb.

TONE: Quiet and still, bra. Your movements are crooked and tipsy.

ROSHAD: If not my feet, then your voice for how loud you quiet me.
  (*Roshad removes his shoes and holds them up. Azure wakes up suddenly from
  a nightmare kicking and punching the air frantically.*)

AZURE: Aaaah...Up and down this street, you hear me...

TONE: 'Zure... 'Zure!

AZURE (*repeats*): All over this concrete, you're gone listen to me...listen to
  me...listen to me. (*Tone catches her swinging arms. She looks around and
  recognizes her surroundings. She catches her breath.*)

TONE (*to her*): Chill...

  (*To Roshad:*) See. It was the scent of your stank ass feet.

  (*To her:*) Rest.

AZURE: I should get to my own nest.

TONE: Rest. Adlib tonight.

AZURE: What day is it?

ROSHAD: Thursday.

AZURE: A set of seven brights since I buried my knight. What time?

TONE: Late black, too late to drive back. Plus, these times ain't normal.
What's gone down outweighs the formal. It's okay for you to stay. Rest.

AZURE: I buried rest in his grave! Flowers and verses, hymns and hearses.
Rest is buried so I am up.

TONE: You just laid down and have been up all day. Peace. Be still.

AZURE: Just don't feel right to chill.

TONE: Shit to do.

AZURE: The police and the people and the protests.

TONE: The protest is a finished fest. Tonight rest.

(She finally sits on the couch beside the drunken Roshad.)

AZURE *(to Tone)*: You spoke well today.

ROSHAD: Well, he spoke.

AZURE *(to Roshad)*: You are blitzed.

ROSHAD: "Grabbed my forty. Then I reminisced."
The el I inhaled was a powerful god sho'nuff.

TONE: And powerful more because you worshiped two idols tonight.
Your religions mixed have you twisted and off-sight.
He chases spirits with the spirits.

ROSHAD: I am a left-handed priest. I need a little buzz to breathe. *(Roshad sits. He whispers a drunken song. Mary J. Blige and Method, "You're All I Need.")*

ROSHAD: *(Raps)*: "Shorty you were there for me. Anytime you need me/ For real, Girl, it's me and your world/ believe me/ Nothin' makes a man feel better than a woman/ Queen with a crown that be down for whateva'. There's a few things that's 'Forever My Lady'. We can make war or make babies."

(His fervor grows as the others join along, forgetting the present in the nostalgia. Deep and Street Knowledge create the music that they hear in their heads.)

ALL: *(Rap:)* "Back when I was nothin', you made a brother feel like he was something. That's why I'm with you till this day, boo, no frontin'. Even when the skies were gray, you would rub me on my back and say, 'baby, it will be okay,' and that's real to a brother like me, baby. Never ever give my "AAAH" away. Keep it tight. Aight."[1]

ROSHAD. Yo, that was the time.

TONE: Tick tock.

AZURE: Those were the lines.

TONE: Say word.

---

1. Smith, Clifford (Method Man), Robert Diggs (RZA), Nickolas Ashford, and Valerie Simpson. 1995. "You're All I Need/ I'll Be There for You (Razor Sharp Mix)" on *I'll Be There for You*. Performed by Mary J. Blige and Method Man. Def Jam Music Inc./Polygram Int.

ROSHAD *(to Tone)*: Oh, draw back the day when you, me and Deep got caught choking in the dorms. Almost got expelled for a spell.

TONE: Junior year, before we moved in here.

AZURE: Told y'all about choking in the dorm.

ROSHAD: We'd done the shit a million times before.

TONE: Yeah, but you didn't put the towel up under the door.

AZURE: Slippin'.

ROSHAD: The towel was tight. The R.A. was just trippin'. Plus you was burning them wack ass incense hardly covering up the scent.

AZURE: Y'all wouldn't have been in the room if you had any sense.

TONE *(laughing)*: We had to do community service down at the... soup kitchen.

ROSHAD: ...soup kitchen. Yeah. That's when Deep started talkin' about he'd found his mission. Said, "If you're only serving self...

TONE: ...That service is in vain"...

AZURE: That is when he started to change.

TONE: I couldn't believe it when he took a semester off to follow his call.

ROSHAD: Changed his major, stopped smoking, talking 'bout he was high off the Spirit. Started quoting scriptures and shit. I had his back on most fronts, but on that he was solo.

TONE: I know. I never thought he'd to Seminary go.

AZURE: And he never will now that he's been killed. *(Beat.)*

Each day the cop's story changes to something stranger.

First, Deep was suspected to be a dealer of drugs,

but all the world knows that he was in no way a thug.

Then the officer said he followed him across three counties,

'cause he thought Deep was another wanted for a bounty.

They claim that he rammed his car into the policeman's ride for no reason, but without reason, why ram? And how twice rammed? And why did the policeman then allow Deep to get back into his car without cuffing him if he was wrong?

ROSHAD: Tomorrow they'll have a new song.

AZURE: It has to be more than just a random mistake!

ROSHAD: The cop that popped Deep was a former student, a man of Mecca's mind.

AZURE: The ironies cannot be ironed with the mind.

ROSHAD: He and Deep even shared the same last name. Lawrence...

ALL: ...*Smith*...

AZURE: ...but Deep's mother says there's no relation.

ROSHAD: Maybe their great fathers plowed the same plantation.

AZURE: Maybe he already knew Deep, and was settling an old beef.

TONE: Scholar your thoughts. No conspiracy theories.

AZURE: Makes as much sense as anything else we've been briefed.

TONE: Pure and true.

ROSHAD *(whisper rises to a chant)*: No justice, no peace, no crooked police.
No justice, no peace, no crooked police.
The people united will never be defeated.
THE PEOPLE UNITED WILL NEVER BE DEFEATED.
WHAT DO WE WANT? JUSTICE.
WHEN DO WE WANT IT? NOW. Just don't feel right to chill. *(Roshad bursts up from his seat, and heads to the door.)*

TONE: Where you gonna go?

ROSHAD *(to Azure)*: Just to the porch to smoke this dro'.
You heard from Deep's mother?

AZURE: She sends her love to you and Tone.

ROSHAD: Send back my love the next time she phones. *(Roshad exits, leaving Tone and Azure alone. Beat. Tone begins to exit.)*

AZURE: Thanks for letting me stay.

TONE: Stay as long as you like.

AZURE: I'll be aight.

(Tone exits to his room down the hall. Once she is alone, Azure pulls a journal from the cracks of the couch and reads.)

AZURE *(reads)*: "I'm holding on to the memories and the possibilities of our laughs in love." *(To herself:)* A poem about us no doubt.
(Reads:) "I'm holding on to the memories and the possibilities of our laughs in love."
(She flips the page)
"Move the scale away from the bed."
No doubt. No doubt. Oh. *(She grabs her side in pain. As she reads Deep's journal, she hears him saying the same words in a rapid slam poetry cadence.)*

DEEP: I'm holding/holding/holding on to the memories, to the possibilities/ to the memories, to the possibilities of our laughs in love.
Laughs in love echo in my mind/ in my mind/ in my mind.
Oh how we would swing on our imaginations,
slide into sand with no boxes/no boundaries,
on the playground of our passions,
learning rules just to break them.
If you'll lie, you'll steal/lie you'll steal.
I lie inwith/inwith/inwith you,

stealing kisses until I'm imprisoned by your eyes.
Some fall in love. I fell inside your eyes, and rolled down your cheeks, trapped in a salty tear, destined to hurt you, even though I loved you.
When I praised your fill, you'd cry still.
Remember the odes I sing. I'd breathe:
"There's a ring 'round the full Moon.
'cause all my thoughts revolve around you
Turned me into a night creature,
hungry, howling at your fullness,
searching for you my...preyed for your stay,
kissed your crescent into the cracks of day."
But when I praised your fullness, you'd dull this,
'cause you didn't want to be full. Didn't want that shape to show.
Too many niggas figuring on that shape.
You're afraid of mental rape from the geometric study of your body.
Too many "God Damns!" too many one-nights stands, too many wandering hands, too many mini-men trying to find wholeness at your soul's expense, so you tried to change it for your own happiness.
You know I've been through every shape under the sun with you, My Moon.
From Full to Quarter to Crescent to...
I've been through every shape under the sun with you, My Moon.
From full to Quarter to Crescent to...
(*She begins to stare at herself in the mirror. She then, slides a scale from its hiding place under the couch and stands on top of it.*)

AZURE	DEEP
"I can't see me like you see me,"	"I can't see me like you see me." Says she.
I tried. The mirror lies and steals my eyes into madness.	
	Holding up a dress. Saying:
"How do I look in this?"	
	He says, "From Full to Quarter to Crescent to...blur." She says:
"I want to look like her."	
	Flippin' through...
Vogue/Cosmopolitan, Vogue/Cosmopolitan.	Vogue/Cosmopolitan, Vogue/Cosmopolitan, There's nothing more beautiful than the Moon African.

Vogue/Cosmopolitan Vogue/Cosmopolitan,

Vogue /Cosmopolitan Vogue/Cosmopolitan,

There's nothing more beautiful than
the Moon African.

Gotta be slim/Gotta be slim… Gotta be slim/Gotta be slim…
From full to quarter to crescent to…

Gotta be slim/Gotta be slim… Gotta be slim/Gotta be slim…
From full to quarter to crescent to…

Gotta be slim/Gotta be slim… Gotta be slim/Gotta be slim…
From full to quarter to crescent to…
(Screams) MOVE THE SCALE
AWAY FROM THE BED.

DEEP. From full to quarter to crescent to…Dead…you eat today?
  (Pause.) Why didn't you eat? *(Azure bends over the toilet and vomits.)*
  Did you eat today? Don't you think your Mom should know about this?
  What's wrong baby? What's wrong?

*(Inside the bathroom we hear the sounds of vomiting. Tone enters, dressed for
work, wearing a fugitive recovery uniform. He hears Azure inside the bathroom.
He stops to listen. The toilet flushes and Azure exits exhausted from the bathroom ordeal. Tone tries to skirt away into the kitchen. Azure opens the door.)*

AZURE: What?

TONE: What?

AZURE: How long you been standin' out here? What did you hear?

TONE: Nothing. I gotta go to work. I'm just fixing some food to eat.

AZURE: Your eyes were fixed over here when the door opened.

TONE: Well, my concentration was broken. *(Tone finally throws his bottles
  away.)*

AZURE: Concentration broken how long?

TONE: As long as I care to stand in my kitchen in my home.

AZURE: My fault. Your home and my mouth too wide in it.

TONE: Too wide indeed. Wide enough to vomit what your body needs.

AZURE: How long were you lurking in the cut?

TONE: Long enough.

AZURE: Whatever you think you know, don't count that as a fact you can
  trust.

TONE: The facts get slimmer and slimmer right before us.
  Come on. We are friends, not by Deep alone but by our own bonds and
  promises unbroken. We have spoken of this before while you were in the core
  of a place depressed. And even when you and Deep could not converse,
  I was an ear to your vexed verse.

AZURE: If rapped on before, there's no need for it to be touched on again.

TONE: Don't feel that you have no ears to listen now that Deep is gone. I gave ear to him and the other was there for you with a divided heart at times. Now you have both drums and my whole heart for your rhymes...

AZURE: ...I'm fine. I don't want to be anybody's project.

TONE: Respect.

(Beat. Awkward.)

AZURE: Haven't seen you rock this gear in a minute.

TONE: As much as I hate the shirt, I had to go back to work.

AZURE: Just can't see you bustin' any brothers?

TONE: Brothers and all others, whatever the description. Depends on the mission.

AZURE: Just an unlikely job.

TONE: Gotta eat. Gotta make the ends meet, you know?

AZURE: Dry-long-so.

(Beat.)

All the time I've known him I wanted to know the thoughts he sealed in these pages quilled. Mind wandered cross a whole host of hiddens. His words were truly his mistress. Wondered what was in his secret art. Always felt I knew him in part.

TONE: No man can reveal all of his heart.

AZURE: This I know more than any other.

TONE: And Deep was a complicated brother.

AZURE: Complicated to the point of confusion.

What I've peeped more than anything else is that he was human.

TONE: And that you couldn't read before you began to scroll?

AZURE: I did know, but didn't grasp in the same way as I hold his human-ity today.

A man's fears, his hopes, his dreams unspoken,

his faults unveiled to the point of complete humility,

makes a man more of a divinity,

more loved than before,

when he could close his heart's doors.

TONE: You catch the vapors as if he stands here restored.

AZURE: Catching vapors. Yes.

Holding nothing. Yes, nor being held.

I wonder if it's a sin to have a jones for his soul gone home,

to lust after his ghost, the specter of my sensuous memory,

which remembers our acts in parts and resurrects the art of our intimacy?

I wonder is it a sin. *(Beat.)*

TONE: Never thought of that before,
  how you can still have a jones for a soul gone home.
  But it is a feeling I've almost known.
AZURE: Didn't know you had the heart to love any soul.
  Thought you were a man of steel.
  Stealing the hearts of others but never letting them in.
TONE: I have loved and lost in one breath.
  Yet, not lost, for how can one lose what one has never held in truth.
  I have lost unrequited, untapped, untouched, and worst of all, "un-confessed."
  But I have never lost a love to death.
AZURE: Then confess to your love, whoever she may be.
  If she be, confess.
  Because of death, confess.
  Life is too short to wait.
TONE: It's already too late.
AZURE: Then she is already wed and hitched?
TONE: Ain't life a bitch.
  Plus, I am safe at this base.
AZURE: Safe?
  What a treacherous place.
  Safe.
  Funny how fortunes flip,
  how the fears in past years can become the desire of your lips.
  All those nights I refused him I had no idea that I might soon lose him.
  Wouldn't let him feel this…
TONE: Because of your eating illness?
(Beat.)
AZURE: Yeah. Yeah.
  While he tried to keep our union pure,
  I know it was too much to endure.
  I've already seen lines penned about his frustration in his pages.
  Love passions melodic,
  passion never manifest into flesh erotic.
  Long before he told me, I knew that he'd broken the covenant we built.
TONE: How did you know?
AZURE: It's a woman's gift to know men's guilt.
  Once when I touched his hair,
  I could feel another woman's care in its layers. A shock from his locks was she.

TONE : A shock?

AZURE: A fire for another.

Electricity that wasn't mine, sparked from a lover.

I ducked the thought for a long time,

that some other woman had weaved herself inside his mind,

but I could not ignore that shock from his head.

His locks put me in a state of dread.

More than anything else I blame myself for his moments of stealth.

It was my fault, a product of my mental health.

Plus, with my fading weight, I was no longer the leg and lip and lay I'd been on prior dates when we first touched tongue to tip and heart to hand.

It wasn't hard to guess that he couldn't deal with me being less,

but I cherished "less."

I made "less" my goal,

made his eyes my scale.

The way he looked at me, that's how I could tell my weight.

I made his desire my barometer, his expression my mirror.

I used his frustrations to determine whether or not I was slim.

This is how I kept my love away from him.

Safe.

What a treacherous place.

(Tone kisses her. There is an awkward moment. She kisses him back. Now it is even more awkward.)

BOTH: My fault.

(She looks for a place to hide but finds none. Tone grabs his things for work and exits outside to catch his breath. On the porch, Roshad rhymes a verse to Biggie's "Somebody's Got to Die" as he sips his ale.)

ROSHAD *(raps)*: "...*I open up the door pitiful. 'Is he in critical?' Retaliation for this won't be minimal/ Cause I'm a criminal way before the rap shit. Bust the gatt. Shit, Puff won't even know what happened...if it's done smoothly. Silencers on the Uzi. Stash in the Hooptie, my alibi any cutie with the bootie that's done Fucked Big Pop. Head spinning/ reminiscing bout man C-Rock....*"[2]

Yeah that's what we need. Some Big and a swig." *(Roshad takes a drink from the bottle, pours some of the drink onto the ground.)*

TONE: How's the ale?

---

2. Wallace, C. (Biggie), Sean Combs, A. Hester, Nasheim Myrick, and Carlos Broady. 1997. "Somebody's Gotta Die." Performed by Notorious B.I.G.. Bad Boy Records/Arista Records.

ROSHAD: Sailin', but not far enough away. *(Roshad offers the bottle to Tone again, who takes it this time and downs a large gulp.)*

ROSHAD: Off to work?

(Tone nods.)

We find out tomorrow huh?

(Tone nods.)

With all the excitement, you probably wouldn't get any sleep before the indictment.

TONE: Can I tell you a secret?

ROSHAD: Hush hush, down low.

TONE: You know I have never loved a woman.

ROSHAD: Mack daddy to the end. If you in, get her friend too.

You don't love them hoes, something I always knew.

TONE: I have played more hearts than a gambler hands of cards, and stained more lily whites than a hooker in a hoe house.

ROSHAD: 'Bout it with the ladies you be and with much respect from me 'bout that point.

TONE: And on that point Deep gave me counsel often, saying,

"love is better than lust,"

and thus I abstained from bustin' a nut for a time to search for love,

and did find in an unfortunate pair of eyes.

ROSHAD: A skank skeezer. But no surprise.

Men choose not the arrow of love.

TONE: The last is sound, but the first is off pitch.

Neither skank nor skeezer is she.

ROSHAD: Then why unfortunate? Who is the bitch?

TONE: Bitch neither, but a queen to each. *(Pause.)*

But some reveal too much when love leaks.

Her name I do not intend to breach.

ROSHAD: Then call it not a secret but a half-truth to which my mind reaches in want. You foreplay and tease.

Call us not blood, but half-brothers with half-truths and half-loves. Who is she? Let me know your passion.

TONE: A married passion.

ROSHAD: With ring and papers to boot?

TONE: By God and priest in Church.

ROSHAD: In love? You?

TONE: Fallen and defeated.

ROSHAD: Then Love is a bitch after all.

But he won't catch me with his poisoned arrows.

Those who love must lose one way or another.

Give me my killing under the covers.

TONE: My brother. *(They shake hands and laugh. They both take a swig from the bottle.)*

TONE: What is this we're drinking anyway? *(Reads:)* Rasputin?

ROSHAD: Rasputin. *(Playfully.)* There will be no disputin' it.

TONE: Never had it before. *(Roshad displays the label of the bottle, which depicts Rasputin's face.)*

ROSHAD: Ha ha! This man, this mug on the cover, played servant to the Russian Czar just before the First World War.

His fame is in the histories carved wholly as both a lowly priest and a holy a pimp with a perfected piece.

When the Czar's only seed Alexei was plagued with a tendency to bleed, the Czar searched the land for a man who could heal his son's issue.

But none far-off or familiar could heal his son's hemophilia.

None but Rasputin.

With a hypnotic trance he could calm the prince's qualms,

so his healing hands were fanned by the whole country's palms.

Being close to the son and seed got Rasputin in good with the Queen.

He became Queen Alexandra's key confidante,

which meant Rasputin copped whatever he wanted.

One day the Czar was called by war to defend his throne,

and was forced to leave his seed and Queen alone.

That's when Rasputin made a move on his home.

He went from confidante to comfy in the queen's arms raising her pants with his tantric charms.

Rumors of her britches' breach soon reached the Czar,

but to believe the gossip might do his son harm,

so he closed his eyes and ears to the shame when Queen Alexandra denied their blame.

Soon Rasputin dicked each duchess and dame,

gaining acclaim at expense of their name.

So despite the Czar's fear that the pimp-priest might bleed his brat,

the Romanov aristocrats set their own trap.

They gathered their forces and mixed together a potion that could kill 6 horses.

They poured this tonic in Rasputin's brass grail and waited for their poison to send him to hell.

But somehow this pimp-priest smelled their agenda.

He drank the grail in a gulp and told his body not to surrender.

With their foiled plan, the Romanovs increased their bloody hand, taking
aim with gun,
busting gat in his fat, five times.
Putting up their quiver, they dragged his body to the river,
not knowing that Rasputin's body still shivered.
Alive but beneath breath's surface, he fought to free himself from their
quick coffin, almost surfacing from watery death, but in that struggle for
life, he ran out of breath.
But some of this could be myth.
Many tellers differ in this tale. Believe it if you wish.

TONE: And like every myth there lies truth in it.

ROSHAD: What lies true?

TONE: That there lies a little Rasputin in each person's brew.

ROSHAD: Pure and true. We are all pimps and priests, healers and killers,
good and evil. Here. One of the unopened six-horse potions. *(Roshad
opens another beer and hands it to Tone.)* There's enough Rasputin in me.
Put a little of him in thee.

TONE: There's enough in me. I should just let this course run. *(Tone refuses
'Shad's offer and finishes off the bottle in his hand.)*
You going back next semester? *(Pause.)* Next year?

ROSHAD: Playin' it by ear.

TONE: If by ear you play it, to whom are you listenin'?

ROSHAD: To myself and own heart, which is the only right position.
Right now I'm chillin'.

TONE: Freezin' in fact.
Might seem to some frozen in the same place and time while the clock forward winds. 'Zure and I've already walked while you're not near the line.

ROSHAD: A junior by their records, but fuck it.
I got my own records to scratch until I hear my calling.

TONE: If you're playing it by ear, you'll soon be too 'def' to hear clear from
the loud speakers and too drunk to comprehend from the beers.
Your calling is higher than passin' out flyers at every shin-dig where wigs
shake their ass.

ROSHAD: Nobody's making an earning at what they're stamped for learning.
'Zure's at home with her mother.
You're a hound dog that catches the scent of escaped brothers.

TONE: Fugitive Recovery Agent, Shad.

ROSHAD: Don't take it personal, god. I just hate those vines.

TONE: It's just for the mean time.
I just did some interviews. I'm just waiting for the news.

ROSHAD: Why the fuck do I need Mecca's seal to work outside my field?

TONE: Who cares what field you sow as long as you don't blow the money you owe.

ROSHAD: I had to get these new turntables.

TONE: Well wait till your tables turn and you're financially able.

ROSHAD: Yo, I made it this far without motherfuckin' father, son.

TONE: Aight. I'm done. Plus I gotta run. *(Tone exits. Roshad pours some of his Rasputin on the ground.)*

ROSHAD: Big. Pour a little liq'out for Pac too. *(He pours out a little more.)* And here, Deep. The rest is for you. *(He empties out the bottle onto the ground. Deep appears in the yard.)*

I know you don't like the booze, but in this case you might approve.

DEEP: Roshad.

ROSHAD *(startled)*: What happened?!

DEEP: Roshad. *(Roshad turns and sees Deep's ghost.)*

ROSHAD: AH! Sh… Is it you, the face of sorrow's song? What in heaven is gone wrong? Knowing your soul has taken to the air, you should rightfully be there. Did I not see your corpse in a coffin lain?

DEEP: Say word.

ROSHAD: Have I not heard the gore of how you were slain?

DEEP: Say word.

ROSHAD: 'Less that gore was a dream, and all that it seemed I witnessed:
    the masses being moved by your passing,
    the Nile of your mother's tears,
    the cry of your peers,
    'less all were the elements of some nightmare to which I have now woke to find you present. If all these events were a mind trip, I'd count it a blessing from your lips.

DEEP: Those scenes are no dream, but are your present past.

ROSHAD: Then dream is now's flash?

DEEP: Pinch yourself and you won't awaken.

ROSHAD: Then am I sleep too, corpse never to be shaken?

DEEP: From the poison you've inhaled, you could be close,
    but you are no ghost from an overdose.

ROSHAD *(relieved)*: Since you are gone, I am not dope enough to cope.

DEEP: You know these drugs give no hope. But be of good cheer. For you there's still tomorrow, and life's length will make these feelings extinct.

ROSHAD: Neither time nor distance will fill my thirst for vengeance.
    The whole world is off balance since your death.

DEEP: I know no Death, son. Life for me has just begun.

The joke of Rapture is that there's more laughter Here After.

I count my life lost as wealth. What you avenge, you avenge for yourself.

ROSHAD: For the officer's health, do not haunt me with your goodness.

It is better for the officer's life for you to pressure me to take drastic measures.

Then I might play the punk and bail from the call to war.

But your forgiving spirit gives scores to taking up sword.

DEEP: God's word is the sword.

ROSHAD: Pure and True.

And God's Word is filled with wars and warriors, Death and destruction.

Many men are killed at God's instruction.

DEEP: I am God's messenger here.

ROSHAD: 'Bout that I have no doubt, but it is up to me to hear.

DEEP: Then let me make it clear.

Forget about force.

Let the universe take its course.

Let what's sown be reaped. Let what's last become first.

Let Yah make blessings of this curse.

This is God's wheel.

ROSHAD: And your will too?

DEEP: My will in His, the only way to live.

ROSHAD: Then His will I will do. I accept His call.

DEEP: Then you will be blessed for giving him your all. *Yah-oh-eh Ro-eh*!

ROSHAD: Same as you say.

DEEP: *Yah-oh-eh Ro-eh*!

ROSHAD: He has given me my calling today. I hear it beyond the words we say.

DEEP: His inspiration often increases Man's sensation.

What passion do you overstand?

What is your station?

ROSHAD: Your station first and then my worth.

That you *are* an Angelic Messenger, full of patience and mercy, love and kindness.

You are Osiris.

And I am an Angel of Death. Meant to take the officer's breath.

DEEP: I thought this passion you'd left.

ROSHAD: Your goodness has only confirmed what I'd guessed.

And what I might've done with my own zeal I now see is God's will.

You have turned "might" to "must," a loaded gun to a gatt that busts.

I am called to burn bones and break bones dead.

It is the same as Malcolm said, "There is no revolution without bloodshed."

DEEP: And Christ was already thoroughly bled in sacrifice. There's no need
to take another's life.

ROSHAD: No need for your side since truth is a two-edged knife.

You are the side of surgery; I am the edge of injury.

All those that walk like you need a protector to make the world a respecter.

DEEP: God is my Protector. *(Roshad walks up to Deep, places his hands out to
touch him, but Deep recoils, knowing that physical interaction is impossible.)*

ROSHAD: Then why are we here?

DEEP: This is an understanding, but I meant for you to stand over.

ROSHAD: I will stand over his body while you hover over our souls.

DEEP: That is not the will of Jove.

ROSHAD: God is more than good, more than loving and kind to men.

I am His earthquake and His whirlwind.

I am His flood and His flame.

I am His Rod.

These too belong to God. *(Deep disappears.)*

Scene Two:
*(Late black, but nearing early bright. Azure awakens suddenly as if from a
nightmare kicking and punching the air frantically.)*

AZURE: Aaaah!

Up and down this street, you hear me?

All over this concrete, you're gone listen to me!

Listen to me. Listen to me. Listen to me!

(She looks around and finds herself on the couch, bruised from her dream.)

Each time my eyes make sleep's mistake, I wake up black and blue,

bruised from tossing and turning in dream's ship,

a nightmare that manifests in colors here.

Aaaah.

Black and blue.

(In pain.) Is it not true that I wore these same hues in my dream's scenes?

And in those false arts I am cast in dual parts,

both the black body abused and also the blue abuser,

who swings and stings with Billy club to smack the strongest offense on
this present tense.

Black and blue.

I overstand why I am abused like my lover,

but why am I cast in the enemy's colors. *(Beat.)*

It's your fault, a fat fault.

Get your fat ass up, and work that fault off. *(She looks at her frame in the mirror, driving her to start her early morning aerobics. She throws jabs into the air.)*
One.... two... three... four... five... six... seven... eight... nine... ten. *(She throws jab, right-cross.)*
One... two... three... four... five... six... seven... eight... nine... ten. *(She continues to punch.)*
No fatty foods, no red meats, no sweets.
Instead, the edges of bread, the whites from an egg, the skinny to stay skinny.
No more carbs. That's just sugar in disguise.
Sugar turns to lipid, which turns to fat, which adds to this,
which adds this, which adds to this...

AZURE

It can't be me.
I don't have anything else to burn.

ALTER

If you weren't fat, Tone wouldn't have kissed you like that.
It's your fault. It's all your fault.
Do you think Deep would've been killed that night if you hadn't run him off?
You were the one that made him take flight at late black.

AZURE

This is just another attack.

ALTER

I knew you'd push him away.
I told you he wouldn't stay if you got too slim.

I told him to leave,
because it would be better for him.

You don't deserve a man like him anyway.
You didn't have the goods to make him stay.

You told me to lose it.

With you fading into thin air like a crack-head's ass.

You just said I was fat. Now you're
saying I was too slim for him?

> Oh. You think you can fight me? Is
> that what this is? Without me, you
> don't know how to live.

(She measures out a jab, right-cross, uppercut.)
Jab, right-cross, uppercut…
(She repeats the three-punch combo.)
One…two…three…four…five…six…seven…

> Swing all you want you can't hurt
> this. The more you swing, the more
> you serve my purpose.

One…two…three…four…five…six…seven…
(She continues punching. Roshad enters from his room. He watches Azure for a while. She's so focused that she doesn't notice him.)
One…two…three…four…five…

ROSHAD: I can almost see who you're punching.
AZURE: I guess I should take that as a compliment.
ROSHAD: Ain't hittin' like no bitch that's for sure.
  Best to guard your grill if you fuck with 'Zure.
AZURE: Just aerobics, something to get the blood flowing.
ROSHAD: Blood flowing indeed. Left, right, cut to make a nigga bleed.
  I see your intent.
AZURE: You early up and late to bed?
ROSHAD: Let the dead bury the dead. I got no stomach for sleep.
AZURE: My spirit knows not night from day,
  as if Deep were the lamp that glowed my way. *(She starts back jabbing again.)*
  What's the tick, I wonder?
ROSHAD: I'm sure the tele' will tell us the numbers. Plus, we could use the
  morning news.
AZURE: No! Not the oracle that bears sad blues.
ROSHAD: But I just wanna…
AZURE: …No. Not the medium that suffering screens.
  Be not Pandora. Do not open its scenes. *(Still punching.)*
ROSHAD: It's just the TV.
AZURE: And the devil's throne in every man's home.
ROSHAD: Okay. Have it your way. *(Roshad exits to his spot on the porch.
  Azure stops her workout and follows him outside.)*
AZURE: My bad. It's your house. Who am I to put you out?

ROSHAD: Don't sweat it. I get it.

You're just trying to dead your mind to the headlines. It's cool.

Plus, television is fucked up. That's the general rule.

Better to begin the day in nature's Tao.

AZURE: It's just easier to be here than at my mother's house.

ROSHAD: Seems like all of this would make you and your moms closer

AZURE: Yeah, well everything doesn't work the way it's supposed to.

ROSHAD: Don't know why you're still stuck in the 'burbs anyways.

Your mother's house is far from Broadway.

I mean, I ain't no expert, but you at least gotta be in the mix to make the shit work.

AZURE: It's just been hard to make that transition.

Spent two weeks in the Apple, had a place in its core, the whole nine.

But my mind was restless the whole time.

Anyways, now I have no time for plays.

The only thing that matters today is the way the indictment sways.

(Pause.)

ROSHAD: What if they don't indict him?

AZURE: Don't give that voice.

ROSHAD: How will we then fight them?

AZURE: That's not even a choice.

ROSHAD: Says who? How many times has dirt like this been swept under the rug?

AZURE: We have too much public support for this thing not to go to court.

ROSHAD: Support? Even if the D.A. does indict, that's but the first blow of the fight.

They'll give just enough honor to quiet the throngs,

but not enough justice to right the wrong.

Some of those suckers outside with picket signs gone celebrate just 'cause they set a court date.

They'll probably frame the event, hang it on their wall to trophy. They'll tell their children the great feelin' of standin' up for right against injustice in their times.

Use our chants as lullabies, if they remember the lines.

You know how many of them 'bougie' ass bastards up at Mecca just want to be in the number? But they don't believe in the number's power.

Niggas like that fade by the midnight hour.

At the flag pole, before the protest, remember the race we said we'd run?

AZURE: We said we'd walk seven laps 'round the Court House.

ROSHAD: Seven laps my ass. A memory lapse is what passed.

(Mocking) We vowed "We would March seven laps 'round the Court House
like Israel at Jericho's walls.
We would make our voices like a trumpet's call.
We would make the walls fall."
That's easy to say when you're caught up in the feeling.
But their emotion didn't out measure the length of the building.
While you were inside, behind enemy lines,
some walked three, others four, a few lapped five,
but I'm the only muthafucka that walked around seven times.
So let's see how the shit plays out down the line,
once everybody's tired of protesting,
when it ain't cool to miss class no more,
when they poll our passion by the final verdict,
we'll see how many candles are still lit.
AZURE: Hush, 'less you blow out the hope I have lit.
ROSHAD: My bad.
Though their stamina I don't trust, I realize that you must.
AZURE *(to herself)*: And once the officer is blamed, it may unchain me from
shame.
*(We hear the sound of a car arriving and then a door slamming. Tone walks up
onto the porch.)*
TONE: Are we all owls, with no sleep?
ROSHAD: Our miseries our company did keep.
TONE: You cool?
AZURE: Yeah, yeah. You?
ROSHAD: What happened?
AZURE: Nothing to resurrect.
ROSHAD: Respect.
*(Tone walks past them and into the house. He turns on the television, a habit-
ual morning motion. Each time he flips through the channel, Street Knowledge
morphs into another identity. First up, SK acts out a music video with SK Evil
using a southern hip hop cadence while SK Good booty shakes and bounces to
the rodeo sound.)*
SK EVIL *(raps)*:
  "I'm a hustla, I'm a
      hustla homie
  I'm a hustla, I'm a I'm a
      hustla homie . . ."[3]

3. Reese, Brian Adrian (Cassidy). 2005. "I'm a Hustla." Performed by Cassidy. J. Records Sony
BMG Music Entertainment.

(Channel Flips. Roshad goes back inside. Azure follows.)

SK EVIL: Try this new "fat-melting" pill that works better than risky prescription drugs to subdue your appetite, invigorate your mind-body-and spirit and transform your mood from crappy to happy. See these amazing results.

SK GOOD: I've been using Disintegrate for just two months and look what it's done for me.

SK EVIL: *(holding up pants)*: These are the pants I wore before.

SKGOOD *(holding up pants)*: Now they don't fit me anymore.

SK EVIL: From Crappy to happy

SK GOOD: From Crappy to…

(Azure cuts off the television.)

AZURE: You know what I should do? I should fix you boys something your ribs can cling to.

ROSHAD: Shit. I'm wit' it.

TONE *(to Azure)*: You hungry, Zure?

AZURE: Sure. Plus, we all need our strength to endure.

(Azure goes into the kitchen and prepares breakfast, cutting, slicing, stirring and peeling. Roshad cuts back on the television. He finds a channel he likes. The sounds of Explosion come from the television.)

SK EVIL: The second phase of the Insurgency in the Middle East may have officially started.

(Roshad flips channel.)

SK GOOD: Jackson's lawyers are calling the charges of molestation ridiculous…

(Flips channel.)

SK EVIL *(A cartoon)*: My strength is replenished when I eat me spinach. I'm Popeye the sailor…

(Flips channel.)

SK EVIL: "I'm a hustla. I'm a I'm a hustla, homie."

ROSHAD: Damn she got a phat ass.

(Tone takes the remote and flips the channel to a cartoon, fighting scene.)

SK GOOD: There's only one way we can stop him! If we combine our powers together!

SK EVIL *(straining through the pain)*: I don't know…how much…I have left!

SK GOOD: We have to try!

SK EVIL: Okay. On the count of three. One…

SK GOOD: Two…

(Channel flips.)

SK GOOD: Hi, I'm Kristen Ross. And I want to show you how to get that smashing new sexy body you envision.

(Channel flips.)

SK EVIL: Eat less, burn more fat and lose weight automatically.

(Channel flips.)

SK GOOD: I don't know what he sees in that heifer. I gave him the best years of my life. I'm gone kick that fat %#bp%#$ (@bp*@ . . .

(Channel flip.)

SK EVIL: In the last ten years there have been ten thousand black on black homicides.

SK GOOD: This figure comes from the most recent AP national crime...

(Channel flip.)

SK EVIL: Wave your hand if you believe that God can do a miracle in this room tonight. All the way up in the balcony. *The Son...(He holds his holy hand up to Good. She falls out.)*

(Channel flips.)

SK GOOD: Throughout the ages the sun has been recognized as the main source of light for our planet. However, visible light is only one of many wavelengths in the electromagnetic spectrum.

(Street Knowledge of Evil pop-locks, becoming like a wave. He morphs into a football player holding a football on a football field.)

These wavelengths range from the shortest and consequently the strongest, Gamma Rays to the longer radio waves, which could at times be as small as a football or as long as a football field. If your television uses an antenna, radio waves are being received by your television in order to watch this very program.

(SK Evil changes into an antenna.)

SK EVIL: Other wavelengths in the electromagnetic spectrum will also sound quite familiar if you have been to the doctor or the dentist to get an X-Ray. Our viewers may have experienced extreme sunburn in the summer from Ultra-Violet Rays. And many households, as well as public security systems, use Infrared. In fact, the remote control that you used to change to this channel uses an infrared.

(Roshad snatches the remote from Tone. Channel flips.)

SK GOOD: ...MECCA University student, was killed after an altercation with K.G. County Officer Lawrence Smith, no relation, last Thursday. Smith has stated that he was defending himself in a dangerous circumstance. The students of Mecca and other community activists are hopeful the grand jury proceedings scheduled for today will result in an indictment of Officer Smith.

(Azure cuts off the television, having finished cooking.)
AZURE: Breakfast.
(Roshad and Tone rise to go sit around the table.)
ROSHAD: No wonder Deep kept his hooks in this fish.
AZURE: Stop.
ROSHAD: Girl, where you learn to burn like this? I didn't even know we had all that up in the cabinets.
TONE: Hold your horses before we start grabbin' it.
ROSHAD: Got a brother frisking his whiskers.
TONE: Grits.
ROSHAD: Damn. Got a brother licking his chops.
TONE: Salmon croquets.
ROSHAD: Pan-stacks to make a brother open his belt and lay back.
TONE: Fruit salad, to sugar my palette. *(Both guys are about to eat the food standing.)*
AZURE: Woe. Before you force full your face, let's say the grace. *(They bow their heads.)*
Heavenly Father…It's been a minute. At least a set of seven brights since I stepped to you right, or maybe more, maybe even from before. *(Beat.)*
Thank you for these friends. Bless this food we eat, so that it will come to good ends.
Make the energy we eat fuel the warrior within for our enemy's defeat.
May the ones we fight bite their own tongues with their lies.
May the pain they realize uncover their disguise.
May they trip and be trampled in their own words so that their hearts might be overheard. If you find worth in my Love, whom you formed from birth,
do not let our enemies escape without hurt.
Strike our foe's path with your furious wrath, and crush their regretting cries under your vengeful tide.
If you be God, if you be fair, do these things to prove that you're there.
(To the guys:) I'm done.
(Pause.)
ROSHAD: Amen.
TONE: What's the line on this meal?
AZURE: It's a steal.
AZURE: Just wanted to do something nice for y'all for letting me hang behind your walls, for being there when I call, for putting up with my changing seasons.
TONE: We see how fast your world is spinning, so we know the reasons.

(Deep enters, but only in Azure's mind.)

ROSHAD: Damn shorty. You working the kitchen like one of them britches from down south.

TONE *(to Roshad as he munches)*: Watch your mouth.

ROSHAD *(To Tone as he munches)*: I said britches. Not bitches. Britches. Cause she keep your belt unbuckling to the next inch. I had one of them once. Shawty from down south. She knew the way to a man's game. Plus, she had a nice frame, looking just like what she was cookin' ya'mean. Shawty was home cooking and a barbecue too.

TONE: She was a fine dinner, huh?

ROSHAD: Stacked like pancakes. She had a brother on swole' too. Remember freshman year, when I first came to the verse', I was skinny as a rail, held my britches up with a shoe string…

TONE *(to 'Zure)*: …You gone eat something?

ROSHAD: …Food was so good she had me thinking that I should put the relationship on lock before I ran out of lease.

AZURE: I like watching you.

ROSHAD: Damn, Shawty was a dime piece.

TONE: It's good. You should have a piece too.

ROSHAD: What happened? *(Pause.)* What? You don't want yours?

AZURE: I'm good.

TONE: I thought we all needed our strength?

(Realizing what's going on, Roshad looks at Tone.)

AZURE: There's as much strength in swallowing none as there is in swallowing the sum…and at their extremes those opposites are the same shade.

TONE: Aight, Zure this game is played.

AZURE: This is no game. I have seen Deep, himself, do the same.
Fasting for strength for days on in, with prayer and supplication till he receives the answer to a situation.
Even so, I will find my fuel, more fuel from hunger's duel.

TONE: When did you come to this decision?

AZURE: While we blessed the meal it entered my mind. And its entering during that time, I'll take as a holy sign. *(Pause.)* What? Stop tripping.
It's my fate to wait. You carry on. Clean your plate. *(Azure goes over to the television and cuts the volume back up again.)*

ROSHAD: Yo, she don't want to eat, you can't make her eat. *(Roshad takes her plate and rakes her food on to his.)*

AZURE: Eat up. Today, Justice serves an early weight. We best get dressed to see what She fates. *(She exits to Deep's room to get ready. Lights fade.)*

Scene Three:

(The courthouse. A bench outside the grand jury proceedings. Azure returns from the bathroom, sick to her stomach. Deep's mother, played by Good, waits nervously on the bench.)

MOTHER: You okay? *(Azure tries to hide her pain.)*
I know full well how this hurt pricks the heart sick.

AZURE: Is there any cure for this malady but to endure.

MOTHER: God knows what course will heal.

AZURE *(sarcastically)*: God knows why God did kill.

MOTHER: T'was not God that dressed this shroud.

AZURE: But it was He that allowed.

MOTHER: I never knew the sum of your passion for my son until this tragedy stunned.

AZURE: I can only imagine how you must feel during this ordeal.

MOTHER: Though, before his death, he pledged not his life, your love for him is as thick as a wife's.

AZURE: I am not quite a widow born, but have been marked as one to mourn.

MOTHER: Pure and true. The marks from death are left on the living and make crossed the doctrine of Christ's forgiving. It is Deep's marks from birth that torture me more than the wounds on his corpse, for they were symbols of promise and hope, a gift with many joyful days to ope'. His marks of birth; a raised diagonal line at the small of his spine,
a pearl impressed on the left of his chest,
and a dark crescent moon near the pyramid of his pelvis.
Have you not beheld this?

AZURE: Yes.

MOTHER: Don't be ashamed, dame, since we are nearly the same name.

AZURE: We were making plans.

MOTHER *(lovingly)*: And he concealed his quest for your hand. That devil.

AZURE: That level we felt better kept on the hush.

MOTHER: Such is the way with a boy and his mother's trust;
no man, young man, my son, since his maturity had just begun.
(Tearing:) There are so many disasters a mother foresees to dodge from the day when her child is weaned.
Watching his head as he nears corners and sharp edges, watching his feet as he takes his first steps and flops,
making sure they don't get twisted, removing the harmful stumbling blocks.
Scanning the floor's dimensions for any irregular indentations

lest he lose his footing and trip.

I was blessed with a third eye to spy any possible slip.

What's that in your mouth? What are you getting into now?

And even when they get too old to rock, the mothering never stops.

"Don't ride your bike beyond this block...and be back by dinner time."

No longer afraid of what he has in his mouth, but instead, of what he has in mind. Especially since there are so many mistakes and mishaps, pitfalls and traps left to keep a black boy's growth under wraps,

so many forces that strive to claim the eighteen to twenty-five.

Do you know how careful my mothering had to be? Yet, none of this could I foresee?

(Azure comforts her.) But now, give me this hand that kept closed your plans together. Tell me more of his life, since you were nearly wifed. Give me, his mother, the perspective of your lover.

AZURE *(blushing)*: That's strange.

MOTHER: Please. And do not be too discrete with heat. Give me enough to laugh as much at Josh, the man, as I giggled at him when I held him in hand.

AZURE: What do you want me to tell?

MOTHER: Whatever love-joy over-swells. But since you are the actress, make sure you tell it as well. *(Pause.)*

AZURE: It was my twenty-first birthday.

Knowing my major, he made himself the stager, and put the lines that would be spoken to me on that day to play. And then he cast these lines to his friends and mine

and blocked their movements in my path.

The first key was his path, which was designed to never meet with mine.

This was to make me wonder where he was, and hunger also because.

Then to Jen he gave the words for me, "You look like a queen."

And with Crystal was the scene called "the figure so fair."

And it was Roshad that marveled over my hair, and he also that hinted about what to wear,

which was where I began to catch on that something was wrong or right, because he urged so much, "wear that red dress tonight."

"Wear where?" I asked, "and when?" It was Tiffany that gave me the time then. The most fun was Tone, who arrived when the time was ready, and with his coming, he threw at me confetti. He then revealed his worthy position, and explained the details of his mission.

He was the horseman, and it was his job to carry me to the joint. "To what joint?" I asked, and he passed me the blindfold for my eyes to cover.

MOTHER: And he carried you blindfolded to your lover?

AZURE: He led me from point to point until…

MOTHER: What was the joint? What was the joint?

AZURE: When the horseman unveiled my eyes, you wouldn't believe the surprise.

MOTHER: What had he done?

AZURE: We were on the stage of the university theatre, which he had lined with rose petals leading to the set, which was a bench, a bed and a table candle lit.

The prepared props for the night's act and scene were sides of basmati rice and a gravy well spiced, plus baked chicken plates and of course a birthday cake.

He pressed play somewhere off-stage left, playing a ballad that took away my breath, shredding the shadows to the 'shas' of Sade.

And that was just the beginning of his walk towards me.

He crept out like the shadow, wearing some mean orchestration,

and offered his hand to cut the rug, before we cut the cake, before we cut out to a more comfortable place.

Magnetically charged, I seemed to never leave his charms that night,

that night, like the air was humid from a champagne rain that night.

From the table to the bench to the bed, that night, we dreamed our lust out loud and made those wishes proud that night.

If the empty seats did watch,

they had never seen a show that loved as much,

and at times, so help me, I did hear them applaud, "Take it slow, take off, ride, swing, sail, jam, have a ball, too much, go on girl, high, hot, sss" (sound of sizzling),

until we had reached every emotional phase

that can come from a stage.

Last of all, he gave me the day on the printed page.

And when I did open his play I saw what I did say to others and what they had said to me. On that night, when I saw how well he drew me,

I felt like he truly knew me.

MOTHER (crying): And because of you I know him more too. (Recovering.)

But for the wisdom of years, let us dry these tears of joy and pain

and let our emotions no more reign.

No more laughing or smiling, weeping or wailing,

lest the oceans in our eyes prevent us from prevailing.

Yes?

AZURE: Yes.

MOTHER: Despite this unrest, we don't need the damsel in distress.

And when they do grant the indictment, it is no cause for excitement.
You are an actress, so consider what you have learned in craft good practice.
Whether there be joy or sorrow in your soul,
if ye be moved, put your emotions under control,
using that same passionate potion to put the world around you in motion.
Strength. Since we are on enemy ground. Put on an armor of dignity,
and shawl yourself with invincibility.
Transform your tears into spears and take a clear peek at the officer's conviction, the goal we truly seek.
Yes, daughter?

AZURE: Yes ma'am.

(The sound of a gavel striking. Roshad and Tone enter and sit down on the bench next to Azure and Joyce Smith. Street Knowledge of Evil enters, dressed as a juror.)

GRAND JUROR STREET KNOWLEDGE OF EVIL: After review of the facts, evidence and careful cross examination of Lawrence Smith, we have come to the conclusion…that the officer accused was working within the latitude of his power and position. This is an unfortunate accident, not a crime.

Being a police officer within this city is one that requires split second decisions. In this dangerous and demanding environment, it is needless to say that mistakes are made. It is in the best interest of the greater good to protect those that protect and serve us all. This department expresses our deepest sympathies for the friends, family and classmates of Joshua Smith.

(Roshad storms out of the room. Azure lets out a wail. Tone reaches to comfort her but realizes that he can not. He walks off slowly. Joyce/Mother transforms/pop-locks back into Good and begins to sing. The juror turns back into Evil. Azure is left on stage with the gods hovering.)

SK GOOD *(sings)*: DRIFTING, DREAMING, IN AN AZURE MOOD
STAR DUST GLEAMING, THROUGH MY SOLITUDE
I'M NOT WANTED, I'M SO ALL ALONE
ALWAYS HAUNTED BY THE DREAMS I OWN
BUT THOUGH I'M TORMENTED
I MUST BE CONTENTED
DRIFTING, DREAMING IN AN AZURE MOOD
DRIFTING, DREAMING IN AN AZURE MOOD[4]

END OF ACT ONE

---

4. Ellington, Duke and Irving Mills. 1937. "Azure" on *Ella Fitzgerald Sings the Duke Ellington Songbook* (1957). Performed by Ella Fitzgerald. Verve.

ACT TWO

Halftime:

(Street Knowledge of Good and Evil play the role of drum majors as the cast of characters march across the stage making the noise and motion of a HBCU Marching Band at a halftime show.)

SK GOOD: WHAT TIME IS IT?

SK EVIL: SHOWTIME!

SK GOOD: WHAT TIME IS IT?

SK EVIL: SHOWTIME!

(Creating all sounds with hands and mouth, the guys play the base, tuba and trombone of Cameo's "Talking Out the Side of Your Neck." Creating all signs with hands and mouth, the ladies are trumpets and sax.)

SK: HEY! YOU'RE TALKING OUT THE SIDE OF YOUR NECK
  HEY! YOU'RE GONNA GET WHAT'S COMING TO YOU YET.

SK GOOD: *(Flows like a beat poet.)* What do you do when the marching is
  done?
  When the battle's lost and won,
  When the war is just begun,
  When the bullhorns are bullshit,
  When it's no longer about headway,
  'cause you're not making headlines,
  When there are no more high profiles to smile and pose for pictures,
  When all of the messengers ran out of Scriptures.
  No more of Jesse's rhymes. No more Al's club Sharp.
  No more millions men and children March.
  When there're no more Malcolms to X.
  They've all been shot.

(SK Good kicks, waves and punches like a drum major. SK Evil falls as if he's been hit.)

  When all Farrakhan does is play the violin.

(Good conducts as the band turns into an orchestra and pantomimes playing Barber's Adagio. She continues to conduct as SK Evil rises from his "death.")

SK EVIL *(Martin Luther King)*: We have walked through desolate valleys and
  across the trying hills. We have walked on meandering highways and
  rested our bodies on rocky by-ways. Some of our faces are burned from
  the outpourings of the sweltering sun. Some have literally slept in the
  mud. We have been drenched by the rains. Our bodies are tired and our
  feet are somewhat sore.

(The violin segues into the "Battle Hymn of the Republic" with a military stomp.)

SK GOOD *(at the same time; sings)*: MINE EYES HAVE SEEN THE GLORY OF THE COMING OF THE LORD/HE IS TRAMPLING OUT THE VINTAGE WHERE THE GRAPES OF WRATH ARE STORED/HE HAS LOOSED THE FATEFUL LIGHTNING OF HIS TERRIBLE SWIFT SWORD/HIS TRUTH IS MARCHING ON/GLORY, GLORY HALELU-JAH/GLORY, GLORY HALELUJAH/GLORY, GLORY HALELUJAH/HIS TRUTH IS MARCHING ON.

SK EVIL *(at the same time)*: Yes, we are on the move, and no wave of racism can stop us. We are on the move now. The burning of our churches will not deter us. The bombing of our homes will not dissuade us. We are on the move now. The beating and killing of our clergymen and young people will not divert us. We are on the move now. The wanton release of their known murderers would not discourage us. We are on the move now. Like an idea, whose time has come. Not even the marching of mighty armies can halt us now. We are moving to the land of FREEDOM!!!

(The sounds of gunshots created from a snare clap. He falls. She falls next. Their death drops creating a body wave. The rest of the band scatters for cover. Beat. SK Evil lifts up his head.)

SK EVIL: What do you do when it's all shot and then forgot?

SK GOOD: Up!

SK: Break it down!

(They jump up again. The band gets back in line. The snare taps them into the classic MEAC band popular music break down. They do a routine of three 15-second popular hip-hop vignettes. When the routine is done, the snare claps again, and the halftime show ends with a traditional band exit, leaving Street Knowledge…)

SK: Yet…

When protests give way to partying fests, and life settles back to its norm, there are still those left unable to rest, who wonder how hurt will transform.

Scene One:

(Azure reads from Deep's journal.)

AZURE: "A story for my child when it's time for bed."

(To Deep) This was a hint that you were thinking ahead.

DEEP: Inside the green egg sleeps a tiny caterpillar, all curled and hunched.

After a week of stillness in its egg shaped house,

it wakes up and decides to peek its head out.

"I'm hungry!" it says.

(He performs it like it's for a child. Azure reads along in a whisper.)

AZURE *(laughing)*: I can see you beside the baby bed.

DEEP: And for the next five days it does nothing else except munch, munch, munch. It munches nettle leaves for breakfast, lunch and din' until it's so big and fat that it burst out of its skin. Then you know what? It keeps on eating. The green leaves are tasty. It can't stop itself from treating. Munch, munch, munch. For ten days straight it eats till it's eaten so much and grown so big that it sheds its skin again. Now this might blow your mind, but the caterpillar outgrows its skin two more times.

(Azure begins to play as if she were really telling the story to a child.)

AZURE: But life is dangerous. It has to use its head when birds swoop down to eat it. It drops into the leaves below, by means of a silky thread, like Spiderman, but not a spider, 'cause it's a caterpillar. This is the way it escapes harmful killers. When the birds give up on having a juicy caterpillar for a snack, it uses the silky thread to pull itself back. At three weeks old, it's as grown as caterpillars grow. Probably say it's about as big as your toe. Grown enough so that now it stops eating. It goes deep into the nettle bush, and then begins weaving. She weaves a bed on the back of a big old leaf and, just like you, prepares for sleep. She has to get used to her new room, 'cause she'll spin a lot of time inside this cocoon. After about two weeks of sleeping and hoping, the caterpillar cracks the cocoon open, but we no longer see the caterpillar that escaped death. She emerges from the shell and takes her first breath. She pushes some juice into her wings. Wings you ask? Yes, wings I say. When the juice has filled the four covers, she is wearing her beautiful colors. And once its wings are adorned...

DEEP/AZURE: THE BUTTERFLY IS BORN!

AZURE: She stretches her beautiful wings this way, and then begins to play. Whooh. Riding the breeze. Whooh. Going wherever she pleases. Whooh. High with the birds, she takes flight. Flying, it feels so light.

(Azure has gotten so wrapped up in the story that by this time her limbs have become wings and she seems to be ready to take flight. Azure closes the book and walks into the kitchen area. She pours a bowl of cereal and milk, holds the spoon up to her mouth. Tone enters. She almost takes a bite, but then lowers the spoon to the bowl and slides it away from her.)

AZURE: No. Not for you.
Instead, the edges of bread, the whites from an egg, the skinny to stay...
Sometimes I wonder, "Why don't I just grab a gun, or slit my wrist, or take a dive to quicken the ride instead of killing me softly?"
I'm tired of this torture.
No matter how much I lose or gain, I'm still in chains.

I don't understand what I do; not eating,
eating but throwing it up,
loving Deep but pushing him away.
What I want to do I do not, but what I hate I do.
No. Not for you.
(She pushes the bowl further away.)
"O that this too too solid flesh would melt, thaw and resolve itself into a dew,
Or that the everlasting had not fixed his canon 'gainst self slaughter."
I'll just have water.
(She drinks water.)
Without Deep to live for, I'd have been a dead daughter long before.
And now I wonder how I'll rebirth without what he made life worth.
He was a jewel pressed to precious, heated to heavenly ice,
more perfect than any pearl or diamond crystallized.
But do not give dogs what is sacred.
Do not throw your pearls to pigs.
Boss Hogs know not the cost of what they trample under their feet.
Fuck the police!
Ay, fuck the presidents, the principals, the political activists.
All of them are pacifist!
The governs and mayors of these three county-states,
none of the magistrates know your going rate.
But this has been the case since the race entered Liberty's gate by shipped flight.
This has long been the price of a Black man's life.
(She slumps, exhausted. She pulls down a bag of bread from the counter, pulls out a few slices, and begins to eat its edges.)
I'm tired.
TONE: In that you are not alone.
AZURE: I had no idea you were home.
TONE: In my room. Lying still in a stare. *(We hear the sounds of a festival outside.)*
You can hear the sounds of the festival from here. Sounds coming all the way from the avenue. Oh, that's Mecca's marching band playing right now.
That might be good for you, to go, to get out of this house.
AZURE: I hate crowds. Plus, the music is too loud.
Not for me.
TONE: Are you sure? You could use some fun.
AZURE: How is it fun? Go if you like.
I'm not the one.
TONE: It's just a festival. What's your beef?

(Deep enters. He sits down at the table to eat.)

AZURE: My beef is the meat market atmosphere.

  Those who go, go to show,

  everybody fronting, everybody hunting,

  When I did show up, not even showing enough,

  I had a guy tell me they'd wear my thighs as ear muffs.

  I don't want to be weighed, marked and priced by how much I entice.

  Shit is spoiled.

DEEP: Is that all you're gonna have?

TONE: Is that all you're gonna have?

AZURE *(to Deep)*: Yes. *(To Tone:)* What happened?

TONE: The edges.

AZURE: That's the only part I like.

DEEP: You have to eat more.

TONE: That's all you've had today, I bet.

AZURE: I forget.

TONE: You forget?

AZURE: Forgot. Today, yesterday and days before run together into one score.

DEEP/TONE: You should eat more.

TONE: What are you trying to get out of this?

AZURE: Just the crust…

TONE: …Not the bread. You're tired, you said.

AZURE: I'm fine.

DEEP: You promised me that you were gonna start eating three times. *(She ignores him.)* Okay. If that's where your strength lies, neither will I. *(He pushes his bowl away.)*

AZURE: Does every car run off the same amount of fuel? Is every animal the same way fed?

DEEP: We are the same 'animal'. You need more than bread.

AZURE: This is my body.

DEEP: And God's temple.

AZURE: Is it God's temple just as much when you're in the heat of touch, the sweat of lust, the flight of fuck?

DEEP: This is not about my pleasure.

AZURE: Then what does it matter how I'm measured?

DEEP: It only matters to me because it means so much to thee.

AZURE: My matters are not your weight. Let your worries dissipate. *(Deep storms out of the house. We hear the sound of a car screeching and driving away.)*

TONE: What are you trying to get out of this?

AZURE: What are you trying to get out of this?

TONE: Out of what?

AZURE: You tell me who you're trying to be. *(Azure closes up the bread bag.)*

TONE: You asked me if you could stay here, and that's fine, but I can't watch you do this and stay behind the lines. Not in my house.

AZURE: Not in my house? Wow. I guess not. Just like my mother. I should've known you would eventually kick me out.

TONE: I'm not.

AZURE: You just said you were. Have you so soon forgotten? As a matter of fact, I had no doubt that you would kick me out. That confirms that I *am* the worm that makes y'all squirm. Look at me. You, my mother, Deep. That makes it complete.

TONE: I'm not kicking you out.

AZURE: But you are.

TONE: No I'm not.

AZURE: But you are. Just like them. Except with Deep, *he* left. He got in his car and...*(She starts to break down.)*

TONE: You said yourself that you were tired, so what is it that you truly desire?

AZURE: You know, you would be a good spy.

TONE: What?

AZURE: You and my mother ought to team up. Let's see what else 'Zure has dreamed up. You could be a dynamic duo. You could even check my stool for evidence to see how much food I've touched...*(Mocking.)* Since you want to be all up in my shit so much. *(She goes in Deep's room to get her stuff. She gives him back the keys. Tone is dumbfounded.)*

TONE: You don't have to leave.

AZURE *(from the room)*: No, you're right, and you've made me believe.

TONE: You don't have to go.

AZURE: You shouldn't have to put up with this any more.

(He picks up the bread she's left and begins to eat the rest of it. She sees this, and it stops her.)

AZURE: Deep would do that too. When I'd eat the edges for less, he'd eat the bread that was left. *(Beat.)* I'm sorry. What I want to do, I do not, but what I hate I do.

TONE: I know that same song. It changes its licks on you for cool tricks...

AZURE: ...Leaving your feet off the tick, all made up and nowhere to go. In what way do you know it?

TONE: In many ways. Come to the mirror for one revealer. *(She follows *him to the mirror.)* When I look in the mirror, at times the reflection is unfamiliar.

AZURE: This one I also know. How so for you?

TONE: I see the skeleton inside of me, death's ivory machinery, and then returns my flesh that left. But still I see the face of death as if my body had been rebuilt and modeled after guilt.

AZURE: This I know too. What is the crime?

TONE: I know not my crime, but I fear what I might design.

You know a few days after Deep's death, I had a fugitive in my sights, and I let him steal away into the night.

The guilt of the fugitive was no question as I aimed my Wesson at his name,

Tyrone Simpson.

His offenses were well listed,

but how many of his crimes have the system assisted?

I should have radioed for back-up long before he stood in my sights, but for some reason, turning him in just didn't feel right.

I dropped my aim and whispered,

"Run, save yourself. If you're caught, you'll be caught by someone else."

I still don't know exactly why I did it.

AZURE: Maybe it's time to quit.

TONE: Maybe it *is* better to stall for your true call than to carry on with a path that feels wrong.

AZURE *(looking in the mirror)*: Tell me, what do you see? Am I fine?

TONE: What do you mean?

AZURE: My form? Is it fine to you?

TONE: I don't look at you like that, you know.

AZURE: But if you did?

TONE *(pause)*: No. Not for my taste, no. You were before what I would have killed for, but not any more.

AZURE: You would have killed for? What shape did you once see?

TONE: Must I?

AZURE: On your opinion my trust lies because I cannot trust my own eyes. Please.

TONE: What do you mean?

AZURE: The eye not only inspects, it projects, and mine are made blind by what I have inside. I am like Justice in these times, whose vision is clearer when her eyes are covered, but when she peeks she brings a distortion to the weighed proportion. No matter how the scale figures, sometimes it seems that I'm getting bigger. *(She gets onto the scale.)*

TONE: That's absurd. Each day you weigh in lighter proportions. This is a clear distortion.

AZURE: This quenches a little, but feed me more. What did you see before?

TONE: When Deep was first for you gassed, he compared your math to an hourglass, swearing that in the clear vision of you, he could watch time pass from your movements to know the dial of the day.

AZURE: And did you see me this same way?

TONE: When I saw you, I saw why he did say.

AZURE: But now?

TONE: But now that you hunger, I feel this way no longer.

(She gets off of the scale.)

AZURE: I will give you my reason now, though it may seem no reason to you,

but even still, this is the meat behind what I now do.

In the seven nights since the indictment was refused, I did lose myself inside dreams of the crime scene. Each day I ate less, and the dreams they seemed more vivid.

TONE: Why would you want to relive it?

AZURE: All of the details in my dream's tale are in line with what's factual, with what's been said in report; yet in my dream's scenes, I'm screened a bit more.... even the haze of events that led up before. Since there is no other means to proof, I have chosen this search for truth.

TONE: No. No. This, your reason you have wrapped around your usual starvings to justify a greater cause. The murder was not your fault.

AZURE: I know.

TONE: No. Look at me. *(He grabs her, lovingly.)*

It was not.

AZURE: Stop.

TONE: It was not.

AZURE: I didn't say it was.

TONE: It's written all over your spell. You do this to punish yourself.

AZURE: This may well be, for, in my dreams, I *am* the cop that popped him and also the one killed. But this is the only way that I know to heal.

TONE: Heal? This is no medicinal course. Of course, food deprivation is given to bad dreams and hallucination. This is no pill to trust.

AZURE: There is something else my core reaches for.

TONE: Let it reach for more than the sum of breadcrumbs.

AZURE: I thought you could listen. But I see you can not.

TONE: I'm sorry. I forgot. I can listen. What's your mission?

AZURE: I have gone from eating some to none, and though lessened limbs and a lap slimmed have long been my lust, this new fast has revealed the truth's path. When I am hungry, I become the seer. And that eye's view sheds new light on Deep's case. I see another face, and signs aligned for an accomplice to the crime.

TONE: Another face? Who?

AZURE: Not with clear color or grooves to form any proof, but a face, I see.

TONE: And what signs?

AZURE: A familiar voice, unidentified, with which the muffled truth is testified; the scrambled digits of a phone number that the officer tried, and other numbers to count, but I'm not sure what sum surmounts, but as it were, Deep's twists and turns on that dark route are unblurred at times as if I'm looking through his very fearful eyes.

TONE: If what's clouded became clear to you, you might find the truth near to you.

AZURE *(to herself)*: I have no other track to trust. *(She gets up to leave.)* I'll be back later.

TONE: You might need these. *(He holds up the house keys.)*

AZURE: What happened?

TONE: Twister to the slammer. *(He gives her back the keys to the house.)*

AZURE: Right.

TONE: Keep it light.

(She exits.)

Scene Two:

(Azure comes to a quiet road. She is exhausted from her walk. She puts her hands on her knees to catch her breath.)

AZURE: Deep.

My soles follow your soul's past paces,

where you did steer on that night when you did fear,

and I could not rest until I found my stance here.

According to their words, this is the place where it all occurred.

On Johnson, off of Jefferson, like most crimes of the city-states, between two dead presidents. Are these still the skid marks? Are these the car's broken parts?

How did you die? And why? I've been listening for God, but truth be told, I don't trust His lie;

how he shaped you with such promising flesh and then broke your breath before you could bless.

If I hear His voice now, I won't be a believer, nor will I know Him from the Deceiver. Open my eyes to the visions of truth deferred, and my ears to the proof of the unspoken heard.

(She catches a cramp in her thigh and is put down to the ground. She struggles to get up, but has to just straighten her leg out on the ground.)

Get up! Get up! Aight. I'm aight…*(She cramps up again. Falls.)*

…Aaaah! *(She gets up and falls back down again.)*

Aaaah! Look at you! Look at you now. Stupid. You walk all the way out here with no way back? Stupid. Still. Just rest. Just lay. *(She is about to lose consciousness)* Might as well make your mark here too. You're on the brink of it anyway. Nobody will even notice. Just fade away. *(She tries to get up again, but she cramps up.)*

No! Get Up! *(Delirious:)* Oh God! Help!

SK GOOD: Are you sure, Zure?

SK EVIL: Zure, are you sure?

AZURE: What happened? *(She looks around for the source of the voice.)*

SK GOOD *(echoing 'Zure)*: What happened?

SK EVIL *(echoing Good)*: What happened?

AZURE: Hello?

SK GOOD: Hello?

SK EVIL: Hello. *(Sings show tune from Cheers:)* Sometimes you wanna go…

SK *(sings)*: *Where everybody knows your name.*

AZURE: Who's there?

SK *(sings)*: *And they're always glad you came…*

AZURE *(sings)*: *You wanna be where you can see,*
   troubles are all the same,
   You want to go where everybody knows your name.[5]
   (Speaks:) Hello?

SK GOOD: My fault.

SK EVIL: My fault.

SK GOOD: My fault.

SK EVIL: My fault.

AZURE: Oh. Nothing to fear.
   It's my own voice that I hear.

SK EVIL *(to 'Zure)*: You fear your own voice more than any and all.

AZURE: What happened?!!

SK EVIL *(to Good)*: She asks for truth's eyes,
   but to herself, she lies.

AZURE. Who is it that calls unrecognized?
   Show yourself.

---

5. Gary Portnoy and Judy Hart Angelo. 1982. "Where Everybody Knows Your Name." Addax Music Company Inc.

SK EVIL: This is the not-quite widowed mourner of the one who was killed
on this very corner.

Answer her no more.

She knows not what she asks for.

SK GOOD: Don't be so quick to close the door. She reaches for us from the
depths of her core. See how high her soul vibrates.

SK EVIL: But consider how she got to this state.

By feeding delinquency she reaches our frequencies.

What she wants to hear should be forbidden to her ears, for her sake.

If she receives well our reception, will it cause her self deception?

SK GOOD: It is not our place to be judges of the path the soul trudges.

AZURE: Show yourself!

SK GOOD: She has knocked again.

We must begin.

SK (unison): What up, god? (They are still not visible to her, but she is privy to
their glory and the visions from their imagery.)

AZURE: Who? What? When? Where? How?

SK: We are Street Knowledge...

SK GOOD: Of Good.

SK EVIL: And Evil.

SK GOOD: He is the Undercover, and I am his Twin Lover. I am Life ...

SK OF EVIL: ...and I, Death. I am the vice verses.

SK GOOD: I am the blessings.

SK EVIL: While I am the curses.

SK GOOD: I'm the Virgin Mother that's holding the day's birth.

SK EVIL: And I'm an ill Muthafucka that's holding the night's dirt.

SK GOOD: I understand why you're here...

SK EVIL: I'm the wise guy you fear.

AZURE: If you hold knowledge of recent events of this street,

then maybe you can tell me what happened to Deep.

SK: Are you sure you can endure this truth cured pure?

AZURE: Cancerous blame is far worse.

You must help me cure guilt's curse.

SK EVIL: Ignorance is bliss whether true or false.

AZURE: I want the truth, whatever it cost.

SK EVIL: Very.

SK GOOD: Well.

(They conjure. Street Knowledge opens Azure's third eye to the vision. In break
and pop-lock fashion they reenact the action. Deep enters. Street Knowledge
makes the sound of the car and any other sound effects as well.)

DEEP: Left 'Zure's house with door slams and god damns, hurling curses as
I hit reverse.
Swore I'd never go back to be again pushed away,
though I loved her too much to truly stay away.
My breath came to a psalm and calmed to a coast outside of K.G. on the
outskirts of the city.
That's when I noticed behind me brights blinding,
following closer than comfort. Wasn't the first time
that day the tingle of predator's eyes pricked at my neck,
and stomach.
*(SK Evil uses two flashlights in hand to create the headlights and pop-locking
and martial arts movements to create the car chase.)*
Outside the center where I work,
Cross the street from the church.
I decided I would stop for gas to see if he'd go past.
(Deep's gaze watches the car go past him.)
Yep. The same gold colored Lexus.
Or maybe it's just a coincidence.
Tank drank six dollars and 3 cents of oil steal,
a small price to pay for security's feel.
Down the road a ways towards home's direction,
and again in my mirror came the bright reflection.
I prayed for Jove to drive the rest of the way home.
Pressed light on the gas.
round curves and swerves,
sang myself a hymn to calm my nerves.
(Sings:) "What a fellowship, what a Joy Divine
Leaning on the everlasting arms."
(Speaks:) Still there
STREET KNOWLEDGE: Over hills...
DEEP: Still there...
STREET KNOWLEDGE: Sharp turns...
DEEP: Still there...
STREET KNOWLEDGE: Between cars...
DEEP: Still there...
DEEP/ STREET KNOWLEDGE: Took an exit towards Fairfax, but he was
still laying back. Just back far enough to make it seem like nothing.
DEEP: Could be nothing. I stopped the car...*(Sound of the engines running
idle.)*
STREET KNOWLEDGE OF GOOD: In the middle of the road...

STREET KNOWLEDGE: In the middle of nowhere…nowhere…nowhere. *(Beat.)*

DEEP: Pressed hard on the gas to a pace that was fast
  Foot on the floor…Zooming round curves and tight swerves,
  Still there…

STREET KNOWLEDGE OF EVIL: …Over hills…

DEEP: …Still there…

STREET KNOWLEDGE OF EVIL: …Sharp turns…

DEEP: …Still there…

STREET KNOWLEDGE OF EVIL: …Tires burn…

DEEP: …Still there…

STREET KNOWLEDGE OF EVIL: …Still there, still there…

DEEP: …Still there…

STREET KNOWLEDGE OF EVIL: Still hanging behind far enough.

STREET KNOWLEDGE OF GOOD: Far enough to make me feel crazy.

DEEP/SK EVIL: …Almost got myself lost trying to lose him. Surprised I didn't get stopped by a cop, but I knew I couldn't just stop.

DEEP: Now where?

STREET KNOWLEDGE: No where, no where yet.

DEEP: Let's see if he tries to come through this dead end. If he heads down this track, then he's got to reverse and turn back. No way it's a coincidence then.

SK GOOD *(sings in a run)*: Patience.
  A man's wisdom gives him patience. It is to his glory to overlook an offense…

SK EVIL: …To everything there is a season and a time for every purpose…

SK GOOD: …Through patience a ruler can be persuaded, and a gentle tongue can break a bone….

SK EVIL: …A time to kill and a time to heal…

SK GOOD: …time to tear down and a time to build…

SK EVIL: …time to search and a time to reveal…

SK GOOD: … time to keep and a time to throw away…

SK: …time to be silent and a time to…

(Street Knowledge of Evil points his flashlight/heads down the path. Sounds of a car on an unpaved road.)

SK GOOD: The driver realizes it's a dead end and stops.

(Street Knowledge of Evil pop-locks to transform into the officer. Deep gets out of the car.)

DEEP: What are you following me for? *(Deep moves toward the car.)*

OFFICER: Back in the car. Close the door, and put your hands on the steering wheel. *(Officer turns on his red and blues now and gets out of the car. Deep stops his approach.)*

DEEP: I saw your car pass me when I stopped for gas. And you've been behind me for more than my last four turns. What have I done to make your tires burn?

OFFICER: I'm the one asking the questions here!

DEEP: If I can see a badge, sir? Can't tell who you are from the looks of your car, plus with the plain clothes…

OFFICER: Get back to your car. Put your hands on the wheel. *(The officer draws his weapon.)*

Do you know how fast you were driving? Why so fast? You got something you hiding? You got drugs in the car? Pop it.

DEEP: Aight. Stop it, man.

OFFICER: Pop it, I said. *(Deep reaches to pop the trunk.)*

DEEP: You're really searching, man.

OFFICER: That's right. I'm searching. *(The officer still searches the trunk. Deep takes a beat and then cranks up the car and slides it in reverse, bringing the officer back around to the front of the car waving his weapon.)*

OFFICER: Shut off the car, and slide out slow.

DEEP: You just told me to get in.

OFFICER: I give the orders. You follow.

(Deep doesn't move.)

DEEP: Whoever you think I am, you're mistaken. You never even asked me for my license and registration. Can I see your badge?

OFFICER: Shut off the vehicle!

DEEP: PUT DOWN YOUR GUN!

OFFICER: SHUT IT OFF NOW, DAMN IT!

DEEP: PUT DOWN YOUR GUN!

OFFICER: YOU'RE UNDER ARREST!

DEEP: PUT DOWN YOUR GUN!

SK GOOD *(sings)*: *There's nothing new under the sun.*

DEEP: Foot on the gas, GAS TO THE FLOOR!

SK GOOD: Crash through the right door of the golden Lexus!!!

ALL *(scream)*: CRASH!

(Their confessions:)

DEEP	OFFICER
I used my vehicle as a weapon…	…The suspect used his car as a weapon…
…crashing my car…	…crashing his car into mine…
into the officer's	I shot once through his shield…
unmarked Lex…	

The first shot through the window
shield missed...

...He backed up for a second.

...I rammed my car into his again! I shot...

Four shots spit... ...Four shots...

...Three shots...hits... ...Three hits.

SK GOOD *(sings)*: To everything there is a season and time.

OFFICER: Oh shit. Shit. Oh shit. Shit.

SK GOOD *(sings)*: A time to be born, and a time to die.

OFFICER *(into phone)*: I fucked up. He's dead. *(Listens.)* I mean, he's dead.
  (Listens.) No, he's dead, he's fucking dead. Shit. Shit. *(Listens.)* I killed him.
  (Listens.) This is Johnson road and...fuck. Relax. *(To himself:)* Relax. *(Lis-*
  tens.) No, Fairfax. *(Listens.)* I followed him. You told me to follow him,
  didn't you? *(Listens.)* I didn't mean to kill him. *(Listens.)* He tried to ram
  his car into mine. What was I supposed to do? I shot. Shit. Shit. Huh? *(Dial*
  tone.) Hello? *(He reaches for his radio.)*...I have a suspect down on Johnson, off of Jefferson...

(Deep pop-locks out of his body and flies away. The Officer pop-locks back to Evil.)

AZURE: Wait. WAIT! There's more.

SK: We've said all we can say.

SK EVIL: Played all we can play.

SK GOOD: The first fruits were strange.

SK EVIL: The rest are forbidden.

SK GOOD: You must follow your core

SK EVIL: To discover what's hidden.

AZURE: Why was the officer following Deep so many hours before?
  I will not sleep or slumber or eat from hunger till you reveal what's hidden
  under.

SK EVIL: Very...

SK GOOD: ...well.

SK EVIL: We will point past the name of the blame.

SK GOOD: and instead show you his number.

SK EVIL: This will reveal all that you wonder.

AZURE: The number?

SK EVIL: The number chested above his heart.
  This will fully spell what you now know in part.

SK *(echoing each other)*: One, one, four, four, two, two, eight, eight, five, five,
  seven, seven.

AZURE: One, four, two, eight, five, seven? One, four, two, eight, five, seven.
  (Azure repeats. She passes out.)

Scene Three:
(House. Tone is dressed for work. He drinks a Rasputin. He loads a weapon expertly. He seems to be pumping himself up for something. He takes another swig from his beer. Roshad enters from the street, equally as focused.)

ROSHAD: I can almost see who you're shooting.
(Tone quickly recoils his weapon, spinning it into hiding with lightning speed, but not too fast for Roshad to see.)
ROSHAD: You don't have to.
TONE: My fault. I shouldn't have this out in front of you.
ROSHAD: I told you it's cool. It's not like I don't know you play with guns.
TONE: I wouldn't say play. My aim ain't no game.
ROSHAD: Fair you've been. *(Roshad drops some bills in front of Tone.)*
   Count it. Matter fact, let me make two months exact. *(Tone counts the money.)*
TONE: You don't have to.
ROSHAD: Fair you've been.
TONE: Why vault? This month's is my only want from you.
ROSHAD: I told you it's cool. Better to get it now before later when I'll run.
   Count it. It's a fact that I'm not good at managing stacks, so get it while
   I've got…before it's all been shot.
TONE: This cash is not hot? How did you get this stash?
ROSHAD: I ain't selling hash? That biz is broken.
TONE: Then how did you get enough paper to set us right and still have
   enough to waste during your nights? I sense some caper unspoken. You got
   a gig this big?
ROSHAD: Naw, another broken biz. No more gigs for this kid.
TONE: You giving up the turntables?
ROSHAD: I've already sold and emptied my stables. Look for yourself. In
   my room. No more record bins holding the day's spin, no more day's gone
   round with my sound, no more mic cords, wires and cables. Go. Focus on
   my hocus pocus, my empty stables. *(Tone exits out to what is down to hall
   to look.)*
TONE: It's gone! *(He returns.)*
   You've made a ghost of it.
ROSHAD: At least most of it. I still have some classic hits and mix tapes in
   the dark lits. But all these are either too rich or too poor for the market,
   and too foolish to hock. But these are only mementos of the former stock.
TONE: I'm shocked. I thought they meant so much to you.
ROSHAD: The better to make the bull for my sacrifice than some bull shit.

TONE: At first I thought it was crack you sold, but now I think it's crack you've smoked. What force or fear has steered you here?

ROSHAD: It's only that my calling has become clear.

TONE: A calling? How sound?

ROSHAD: Clear I said. Focus.

I traded in my fun to buy me this gun, and stored up a stash in case I have to run. (*Roshad reveals a 9-millimeter.*)

TONE: And where does this aim at its end?

ROSHAD: I want to help you catch what's criminal and crook.

TONE: Officer Smith?

ROSHAD: There is my hook. The very same name.

TONE: You can't be serious. Have you gone berserk?

ROSHAD: I have already spent my purse on my tools for work. (*He handles the gun.*)

Follow my means and leave the rest in my hand.

My course is to use your resources as a member of the force; radio, records, contacts, the skinny and the inside scoop to find the route and patrol of the officer that struck our souls with blues. Upon that news you will set me in position and sight to take the officer's life one night. I have been given the nerve to make sure justice is served. Call my life a sacrifice to set what's unfair back square. I have been given the nerve, and will not hesitate on that date. This will set the world back spinning.

TONE: Let us concentrate on life's next and let alone death.

ROSHAD: Death let's no one alone but is always fast approaching in chase. My beef is with he that hurried death's pace.

TONE: If you do this, you hurry the pace of your own!

ROSHAD: In this purpose, I know I'm not alone!

Have you not stared at death face to face in place of life in these past brights and nights? I have. I have made his skull my favorite meditation, since it is inevitable, our confrontation. And in my mourning sentiment, with the end of life I have become intimate.

Death is merely a lover that pleases with a smother holding our pants in panic to a climax relaxed. With this focus held, I have felt the ghost in this shell be expelled from the cell where it's now held, and when that breath came back, death made my life more exact.

Man has no cause to fear the skull if his life is lived full. I know that you like I have had many waking nights, wondering where your allegiance lies, wondering how a brother dies and we make no tries to avenge his blood's cries. Vengeance is not a cure for what hurts, for what's lost no one can return. But what burns worse is what Deep's life was worth.

What he birthed in me to make me who I am. Nay, I am not unless he is. And the same is true of you. We have all made each other into iron; and used those edges to brother one another.

I have traded in my purse for his worth. And that is not enough to leave for I know that this is not life only because we breathe. It's what we believe, what we leave. And though Deep's life was a tree blessed, when we die ourselves, look at the legacy we'll have left from his death; that it cost nothing to claim a black man's breath? Is this what you believe? Can't you see? We are dead. Not he.

TONE: The officer is black too, and a crime by us would be as dark as his, one less brother left to live.

ROSHAD: Deep was our brother! Fuck that muthafucka! When I came in even, I saw you load your gun with what's right. I saw your intent well open, for I have held that same focus in my sights.

TONE: No. These are not the weapons he would have us use to fight.

Though murder and revenge taunt me, it is his kindness that haunts me.

ROSHAD: And it is that kindness that sends me to this end the most.

Have you not felt this ghost?

(Tone nods his head.)

ROSHAD: Then side with me.

(Beat.)

TONE: Ride with me. *(They shake.)*

The officer is on duty. In these nights since the indictment, I have not been back to work, but have made it my night's business to track the route and course of our enemy on the force.

ROSHAD: I knew you'd considered this before. I knew.

TONE: Not with you.

ROSHAD: But I knew. Now this feat will be more complete with me in the passenger's seat.

TONE: Then let's roll, and hope that this violence settles our souls.

(They exit to the street.)

Scene Four:

(The sounds of a car door slamming. The officer, played by SK Evil, walks into the scene, wearing a uniform this time.)

OFFICER: By my word, this is the place where it occurred. These are still the skid marks, and here, some of his car's parts. Here is where he backed up his drive. And here is where his body did lie when they pulled him from his ride. And here…*(He sees Azure's body lying on the ground.)*

Here is another body… *(He checks her pulse.)*

...barely alive. Ma'am? Ma'am? *(He pours water on her face...and some in her mouth.)*

AZURE: Huh?

OFFICER: Are you okay?

AZURE: That way.

OFFICER: What way?

AZURE: I'm walking. I can make it.

OFFICER: You *were* walking, but you fell faint.

AZURE: I ain't...I ain't...I ain't the damsel in distress.

(He tries to pick her up.)

SMITH: You're delirious. I'll carry you to the hospital in case it's something serious.

AZURE *(coming to)*: No. No hospital. I'm fine.

OFFICER: You were passed out here near Death, and he would have surely touched you if you had been left. I'll drive you to the hospital. Come.

AZURE: Don't bother. Just give me more of that water. *(He gives her the rest. She gulps it quickly.)* I'm fine. This I say with assurance since I have no insurance. *(She begins to walk again.)*

See. Now my gait is again straight.

OFFICER: Wait! You headed back to the city? You headed east? Let me drive you back to the city at least.

(SK Good comes and places two seats side by side)

Here's my car. See. Where are we headed? Nothing's too far.

(She has trouble opening the door. He slides inside and unlocks the door for her.)

Oh, I have to let you in from inside, since I now have that dent.

AZURE: What happened?

OFFICER: Nothing. Just had a little accident. This ought to get us their faster. *(He cranks up the car and starts to drive. He places the red and blue light above his car.)*

OFFICER: What's your name?

AZURE: Azure.

OFFICER: Azure. I like that name. That's nice. That's pretty. Where are you from?

AZURE: From the 'burbs, but I'm crashing with some friends in the city.

OFFICER: So why are you out in this wilderness alone?

AZURE: I was soaring over these city-states, piecing together the parts from the art of my lover's end and did crash at this path.

OFFICER: Your lover's end? At this path?

AZURE: Because this was the end of my math. Yet not the end of the work that brought him to hurt. He was murdered by a cop who lied and was never tried.

OFFICER: I know that case well, both from its local tales and all its blues in the news. I'm sorry.

AZURE: Dry-long-so.

OFFICER: You had no kids with him though?

AZURE: None.

OFFICER: That's good that he had no kids left.

AZURE: Why are you glad at this theft? That the possibility of a baby's gift is a mist is but another sin to list.

OFFICER: Glad that there are less left to miss him.

AZURE: You have kids?

OFFICER: Two. One son, and a daughter whose crawling has just begun.

AZURE: And a wife too?

OFFICER: Not quite, but I will marry her when the time is right. (Pause.) You went to Mecca?

AZURE: Graduated, last year.

OFFICER: I went there for a few semests', but life wouldn't let me finish the rest. (Pause.) I'm sorry for your loss.

Being an officer I know the other side of this affair that seems unfair to you.

We are called as cops to break the boundaries in order to enforce them. But there are some that take extra liberties, irresponsibly; breaking the law for their own ends knowing the system will cover their sins.

AZURE: Pure and true. Even now, your red and blues siren us beyond the Law's lines to get us to my house in no time. No, not for my good. Cut off your sirens. Drive as you should.

(He cuts off the sirens and drives slower.)

OFFICER: Peace. I understand your grief.

AZURE: And the officer was black too. You would think he would be less likely to strike his own. (Beat.) Forgive me.

OFFICER: No, you have a right to spit this. It is true. There are men on the force with this weakness. The force only magnifies what always lied. I have seen cops take bribes, sell drugs, play thugs, and any and all crime within our ranks.

AZURE: The one that killed my love sits not above this bank. He cast my love in the role of the accused, destined to lose because of his hue.

OFFICER: I am sure that your love was a prince, but sometimes seeing so many brothers arrested can make a cop's eyes infected, even the eyes of black cop.

(Together:) The eye not only inspects…it projects

AZURE: …it projects. Pure and true! And that alone could be enough for the officer to single out my love to bring him to his end, but there still seems to be more to this sin.

OFFICER: It was surely some strand of this mind, with some other factors intertwined. Who knows? Who knows what he projected?

AZURE: But don't you see that when you remove your badge and uniform, you will be treated by the same norms? *(Azure begins to look at him closely.)* You're from K.G.

OFFICER: You well see.

AZURE: Why are you in this district? Is this not outside your jurisdiction?

OFFICER: I'm not here because of what I earn. I'm here because of how my heart burns.

AZURE *(reading his badge)*: 314693.

OFFICER: 314693, that's me.

AZURE: Is that the seal you always wear?

OFFICER: Same seal…ever since I took its swear.

AZURE: Officer Smith?

OFFICER: Smith is printed plain, and yes, Lawrence is my first name.
   And you are the not-quite widowed dame of the Prince slain.

AZURE: Why did you return to that place of pain?

OFFICER: To unravel my unrest.

AZURE: Then confess.
   What was held in suppression because of your profession, free it now in open confession. *(Pause.)* Tell me why you followed him before that night's tour. Outside the center where he worked, when he stopped by the church, you were there. Why? That's right. I know that night wasn't the first time you had him in your sights. *(Beat.)* Then let me out. *(She reaches for the car door. He locks it.)*

OFFICER: No. Not yet.

AZURE: Let me go.

OFFICER: Just let me drive you back. *(Beat)* It wasn't supposed to go this way.

AZURE: What way was it supposed to go? *(Beat)*
   I know there was a number of another name who's to blame.
   1-4-2-8-5-7…who is he?

OFFICER: What words I have about this I must swallow them.

AZURE: If the Prosecutor knew that you were following Deep earlier that day, they would have to reopen the case. *(He stops the car and grabs her face.)*

OFFICER: Shut up! Shut up…Shut your trap for your own good. I have more power at the end of this club than any judge's gavel. Do you overstand? Overstand that my word is over yours, and no word is bond until I enforce it! No matter how many people you got screaming along with moans and megaphones to be heard it still ain't as loud as my whisper. Are you a listener!

AZURE *(in pain)*: Yes!

OFFICER: The powers that be were never thinking about prosecuting me. There will be no more legal actions. However I said it happened is how it happened. Case closed. Ain't no more to be exposed. *(He lets her face go. She unlocks the door again, and manages to get out of the car this time. Beat. We hear the sound of the car door closing, and the car driving away. Smith transforms back into SK Evil and is again invisible to her. A relieved Azure watches the car drive away into the distance.)*

AZURE: I'm not surprised that you kept your deceit hid,

but this lie shows more than the truth you give. *(Azure exits with new strength.)*

Scene Five:

(Azure enters from street, exhausted. She goes into the house, places her head under the faucet and drinks. She pours cereal into the bowl.)

AZURE *(repeats in a whisper)*: One, four, two, eight, five, seven…*(She puts down the bowl of cereal. Outside, Tone and Roshad enter.)*

TONE: Take that shirt off before someone sees you out here.

ROSHAD: Let me my victory wear before I dispose of these clothes.

TONE: Not inside yet. 'Zure is home. Off, before she sees that we have killed.

ROSHAD: There. I am exposed. *(Roshad removes his bloody shirt to reveal a bare chest.)* Aah! I have no guilt about the grave that I've built.

If not for your sake, I'd build a sepulcher above ground so his body could be found,

and write on that tomb the names that brought him to his doom.

TONE: If you had listened to me, your kill would've been cleaner. There was no need to get that close.

ROSHAD: I wanted my feel of the blood spilled, to dip my hands in the river of his life while it drained,

to watch him struggle in vain as he realized life would never return again. You cut that sport too short for my taste.

When a little of his blood did waste, I felt my own red race quick to make me stiff.

And once that rouge through veins pushed me, revenge became the sweet-
est joy next to getting pussy.

I wanted to hear him put his hurts in a verse,

but when he was near words, you shot him in the face first...

TONE: ...Sh!

ROSHAD: ...a sport too short. *(He looks through the screen door.)*

Azure *is* home. Let's tell her what we've done, that we have become Justice's
sons,

that we have brought the badge and number of the one who put her love
to slumber. *(Roshad reveals the officer's badge.)* She will wish she was there
to stare while we put him on trial.

She will wish she was there to see how we made ourselves the jury and
judge of his fury.

TONE: No! She can never know. Never. No.

Let's get inside. I retrieved these sleeves from my back seat. Here.

Wear this shirt to cover our work. *(Tone puts Roshad's bloody shirt in his
workbag, along with the badge. Tone hands him another shirt, a fugitive recovery t-shirt. They enter the house.)*

AZURE: Roshad, you in uniform too? That's funny.

ROSHAD: What laughs at it?

AZURE: The two of you wearing the same vines? Funny.

ROSHAD: For me this is not the norm.

Lord knows I hate a man in uniform. *(Roshad leaves to remove the shirt.)*

AZURE *(reads Tone's badge)*: 1-4-2-8-5-7. Funny.

TONE: What laughs at it? *(Long silence.)*

What joke is unspoken?

AZURE: A joke of a riddle broken.

TONE: What do you mean?

AZURE: The evidence of things unseen. Though I fear to have faith in these
numbers to reveal what I've wondered.

TONE: Give it to me straight.

AZURE: How can I make straight a crooked place? 1-4-2-8...Enough. This
course is too rough. What will I find when I unwind these signs and
wonders?

TONE: Are you under some spell?

AZURE: Are these numbers from heaven or hell?

TONE: What's wrong?

AZURE *(confused)*: 1-4-2-8-5-7.

These are the numbers of the name of the man who is to blame for Deep's early roam home. Your number, your name. Unless this is some sordid spirit's game?

Are you to blame? *(Silence.)*

ARE YOU TO BLAME!

1-4-2-8-5-7!

Answer me! Whether true or false, good or evil, answer now!

You have been silent long enough!

TONE: Yes! I never meant for it to mount up like it did. You were just a speck in my eye, a single sin. I watched you put yourself in Deep's shadow. He could do no wrong in your eyes. All the while yourself you despised. Do you know what hell it is to love someone that hates themselves so much, to keep that lust hush, to never get to touch?

While they die from no hope, you hold the antidote.

AZURE: No, this was not about me, no.

TONE: I, the acute angle in this love-triangle, knew there had to be some soiled ground Deep still trod and I wanted him to drop his facade. Sure, he was in love with God, but addicts don't kick habits that quick, especially when their weakness is women's lips. I knew better. We used to run together.

ROSHAD: *No!* We buried the killer tonight. *(He slams the officer's badge on the table.)*

314693, that's him. We made ourselves judge and jury of his words, on the outskirts, near the 'burbs, so no one heard.

TONE: I never meant to cut him so hard as to do him real harm. I wasn't trying to make you leave his arms for my charms. I was still content with loving you from a distance. I knew there was no hope for my hidden feelings, because your love's hue would never pale. But I would be the rock to balance the scale. I would catch him in a lie to bring his image to size in your eyes. Find a little dirt on him, catch him in a blunder. I didn't mean to bury him under so much. Got in touch with a brother I knew from when I first got into the bounty-biz. I phoned one Lawrence Smith for the job-caper. Pushed him a little paper. Plus, he was eager to repay a favor. I saved his ass one night late when we were out on a chase. The whole point was that Deep was never supposed to know he was being followed. That point was dull, not sharp enough to stab his tomorrow. But these cops get carried away often, and when they do, others get carried in-coffin. This was the case with Smith, and the fraction of the infraction that I never fashioned. I have no idea what brought Smith to this murderous passion, whether this was his everyday occurrence or a spur of the current. I know not whether it was Deep's confidence or some other offense…

AZURE: It was you that gave him room for the incidence.

TONE: Pure and true.

AZURE: You were the one who put him on the beat that Deep trod!
  You were the one that tried to play God!

TONE: My fault. I am the one that opened Death's vault, but believe that I
  have kept my part in this play secret to protect you from further pains.

(Roshad aims his gun at Tone.)

AZURE: Put the gun down, Roshad!

(Tone draws his gun.)

ROSHAD: I don't understand! You were his main man. I was his right rod.

TONE: We are all pimps and priests, killers and healers, good and evil,

ROSHAD: A little Rasputin in each person's brew.

TONE: But despite these faults you've found anew
  Do not doubt the love that lies true in us.
  I'll show you now that you can trust...

(Tone puts down the gun. Roshad shoots Tone once. He falls. Roshad stands over his body.)

ROSHAD: We were brothers, all of us! *(He finishes him off, shooting him four more times. Then Roshad points the gun at Azure.)*
  Were you fucking him? *(Silence.)* Are you the cunt that caused this punk to play the Benedict?!

(Azure pulls down the box of Life and pours the cereal into a bowl until it over-flows. She sits down at the table with the bowl in front of her. Roshad keeps his gun aimed at her.)

AZURE *(in a daze)*: No need to torture me. I've already 'tired that task.
  No matter how much I lose or gain, I'm still in chains. I don't understand what I do. What I want to do, I do not, but what I hate I do.
  I have no control of what unfolds, so I give up. I had no power over Tone's plan, no say in the officer's hand. I can't even keep straight the numbers of my weight. So if you are Death's angel sent to kill, then do what you will. What else can I lose?

(Azure shakes the bowl and clears the table so that the excess around her falls to the ground. She pours in the milk and takes a bite. Roshad watches her eat, and after a moment lowers his aim. He walks out of the house and breaks down cry-ing on the steps.)

STREET KNOWLEDGE OF EVIL: Now life was still dangerous.

STREET KNOWLEDGE OF GOOD: She still had to use her head when
  birds would swoop down to eat her.

STREET KNOWLEDGE OF EVIL: She would drop into the leaves below, by
  mean of a silky thread.

STREET KNOWLEDGE OF GOOD: ...like Spiderman, but not a spider, cause she was a caterpillar.

STREET KNOWLEDGE OF EVIL: This is the way she escapes the harmful killers.

STREET KNOWLEDGE: When the birds give up on having a juicy caterpillar for a snack, she uses the silky thread to pull herself back.

THE END

GLOSSARY for Deep Azure

Barbecue—(jazz) (n.) A beautiful lady. Girlfriend material.

Beef—(jazz) (v.) To state. To announce. (hip hop)(n.)A problem or issue with something. Conflict. Confrontation. (v.) To cause conflict or confrontation: i.e., Tupac beefed with Biggie.

Bible—(jazz) The truth without a shred of doubt. The gospel truth.

Boat—(hip-hop) (n.) Short for "love boat." PCP that has been sprinkled onto marijuana. Invented in DC during the 1980s.

Black—(jazz) Night.

Blitzed—(hip hop) Drunk. Twisted.

Bloods—A gang founded in Los Angeles in the early 1970s. The organization has since spread to numberous cities and towns throughout the world. They are known for wearing the color red.

Boss Hogs (hip hop)—Police. Racist police. Related to the television show, *Dukes of Hazard* and the term "pigs" used by the Black Panther Party in the 1970s.

Bougie—(adj.) A slang word derived from the word bourgeoisie. Bougie has a negative connotation because it insinuates that the described person or thing is trying to be of a higher class, better or more important than others. It has been used by African Americans to refer to the Talented Tenth and affluent African Americans as a comparative to other economic and social sectors of the African American race.

Bout it—(hip hop) (adj.) Ready, willing and able. Dedicated. (v.) To commit or dedicate oneself.

Build—(hip hop) (v.) (1.) To develop. To brainstorm. (2.) To construct a plan.

Bust a nut—(hip hop) (v.) Ejaculate.

Busting—(v.) (1.) To shoot a gun. (2.) To catch someone doing a crime.

Buzz—(adj.) Tipsy. (n.) The state of being tipsy. Slightly inebriated.

Catchin' vapors—(hip hop) (v.) (1.) To become consumed with someone else's popularity, hype, or glamour. (2.) To become overwhelmed with emotion suddenly. (3.) To grasp at what is gone.

Cool tricks—(n.) (1.) Fun. Good Time. (2.) Clever prank.

Crips—(n.) A gang founded in Watts during the early 1970s. The organization has since spread to numerous cities throughout the world. They are known for wearing the color blue. **Crip, Crippin (v.)** To gang bang.

Def—(hip hop) (adj.) Nice. Appealing. Stylish. Similar to dope, fly, hot, fresh.

Dime piece—(n.) A measurement or rating of women from one to ten; a dime piece is a ten.

Draw back—(v.) Paint a picture of the past in your mind. Reminisce.

Drive-by—(n.) A murder attempt in which assassins fire at their victim as they drive past them.

Dro—(n.) A potent marijuana grown with high levels of THC, mainly because it is seedless. Seedless marijuana is commonly grown using hydroponic techniques, which cultivate the production of cannabis using fertilized water and no dirt.

Dry long so—(jazz) "That's Life" or "That's fate" or "Just like that."

Early black (n.) Evening.

Early bright (n.) Morning.

El—(n.) (1.) God. A word of Babylonian and Hebrew derivation. (2.) (hip-hop) Short for El Producto cigars. Marijuana rolled inside a cigar to create a blunt.

Fine—(adj.) Handsome. Sexy, beautiful.

Fine dinner—(jazz) A good looking woman.

Frisking the whiskers—(jazz) (v.) To warm up for a swing session.

Front—(v.) (1.) To pretend to be that which you are not. (2.) (n.) A false face, demeanor. (3.) A show put on to impress.

Gat—(hip hop) (n.) Although the term originates from Gatling gun, it has been used to describe any fire arm.

god—(hip-hop) (n.) A term of endearment from 5% Muslim lingo to acknowledge the divinity in man.

Hook—(hip hop) (n.) A chorus in a hip hop song. A refrain that is repeated. It is also used in a freestyle battle or cipher to get the emcees in sync with one another.

Hush hush, down low—An assurance that what's said in secret will stay secret.

Jones—(n.) Yearning, strong desire for something. Hunger. Craving. (v.) To want, crave, or desire.

K.G.—(n.) County near Mecca University.

Lampin'—(hip hop) (v.) To relax. To lay back with lethargy.

Licks—(jazz) (n.) Hot musical phrases.

Licking the chops—(jazz) (v.) See frisking whiskers. A preparation to perform.

Line or line on—(jazz) (n.) Cost.

Mack daddy or mack—(n.) (1.) Ladies' man. (2.) Art of seduction. (v.) (1.) To flirt and successfully woo a love interest. (2.) To seduce.

Mad—(hip hop) (n.) A whole lot. An unfathomable amount.

Mug—(n.) (1.) Muthafucka. (2.) (n.) Short for mug shot. (3.) (v.) A threatening stare. Short for to mean mug. Evil eye.

Nigga—(n.) "Nigger" is derived from the Spanish word *negro*, which simply means "black." The word *negro* came to the English language through the Spanish and Portuguese slave trades and the subsequent caste system. White supremacist views that justified the continuation of chattel slavery and the trans-Atlantic Slave Trade became central to the meaning of "Nigger." Those views claimed that the African was subhuman and his subhumanity was supported by Biblical interpretations of the curse of Ham. Some African Americans have made a distinction between the words "Nigger" and **"Nigga."** The latter can, in this interpretation, be a term of endearment friend, brother. While some people believe that a different spelling, pronunciation, and contextual meaning infuse a sense of pride and defiance into the word, there are others who argue that it is impossible to separate the meaning and spelling of "nigga" from its profane history. In general, the use of either term by whites, "nigga" or "nigger," regardless of its context and/or intention, is viewed as derogatory by many African Americans. Despite the stigmas on the word, hip hop has made the word common to people of different races throughout the world, some of whom belive that the word no longer carries a racial distinction.

Off-time Jive—(Jazz) (n.) (1.) Sorry excuse. The wrong statement. (2.) Untimely offense.

Peep—(hip hop) (v.) (1.) To look at something. (2.) To check something out.

Phat—(hip hop) (adj.) Dope, fresh, nice, attractive, pleasing.

Pigs—(n.) A term used for the police by the Black Panther Party.

Po-po—(hip hop) Police.

Pure and true—A truth that cannot be argued, e.g., "I can't argue with that."

Respect—(hip hop) A salute or action of honoring. It can also be used as an apology or to reestablish a working ground for conversing and interaction once personal barriers have been crossed.

Right Rod—Best friend. Denotes the use of a guidance and protection. The staff and rod of a shepherd.

Say word—(hip hop) Like "Amen" in church. "Yes." Also said, "Word" or "Word up."

Semi—(n.) Short for semi-automatic weapon.

Set—(jazz) (n.) A smaller division of members within a larger gang that share common initiations, codes, territories, business, and enemies. In the same gang, one set can have beef or conflict with another.

Set of seven brights—(jazz) (n.) A week.

Shawty—(hip hop) (n.) Southern term for a cute girl. A cutie. A fine woman, especially a fine woman that is short. Similar to the Northern term "shorty."

Skank—(hip hop) (n.) or (adj.) (1.) A scandalous woman. A freak. (2.) Whore, prostitute.

Skeezer—(hip hop) (n.) A nymphomaniac, a freak.

Slide your jib—(jazz) (v.) To express one's self openly. To talk freely.

Sling—(hip hop) (v.) To distribute drugs. Usually identified with drugs, i.e., "Slingin' crack rock."

Slug—(hip hop) (n.) Ammunition, shot from a shotgun barrel, powerful enough to knock its victim off of their feet.

Spell—(n.) An emotional or spiritual trance.

Spit—(hip hop) (v.) To deliver a rhyme, written or freestyled (improvisation), e.g., "The emcee spit a nice lyric at the cipher."

Sun—(hip hop) (n.) A term of endearment that acknowledges the divinity in man.

Sweat—(v.) (1.) To worry. (2.) To obsess over. (3.) To have a crush on. (4.) To chase after an object of one's affection.

Take it slow—(v.) Be careful.

To a T—(adv.) Exactly. Precisely. Perfectly.

Twisted—(adv.) Drunk. Blitzed.

Twister to the slammer—(n.) key to the door.

Vines—(n.) Clothing. Threads. Gear. Clothing.

Wack—(v.) To murder by order. (hip hop) (adj.) Distasteful. Terrible. Awful. Not hip. Untimely. Wack is the opposite of def, fresh, hot, dope.

What happened?—"What did I miss?" Often used by New Yorkers in the strangest contexts. It is similar to "What?" or " hunh?" but much more versatile. In the play, it also reverberates the deep desire of all of the characters to know "what happened" on the night of Deep's death and that they are all "missing something" since his passing.

Yahweh Roeh—*Yahweh,* a name for God in Hebrew. The Self Existent One. *Roeh*— my shepherd or protector, my guide, my vision. God the Protector. God the Shepherd.

Ya Mean—(hip hop) (phrase) "You know what I mean?"

Hip Hop Theater Plays

As with the poetic works in the previous part, this group of plays also requires a deep understanding of Hip Hop culture and its performative elements. *Welcome To Arroyo's,* by Kristoffer Diaz, reclaims the role of Latinas and Latinos in the birth of Hip Hop culture by focusing on a mystery around the identity of an early Latina DJ. The play treats a generational divide in a Boricuan family, especially when a teenager's fervent commitment to the Hip Hop element of Writing causes a conflict of values in the family.

The play also incorporates a Hip Hop twist—the onstage chorus consists of a DJ and an Emcee who are integral to the storyline and also step outside the narrative to share commentary and play other roles. This device is certainly not unprecedented in scripted drama, but it takes on a different valence when presented within the world of Hip Hop Theater. The characters Trip and Nelson connect with the audience in a uniquely Hip Hop manner, and they fulfill the role of the African *Djeli,* using the storyteller's techniques of praise and abuse found in traditional *Djelia* (as discussed in the introduction). Significant, too, is the playwright's insistence on a plural society—many different ethnicities are represented in the play, and this, too, is the immutable fact of Hip Hop. For a Hip Hop audience accustomed to seeing the myth of a monochromatic, televised version of New York depicted in such television shows as *Friends* or *Seinfeld,* this play presents New York as it is and as Hip Hoppers experience it.

The central element of *In Case You Forget* by Ben Snyder is also Writing. The protagonist, Jim/Kaptn, is a young man who leads a graf crew. He is about to go to prison for his illegal public art practice and struggles with his community and his on-again, off-again girlfriend as a result of his passion for his art and Hip Hop. This is a familiar Hip Hop narrative, not only in the United States, but abroad. Hip Hoppers often have to choose between, on the one hand, family, friends, and financial stability and, on the other, their social, political, and creative convictions. These pressures and the fear of being seen by one's peers as a "sellout" can cause ruptures in social relationships and networks when an individual commits to Hip Hop as a lifestyle or culture. The alternative is to take the expected and accepted path and keep Hip Hop on the back burner. To someone from outside the culture, this may not seem such a wrenching identity crisis. However, for many Hip Hop heads, to turn one's back on Hip Hop means abandoning one's sense of personal truth. Snyder's play explores the depths of this conflict, as Jim moves through various relationships and begins to have a better sense of his place and power in the world.

Finally, *Blurring Shine* by Zakiyyah Alexander is a scathing, satiric indictment of the industries that exploit the young people—specifically the young men—of Hip Hop culture. The play takes tremendous risks, in terms of style and content, in its representation of the ways which Hip Hop is marketed to young people from urban environments, suggesting a nefarious manipulation of product placement, rather than more widely accepted practice of trend prediction. Alexander narrates the relationship between Luther, a high-powered executive who has risen above his poor upbringing, and Shine, the younger half-brother he left behind, who lives the life that has been marketed to him as "authentically" Hip Hop.

This story of class and generational differences is intercut by an analysis of pop culture through the eyes of the Speaker, a television talk show host whose personality is not as exaggerated as the play's hyperreal framework may suggest. Alexander masterfully reveals that the tragic and extreme ways pop culture has interpolated Hip Hop is often an exaggeration or grotesquerie of itself. Take, for example, Nelly's "Tip Drill" video or the brutal industry murders of several Hip Hop music legends. When a frame is drawn around these iconic moments of contemporary popular culture, they are just as absurd or tragic as any play could make them—parallels can be drawn to Jacobean tragedy, Fernando Arrabal, Antonin Artaud, as well as the legends of ancient Kemet, Japan, or India. Each civilization has its own history of brutality, and *Blurring Shine* looks at the ways in which this plays out in a Hip Hop–inflected world.

One of the play's most searing moments relates to Spokenfo, a relatively minor character in terms of stage time, whom the Speaker painfully exoticizes for his Blackness and Hip Hop–ness. When this character is finally allowed to speak for himself, he attempts to communicate through the vernacular of Hip Hop, an act that represents self-determination and freedom within the culture. However, Spokenfo has lost the ability to speak anything but this vernacular and it imprisons him—he cannot express himself or make himself understood. He has effectively lost the ability to communicate, and the audience watches him struggle with the painful self-realization of his now diminished capacity for self-expression. He cannot, it seems, understand what is happening to him; yet he knows he is flailing. While Alexander does not specifically identify as a Hip Hop Theater playwright, her deep knowledge of the culture allows her to cast a critical eye on the global marketplace's complicity with the less than positive values that corporate greed has knowingly instigated and bred in the culture. This is a play that will be read for years to come as a means of understanding capitalism's impact in our time and its exploitation and manipulation of young consumers.

By Kristoffer Diaz

Welcome To Arroyo's

CHARACTERS:

ALEJANDRO ARROYO: Male/24/Puerto Rican. Owner of and bartender at Arroyo's Lounge.

AMALIA (MOLLY) ARROYO: Female/18/Puerto Rican. Graffiti artist. Angry graffiti artist.

TRIP GOLDSTEIN : Male/24/Jewish. DJ/rapper at Arroyo's.

NELSON CARDENAL: Male/24/Asian-American. DJ/rapper at Arroyo's. (Note: Nelson refers to himself as "Pinoy," marking himself as being of Filipino descent. If played by a non-Filipino, feel free to change that line to a more appropriate reference—"my Japanese ass," or "my Hindu ass," for example.)

OFFICER DEREK: Male/22/African-American. Rookie New York Police Officer. New to New York.

LELLY SANTIAGO: Female/24/Puerto Rican. Suburban college student.

SETTING

Arroyo's Lounge.

The Arroyo family apartment.

A back alley behind the police station.
The Lower East Side of New York City.
Right About Now.

A NOTE ON THE DJ BOOTH

The DJ booth should be visible on stage for the majority of the play. Trip and Nelson will play music and make comments from there throughout.

A NOTE ON MUSIC AND OTHER POP CULTURE REFERENCES

The text suggests certain songs for certain moments in the play. While it's not necessary to use the exact songs mentioned in the text, the inclusion of music—current, evocative, popular music—throughout the piece is very important. The same should hold true for pop culture references. Use your judgment.

A NOTE ON SCENES

Scenes are generally divided according to plot points—not breaks in the action. Scenes marked "continuous" are just that and unfold in the same location with no interruption. There should be no blackouts, even when switching locations, unless noted in the text.

A NOTE ON NEW YORKERS

Four characters in this play (Alejandro, Molly, Trip, and Nelson) are lifetime New Yorkers. This is their most important character trait. Like most lifetime New Yorkers, they've got that unique mix of strength and weakness, rough edges and constant humor, tough exteriors and easily bruised hearts. These characters are ultimately unified by this bond. The two outsider characters (Lelly and Officer Derek) are not part of this community—and that's probably their most important character trait.

◆

PRESHOW
(TRIP and NELSON onstage as the audience enters. They are playing upbeat party hip-hop from their DJ booth—this is the music we'll hear in virtually all the bar scenes, unless otherwise specified.
LELLY, seated at the bar. She's got books and notebooks and papers everywhere. She's clearly researching something. Messily. Trip and Nelson pay Lelly no attention. And vice versa.)

• 1
(Lelly turns, addresses the audience. Music stops.)
LELLY: Kool Herc. *(PROJECTION: A photo of Kool Herc.)*

Grandmaster Flash. *(PROJECTION: A photo of Grandmaster Flash.)*

Afrika Bambaataa. *(PROJECTION: A photo of Afrika Bambaataa.)*

These three men are generally acknowledged as the forefathers of what we now know as hip-hop music and culture. With any justice, this esteemed group will someday include a fourth name: Reina Rey.

It has been said, by at least one hip-hop historian—probably less than five—okay, probably less than three—but definitely at least one—that in hip-hop's earliest days, there was a *Boricua*—I'm sorry, you might not know what that means—there was a *Puerto Rican woman*—who could rock a microphone in English and Spanish with only herself as her DJ and no one's ever heard of her and that's tragic but at the same time it's astoundingly awesome and I'm getting overexcited and ahead of myself and okay I'll stop.

In 1980, just as hip-hop became hip-hop, Reina Rey disappeared.

And no one knows anything about her.

If somebody—for argument's sake, let's say, I don't know, *me*—ever cracks the mystery of Reina Rey, she or he, or me, instantly becomes one of the foremost experts on the creation of hip-hop culture; and she or he or me becomes an integral component of Latino cultural history; and she or he or me, at that moment of discovery, validates her or his or my entire existence, especially if she or he...or me...is, say, a nerdy little Puerto Rican girl with a lot to prove. *(Pause.)*

I think. I might. Have figured. It out. *(She gathers her books and exits.)*

• 2

(Trip and Nelson, playing to the audience. The music is back.)

TRIP: Ladies and Gentlemen, you have found your way to the hottest watering hole South of Houston Street. My name is Trip Trizzy, this is my partner Nelly Nel, and we'd like to welcome you...to Arroyo's.

NELSON: *(Rapping:)* Welcome to Arroyo's/where the players play/we serve them black white/purple striped/straight and gay/you could hear the girls say/on Avenue A...

TRIP: "Trip Trizzy/gets busy/like his name was E-bay..."

NELSON: And he may/indeed/give you what you need...

TRIP: If you pricketh this Jew/doth not he bleed?

NELSON: Trip rhymes...

TRIP: At light speed...

NELSON: Trip's dope...

TRIP: So take heed/and since I ripped the mic first/son, follow my lead/ Nelly Nel...

NELSON: Cardenal/spitting rhymes for y'all/I slam the mic so hard/could call it basketball...

TRIP: Nelly Nel...

NELSON: Coming at you/from the Lower East/downtown baby/is where I eat my feast...

TRIP: Nelly Nel/give them hell...

NELSON: Jail cell/to oil well/first bell/to death knell/dude, you should have bought a Dell/I make the crowd yell/and I rock the hair gel/and I could rhyme all night but we got stories to tell/YUP! *(The music shifts to an old-school track: think Eric B. and Rakim's "I Know You Got Soul.")*

TRIP: So just throw your hands in the air/and get dirty like Double Dare/and if there's Nair/in your hair/at the county fair/let me hear you say oh yeah...

NELSON (AND AUDIENCE): Oh yeah!

TRIP: Oh yeah!

NELSON (AND AUDIENCE): Oh yeah!

NELSON: It's time to do it old school/cause yo, we're on a mission...

TRIP: Nel, drop out the beat/so they could hear/the exposition...

NELSON: Here's a little story that must be told/about a Puerto Rican brother/24 years old/he's our boy Alejandro/and he owns this place...

TRIP: He loves this spot like he loves his own face...

NELSON: The superstar of the bar...

TRIP: The Sphinx of mixed drinks...

NELSON: Tending bar so fast, I wonder when he thinks/see, he lives upstairs/and he works down here...

TRIP: And I ain't seen him out this building in like half a year. *(Music out.)* For real. That dude don't leave.

NELSON: *(Speaking, to audience:)* At the sound of the scratch, Mr. Alejandro Arroyo will unlock that front door.

(ALEJANDRO enters from the apartment, walks to the front door.)

TRIP: And when he does, this lounge—his lounge—will officially be celebrating its one-month anniversary.

(An abrupt loud SCRATCH on the turntables as Alejandro unlocks the front door.)

NELSON: Happy anniversary, Al.

(Alejandro walks behind the bar...and waits.)

ALEJANDRO: Today's gonna be the big day.

TRIP: Hells yeah, Al.

NELSON: Today's the day that Arroyo's becomes the most popular lounge in Manhattan.

(More waiting. No customers.)

NELSON: *(To audience:)* Today is not the day.

TRIP: Six months ago, this place was the hottest spot in the Lower East Side.

NELSON: Only it wasn't a lounge. It was a bodega. The dopest, most no-frills-est bodega in creation.

TRIP: Everybody in the neighborhood came through here, either to buy cigarettes or lotto tickets or those little mint breath things you put on your tongue and your eyes get all watery and...

NELSON: *(Cutting Trip off mid-rambling thought.)* And Al's mom was sitting right where he's standing now. Six Months Ago.

TRIP: Only she wasn't behind a bar. She was behind the front counter.

NELSON: And now she's not here. The bar is. And the customers—well, there ain't many of them around either.

TRIP: But patrons or not, we're open every night. The whole night. Al tells us:

ALEJANDRO: *(To Trip:)* The sign says eight to four, then we're open eight to four.

NELSON: And then we tell Al:

TRIP: Ain't like we getting a rush at 3:45. *(To audience:)* To which he says:

ALEJANDRO: People need to know they could count on us.

TRIP: And we tell him there's nobody here to count on us and people won't just come through only for drinks...

NELSON: *(To Alejandro:)* ...and yo Al, maybe if we gave people something to watch, some entertainment or something...

TRIP: *(To audience:)* But Al don't like gimmicks.

ALEJANDRO: A deli needs to be a deli. A bar needs to be a bar. We do what we're supposed to do the way we're supposed to do it. The customers will come.

NELSON: And if we argue, he says:

ALEJANDRO: It worked for my mother. *(Alejandro goes back to the bar.)*

TRIP: You can't argue with fresh wounds.

NELSON: So we keep working. Exactly eight to exactly four, every night. By two minutes after four, me and Trip are long gone.

(Alejandro starts to clean the bar.)

TRIP: But Al ain't. He's just getting started on cleaning. Wasn't no one here to get the bar dirty, but he's cleaning.

NELSON: Cleaning ain't even the right word though. He's sweeping, mopping, down on his knees scrubbing scuff marks you can't even see off the bar rail.

TRIP: Gets this place cleaner than a Will Smith CD.

NELSON: And it's not like he exactly could get away from it by going home. *(Alejandro finishes cleaning and heads upstairs to the apartment.)* He lives right upstairs.

TRIP: So his whole life right now is up and down, from his cramped apartment to his underperforming bar and back.

NELSON: And that's all he does.

TRIP: Everyday.

NELSON: That's it.

TRIP: We got nothing else to show you.

NELSON: Bet you wondering why you came to see this play.

TRIP: You fucked up. We got nothing.

(MOLLY, at the police station.)

MOLLY: Ma! Yo, Ma!

NELSON: Oh yeah. He got a little sister.

• 3

(Projection: Molly's mug shot. The name reads ARROYO, AMALIA. The charge reads VANDALISM.)

MOLLY: I gotta talk to you about your son, Ma. *(Molly turns to the mug shot and begins to spray paint over it.)* That kid ain't got no life anymore. Go to work, feed the family. Go to work, clean up after the family. That's all he does, Ma. I tell him though. I tell him that shit kills you, then you dead, and nobody outside your little circle even remembers you. That's what happened to you, Ma.

It's a disease. It's fucking O.P.R.F.S.: Obsessive Puerto Rican Folk Syndrome. Makes you think all that shit—like his bar, like the deli you wasted your life in—makes you think all that shit's worth something. You had it. And your son Al got it now. You gave him that deli, you gave him the fucked-up genes. You gave him your fucked-up heart. But me? I got the little tiny good part of you. I got the clear-headed DNA. The unblocked arteries. I ain't getting infected. I'm an artist. *(Molly finishes painting and steps away from the wall to reveal that she has written the name MOLLY, big and bold, over the mug shot.)* I'm the only healthy one ever lived in this family. *(She exits towards the apartment.)*

• 4

(Alejandro, making breakfast in the apartment. MOLLY stomps in.)

MOLLY: Don't tell me I'm late.

ALEJANDRO: It's four-fifteen AM, Amalia.

MOLLY: My name is not Amalia. It's Molly. I'm not late.

ALEJANDRO: You told me you'd start getting home earlier.

MOLLY: I don't have a watch. I'm an artist.

ALEJANDRO: I'll buy you a watch. A nice artistic watch.

MOLLY: Watches are enemies of art. Watches are called watches cause they're for people who watch. You watch watches, you watch time, instead of actually doing something with that time.

ALEJANDRO: You're doing something with your time? I thought you was just out there writing on walls.

MOLLY: And I thought you were just downstairs making Long Island Iced Teas.

ALEJANDRO: That's my job.

MOLLY: Writing on walls is my job. Nah, fuck that—writing on walls is my calling.

ALEJANDRO: Your calling is illegal.

MOLLY: Your job should be illegal. Alcohol kills bodies. *(Molly grabs a plate of breakfast.)*

ALEJANDRO: Stress kills bodies. Alcohol at least lets your body enjoy being killed.

MOLLY: Your body would enjoy getting up out of this building once in a while...

ALEJANDRO: So I could do what? Scribble my name on a park bench?

MOLLY: When was the last time you even saw a park bench?

ALEJANDRO: When was the last time you were home before daylight?

MOLLY: When was the last time you had sex? *(Silence.)*

ALEJANDRO: That got nothing to do with nothing!

MOLLY: Generations of Arroyos are disgusted by your lack of mack.

ALEJANDRO: I got game.

MOLLY: I bet even Ma got more ass than you.

ALEJANDRO: *(Deadly serious.)* Not even six months she's gone and you talk about her like that? *(Silence.)* I got game.

MOLLY: Oh yeah—you're a rock star pouring cheap-ass vodka.

ALEJANDRO: I serve quality vodka. I serve quality everything. And anyway, yeah—bartenders are like one step down from rock stars in terms of game.

TRIP: *(Interrupting from the booth—to the audience:)* And a DJ is like a cross between a rock star and a bartender, so you know how we do. *(To a specific audience member:)* Tell 'em how we do, baby.

MOLLY: All right, if you say you get ass, Al...nah, I still don't believe you.

ALEJANDRO: I ain't asking you to believe nothing.

MOLLY: You might have better luck with the ladies in your bar if, you know, you actually had some ladies in your bar.

ALEJANDRO: *(Forcing himself to stay calm.)* I am telling you. That you need to spend. Five less minutes scribbling your name on some wall that no one is ever gonna see…

MOLLY: I always put my name where people could see it.

ALEJANDRO: And it gets painted over the day you put it up.

MOLLY: No, it don't. Not always. And, and, and, and…fuck you.

ALEJANDRO: You need. To be in this house once in a while. Scrubbing a dish out of respect for the generations of Arroyos who made sure you would have a dish to scrub.

MOLLY: You scrub. You're a bartender. Bartenders are one step up from dishwashers.

(She slides her food across the table at him, and exits.)

• 5

(Trip and Nelson, in the booth. Molly, working on the graffiti she started earlier—her name, big and bold.)

NELSON: Even before her mom passed, Molly was showing signs of rebellion.

TRIP: No smoking, no drinking, she wouldn't touch drugs. Baby Molly's revolution sprayed out the tip of an aerosol can.

NELSON: At first, she only used to hit the front wall of the deli. Her moms would come out with the soap and the vinegar scrub and clean that wall until it shined like new under every fresh moon.

TRIP: Poetic, Nel. Next day, Molly would be back and hit it again. She wasn't real good back then—you couldn't even tell what she was trying to write. As far as Molly knew, her mom never knew who was doing it.

NELSON: Her mom never complained neither. She just cleaned the wall.

TRIP: We all used to think maybe she kinda dug it.

• 5.5

(Continuous.)

NELSON: So I wish we had a better transition for this, but we're just gonna leave Molly working on her graf for a minute, and give you a little heads up:

TRIP: This next scene's probably gonna be censored.

NELSON: Not the whole scene, but there's certain things we ain't supposed to tell you yet. Now look, we don't support censorship—

TRIP: *—Karen Finley, stand up! Robert Mapplethorpe, where you at? (Nelson stares at Trip. Silence. Then…) Lenny Bruce, what! (Pause.)*

NELSON: You're so fucking embarrassing. *(OFFICER DEREK enters, angry. He is not in uniform.)* This is Derek. He's an angry dude.

TRIP: Derek is angry because {BLEEEEEEEEEEEP} without thinking of another guy who shares his {BLEEEP}. *(Trip's words are bleeped out.)*

NELSON: Word. When Derek was in high school, he was a photographer. (Officer Derek pulls out a camera.) He won a photography award. He won a bunch of awards. But while he was making a name for himself like that, {BLEEEEEEEEEEEEP} was making a name for himself by {BLEEEEEE-EEEEEEEP}—so this motherfucker ended up pissed off all the time.

TRIP: So pissed off that he stopped taking pictures altogether. *(Officer Derek throws the camera away.)* He went searching for something bigger. And like a lot of people who saw what happened when we lost a couple buildings in this city, Derek decided to join the NYPD.

NELSON: He became Officer Derek.

(Officer Derek puts on his uniform.)

TRIP: Officer Derek {BLEEP}. This scene needs the ill parental advisory sticker.

NELSON: So you see, we really can't tell you that much about him, except that for last few years of this young man's life, dude has been angry.

TRIP: Look at him. He's angry right now.

(Officer Derek is angry.)

But keep looking.

(Officer Derek comes across Molly writing graffiti. He stops and stares at her.)

NELSON: He ain't angry anymore.

• 6

(Continuous. Molly writes her graffiti. Officer Derek stares at her.)

MOLLY: *(Without looking at him.)* How long you been standing there looking at my ass?

OFFICER DEREK: I just got here.

MOLLY: You're lucky that I'm busy right now, cause it would very easy for me to stick this can down your throat and tag up on your esophagus. But I won't. As a matter of fact, you're double lucky, cause not only will I resist the temptation to feed you some Krylon, but I'm feeling good enough to let you stand there and witness the unveiling of graffiti so fucking beautiful you might aneurysm yourself.

OFFICER DEREK: I wasn't looking at your ass.

MOLLY: You're lying, but that shit's okay—soon as I finish this up here, you ain't gonna be able to look nowhere but dead center of this wall. You know what's on the other side of this wall? The police. Fuck them. They think this their building? They got some ownership issues, cause look right there at who this building says it belongs to. Who does it look like this building belongs to to you? *(Pause.)* Huh? Who, huh?

OFFICER DEREK: I'm a police officer. *(Silence.)*

MOLLY: Fuck you then. What you think, you're gonna arrest me for being an artist? You're gonna put me in jail for being proud of my name?

OFFICER DEREK: No.

MOLLY: That's right, no. You fucking cops don't understand nothing about what I'm doing out here. You see me writing my name loud so the whole Lower East Side could hear it and you think I'm some obnoxious little girl. I am not some obnoxious little girl. I am this obnoxious little girl. *(Molly points to her name. She still has not turned around.)*

OFFICER DEREK: You're Molly.

MOLLY: Damn. Fucking. Right I'm Molly. You're gonna remember that name long after you arrest me and paint my name off this wall—

OFFICER DEREK: I'm not going to arrest you. *(Pause.)* I'm supposed to, yeah. Graffiti's a crime. But...*(Pause.)*...watching you do it is kind of beautiful.

(Molly and Officer Derek make eye contact for the first time. They freeze. Love at first sight. The DJs play an ironic, angry rock love song—something like "This is Love" by PJ Harvey. Blackout on the police station.)

• 7

(Nelson, alone in the booth.)

NELSON: The role of the grizzled but lovable senior officer will be played tonight by Mr. Trip Goldstein. *(Trip, at the bar, wearing a police hat. Alejandro, behind the bar.)*

TRIP: *(As the Officer. To Alejandro:)* She's got the rookie slipping over his own drool! I'm ready to hop on the CB and let all units know we got a riot about to unfold—a laugh riot! HA!

NELSON: *(To audience:)* That dude is mad grizzled, but surprisingly lovable.

TRIP: You walk back there—you know, that's where we go to smoke—and you got the whole picture in front of you. She's standing there, can of paint, guilty like Gilfrey, if you know what I mean...*(Molly, in the same spot we left her, staring into Officer Derek's eyes.)* He's standing there, hand on his gun, jaw scraping the ground like a loose muffler...*(Officer Derek, still staring at Molly.)* And the kicker—the be-all kicker to end all kickers— is right over her shoulder, right in his eyeline...there's her name on the wall. *(Molly's name, still on the wall.)*

ALEJANDRO: On the police station wall?

TRIP: On the back wall, yessiree.

ALEJANDRO: My mother did not bring her up like that...

TRIP: Eh, in my mind, it's victimless crime. Worse things kids could be doing than writing graffiti. Even adds some color to the place, gives me something to read between puffs.

ALEJANDRO: So she's not in trouble?

TRIP: I didn't say that. This is the new New York City. The mayor right now—come to think of it, the last couple of mayors—let's say they're not exactly connoisseurs of street art. We catch graffiti artists in the act, we gotta bring 'em in.

ALEJANDRO: You brought her in? Do I need to go down there? What's the bail?

TRIP: Slow down, slow down. Here's where we go from tragedy to comedy. See, I walk in on them, right? They're staring all google-faced like this is *Desperate Housewives* or something.

ALEJANDRO: Grizzled guy like you watches *Desperate Housewives*?

NELSON: *(From the DJ booth.)* And he cried when *Melrose Place* went off the air.

TRIP: *(As himself.)* Fuck you, man. I'm in character.
(As The Officer.) So I walk into the parking lot... *(Trip—still as The Officer— walks over to the police station, where Molly and Officer Derek have not moved, have not taken their eyes off each other.)* Hey, rookie—we wanna sign you up for the squad softball team. Figure those fire department guys see your name on the roster and go running off with their hoses between their legs.

OFFICER DEREK: *(Turning away from Molly, embarrassed.)* I don't play baseball.

TRIP: We don't need you to play. We just need the name. *(Noticing Molly.)* Oh, I see you ran into our neighborhood redecoration specialist. It's all wrong, Molly. That shade is clashing with the cigarette butts.

MOLLY: I don't know what you're talking about. I don't know anything about paint. I definitely don't know anything about this beautiful, stunning, perfect piece on this boring white wall. I don't know nothing about nothing.

TRIP: I guess somebody else wrote your name on this wall.

MOLLY: *(Fake sweet.)* That's not my name. My name is Amalia.

TRIP: We've given you too many warnings, *Amalia*. I'm assuming a smart kid like you already knows your Miranda rights... *(Trip goes to handcuff Molly. She pushes away.)*

MOLLY: Nah, no.

TRIP: Take another step away and it's misconduct. Put your hand on me again, and that's resisting arrest. Now be quiet and listen to your rights.

MOLLY: I don't need no rights. I'm already exonerated. Ask your boy right there what he saw—it wasn't me writing this genius, brilliant graffiti, I know that.

TRIP: Tell me what you saw, rook, so we can end this and solve some real crimes.

MOLLY: *(To Officer Derek:)* Come on—you know I didn't do nothing. Tell him I didn't do nothing.

TRIP: You gotta show a little more respect, Amalia—didn't the rookie here tell you who he is? You're dealing with a celebrity...

OFFICER DEREK: I'm not a fucking celebrity. I'm a police officer. *(Pause.)* I'm sorry.

MOLLY: Tell him what you saw. Come on, tell him. Fucking tell him. *(Desperately.)* Please.

(Silence.)

OFFICER DEREK: I saw some girl. I can't say if it was her. *(Pause.)* I guess we have to let her go, huh? *(Silence.)*

MOLLY: When you find whoever did it, tell her I'm impressed. *(Molly exits. Trip stares at Officer Derek, then breaks into laughter and returns to the booth, switching back to himself.)*

TRIP: Yo, he got a whole different kinda emotion than angry right now.

OFFICER DEREK: *(Calls after the Senior Officer.)* This is not something to joke about! I deserve to be taken seriously!

• 8

(Continuous. Alejandro and Officer Derek, at the bar.)

ALEJANDRO: That's right. You do deserve to be taken seriously.

OFFICER DEREK: The entire precinct thinks the whole situation with your sister is a joke.

ALEJANDRO: Bastards. So what exactly is the situation with my sister?

OFFICER DEREK: I earned my uniform. I can handle New York. I can handle anything. And definitely some cute girl—I don't care how cute she is. And she's not. Cute. Not. Not cute.

ALEJANDRO: *(Slides a beer in front of Officer Derek.)* Guinness. Good for nerves.

OFFICER DEREK: Nerves? I don't have nerves. I have nerves, nerves of steel nerves, and, and, and she broke the law, and, and, and that's what I'm here to talk to you about. That.

ALEJANDRO: We got all night to talk about Molly. Drink up.

NELSON: *(Interrupting the action. To audience.)* Yo, chill, chill, chill for one second. Y'all don't even realize what you saw my boy do right there.

TRIP: Let me run the track back so we could give the ill alternate DVD commentary. *(Trip winds a record back and the scene resets to the beginning.)*

ALEJANDRO: That's right. You do deserve to be taken seriously.

TRIP: *(Speaking over Officer Derek's lines.)* Right from jump, he puts himself on this guy's side. Two minutes ago, they never seen each other before. Now Al's his biggest ally.

ALEJANDRO: Bastards. So what exactly is the situation with my sister?

NELSON: People who sit at the bar always want to talk about they self. Al always gives them that opportunity. First time you say a word to him, he's asking you for your story.

TRIP: And the thing is, look at his face. He's focused on what the cop is telling him. And it's not because he's talking about Al's sister. This guy could be talking about President Taft getting stuck in the White House bathtub, and Al's attention would be on lock.

ALEJANDRO: *(Slides a beer in front of Officer Derek.)* Guinness. Good for nerves.

NELSON: Soon as that boy gets tense, Al's ready to chill him out. Slip him a beer, slow the kid down. Last thing you need in new bar like this is a agitated cop.

ALEJANDRO: We got all night to talk about Molly. Drink up.

NELSON: Yo, that's my favorite. Play it again, Trip.

ALEJANDRO: We got all night to talk about Molly. Drink up.

TRIP: Naw—I wanna play it even one more time.

ALEJANDRO: We got all night to talk about Molly.

TRIP: He ain't got no intention of talking about Molly. And the cop ain't looking for the end of a conversation anyway. You don't go to a bar to get your problem solved; you just want someone to listen to you. Al listens. That's what he does.

NELSON: And then this next move:

ALEJANDRO: Drink up.

NELSON: My man is only trying to make you drink faster so you buy more alcohol.

TRIP: And you don't even realize it.

NELSON: And you wouldn't mind if you did.

TRIP: And you don't even realize it.

NELSON: And you wouldn't mind if you did.

TRIP: Cause our boy is that damn good. So then the question is how can he be so good…and we still don't hardly have customers?

NELSON: And we'll answer that question. In the next scene.

(Back to the regular scene.)

OFFICER DEREK: There's, there's, there's a reason that I covered for her, and it wasn't anything, it wasn't it wasn't anything like they think—it was about justice, and, and rehabilitation, and I think it may have even been kind of noble—

ALEJANDRO: Two peanuts walking down the street. One was "a salted." *(Silence.)* Cop joke. And a bar joke too, I guess. *(Silence.)* You take things too seriously, buddy. What's your name?

OFFICER DEREK: People think graffiti is a small problem, but, but, but have you ever heard of the Broken Windows Theory? Quality of life crimes—like graffiti—destroy neighborhoods, destroy businesses—

ALEJANDRO: I know some things about business. My mother used to run a business. Right here. Right in this spot. And she made it her business, at that business, to know her customers…and their business. She knew how they took their coffee. Who they were dating—

OFFICER DEREK: —I'm not dating anyone.

ALEJANDRO: I'm not asking you out. I'm just looking for your name.

OFFICER DEREK: Okay. I'm Derek.

ALEJANDRO: You got a last name, Officer Derek?

(Pause.)

OFFICER DEREK: This is a serious outreach that I'm making to you for your sister's sake, and I don't need to be belittled, or disrespected, or—

ALEJANDRO: No, no—who's gonna belittle you, yo? I got nothing but respect—and respect like I got for you deserves a full name. *(Silence.)* I could wait a long time. A real long respectful time.

OFFICER DEREK: Okay. My last name's…my last name is…Jeter. *(Silence.)*

ALEJANDRO: Derek. Like Eric with a D?

OFFICER DEREK: Yes.

ALEJANDRO: And Jeter. Like Eater with a J?

OFFICER DEREK: Yes. *(Silence.)* Derek Jeter, NYPD. *(Silence.)* And your sister doesn't need to know that. And no, I'm not a Yankees fan. I'm from Boston. Outside Boston. Ashland. And I've heard all the jokes, so don't make them, because they're not original, and they're disrespectful to me, not only as a human being, but as a member of the finest law enforcement unit in the United States, who happens to be doing a pretty damn good job of protecting you and serving you even if no one wants to give me any credit for it. *(Silence.)*

ALEJANDRO: Okay. *(Pause.)* Derek Jeter, NYPD—don't forget why you are where you are. You're in the best bar in the Lower East Side. You're here to chill, to relax, to soak up every inch of hospitality that a humble bartender like me can give you. You're not here on business. You're definitely not here to talk about my family—

(The front door flies open. Lelly enters. It's a big theatrical moment. Maybe she's backlit. The entire attention of the audience should be drawn to her.)

LELLY: *(To audience:)* Elisabeth Arroyo probably moved to the Lower East Side sometime in the early-'80s—but you can't really confirm that, and that's kinda phenomenally awesome. You can confirm that she got a job in a deli, worked there for twenty years, and eventually became its owner, two months before she died, which was roughly six months before today.

She was an institution down here. I used to buy Pop Rocks and baseball cards from her—okay, that's personal information, not academic. Forget I even mentioned it.

She never talked about herself, so no one outside her family knew anything about her outside of that deli counter, but I've discovered two bits of mind-blowing Elisabeth Arroyo-related info that I wanna share with you. Okay?

Okay. One: Knowing that I have to out of nowhere spring this all on her son kind of makes me ludicrously nervous, so I keep reminding myself that this is good news, and he's going to love me for bringing it to him, only it's not news, it's just a theory, and this isn't about love, it's about history—the act of historicization is not about being loved. *(Pause.)*

I don't think historicization is a word. *(Pause.)*

Oh. And um, Two: Elisabeth Arroyo's middle name was *Reina.*

(Back to normal. Back to the bar. Lelly enters.)

TRIP: Yo Nel. Is that who I think it is?

NELSON: Oh fuck…why's she here?

LELLY: Alejandro Arroyo?

ALEJANDRO: That's me. I own this place. What can I do for you? *(Pause.)*

LELLY: Some day you and I are going to Grand Marshal the Puerto Rican Day parade on the first ever float commemorating Reina Rey and we'll look back at today and laugh. *(Silence.)* Shit. I didn't mean to just come in and come out and say it like that. *(Silence.)* I have to go. *(Lelly exits.)*

TRIP: Oh, *hell* no.

• 9

(Still in the bar, but later. Officer Derek has exited. Trip and Nelson, talking to Alejandro, who is still staring off after Lelly.)

TRIP: Her name is Lelly Santiago. In related news, she's a skank-ass white girl.

NELSON: She's Puerto Rican, but she's a white girl. Trust me.

TRIP: And if you don't trust him, trust the white boy.

NELSON: You're not white. You're Jewish.

TRIP: That's way too complicated a discussion to get into right now. Bet she got a tattoo on her back over her ass and everything.

NELSON: Probably a dolphin.

TRIP: Yeah. Definitely a dolphin.

NELSON: But more important, Al—check this out. Me and Trip been working for you since this spot came open.

TRIP: Even before that. We helped you turn this spot into a lounge in the first place.

NELSON: I still got a cut on my arm from tearing down the "Arroyo's Bodega" sign.

TRIP: And yo, we seen the difficulties this place has gone through.

ALEJANDRO: We're not changing anything. We do what we say, and the people will come.

TRIP: We know…

ALEJANDRO: It worked for my mother.

NELSON: *(To audience:)* You see? How do you argue against that?

ALEJANDRO: Wait, wait, wait. What you mean, "skank-ass white girl?"

NELSON: I'm not saying we should change anything, but me and Trip, see, we got this hip-hop group thing on the side.

TRIP: We rhyme in our spare time, you know what I mean?

NELSON: We focused, man. We work that shit. We live that shit.

TRIP: Fuck, I wrote Kanye West in as my vote for president. *(To audience:)* What? I'm in New York. It's not like it made a difference.

ALEJANDRO: What you mean "skank-ass white girl?"

NELSON: Skank like skunk, mean she stunk like shit was dank. And when you sniff the stank, slink away from the junk, punk. *(An afterthought.)* Ass white girl.

TRIP: See? We live that shit! Hip-hop, you the love of my life!

NELSON: The reason why you ain't had such good business lately is because…well, it's because you ain't give The Tripnel Cartel—

TRIP: Hot name, right?

NELSON: You ain't give us the mic in the club yet.

ALEJANDRO: I'm saying though…

NELSON: Come on, Al! We got the beats, we got the lyrics, we got the love…

TRIP: We got everything you need to bring the *real* Lower East Side crowd back into your bar.

ALEJANDRO: It's not a bar. It's a lounge.

NELSON: Lounges ain't what the LES is looking for.

TRIP: Real motherfuckers—

NELSON: —motherfuckers from around here—

TRIP: —want to hear other real motherfuckers—

NELSON: —preferably other real motherfuckers from around here—

TRIP: —making real motherfucking shit—

NELSON: —like a motherfucker. Me and Trip can guarantee we bring the local Boricua market back.

ALEJANDRO: I'm saying though—I still don't see why you calling her a skank.

NELSON: How you still even have Lelly Santiago anywhere in your brain?

ALEJANDRO: What she talking about us going to the parade for? I don't even know her ass.

NELSON: You know what we are to Lelly Santiago? We a science project. We a ant farm. She's dubious, son.

TRIP: How she gonna troop on in here from Upstate exploring the LES outback for specimens she could show off to her friends like she the Crocodile Hunter or some shit?

ALEJANDRO: How you know so much—wait, how you know anything about this girl?

TRIP AND NELSON: (*In chorus.*) We the chorus!

ALEJANDRO: What?

TRIP: We know cause she used to live down here, on Norfolk Street, till like fourth grade.

NELSON: And even then she was taking the train to the Upper West Side to go to school with the other dark-skinned geniuses that were too smart and too precious to rot away in public school with us juvenile delinquents and future grown-ass delinquents. I don't know how you didn't know her.

TRIP: First chance her family got, they hauled ass out the LES. And she ain't never came back until she realized that the boy band frat boys she went to school with got all impressed that she was from the "East Village." This ain't even the East Village! It's the Lower East Side! But she don't know the difference. She's the worst worst worst of everything that I'm talking about: a Puerto Rican girl who left this neighborhood when it sucked and only comes back to claim it when shit becomes convenient. Gives your people a bad name.

ALEJANDRO: Hold up, hold up. How I'm gonna take Puerto Rican advice from Trip fucking Goldstein?

TRIP: Don't disappoint me, Al. It's like Rakim said: "it ain't where you're from, it's where you're at."[1]

---

1. Barrier, Eric, and William Griffith. 1987. "I Ain't No Joke" on *Paid in Full*. Performed by Eric B. and Rakim. Universal Songs/Polygram International Inc.

NELSON: And you right here, Al. We got mad love for that. Now put my Pinoy ass on.

TRIP: And put that skank out your head.

ALEJANDRO: She's in my bar. I need to make her happy.

NELSON: It ain't a bar. It's a lounge.

ALEJANDRO: That's right. And in my lounge, my job is to make people happy. That's what I say I do, and that's what I do. Same way it was in the deli for my mom…

TRIP: She's a skank. *(Awkward silence.)* I mean, Lelly. Lelly's a skank.

ALEJANDRO: I got it. She comes back, I'll treat her like anybody else. Nothing more, nothing less.

TRIP: But yo, she's a—

ALEJANDRO: Nothing more, nothing less.

• 10

(Molly, alone in the apartment.)

MOLLY: You saw that, right Ma? Wherever you are, you saw the way that a real woman handles her problems, right? I ain't cleaning no walls or locking myself away cause some cops want to tell me to stop writing. They can't hold me. This whole city can't hold me. And they think some rookie cop can? You saw his face, right? He never saw nothing like me before. They're all afraid. The all of them.

Damn, Ma—I own those streets now. Back of that police station—that's mine. I could be out all night, bombing left, bombing right, and they ain't gonna say nothing. And the only reason I ain't out there now is… *(Long pause as she thinks about it.)*

It ain't cause I'm scared. And it got nothing to do with that cop. *(Pause.)*

I ain't gotta tell you shit. You wanna know so bad, you shoulda taken care of your heart so you still woulda been here.

• 11

(Continuous. Alejandro enters, immediately starts making breakfast.)

MOLLY: Just cause I'm here before you don't mean I didn't come home late.

ALEJANDRO: I met a girl tonight, Amalia.

MOLLY: *(Genuinely excited.)* You met a real girl?

ALEJANDRO: Yup.

MOLLY: *(Remembering.)* My name is not Amalia.

ALEJANDRO: Her name is Lelly.

MOLLY: The fuck kinda name is Lelly? Let me guess. Her last name is like…Von Hofflinger or something. Lelly Von Hofflinger. The Third. Bet she read you her college thesis on the geopolitical ramifications of Eminem's artistry.

ALEJANDRO: How you know she was in college?

MOLLY: If she was in your bar, she wasn't no Lower East Side girl.

ALEJANDRO: How you know she was in the lounge?

MOLLY: Where the hell else she's gonna meet you?

ALEJANDRO: *(Adding salt to the eggs he's cooking.)* Her last name is Santiago. From Norfolk Street. There's something about this girl, Molly. I mean, it ain't even that she's fine—I mean, she *is* fine—but for some reason...for some reason, she was like...salt.

MOLLY: She's like salt.

ALEJANDRO: Like she threw salt and it hit my eye, and I blinked and I blinked and I blinked and it wouldn't go, it wouldn't flush itself out. And yeah, that shit hurt—you got salt in your eye, it hurts—but...I liked it. *(Pause.)* Aight, salt's not the best way to explain it. But I can't shake her and I'm kinda fine with that. I just keep blinking and blinking and thinking how good that salt could taste once it comes out my eye. *(Pause.)* Forget the salt.

MOLLY: Big pimping, Don Alejandro. Big salty pimping.

ALEJANDRO: Forget the salt! You still never did the dishes.

MOLLY: Servants do dishes. Artists contemplate why servants allow themselves to do dishes.

ALEJANDRO: I bet you would do dishes for Derek Jeter.

MOLLY: Artists don't watch baseball.

ALEJANDRO: Not that Derek Jeter. Officer Derek Jeter.

MOLLY: You better start getting out your bar more often.

ALEJANDRO: You know. The angry dude.

MOLLY: *(Freezes in her tracks.) You talked to him?*

ALEJANDRO: What, I'm not allowed to talk to my sister's boyfriend?

MOLLY: I don't have no boyfriend. *(Pause.)* How you know about him?

ALEJANDRO: Arroyo's is the central nervous system of the Lower East Side. Anything happens from Houston to Delancey, I know about it.

MOLLY: What, did he come into your bar and introduce himself?

ALEJANDRO: Yeah. He did. We had a big night.

MOLLY: He got no reason to be there.

ALEJANDRO: Well, now he does. He's a valued customer. And yo, it's better for you that it's him and not the last three cops I had in my bar looking for you. He ain't interested in arresting you.

MOLLY: Why the fuck not?

ALEJANDRO: I think my man got a crush on your artistic ass.

MOLLY: He does?

ALEJANDRO: *(Offering her a plate of food.)* Careful with the eggs. They salty.

(Molly pushes past him and exits.)

• 12

(Trip and Nelson in the booth.)

TRIP: *(To audience:)* At the sound of the scratch, Al will unlock the front door, and Arroyo's will officially be open for business.

NELSON: You might have noticed we do this every night. Al's like that prime meridian clock or whatever. Always opens in 3...2...1...*(SCRATCH...then silence. No Alejandro. They wait. They check their watches. They wait some more.)* He's late.

TRIP: He ain't been late once since we opened. *(Silence.)*

NELSON: I'm scared.

(Alejandro runs in from the apartment.)

ALEJANDRO: I'm not late, I'm not late. We didn't open yet. I'm not late. I was upstairs thinking, that was all.

NELSON: Uh oh. What you think he was thinking about, Trip?

TRIP: What you think I think he was thinking about?

ALEJANDRO: I wasn't thinking about no girl, if that's what you're trying to say...

TRIP: Then how you think you know we think we know what you thinking about then?

NELSON: Yo, I wouldn't even expect her back, son. She's out her place down here.

ALEJANDRO: Whatever. I ain't thinking bout her. *(He goes about his business.)* How somebody you don't even know is gonna come into your place of business, be like "you and me, the parade, laughing, whatever"? Then how she's gonna be like "uh" and walk out and now you think she ain't coming back to explain herself? *(Pause.)* I ain't thinking bout her.

• 13

(Lelly, alone. Outside the bar.)

LELLY: My dad doesn't think I'm doing *real* research. He says all I do all day is look at old party flyers and transcripts of other people's interviews with folks who were there, and yeah, that's all I do, but hey—I found Reina Rey that way, and I didn't just find her story:

I found a picture. One picture.

She had just gotten arrested, her hands are cuffed behind her back, and she's wearing a sweat shirt with those iron-on felt letters spelling out her name—and okay, this is the awesome best thing ever part—she looks like someone I knew.

She looks, somehow, like the woman who sold me my candy when I was a kid. How could I not follow that up? *(She enters the bar.)*

This is a bad idea. *(She exits the bar.)*

Okay. I go back in, and I explain who I am—no—I apologize for being weird, for being weird last time and for being weird in general. Then I explain who I am. Then I go ahead and hit this virtual stranger with the earth-shattering news about his late mother and the history of hip-hop and the future of the world as we know it.

Sounds like a plan.

• 14

(Continuous. Lelly opens the bar door—again, it's a big theatrical moment.)

ALEJANDRO: You're back!

LELLY: Sometimes I start saying what I'm thinking and I say it too fast to not say it even if I don't know what I'm planning to say next...

ALEJANDRO: I knew you'd be back. I was waiting to talk with you...

NELSON: Yo Trip, you remember this song? *(Trip and Nelson, watching this, begin mixing in recorded snippets of their earlier conversation with Alejandro into the music.)*

ALEJANDRO (SAMPLED): "I AIN'T THINKING BOUT HER."

ALEJANDRO: Now if I remember correctly, last time you was in here you didn't end up getting a drink at all.

TRIP: How that song went, Nel?

ALEJANDRO (SAMPLED): *(Music being made from the samples now.)* "I'LL TREAT HER LIKE ANYBODY ELSE/ANY/ANY/ANYBODY ELSE/I AIN'T THINKING ABOUT HER..."

TRIP: That was the jam.

ALEJANDRO: Alls I'm saying is that ain't nobody coming back here two nights in a row and not drinking nothing.

NELSON: What about this one, Trip?

ALEJANDRO (SAMPLED): "NOTHING MORE/NOTHING/NOTHING MORE, NOTHING LESS/I AIN'T THINKING ABOUT HER..."

ALEJANDRO: I know you didn't come back because of the music. And the way we do things at Arroyo's is to make sure every customer walks out happier than they came in. I ain't sure your happiness increased much yet. My mother—that's where I get that attitude from. Worked hard and only cared about her customers and she did what she said—

LELLY: *(Puts her hand over Alejandro's mouth.)* I think your mother wasn't exactly who you think she was. *(Silence.)*

ALEJANDRO: *(Shaken.)* You think what. About my mother?

LELLY: *(Warily.) You don't know who she really was. (Silence.) You start talking and I forget where I am and it comes out. (She exits.)*

ALEJANDRO: *(To Trip and Nelson.)* We're closed. *(Alejandro exits up to the apartment.)*

(Silence.)

TRIP: Now I'm scared too.

• 15

(Officer Derek, at the police station wall. He has a can of graffiti remover. Molly's name is still on the wall. Officer Derek suddenly spins to face the wall, drawing the can, like a gun, directly at the spray paint.)

OFFICER DEREK: This job's harder than hitting a baseball. *(He does it again.)* 19 million dollars you made this year, Derek Jeter. For playing a game. I'm down here. On the streets. Keeping people safe. Keeping *you* safe. *(He does it again.)* What you have ever done for anyone, huh? You learned how to inside-out a fastball into right field for a base hit, made one nice backhanded toss to the plate, and suddenly the world's in love with you. King of New York. Dated Mariah Carey. Not that I'd want to date Mariah Carey. But still. What do you actually *do*, Derek Jeter? *(He does it again. Building his confidence each time.)* Cause I know what I do. I arrest people. I'll arrest you if I have to. Oh yeah, I would. Maybe then people would understand that you don't really do anything for anyone. Maybe then people would appreciate people like me. People who enforce the law. I can already see the headline on the back page of the paper: "Derek Jeter arrested by…Derek Jeter." *(Officer Derek, in a sudden fit of anger, fires the can at the wall.)* You're the one that should be getting rid of her name. You're good at it.

• 16

(Continuous. Molly storms in. Officer Derek nervously hides the can.)

MOLLY: I don't know what kind of sick ideas you got about you and me and some kind of relationship, but you need to put that shit out of your head right now.

OFFICER DEREK: Back to the scene of the crime, young lady?

MOLLY: I didn't commit no crime. And I ain't no fucking young lady. You see my name right there on that wall. You call me by my name…

OFFICER DEREK: And I'd appreciate you calling me by my name right there on that wall. Police. Police Officer. *(Pause.)* That's not my name.

MOLLY: My brother told me your name.

OFFICER DEREK: I told him not to.

MOLLY: I don't give a fuck about your name.

OFFICER DEREK: Really? You're the first person in New York to say that—

MOLLY: —my brother's valuable time shouldn't even be bothered with your name—

OFFICER DEREK: —no one's should. But if it helps your family and the Police Department build up our relationship—

MOLLY: My family and you don't have no relationship except me doing what I want and you doing what I tell you, cop or not. Now turn your ass around and look at who owns this police station you work in. You see right there where it says my name?

(Molly jabs her finger into Officer Derek's chest to push him to look. Officer Derek grabs her wrist and holds it there, finger flush against his chest. Trip and Nelson, in the booth. Molly and Officer Derek, frozen, still visible.)

NELSON: When me and Trip and Al was tearing down the deli to build the bar, Molly used to throw broken bricks at us if we pissed her off.

TRIP: One time they were checking Molly's head for lice at her school, and the nurse accidentally stabbed her head with the chopsticky thing. Molly punched her in the eye.

NELSON: She hates cops.

TRIP: Shit. She hates people she likes.

NELSON: She hits people she hates.

TRIP: But a cop?

OFFICER DEREK: *(Still holding Molly's finger to his chest.)* I am an officer of laws. This is a place of laws. You have respect, you will, for this and for me when you come here. *(Silence.)*

MOLLY: I'm not afraid of cops.

OFFICER DEREK: Fear I'm not asking for here. *(Tense silence.)*

MOLLY: That rhymed. *(Officer Derek lets go of her hand.)* It was cute, *Officer*.

OFFICER DEREK: I don't need smart-assed comments that are smart-assed.

MOLLY: I don't usually get down with cute, but that was, I don't know. Kinda funny. I didn't expect you to be funny. You ain't so bad when you're funny. *(Long silence.)* You didn't paint over my name yet.

OFFICER DEREK: I'm about to.

MOLLY: Took a long time for you to get started.

OFFICER DEREK: They didn't tell me it was my job to clean it.

MOLLY: You don't know what your job is?

OFFICER DEREK: My job is arresting criminals, not painting and cleaning…

MOLLY: Why you gotta paint and clean then?

OFFICER DEREK: It's just today.

MOLLY: Get demoted?

OFFICER DEREK: It's just today.

MOLLY: Did they say it was just today?

OFFICER DEREK: They said to clean it. I'm going to clean it.

MOLLY: See, that's the difference between you and me. Cops tell me to repaint the wall, I ain't repainting the wall. They tell you to do it, your ass has to do it. You're a servant. I'm an artist—

OFFICER DEREK: It reminds me of you. *(Silence.)* Your name. It reminds me of you. Maybe I won't clean it. *(Silence.)*

(Molly calmly crosses to Officer Derek...and punches him in the face.)

• 17

(Trip and Nelson, in the booth. They've been watching Molly and Officer Derek. They play "Mama Said Knock You Out" by LL Cool J—or some other suitable face-punching commentary music.)

TRIP: Yo...we're comic relief.

• 18

(Alejandro, alone in the apartment. Molly stomps in.)

ALEJANDRO: *(Immediately as Molly enters.)* Lelly Santiago. She used to live on Norfolk Street.

MOLLY: Oh yeah? Cool. I punched that cop.

ALEJANDRO: You're sure you don't know her?

MOLLY: It was fun.

ALEJANDRO: She came in again, talking shit like she knows my mother. Like she knows my mother better than me. Nobody knows my mother better than me. And telling me that in my lounge? And not even trying to explain herself...

MOLLY: You probably didn't stop talking about your bar long enough to let her.

ALEJANDRO: Don't tell me I wasn't listening. I'm a bartender. It's my job to listen. *(Pause.)* You punched Derek Jeter?

MOLLY: I might go back there and bust him in his eye again on principle.

ALEJANDRO: No. That's one of my valued customers.

MOLLY: And don't tell me I should apologize, cause I ain't sorry.

ALEJANDRO: All we got right now is the Arroyo name. You disgrace that, and that spot downstairs that pays your bills—that pays for your paint— goes out of business...

MOLLY: And I ain't sorry, and it ain't like he would listen if I said sorry anyway. He's a cop, and I beat his ass, and I got no reason to apologize for nothing.

ALEJANDRO: Don't apologize.

MOLLY: And I don't need no advice from you neither.

ALEJANDRO: Don't apologize. Don't go near there. Don't apologize.

MOLLY: If they're gonna arrest me, I can't change that. Not even with an apology, which I ain't giving anyway. Right? That wouldn't change nothing. *(No response.)* Right? *(Alejandro exits to his room.)* RIGHT? *(Molly keeps looking to Alejandro, even as he has left the room. A LOUD KNOCK on the front door of the apartment. Molly storms over, opens the door.)*

MOLLY: The fuck do you want? *(No one there. A photograph is taped to the door. Molly takes the photo off the door.)* Ma? This is you, Ma? *(Pause.)* You should have shown me this before.

• 19

(Lelly, at the bar. Big and theatrical again. She has a notepad. Aaliyah's "Four Page Letter" plays as she writes page after page.)

LELLY: I go all dumb when I try to say it out loud. She's his mother. So what if I figured out she was Reina Rey? I mean, if I figured out she *might have been* Reina Rey. I can't stand there and spew words at him and not expect him to get offended. So I figured if I just showed him the picture, maybe I wouldn't have to explain.

(Lelly picks up the papers and walks towards the front door of the bar.)

But you can't just tape a picture to a door and expect that he'll understand. *Of course* I'll have to explain. So I wrote him this four page letter. I would enclose it with a kiss...

(Lelly pulls out a hammer and nails the papers to the door.)

...but romance has no role in reformation. *(She exits.)*

(Trip and Nelson, dumbfounded.)

NELSON: Did she just...?

TRIP: With a nail...?

NELSON: In my man's door?

TRIP: I...I got no words.

NELSON: *(To audience.)* Just...just go to the police station.

• 20

(Molly and Officer Derek, at the police station, staring at each other.)

MOLLY: Okay. I realize that...in cases like this...you might look, or you might be looking for me to say...certain things that maybe got said in the kind of house you grew up in, but in my family, and in the way I grew up, we never said...like...we never said...like—the way I grew up, it didn't matter if I was, if I was right, if I was wrong, it didn't matter, cause we fight. We fight. And you could fight with like hands or you could fight with like words, and then you sleep, and then everybody knows that everybody's wrong and everybody's...fine with that. It's a cultural thing, and if you don't understand, then, then, then you a racist motherfucker.

OFFICER DEREK: You're apologizing.

MOLLY: No. I'm not.

OFFICER DEREK: It's been a long time since anyone properly apologized to me.

MOLLY: I'm not. And you asked for it anyway. But you were being kinda nice. For a cop. So maybe...you shouldn't have gotten hit. So...you know.

OFFICER DEREK: Surprising to me that it would come from a girl like you.

MOLLY: The fuck you saying, a girl like me?

OFFICER DEREK: You don't seem like the apologizing type.

MOLLY: I'm eighteen. I don't need to apologize for nothing. All I need to do is change the world and piss off people like you.

OFFICER DEREK: You know what I was doing when I was eighteen?

MOLLY: You were probably a fucking hall monitor. The fuck do I care?

OFFICER DEREK: I was an artist, like you. Not exactly like you—a photographer. When I turned eighteen, the Ashland City paper offered to publish one of my photos—not front page or anything. Page seven. But still. I was a kid. It was a big deal to get into the paper at all. And I was excited. Until we talked about the photo credit. The publisher made the same joke I heard everyday for the last few years: "Derek Jeter? He sucks wicked hard!"

Yeah, I know, it's real funny, right? But that's my name. And I knew right there that this was what it was going to be. That other guy wasn't going anywhere—he was becoming the most famous baseball player in the country. And no matter what I did, no matter how many perfect page seven photos I took, no one was ever going to think of me when they read my name. And I don't know—I didn't really want the photo credit after that. So they ran the photo uncredited. And I stopped taking pictures.

My mom, she has the photo on her refrigerator, probably still. And she put a sticker on it, a label, and it says "photo taken by my son, Derek Jeter." I didn't even want her to do that. But I don't know. I guess it's pretty cool. *(Silence.)*

MOLLY: My mom was cooler than your mom. *(Pause.)* People, some people think that my mom didn't do nothing but sit behind a deli counter, but she ran that deli. By herself. And she raised two kids alone, and she did it in the most shit neighborhood south of the South Bronx.

OFFICER DEREK: You didn't come here to talk about your mother.

MOLLY: *(Cutting him off.)* And maybe, maybe that doesn't sound like shit to you, but I'm not gonna let you not give my mom the credit she deserves. And look...(*She pulls the picture out of her pocket and stuffs it into his hands.*) She was like me—I mean, I'm like her. She didn't back down from no cops, see?

OFFICER DEREK: This is your mother?

MOLLY: Fuck yeah, that's my mom.

OFFICER DEREK: She's getting arrested.

MOLLY: Fuck yeah, she is.

OFFICER DEREK: For what?

MOLLY: I got no fucking idea. Who cares? Look at her—the cops got her cuffed on the sidewalk, and, and, and she got the look, the *I-don't-give-a-fuck* look, cause whatever they got her for, it was bigger than what those cops could ever do.

OFFICER DEREK: Your mom...

MOLLY: It's the same way right now. I'm doing better things than you could even imagine. I'm an artist. My mom—look at that picture and tell me my mom didn't have artist in her.

OFFICER DEREK: Your mom...

MOLLY: My mom was a fucking warrior. Whatever she's doing here, that proves it. My mom, my mom, my mom...

OFFICER DEREK: Your mom was HOT. (*Silence.*)

MOLLY: Stupid. (*She pulls the picture away from him.*)

OFFICER DEREK: I'm serious! Look... (*He moves next to her, pulling the photo back into his hands.*) See, her eyes are all big and midnight black, and same color as her hair, and hair that long? Sexy as sex.

MOLLY: Shut up, that's my mom!

OFFICER DEREK: Serious! Look—and her skin. You have the same skin. This picture right here, with these handcuffs and the sidewalk—that's not your mother. That's you. (*Silence.*)

MOLLY: Stupid.

OFFICER DEREK: No, look. Put your arms back behind your back...(*He bends her arms behind her, as if he was handcuffing her. She resists.*) Relax. Put them back there, and tilt your head like this...(*He pushes her head to the side.*) And let me look. (*He continues to hold her arms behind her with one hand, moves around in front of her, and holds the picture up next to her head. They are chest to chest. Silence.*)

MOLLY: I look like her? For real?

(*Silence. They stare at each other. That same ironic rock love song we heard before is played. They continue to stare. Silence. Molly stomps on Officer Derek's foot, then punches him in the face.*)

• 21

(Alejandro, in the bar, cleaning. Trip and Nelson, in the booth, talking to each other but at Alejandro.)

TRIP: So Nel, check out this purely hypothetical but wildly dubious situation: what would you do if someone defaced your valued property in the most stalker-esque, dubious way imaginable?

NELSON: Damn, Trip. That does indeed sound dubious. I'd probably cut the skank-ass white girl right off.

TRIP: Shh—we keeping it generic. He doesn't need to be thinking about her.

ALEJANDRO: What are y'all talking about?

NELSON: Nothing, man. Nothing. *(Alejandro takes a bag of garbage out through the front door, returns…and sees the letter.)* We was just saying that in the unlikely event someone had damaged our door or something…

(Alejandro opens the letter, reads it, and heads straight for Trip and Nelson.)

ALEJANDRO: *(Reading.)* "The form and function of one's response to familial obligation is as varied as the relative strengths of familial bonds themselves." *(Silence.)* The hell kinda wack lyrics is this? *(No response.)* Y'all didn't write this?

(No response. Alejandro keeps reading, exits towards the apartment.)

TRIP: *(To audience:)* We think we should let him figure this out on his own.

NELSON: He figures out she wrote it, he figures out she's crazy.

TRIP: He figures out she's crazy, he figures out we was right all along.

NELSON: And once he knows we right, he's gonna know we should rhyme.

TRIP: This whole Lelly speed bump turns out better for us than we thought.

(Alejandro bursts back through the door.)

ALEJANDRO: *(Reading from the letter.)* "Implicit in the nature/nurture dialectic is the concept of one's relative locality in the Cosmic Plan." *(Pause.)* For real, y'all wrote this?

TRIP: *(To audience:)* How could he not know who wrote this?

NELSON: *(To audience:)* How could anyone not know who wrote this?

ALEJANDRO: Y'all know who wrote this?

NELSON AND TRIP: *(Nervous ad-lib.)* Nah, nah, no man.

NELSON: Whoever wrote this, the whole thing sounds kinda crazy.

TRIP: Whoever wrote this, I'm staying the hell away from them at all costs. You too, Nel?

NELSON: Yup. You too, Trip?

TRIP: Yup. You too, Al? *(Alejandro is reading the letter.)* Al? You gonna stay away from her—or him, I mean, whoever wrote it, I mean—you gonna stay away from her, or him too, right?

ALEJANDRO: Whoever wrote this is real smart.

NELSON: *Real* smart. Book smart. College smart.

ALEJANDRO: And to go through all this…they must want something.

NELSON: That person definitely got an agenda.

TRIP: An agenda to fuck up your front door.

ALEJANDRO: I bet whoever did this could really help us out with the lounge. *(Pause.)*

TRIP: Damn.

ALEJANDRO: It couldn't hurt to talk to 'em, right?

NELSON: Damn. Yo, you know what I'm thinking, Al? I'm thinking you should just trash that letter.

TRIP: Word. You got other things to be thinking about. Like…well, like you already know me and Nel could rhyme, but you don't know that we could do magic. *(Trip grabs the letter and crumples it up.)* Abracadabra! *(Nelson blows on the letter and Trip throws it over his head behind the bar.)* See? Magic.

NELSON: *(To audience:) Desperate times, you know?*

(They head back to the booth. Alejandro runs back behind the bar, and drops down out of sight looking for the letter. The front door of the bar opens. Lelly enters, searching for the letter.)

LELLY: Fuck. He's already reading it. *(Alejandro slowly rises from behind the bar, reading the letter.)* Fuck. You're already reading it.

(Trip and Nelson, speaking to the audience from the booth.)

NELSON: We recognize that y'all might be interested in the little thing they got going on there, but me and Trip can't take all that dubiousness in one sitting.

TRIP: We gotta snap that shit into little dubious morsels to diffuse the dubious essence.

NELSON: And so, as protest, we step in and kick the action back to Baby Molly.

• 22

(Molly, alone in the apartment, looking at the photo.)

MOLLY: You saw that, right, Ma? You saw what he pulled—"oh you look like your mom oh she's hot oh let me touch you." I'm showing him pictures to defend you, not for him to get close and comfortable. And he says I look like you in that handcuff picture? Nuh uh, no offense, no way. Not Molly. *(She starts clearing dishes from the table.)* You heard that, *Officer?* I ain't cuffed, I ain't never cuffed. I ain't down with the sickness you spreading. You think a badge gets you uncuffed? No. You know what your job description says? Civil. Servant. People like you, you go to work, you get shackled. My brother Alex, he gets shackled. Me, I got paint. I got razor-edged paint cutting my wrists loose before I get locked in. (*She slams the dishes into the sink and starts washing them.*) And and and and you don't take my paint off that wall, because you know, somewhere you know that it could cut you loose, and that's all you want to see is someone cut you loose, same way the whole world wants to get cut loose. But Molly can't cut your wrists alone—you got to hold your hands out! Hold out your chains and Molly's truth shall set you free! (*Molly holds out her hands, full of soap and holding a dish. She just now realizes what she's been doing.*) Motherfucker!

• 23

(*Alejandro and Lelly, in the bar, same positions we left them in.*)

LELLY: Fuck. You're already reading it.

NELSON: (*Cutting her off from the booth. To audience.*) Yeah, see, we're still not ready to listen her speak, so what I'd like to do now is...

LELLY: (*Walking over to the DJ booth.*) Hey!

NELSON: (*Shocked.*) Um. Hey. What's up, Lelly?

LELLY: You can't stop me from talking to him.

TRIP: Oh. Okay. (*Pause.*) Wait, wait, wait—how'd you even know we were talking about you? We're in a whole different theatrical reality! How'd you do that? How'd she do that, Nel?

LELLY: Everything that you've said about me—about the white girl, about abandoning the Lower East Side, about me having no right to come back here—it's all true. Except for the tattoo. It's not a dolphin. It's tribal. But other than that, you're completely right.

NELSON: That's right, we're right.

LELLY: But I'm here to change it. All of it. I'm here for redemption. So if you, kind Nelsoncrantz and you, sweet Goldsteinstern, will excuse me, I've got an indecisive prince to compel into action. (*Silence.*)

NELSON: (*To audience.*) What I'd like to do now is sing Led Zeppelin's classic "Stairway to Heaven," in its entirety, *en español*...(*Lelly unplugs Nelson's microphone. Lights out on the DJ booth.*)

LELLY: Fuck. You're already reading it. I was kinda hoping I could come steal it back off the door before you found it. And now it's all worse than I made it the last two times, cause you probably think I'm some stuck-up neo-white faux-ethnic girl who can only express herself in some over-intellectualized heady mastubatory mumbo-jumbo letter and oh my god. You have me rambling again. This is a bad idea. I should go.

ALEJANDRO: No. You ain't leaving. I got questions. *(Reading.)* "The personified manifestation of the unheralded parallel between literal and spiritual service..." *(Pause.)* I don't even know how to ask a question about this.

LELLY: I can explain why I said what I said about your, you know, your mother...

ALEJANDRO: You will. First you need to explain this letter.

LELLY: Some chick spazzes out on you for days, then writes you a rambling, incoherent letter of introduction like this is *Dangerous Liaisons*, and you take the time to figure out what she's saying before kicking her out?

ALEJANDRO: It's keeping me from doing my job.

LELLY: I know. I can go.

ALEJANDRO: It's keeping me from doing my job because I'm thinking about it too much. I tell my customers I'm going to give them complete and undivided attention at all times, and this letter's making me a liar. Plus you're a customer, so you deserve my attention as much as anybody else. Now you got it. So go ahead.

LELLY: You have the best answers. Okay, for that, you definitely deserve a real explanation. *(Lelly pulls a plate of sushi from her bag.)* This is sushi.

ALEJANDRO: My real explanation is sushi?

LELLY: I have to go slow to stay focused when I'm explaining myself, especially to you, especially about this. *(Starting again.)* This is sushi.

ALEJANDRO: I know.

LELLY: Of course you know. You live in New York. What do you think about sushi?

ALEJANDRO: I think it's nasty.

LELLY: No, but what do you *think* about sushi?

ALEJANDRO: I don't know—it's fish and it's not cooked and it's nasty.

LELLY: I think about sushi, I think about Japan. It's an archipelago—I mean, it's a bunch of islands, so they fish. Fine, that makes sense. Then I think about the fact that they don't cook it. Then I think about eel. And crab roe. And seaweed—especially the seaweed. How did they end up eating all these really awesome obscurities that nobody else eats? We use salt and pepper, they use wasabi and ginger. I mean, wasabi and ginger? Where did that genius come from? I think about how what they eat affects their body types, and their body types affect the amount of energy they have, and their energy affects the way they live, and the way they live affects what they produce, and that affects what we produce, and that affects what I eat, whether I turn around and eat sushi or not.

ALEJANDRO: You think all that? From sushi?

LELLY: To start, yeah.

ALEJANDRO: Damn. When the hell do you eat?

LELLY: And you're probably wondering what this has to do with you, and it really doesn't have anything to do with you, except that…well, lately I've been thinking about you the same way I think about sushi. *(Silence.)*

ALEJANDRO: How much Trip and Nelson paid you to fuck with me?

LELLY: I couldn't imagine having to be paid to fuck with you. *(Silence.)* I mean, you're a bartender. *(Silence.)* Bartenders do important work. Some guy comes in after having his heart broken—he gets his drama out of his system here and goes home ready to make it to the next day. Teachers burn off the stress of mandatory testing and escalating violence with a beer and some good company. Big business gets done over rounds of shots. You help couples get formed in here. Babies get made in your bar—I mean, not made, but planned—I mean, not planned, but the process gets started and you start it.

ALEJANDRO: Yo, I'm a get my sister and you tell her exactly that same thing you just said.

LELLY: I have a lot to say to her. And to you.

ALEJANDRO: She don't do nothing but write her name on the police station all day. And I do all that that you just said. And she got the nerve to say all I do is serve drinks?

LELLY: Those drinks—and by extension, this bar—and by extension, you—make up a central concentric circle of this neighborhood, which happens to be one of the central concentric circles of New York City, which, as everyone knows, is the center of the universe, which makes you one of the central concentric circles of the center of the universe in a way, and oh my god why am I saying concentric so much like an arrogant neophyte college student and oh my god, neophyte?—I'm doing it again. I'll shut up now.

ALEJANDRO: You can't shut up—all I know right now is you think I'm sushi in a center circle.

LELLY: The fact that you're sushi in a center circle—it's concentric circle, but your way sounds better—all it means is that…all it means is this: what did you think of the picture?

ALEJANDRO: What picture?

LELLY: The picture from your door. *(No response.)* You didn't see the picture? *(Silence.)* I really have to go.

ALEJANDRO: You can't go! Now I got more questions about everything you just said…

LELLY: But you didn't see the picture. And that means you don't have the picture and without it, there's no way I can explain to you who your mother used to be. *(Silence.)* I'll be back. I promise. *(Almost gone.)* Try the sushi. *(Lelly plugs the DJs' microphone back in and exits. Trip and Nelson, in the booth.)*

NELSON: (Singing.) "Y esta comprando/una escalera/al cielo…"[2] (Playing a recording of a crowd cheering.) Gracias! Gracias mi gente!

• 24

(Molly, angrily scrubbing the floor. Alejandro enters.)

MOLLY: If you say one sound about me cleaning this house, I'm busting your ass.

ALEJANDRO: I need a dictionary and a fork.

MOLLY: It don't mean nothing if I do the dishes—I just did 'em. Ain't no reason why.

ALEJANDRO: You wash the forks?

MOLLY: I washed everything.

ALEJANDRO: Nice. *(He grabs a fork from a drawer, then exits back to the bar—hardly ever looking at Molly. Molly follows him.)*

MOLLY: You ain't even gonna ask what happened? I ain't gonna tell you, but you could still ask.

ALEJANDRO: Yo—

MOLLY: I ain't gonna tell you!

ALEJANDRO: —maybe I should use the chopsticks. *(Silence.)* I'm saying, they give you chopsticks, they don't give you forks. They gotta have a reason for that. And maybe you don't use the chopsticks, you don't get the same effect or something. Maybe it don't taste the same. Maybe I don't need the fork.

MOLLY: I punched your valued customer again. *(No response—Alejandro is staring at the sushi.)* I ain't saying that's why I'm cleaning. I'm just telling you cause I know you want to know. *(No response.)* And I'm a go down there now and I'm a bust that angry motherfucker in the face one more time. And no way I'm apologizing—he's the one out of line. You chose to be a cop, be a cop. You supposed to clean something, clean it. You supposed to arrest somebody, arrest her. If you ain't gonna be a cop, then why you a cop? *(No response.)* I'm saying, that ain't why I'm cleaning. I'm just telling you.

ALEJANDRO: (Never looking up from his sushi.) I actually might eat this.

(Molly stomps out through the front door. Alejandro, chopsticks in hand, just sits and stares at the sushi.)

---

2. Spanish translation of Page, Jimmy, and Robert Plant. 1971. "Stairway to Heaven" on *Led Zeppelin IV*. Led Zeppelin: Atlantic/WEA.

• 25

(Officer Derek and Molly, at the police station, staring at each other.)

MOLLY: I'm sorry. *(Silence.)*

OFFICER DEREK: I don't believe you.

MOLLY: You know how many black eyes I gave my brother since we were kids?

OFFICER DEREK: I don't believe you.

MOLLY: You know how many times I apologized to him? I ain't saying it again to you. Far as getting injured in the line of duty goes, you're a cop. You got off easy. *(Officer Derek turns to leave.)* Now you walk away? I'm a eighteen-year-old girl. You're a grown man. You can't look in my eyes when I scream at you? Yeah, I knocked your eyeball four inches deeper than standard issue, and yeah, I did it twice, but no, you cannot not believe me.

OFFICER DEREK: It's fine. You're sorry.

MOLLY: You don't have to be so fucking calm—if you're mad, be mad. Otherwise, I do not say to anyone what I said to you. You tell me right now that everything is cool and everything is understood…

OFFICER DEREK: That's fine. I believe you.

MOLLY: You believe me?

OFFICER DEREK: Fine. Yeah.

MOLLY: And I'm cool? With you?

OFFICER DEREK: Fine. Sure.

MOLLY: I don't believe you. *(Officer Derek, frustrated, goes to leave again.)* I'm playing, I'm playing. Thank you.

OFFICER DEREK: Right. Whatever. I have to go back to work.

MOLLY: I brought another picture. I don't have anyone else to really show it to, and you kinda dug the last one, right?

OFFICER DEREK: It was okay.

MOLLY: My mom had you tripping on your tongue.

OFFICER DEREK: It was okay.

MOLLY: You'll like this one. You ain't got time to look at one?

OFFICER DEREK: No.

MOLLY: It's a really good one. *(Pause.)* And I promise I won't hit you again.

OFFICER DEREK: I'm not going to look at it. *(He looks at the photo.)* This is the same picture.

MOLLY: You wouldn't have looked at it if I told you.

OFFICER DEREK: I have work and I need to get back to work…

MOLLY: Wait. Why do you think she got arrested?

OFFICER DEREK: How would I know?

MOLLY: I don't even know either. But whatever it was, it was right. She was right. Look at her face...

OFFICER DEREK: She looks like you.

MOLLY: Shut up! Stupid. Way she looks right there, she believes completely in whatever she did. You even know how that feels? To be that right? About anything? And then to have a picture of it? And then to show it to your kids? Do you even understand that?

OFFICER DEREK: No. *(Pause.)* Graffiti is a crime. Next time you're caught, the police will arrest you. Goodbye. *(He turns to leave.)*

MOLLY: I still talk to my mom. She's dead. *(Pause.)* Her heart stopped working. One hundred and eighty four days ago. She pushed it too hard. That's what I tell her. *(Pause.)* She doesn't talk back. I'm not crazy. I talk to her, and I tell her things. I tell her when I do something wrong and I think I wouldn't have done the wrong thing if she was around still. *(Pause.)* But nah, she doesn't talk back.

OFFICER DEREK: Maybe she does, but you don't know that it's her.

MOLLY: I don't know where this picture came from. Cause it was taped to my door. And my brother wouldn't have done that. He's too clean. And who else is there? *(Silence.)* I think she sent it to me.

OFFICER DEREK: She probably did. *(Pause.)* My mom told me one time that when she dies, she's gonna call my name. That's why I don't change it. Even though I hate it. She's gonna call my name, and she's gonna tell me that she loves me, and she's gonna make sure I keep being who she raised me to be. It kind of made me cry when she said it. And that made her cry. And I apologized. And I meant it. And my mom just kind of smiled and hugged me and then she made me some soup and we didn't even talk about it again. *(Pause.)* I don't know. I guess that was kinda cool.

MOLLY: You think it's my mom? Seriously?

OFFICER DEREK: Seriously.

MOLLY: Why am I telling you this?

OFFICER DEREK: Cause I'm listening. Thank you for telling me. *(Silence.)*

MOLLY: Do you believe that I'm sorry now?

OFFICER DEREK: Yes.

MOLLY: Cause I am.

OFFICER DEREK: I know...*(She kisses him. Hard. Silence.)*

MOLLY: You're not going to take my name down, are you? *(Silence.)*

OFFICER DEREK: You're kidding, right?

MOLLY: Are you?

OFFICER DEREK: This, this story, your mother, this picture, this, this, this all is...about graffiti? To keep me from erasing your graffiti?

MOLLY: No, I was asking for you.

OFFICER DEREK: Sucker me in, sweet and apologies, smile for once at me after all anger and cheap shots? I am an officer of law. Punk kid, thinks punches get thrown, then you can kiss and make up…

MOLLY: No, I was asking for you. I want you to keep it up for you… *(Officer Derek takes her hand…and spins her face first up against the wall. That same ironic love song again.)*

OFFICER DEREK: You got some agenda, I don't know, but I am a grown man—fuck a cop—I'm a grown man. You're a kid, a kid who thinks you can flirt and smile and try to kiss and try to intimidate a grown man like a kid…

MOLLY: No, I want you to keep it up for you, it's yours, you like it, I want you to have it…

OFFICER DEREK: I deserve more respect than this! *(He holds her against the wall with one hand, pulls the can of graffiti remover from his pocket with the other. He sprays the remover dead center of Molly's name. The music is getting louder.)*

MOLLY: STOP! That's yours!

(The music drowns out Officer Derek's voice. Officer Derek tosses the can on the floor, and starts scrubbing Molly's name off the wall with his sleeve, holding her against the wall, forcing her to watch. Lights out. Music out.)

INTERMISSION.

•

• ACT TWO

• 26

(Alejandro, still staring at the sushi.)

TRIP: *(To the audience.)* The role of the scholarly yet thirsty patron will be played tonight by the lovely and talented Mr. Nelson Cardenal.

NELSON: *(At the bar, as a customer.)* Hello there, barkeep. I've inhabited New York City for many a year, and I've recently heard tell of your prowess as both mixologist and conversationalist. As I now find myself in need of refreshment, both liquid and spiritual, I've concluded that you are precisely the man to see. *(No response.)*

TRIP: Al. Yo, Al! AL!

ALEJANDRO: Huh? What happened?

TRIP: Get ya mind out ya food, son. You got a customer.

ALEJANDRO: (To the customer.) What you think about sushi?

NELSON: I beg your pardon?

ALEJANDRO: This is sushi. What do you think about it?

TRIP: *(To audience:)* And yo—that dubiousity goes on all night. *(As a customer:)* I need a drink.

ALEJANDRO: But what do you really <u>think</u> about sushi?

NELSON: *(As a customer:)* Can I have a—

ALEJANDRO: Sushi.

TRIP: Let me get a—

ALEJANDRO: Sushi.

NELSON: But—

ALEJANDRO: Sushi?

TRIP: But—

ALEJANDRO: Sushi!

NELSON: *(Back to himself.)* Stop with that shit! You don't even eat sushi.

TRIP: You got a whole plate of it sitting there all night. You ain't touched it.

ALEJANDRO: I'm thinking about it.

NELSON: What you got to think about? You bought it, you eat it.

ALEJANDRO: I didn't buy it. And I ain't saying I'm a eat it. Saying I'm thinking about it. *(Pause.)* What do you think about it? *(Silence.)*

TRIP: Oh. No. She got to you.

NELSON: She got to you. We told you.

TRIP: We told you. She's trapping you.

NELSON: You ET to her, son. She gonna do the science on you.

ALEJANDRO: Ain't no science—maybe me and her could play doctor, but that's it…

NELSON: Don't try to turn this into her being on your dick.

TRIP: That girl don't get on nobody's dick without telling you to turn your head and cough.

NELSON: You're being examined and you don't even realize that the little hospital robe leaves your ass hanging out.

TRIP: We actually had customers tonight too. Damn.

• 27

(Lelly, outside of the bar.)

LELLY: I thought we lost the picture. *(She holds up a photo.)* Thank God for scanners.

• 28

(Continuous. Lelly enters the bar.)

LELLY: I found the picture. A copy of it.

NELSON: Yo, she's like our best customer. But she never buys a drink.

ALEJANDRO: Put that picture away, cause I got something I'm gonna ask you, then I got something I'm gonna tell you, and then you could show me what you got.

LELLY: If I don't show you this now, I'm going to get nervous and then I'm gonna get confused…

ALEJANDRO: You're gonna get nervous and confused anyway.

LELLY: That's probably true.

ALEJANDRO: So yo, tell them, these two guys back here, exactly how important a bartender is to the universe. Tell them like you told me.

LELLY: Very important.

ALEJANDRO: Sushi in a center circle.

LELLY: Absolutely.

ALEJANDRO: Oh. I understand for serious now.

LELLY: Can I show you the picture please?

ALEJANDRO: But here's my question though: if a bartender is so important, then by extension—see, I said that like you, "by extension"—then a lounge is so important too.

LELLY: By extension, yeah.

ALEJANDRO: Then how come we don't get the kinda customer numbers we should be getting?

TRIP: How you gonna ask this suburban girl? She don't know nothing about Lower East Side nightlife.

LELLY: Your genius DJ's right. I don't.

TRIP: Yo Nel, she said I'm a genius.

NELSON: She got jokes.

TRIP: Oh. That was a joke.

LELLY: Honestly, all I know these days is hip-hop history. That's why if you let me show you the picture…

NELSON: You know what has four thumbs and is hip-hop history? This guy *(pointing to himself with his thumbs)* and this guy *(Trip points to himself with his thumbs)*. The Tripnel Cartel. We're history that ain't even happened yet. We're the future of history. What you know about that?

LELLY: Nothing.

TRIP: That's right. Cause if you knew something about hip-hop history, you'd know how to answer my man's question. You'd tell him if he put us on in here some night, we'd pack this place tighter than my rhyme scheme.

LELLY: Sounds like that would work.

TRIP: Now she got jokes again.

LELLY: I think that's actually a really good idea, Alejandro. The beauty of a place like this is unity—making people feel like they belong to something they can't get anywhere else. Local artists—that seems like a great way to get started on building a community. *(Silence.)*

NELSON: Yo, this girl is mad smart.

ALEJANDRO: I told you she was. And I told you she got ways to help Arroyo's get up on its feet. So Lelly, you got a cool way to describe this idea? Like some kinda Japanese food term that could sum it up?

LELLY: I mean, no. Basically it's a community center. For adults. With alcohol.

TRIP: She *is* good. I'm a start practicing right now. *(Trip and Nelson disappear into the background.)*

ALEJANDRO: *(Can't contain himself.)* I have eaten the sushi! *(Silence.)* Now you got me spitting words out like you.

LELLY: You tried it?

ALEJANDRO: Took me a while, but yeah.

LELLY: You don't understand—when I ate sushi for the first time, it changed my whole head. It's so different, a product of a completely unique worldview, a different approach to not just cooking, but eating. Not just eating, but life.

ALEJANDRO: Uh. Yeah.

LELLY: Sorry. Did you like it?

ALEJANDRO: You know how you eat sushi and it makes you think all those things?

LELLY: Completely unique worldview.

ALEJANDRO: It made me think too. About how I can't believe you're Puerto Rican and you eat that nastiness.

LELLY: Well, I am. And I do. *(Pause.)* I didn't think you would even try it.

ALEJANDRO: You asked me to.

LELLY: God, I need to show you this picture.

ALEJANDRO: You know what the sushi made me think about?

LELLY: My brain and my heart are both going to fall straight through my stomach if you say that it's nasty again.

ALEJANDRO: Nah, it made me think about how I had never even tried it, but I was convinced I didn't like it. And when I tasted it, I was kinda right. It was ass.

LELLY: Here I am, rambling about unique worldviews and unimaginable Eastern paradigms…and the sushi is ass.

ALEJANDRO: Thing is, it was ass in a different way than I expected.

LELLY: So it wasn't as bad as you thought?

ALEJANDRO: Nah. It was worse. But it was worse different than I thought.

LELLY: You're trying to make me feel better about giving you something you hated.

ALEJANDRO: It didn't taste like I thought...so it could have tasted good, you know? Makes you think when the stuff you thought you knew was wack ain't really wack—at least not wack like you expected it to be. And that's kinda a whole new view of the world too, right?

LELLY: That's exactly what it is. *(Silence.)*

ALEJANDRO: So...you wanna show me that picture?

• 29

(Molly, alone at the police station. Sitting against the wall, under her name— which now has a huge hole in the middle. Silence. She does not move.)

• 30

(Back to Alejandro and Lelly at the bar.)

LELLY: Have you ever heard of Reina Rey?

ALEJANDRO: Only from you. And since you the one mentioning her, she must be a major figure in hip-hop history or some shit.

LELLY: She should be.

ALEJANDRO: See? I got you all figured out, Lelly Santiago.

LELLY: Reina Rey was one of the first real party DJs. *(Trip, in the booth, dressed as a 1979 old school hip-hop pioneer.)* In 1979, a Bronx party DJ was responsible for one thing: making the good part of a song last forever. *(Trip demonstrates, extending the break on a classic B-Boy song. This should take a while. This should be very impressive.)* Reina Rey made her way into that world of the early DJ.

She studied their techniques.

She shut out their sexist shit-talking.

She fought her way onto the tables.

And pretty soon, Reina Rey was better than damn near every boy she battled.

ALEJANDRO: And she's a local artist?

LELLY: Reina Rey was also one of the first real party MCs. *(Nelson, as a 1979 hip-hop pioneer.)* In 1979, a Bronx party MC was also responsible for one thing: moving the crowd. *(Nelson demonstrates, freestyling an old-school party rhyme. This should involve the audience in some way. This should also be very impressive.)* Reina Rey could rock a party with the best of them.

In English *and* Spanish.

With only herself as her DJ.

And nobody's ever heard of her.

ALEJANDRO: And you're going to show me a picture of her.

LELLY: *(Blurting it out.)* And she was your mother. *(Silence.)* That's my theory. *(She hands him the picture. Silence.)*

NELSON: *(To audience.)* My mind would be blown right now if I wasn't an omniscient narrator.

LELLY: All those things I just told you—that was your mother. *(Molly, dressed in old school 1979 Bronx style herself... including a sweatshirt that reads "Reina Rey.")* Elisabeth "Reina Rey" Arroyo. The Bronx, 1977, '78, '79, birth of hip-hop. Your mom was there. And her being there changes the world, really. *(Alejandro keeps staring at the picture.)* You don't want to ask *how* it changes the world? *(A classic early hip-hop beat plays. Molly slowly begins to walk towards Alejandro as Lelly speaks.)*

If you can place a Puerto Rican woman at the dawn of hip-hop's creation, not just as an observer, but as a vital participant, you change the perception of all women's entitlement to the form AND you reshape the face of ethno-racial relationships throughout the Afro-Latino Diaspora! *(The music stops.)*

I'm doing it again and I know and I'll fix it. *(The music restarts.)*

Okay. We know that there were women involved back then. We know there were Puerto Ricans involved back then. We don't really know the specifics of a lot of their stories. But I know the beginning of your mom's story, and you know the end, and if we put them together and tell it in its entirety...
(Molly is directly behind Alejandro. Inches away. She reaches out to touch him.)

ALEJANDRO: This picture ain't my mother. *(Molly disappears.)*
(Silence.)

LELLY: Um. *(Pause.)* Um. *(Pause.)* I'm good with faces.

ALEJANDRO: You think I don't know my mother's face?

LELLY: I think it's her.

ALEJANDRO: My mother was here in the Lower East Side in '77, '78, '79...

LELLY: No one in the neighborhood remembers her being around before '80. Do you know what year she came here?

ALEJANDRO: Sometime back then. I don't know.

LELLY: Awesome. And where did she live before here?

ALEJANDRO: I don't know.

LELLY: AWESOME! She never really told anyone where she came from—at least, no one I've found.

ALEJANDRO: Then it wasn't no one's business.

LELLY: Reina Rey disappears from the South Bronx in 1980. No one knows why. I think she got pregnant and started a new life. Here in the Lower East Side.

ALEJANDRO: My mother would have told me that. My mother told me everything.

LELLY: She didn't tell you what year she moved here. *(Pause.)* I don't mean that to be disrespectful.

ALEJANDRO: You should probably leave.

LELLY: Please Alejandro, help me with this. I really think it's her, and I know that we—you and me—can confirm it…

ALEJANDRO: I ain't helping you confirm no lie about my mother.

LELLY: The woman in this picture is not a lie.

ALEJANDRO: She's not my mother either. *(Silence.)*

LELLY: *(Last chance.)* Reina Rey's story changed my life. And it can change the life of any young woman in America, regardless of their race. It can change the life of any Puerto Rican in America, male or female. And it can change the life of anyone who has ever picked up a microphone or spun some vinyl or—if this theory I'm presenting to you is correct— even anyone who has ever given up one true love for a bigger true love. Like family.

ALEJANDRO: Not everybody needs their life changed.

LELLY: You can keep the picture. *(Alejandro looks right at her…and tears the picture in pieces, then throws them on the floor.)* I liked this place better when it was a deli. *(She exits.)*

• 31

(Molly, alone at the police station. Exact same way we left her. Silence. Lelly enters, stares at the graffiti. Silence.)

LELLY: Things fall apart. *(No response.)* "Things fall apart. The center cannot hold." It's a poem. Yeats. Have you read it? *(No response.)* It's an album by The Roots too, but that's not the point. It's a poem about—how can I say what it's about? I can't say what it's about. But I look at that wall, and what you did there says everything I want to say, but it would take me fifteen million words to say it and it still wouldn't make sense like that wall does—

MOLLY: I will. Fucking kill you. If you don't stop looking at that. *(Lelly keeps looking. Molly does not kill her. Silence.)* You talk too much.

LELLY: I think too much. I'm a freak. *(Silence.)* I'm Lelly.

MOLLY: The fuck kinda name is Lelly?

LELLY: My brother couldn't pronounce Elisabeth.

MOLLY: That's my mother's name.

LELLY: Elisabeth Reina Arroyo. *(Silence.)* I'm not like a stalker or anything, so don't worry. I'm doing research—I *was* doing research. My thesis fell apart. Its center could not hold. It wasn't her. Fuck, it wasn't her. FUCK. *(Silence.)* I wish I had a camera.

MOLLY: Should have seen it before he…before the cops fucked it up.

LELLY: That right there is not fucked up. That right there is kinda brilliant.

MOLLY: It got a fucking hole in the middle.

LELLY: So do you! *(Pause.)* Please don't kill me. I mean, it's like…like there's a hole in your middle—not you like Molly Arroyo, like you like everybody. I mean, I know I'm missing something someplace inside me—I think everybody is. And that's there. In what you painted.

MOLLY: You think I *wanted* there to be a hole in the middle?

LELLY: Doesn't matter. This is beautiful the way it is now. The hole just gives it a whole different meaning. *(Silence.)*

MOLLY: Maybe the hole in your thesis gives it a whole different meaning too. *(Silence.)*

LELLY: I really wish I had a camera. *(Silence.)*

MOLLY: You wanna see a picture?

LELLY: You take pictures of your work?

MOLLY: I don't know who took it. It's a picture of my mom. *(Molly pulls out the picture. Lelly does not see it.)* She got writing on her sweatshirt. I don't know what it says.

LELLY: I do.

• 32

(No lights in the bar.)

TRIP: Ladies and Gentlemen, you have found your way to the hottest watering hole south of Houston Street. *(The bar lights start to strobe on and off— Nelson is standing by the light switch, flipping it up and down.)* My name is Trip Trizzy, this is my partner Nelly Nel, and…yo. The hell are you doing with the lights?

NELSON: That's the strobe! We big time—we deserve lighting effects.

TRIP: That shit looks mad bootleg.

NELSON: This place ain't built for performance. This is all the effects we got. *(Alejandro enters. Cleaning. Everything.)* Tell him, Al. Tell him we gotta make this place look classy at showtime.

ALEJANDRO: Bar light bulbs usually last longer than home light bulbs. Mainly because they don't get flicked on and off so much. If I gotta change these earlier than scheduled, it's coming out of y'all's paychecks.

NELSON: Shit, Al. The money we bring in the first night, you could buy bulbs to light the way from Brooklyn.

TRIP: He's wrong about the lights, but he's right about the dough, Al. The whole LES is already excited about it.

ALEJANDRO: Excited about what?

TRIP: You know. This local artists thing. Or more specifically, this Trip and Nelson thing.

NELSON: We been telling some folks some things, and they can't wait to come through.

TRIP: It's what the community been waiting for. Lelly was right.

ALEJANDRO: She was not right. About anything. *(Silence.)* We're not doing it.

NELSON: But Al…

ALEJANDRO: This place was built to honor the memory of my mother. People who don't do that ain't got no place here.

TRIP: *(To audience:)* When he brings up his mom, there's no way to argue it.

NELSON: Unless you get some kinda divine intervention.

(Alejandro has never stopped cleaning for a second.)

• 33

(Continuous. The front door of the bar flies open. Molly enters. Maybe it's backlit—maybe it looks exactly like one of Lelly's earlier entrances. She's got spraypaint. Lots of spraypaint.)

MOLLY: I'm gonna paint your bar.

NELSON: *(To audience:)* Thank God for Molly.

ALEJANDRO: *(Stops cleaning.)* What?

MOLLY: —Your lounge. It's a lounge. I'm gonna paint it.

TRIP: Who are you? You look like Molly, but…who are you?

ALEJANDRO: What happened with that cop, Amalia?

MOLLY: For free. I'm gonna paint it. I even already got the paint. Don't ask me how I got it, but I got it.

NELSON: First you going around punching cops and now you stealing paint too?

TRIP: Bet they got you on that Homeland Security list and everything.

MOLLY: Normally, a wise comment like that would get your ass kicked. But I feel good, and no, to answer your question, I didn't do nothing wrong. I didn't steal nothing.

TRIP: But still, after everything you been doing, now you trying to get to throw your name up on the walls in here?

MOLLY: I ain't trying to do nothing but talk to my brother. But no, I ain't gonna write my name on any of these walls, even if the all of you got down and begged me. I ain't throwing my name up nowhere no more. I got a whole plan for in here already, Alex, but whatever you wanna do, I could work with you.

ALEJANDRO: For serious? You wanna put your work up in my bar?

MOLLY: And I don't want shit from you. I'm making a offering. *(Pause.)*

ALEJANDRO: Yo, remember when you used to write your name on the wall in front of the building?

MOLLY: You knew about that?

ALEJANDRO: You thought we didn't know? Me and Ma used to sit in the window and watch you sometimes.

MOLLY: Ma knew?

ALEJANDRO: I wanted to come out there and snatch that can out your hand. That was Ma's building you was writing on. That was extra work you was giving her. She already worked too hard.

MOLLY: I know. *(Pause.)* Was she mad at me?

ALEJANDRO: She didn't let me come out and stop you. Said you had to practice somewhere if you was gonna be any good. Might as well be at home. She didn't like having to clean the wall everyday. I didn't like looking at the wack mess of paint you was trying to pass off as graf.

MOLLY: I'm better at it now.

ALEJANDRO: I wouldn't know nothing about that.

MOLLY: Cause you never come to look. *(Pause.)* But I ain't holding that against you. I want to paint the bar.

ALEJANDRO: You wanna paint my...our lounge?

MOLLY: Yeah. I wanna paint our lounge.

ALEJANDRO: And you don't want nothing from me?

MOLLY: Nothing. I'm just a humble local artist contributing to the creation of my neighborhood's newest community center. For adults. With alcohol. *(Silence. Alejandro starts polishing the bar, hard and intense and angry.)*

NELSON: Okay. I think this is a family situation...

TRIP: Yeah. Me and Nel are gonna step over here and we just gonna...*(They exit quickly.)*

ALEJANDRO: She got to you.

MOLLY: I wanna do every surface in here in tribute to Ma. Lelly bought me all this paint and she told me everything about how dope Ma was.

ALEJANDRO: My mother was dope before that girl came around.

MOLLY: I could do a DJ mural on this wall right here. And over here I could do a wall about her as an MC. Lelly says that when Reina Rey rocked a party, every high school in the Bronx was talking about it for days after. I got respect for Ma now that I couldn't never have for no deli counter person.

ALEJANDRO: *(Still polishing the same spot on the bar.)* You get your respect for your mother from some white Puerto Rican girl that don't even live in this neighborhood?

MOLLY: And Lelly thought you might be looking to represent the deli too, so we figured I could do one wall like the old sign from the front, you know? Arroyo's Bodega—it's like Ma's whole life right here, all drawn out and illustrated. Lelly says...

ALEJANDRO: *(Still polishing.)* Is this about Ma or is this about Lelly?

MOLLY: This is about me, Alejandro. I'm excited about being from this family for the first time in my life. What difference does it make how I got excited?

ALEJANDRO: *(Still polishing.)* I don't want that kind of paint on my wall. I want these walls clean and simple and the way Ma wanted them.

MOLLY: How the fuck do you know what she wanted? *(Stopping him from polishing.)* And the fucking bar is clean!

ALEJANDRO: She wanted a business that was consistent and solid and gave her customers what they wanted. She wanted to take care of her family. She wanted to raise kids that were smart enough not to fall for any bullshit story from a pretty girl with a college degree that don't mean nothing down here. That's why she put in twenty years of work. That's why she put in twenty years of sweat equity—

MOLLY: Twenty years of sweat equity got her two months of ownership and a heart that quit pumping. *(Alejandro, in a fit of anger, knocks everything within his reach off the bar. Silence.)* Fucking deli ain't even here no more. *(Silence.)*

ALEJANDRO: Picture don't even look like her that much.

MOLLY: It could be her though. *(Pause.)*

ALEJANDRO: You don't think it looks like her, do you? *(Molly shrugs.)* See? Now how you gonna let something that some girl you don't even know tells you about your mother and and and that all she could back it up with is a picture that don't even look like your mom and how you gonna let that change the whole, the whole, the whole history that you grew up with living?

MOLLY: It might be her. *(Pause.)* When I had first found the picture, immediately I thought it was Ma. And I got an explosion, like a pain, you know, in my eyes. The back of my eyes—they got hot. They saw something—I don't know, not like in the picture, like in the, I don't know, in the *possibility* that was in the picture. Ma wasn't usually in a picture that looked like that, not in my head. Not in a picture with that kind of passion, with that kind of willingness to do something wrong cause she thought it was right.

My eyes hurt—maybe I was understanding what you had said about salt with Lelly, you know?

ALEJANDRO: Lelly doesn't have no proof to none of this, Molly.

MOLLY: The only proof I need is that I saw it. Maybe that picture isn't her. Maybe this Reina Rey woman has nothing to do with us—maybe she got hit by a train in 1980 and that's why no one knows where she went. But Alex—*no one knows where she went.* And she might have come here. And she might have been our mom. And for honest, it don't even really matter to me if it's true or not. *(Silence.)*

I can't take a risk that she did something that beautiful and I never even entertained the possibility of seeing it. *(Silence.)*

If you really don't want me to paint in here, I won't. *(No response.)*

Maybe I'll go make breakfast. *(She kisses him on the cheek, then exits up to the apartment. Alejandro goes back to cleaning for a second...then exits. Out the front door.)*

• 34

(Officer Derek, alone at the police station. He is painting the wall. This goes on in silence for a while. Alejandro enters. He stares long and hard at the wall.)

ALEJANDRO: It's gone.

OFFICER DEREK: Of course it's gone, Mr. Arroyo. Can't believe I waited this long to get rid of it. *(Silence.)*

ALEJANDRO: Was it good?

OFFICER DEREK: Mr. Arroyo, I mean no disrespect with this—you're an upstanding member of the community I'm here to protect and serve, but—hundreds of crimes are committed everyday, and I've spent way too much time on this insignificant little drawing incident already—

ALEJANDRO: How'd it make your eyes feel?

OFFICER DEREK: My eyes? I don't have time for this—

ALEJANDRO: Did it hurt? Did your eyes hurt? Were they burning? Was it like an explosion? Maybe it was like salt in a cut or—did it hurt your eyes?

OFFICER DEREK: Is this supposed to be some kind of joke?

ALEJANDRO: Did looking at her graffiti hurt your eyes?

OFFICER DEREK: It didn't hurt. It definitely didn't burn. *(Silence.)*

ALEJANDRO: I don't mean to wish you pain bro, but I was hoping you was gonna say otherwise. *(Silence. Alejandro goes to leave.)* You know she's gonna come back and do it again, right? *(Silence.)* She must have thrown her name up on my mom's deli like two hundred and fifty times, for serious. Ma would paint over it, Molly would throw it back up.

OFFICER DEREK: I am working. I am not interested in stories of your sister's rebellion—

ALEJANDRO: —that shit don't have nothing to with rebellion. It was the way she let Ma know she was thinking about her. And Ma let her know right back.

OFFICER DEREK: I ain't thinking about her.

ALEJANDRO: *(Laughing.)* I know all about that song, Derek Jeter. And I know some things about cleaning, and I could tell that you ain't getting that wall much cleaner than that. *(Officer Derek keeps painting.)* Aight, well, you're still a valued customer, so come by whenever—

OFFICER DEREK: *(Blurting it out.)*—my eyes hurt most of the time. They burn. Constantly. And this sounds stupid, and it is stupid, but it's because of my name. I'm an angry guy. I'm angry because people hear my name, and they think of some baseball player, and they can't take me seriously. I could just change my name, I know, but somewhere, even though I hate it, I love it. I want to be proud of it.

I come out back here every time someone in there makes a comment and sets my eyes burning. I come out here a lot. And one time I come out here, and there she is, pouring her pride in who she is onto that wall and not worrying about how insanely, horribly illegal and stupid what she's doing is, not worrying of the disrespect of getting painted over or arrested or even mocked for it—she had to put that pride out into the world.

And for the whole time I was looking at it, my eyes weren't burning at all. *(Silence.)*

I have to go back to work. Can you give her something for me? *(Pause.)*

Forget it. I'm not going to ask you to give her anything. *(Officer Derek turns to leave.)*

ALEJANDRO: You could give her anything you want. Next week. She's gonna have some art up in my lounge. *(Alejandro stares at the wall again.)* I don't think I dig blank walls so much no more.

(Alejandro exits.)

• 35

(Molly, standing on the bar, bottle of beer in hand, speaking to a crowd of bar patrons. Alejandro is sitting at the bar, inconspicuously, watching all the action. The audience might not even realize he's there.)

MOLLY: So my brother asked me to thank you all for coming out tonight, for filling up Arroyo's and supporting local artists like me. Thank you all for checking out the murals on the wall—I'm glad I could share my work with so many people. And now I got the honor to introduce the reason a lot of you came through tonight: for the first time at Arroyo's…ladies and gentlemen, the Tripnel Cartel!

(Trip and Nelson, performing for the bar.)

TRIP: *(To the audience as the music starts.)* This ain't really what we performed, but I think it'll tell you how we was feeling.

NELSON: *(Rapping.)* The L, the E, the L, the L, the Y, the L, the E, the L—it's Lelly!

TRIP: Now we know you heard us talking bout Lelly all foul/questioning her style…

NELSON: We was just protecting Al/dragging this fine woman through the stank and the sludge/her reputation smudged…

TRIP: Yo, we might have misjudged/she still ain't/no pure saint/thinking that this bar's quaint/suggesting Molly should paint/won't whitewash her white taint…

NELSON: Her still faint/memories of the Lower East/just prove her privilege is deceased/a lot to prove, to say the least…

TRIP: We'll give her thanks but yo, we know/she wasn't sent from up above/but she got Al to show the love/to put me on up in the club/so…

NELSON: Go Lelly/it's your birthday/we gonna party like it's your birthday/[3]

Tripnel gone rhyme like it's your birthday…

TRIP: And since you got us up on stage, you earned some mercy.

NELSON: (Speaking, but still over the music.) But yo, you knew this couldn't all unfold without some controversy…

• 36

(Continuous.)

TRIP: *(Rapping.)* So just throw your guns to the front/Pull out your weed and roll a blunt…

NELSON: If you're ready for hell/with Tripnel Cartel/let me hear you yell…
(Officer Derek slams the front door shut loudly, and thrusts his badge in the air.)

OFFICER DEREK: Freeze! Police! *(Music out.)*

TRIP: We ain't got no weed! We studio gangstas! It's just a image! *(Silence.)*

OFFICER DEREK: A joke. That's what that was. A joke. *(To Trip and Nelson:)* You can play the music again. Please. *(Trip and Nelson turn the music back on. Officer Derek turns to Molly.)* I didn't really think you would really be here. I'm glad you are. *(He waits. No response.)* I did that only because I

---

3. Jackson, Curtis, Andre Romell, and Michael A. Elizondo Jr. 2003. "In da Club" on *Get Rich or Die Trying*. Performed by 50 Cent. Interscope.

didn't know what to say. A joke. It was. I saw you had a drink, and that is illegal and all. I'm not going to say anything about it though. I didn't really expect you to laugh. I brought you something. *(He pulls out a picture, holds it towards her. No response.)*

It's a picture. I don't have pictures of my mom or my family like you do. I don't have that many pictures at all really. I thought you might like this one. It's a picture of your name. *(No response.)* I took it before...before we, uh, cleaned the wall. A whole roll I took. This one came out really well though. And the cool thing, for me at least, is if you flip it over, I put a little photo credit on it. "Photo by Officer Derek Jeter." *(He tries to hand her the picture, but she doesn't take it.)* I won't make you take it. *(He turns to leave.)* What you did in here, on the walls, it's beautiful, don't get me wrong—but you really shouldn't stop writing your name. *(He's almost gone.)*

MOLLY: Hold up. *(Molly calmly crosses to Officer Derek.)*

TRIP: *(From the booth, to the bar crowd:)* Yo, we don't just play hip-hop in here—we got the ill rock mix too!

(That same ironic love song plays one more time. Molly stares at Officer Derek.)

MOLLY: Let me get that picture. *(He hands it to her. She keeps staring at him. She never looks at the picture.)* Thanks.

(She turns and calmly walks back to the bar. Officer Derek exits.)

• 37

(Continuous. Alejandro is still sitting at the bar. He was not watching Molly and Officer Derek. Molly walks straight over to Alejandro. She hands him the picture, kisses him on the cheek, and exits. Alejandro looks at the photo long and hard.)

ALEJANDRO: She's good, Ma.

• 38

(Continuous. The front door of the bar swings open. Lelly pushes her way in and stands close to the wall. There's nothing big and theatrical about her entrance this time. She's carrying a large envelope. Lelly looks over the lounge. She's impressed. Lelly makes her way over to Alejandro.)

LELLY: Hey. I don't know if I'm welcome here tonight, but...

ALEJANDRO: Hell. Without you, there wouldn't be a tonight. You're the Christopher Columbus of hip-hop history. Came along and "discovered" something that already been discovered.

LELLY: I knew this was a bad idea.

ALEJANDRO: And now you wanna freak out and leave.

LELLY: I do. But I can't.

ALEJANDRO: Yeah, stick around. I could stop the music and you could explain every mural on these walls with your big words, and then you could be hailed as the hero of this night so that not only do folks forget that they're here to come to a bar, but that supposedly the star of this whole damn place is my mom.

LELLY: That's not why I came...

ALEJANDRO: Why else would you come? Why would you come in the first place? Why would you start taping pictures and nailing letters to my doors if you ain't trying to make this about you? You trying to make a name for yourself—you don't care nothing about no Reina Rey...

LELLY: I found out who she was. *(Silence.)* I found out who the woman who got arrested was. I tracked down the person who took the picture. They gave me a name. I did my research. Police records, the whole thing. Verified it all. I know who she was.

(Silence.)

ALEJANDRO: Who was she? *(Silence.)*

LELLY: I could take the information in this envelope and publish it, and then I'd be the prodigal daughter, coming back to the Lower East Side as a conquering hero—it would be like I had never left. Scholars and historians and experts from all over the country—maybe all over the world—would come to me, goofy little Elisabeth Santiago, the foremost authority on this one particular aspect of Puerto Rican culture. And they would never, for a second, question if I was Puerto Rican enough to claim ownership. *(Lelly hands Alejandro the envelope.)*

But I'm not going to publish it.

ALEJANDRO: Why not?

LELLY: I like what your sister did in here. And I really like that you let her. *(Pause.)* The reason I came down here in the first place was because I thought, finally, twenty years after I left this neighborhood, I had something worthwhile to contribute to this community. And I was kinda right. Only I thought it was Reina Rey. *(Pause.)* It doesn't matter whether your mom was Reina Rey or not. She'd be proud of this. *(Pause.)* I should go. *(She turns to leave.)*

ALEJANDRO: Next time you come back, I'm buying you a drink for serious.

LELLY: I'm counting on it. Good luck with your center circle. *(She exits. Alejandro sits, envelope in one hand, Molly's picture in the other. He considers each of them. Alejandro tosses the envelope onto the bar, and exits, engrossed in the photo.)*

• 39

(Trip and Nelson, in the booth, to the audience.)

NELSON: Two months after the big local artists night—

TRIP: —the first of many local artists nights—

NELSON: —this was in the *Village Voice*, Best of New York edition:

(Trip and Nelson take turns re-enacting each of the following newspaper/ magazine quotes.)

TRIP: *(Too cool for the room.)* "Sexiest Bartender south of Houston: Alejandro at Arroyo's on Eldridge Street. It's not only the generous buybacks and ultra-smooth mojitos. It's not only the smoldering machismo behind his deep, Latino eyes. No, the sex appeal here lies in his ears: the man actually listens." *(As himself.)* Two months later, we were in *Time Out New York*:

NELSON: *(Young and bubbly.)* "Who cares if the rain never ends, the economy never stabilizes, and we still can't smoke in bars? We just head over to our favorite watering hole-slash-therapy session at Arroyo's, where owner-slash-bartender Alejandro solves the problems of the world over martinis-slash-Cosmos. Lighting up's not allowed, but the effervescent community atmosphere is guaranteed to lighten your load."

TRIP: Then it was *AM New York*:

NELSON: *(Sorta hip, but kinda stuffy too.)* "We love Arroyo's!"

TRIP: Then it was *Time Out* again:

NELSON: *(Even bubblier.)* "We *still* love Arroyo's!" *(As himself.)* And now, at the sound of the scratch, Arroyo's will be celebrating six months of success as the Tupac Shakur of alcohol establishments...

TRIP: The Biggie Smalls of distilled spirit distribution...

NELSON: The Big Pun—do you understand what I'm saying?—the BIG PUN of Lower East Side lounges...*(A LOUD SCRATCH.)* And today's *New York Magazine* calls us:

TRIP: *(Deadpan yuppie.)* "The best lounge you haven't heard of."

NELSON: That's where we're at right now. Making money every night, and Al's getting the credit he deserves. Tripnel Cartel ain't getting the credit we deserve—

TRIP: —I mean, we told him it would happen if he let us rhyme—

NELSON: —but it feels good to us for Al to be seen as the artist he really is.

TRIP: So that's it. Thanks for coming out. *(They turn up the music and ignore the audience, as if the show was over.)*

NELSON: No, for real. That's it this time. Good night, and uh, thank you for coming to Arroyo's. *(They go back to the music.)*

TRIP: Nah, we just fucking with you. You still wanna know what's in that envelope, right?

NELSON: Reina Rey in all her glory. Was she Al and Molly's mom? She somebody else that just up and vanished? *(The envelope is still on the bar.)* You think it matters?

TRIP: Or maybe it just matters if she's really a major figure in the birth of this artform, this culture, this hip-hop that I love…or if maybe Lelly didn't even know what she was talking about. Maybe she made the whole thing up.

NELSON: Wow—that's a brilliant theory I hadn't even considered, Mr. Goldstein.

TRIP: You better consider it, Mr. Cardenal.

NELSON: Consideration is in effect. And the answer—that's right here in this envelope. *(Long pause. Then to the audience:)* But you could do your own research. I'm a DJ. I'm here to party.

(They turn the volume on that upbeat party hip-hop way up. END OF PLAY.)

by Ben Snyder

In Case You Forget

SETTING: Early spring, late 1990s, New York City

CHARACTERS:

(KAPTN) JIM: Idealistic, driven, passionate, 22-year-old from the Lower East Side. Man of color.

(GATO) VICTOR: Easily excited, fast thinking, incredibly loyal, 21-year-old originally from New Jersey. Latino.

KAILA: Wise, strong, playful, 22-year-old from the Lower East Side. Woman of color.

(MARTER) SONNY: Outspoken, rowdy, unpredictable, 23-year-old from Brooklyn. Italian.

WALTER/Voice of DAVE: Large, muscular, rugged, bald headed, white goatee, middle-aged man. Any ethnicity.

Yolanda, Arlene, Kelvis, Avery Veera, Alani, Swedish Girl 1, Swedish Girl 1, Lazer, Clerk, Defense, Prosecution, Judge, and other voices can be either on- or off-stage actors.

GLOSSARY:
"A" = "hey" without the "h"

"Tape Light" is a special light used only for Jim's tape recorder monologues.

◆

Act 1, Scene 1
(A gavel bangs loudly as lights suddenly blackout. At Rise: Tape Light comes up to Jim alone on stage speaking into a tape recorder. These speeches are focused and fierce, with a paranoid urgency.)
JIM: Entry 2146.
(Beat.)
  It's happened.
(Beat.)
  Will rendezvous with Gato in 0800 hours. Preparations must be made.
(Quick beat.)
  Kaptn out. *(Jim stops the tape as lights black out.)*

Act 1, Scene 2
(In blackout there is a flash. At Rise: Lights up to Jim and Victor. Jim has a disposable camera and has just taken a picture. They face the audience, as if looking at a wall.)
VICTOR: *(Eyeing the word "Gato.")* Yeah I know, it's uh, rushed…and that fuckin T, I hate my T's.
JIM: No, I like it.
VICTOR: Thanks.
JIM: You'd think this woulda been buffed by now.
VICTOR: So you tell Kaila yet?
JIM: Not yet.
VICTOR: If I was you man, I'd be over there right now.
JIM: Why?
VICTOR: Are you retarded? How long could they put you in for?
JIM: A couple months at the most.
VICTOR: A couple months!! Why you even talkin to me?
JIM: You hear from Sonny?
VICTOR: He called me up yesterday.
JIM: I heard Kaila's been lookin good.
VICTOR: You fuckin dick! She always looks good.
JIM: I guess.
VICTOR: You guess? *(Flustered.)* How you…How c'you be so—

JIM: What? What?

VICTOR: In a matter of days you go in a fuckin cage. Isn't that like waitin for a shot from the doctor, or like that tooth to get pulled, or that ingrown toenail to get cut out?

JIM: I hadn't thought of it like that.

VICTOR: Well I'm pretty scared.

JIM: But you're not goin. *(Victor gives Jim a book from his backpack.)*

VICTOR: Here.

JIM: What's this?

VICTOR: My moms bought it for you.

JIM: *(Reads the title.)* "Surviving Prison." Tell her thank you.

VICTOR: You'll probly have'ta kill someone.

JIM: I really wanna paint tonight.

VICTOR: Just find someone that looks weak and stab'm in the neck or somethin.

JIM: You ever finish that shit on Delancy?

VICTOR: Then they'll all know…When they see you they'll be like, "That nigga already stabbed a kid, we betta not rape him tonight."

JIM: I kinda wanna do a rooftop.

VICTOR: …but then you could get more time if he dies…maybe stab'm in the shoulder blade or some other non-fatal wound area.

JIM: What are you talkin about?

VICTOR: A, Sonny's got a cousin in Raybrook, thas where they'll send ya right?

JIM: Probly.

VICTOR: When was the last time you spoke to Sonny?

JIM: I saw him when I came by Chino's party.

VICTOR: You been paintin w'him?

JIM: Not since that night.

VICTOR: I know he feels bad about how shit went down.

JIM: *(Uninterested.)* Huh?

VICTOR: Wait, was you there when Lex and Sonny got into it?

JIM: Nah, what happened?

VICTOR: They was talkin bout *that* night. Sonny tried to say it was Lex's fault you got bagged, cuz he was takin so long with his piece. Yo Lex got heated, everyone knows if it was anyone's fault it was Sonny's. He's like, "You little bitch, if you wasn't around the corner breakin windows cops never would've rolled on us in the first place!" Sonny tried to choke Lex so Chino kicked him out.

JIM: When that happen?

VICTOR: Must have been just after you and Dante left.

JIM: You seen Sonny?

VICTOR: Yo he been missin in action for a minute now. But check this shit, yesterday he calls me up outa nowhere, sayin' he wants to go paintin, and he wants you to come.

JIM: He said that?

VICTOR: He said if I could bring Kaptn. Why you don't wanna go?

JIM: Nah whatever. I'm dyin to paint.

VICTOR: Maybe he wants to apologize. No, but I was sayin like, you should ask about his cousin.

JIM: For what?

VICTOR: To help you keep that cherry on your asshole Jim. Soon as you in you gotta find people fast.

JIM: We'll see.

VICTOR: Fuck paintin kid, go piece Kaila.

JIM: You know she paged me the other week.

VICTOR: You call back?

JIM: No.

VICTOR: How can…Jesus Jim, I would not be ignorin a girl like that.

JIM: I been busy.

VICTOR: She don't deserve that. Kaila's a smart girl.

JIM: I know but…I haven't even seen her in…You don't know what it's like to be wi'someone for years.

VICTOR: Me!!? I don't know what it's like to be wi'someone for seconds. The highlight of my date is when her shadow touches my Nike. But you, ya got two days, get the fuck atta here, ya need to be between the sheets. Itsya last chance to get some ass. *(Realizing this sort of rhymes, Victor turns it into a little song and dance:)* Last chance, to get some ass…Last-chance, Get-some-ass…Last chance get-

JIM: That don't rhyme.

VICTOR: How c'you be so fucking calm?! I'm losing sleep! You getting outa the country or somethin? Where you goin? Puerto Rico?

JIM: I just wanna paint.

VICTOR: That's all you're thinkin about?

JIM: That's all I'm thinkin about. I wanna do some shit with everyone.

VICTOR: Should have a writer's party. Like Alani's birthday. Get a few strip-pers, catch tags on they titties.

JIM: No. Not a party, a meeting.

VICTOR: A meeting?

JIM: A meeting.

VICTOR: Whatchyou mean?

JIM: Victor, why you write?

VICTOR: What?

JIM: What made you start writin?

VICTOR: Shut up man. What are you talkin about? Meetings?

JIM: I just wanna get everyone together…

VICTOR: You wanna do a UVK production?

JIM: I wanna talk to the crew. It's time.

VICTOR: Man, it's *time* to invest on some steroids, hit the gym, get musculated, learn to kick box…

JIM: I'll be alright.

VICTOR: You never been in.

JIM: You were in for what, a day?

VICTOR: And thas enough. I was in there contemplatin what would be the quickest and most painless way to kill myself. I kid you not.

JIM: It was that bad?

VICTOR: Worse. Well, I mean..I didn't suck any dick or nothin like that, but, like… take grown men, give'm the minds of angry children, lock'm in small poorly ventilated rooms, throw sexual frustration up in the mix and that's some scary shit. Just *being* sexually frustrated's scary enough, believe me.

JIM: I'll take your word for it. I'm jus'tryin not to think about it.

VICTOR: You think I haven't noticed? You been acting like Cody's retarded little brother sittin around droolin on ya'self. You need to be gettin mentally prepared. We gotta toughen you up. (*Victor starts hopping around, slap-boxing Jim.*)

JIM: What are you doing?

VICTOR: (*In his meanest voice:*) Who's the new kid?

C'mon new kid, Ima make you my bitch.

What you got new kid?

JIM: (*Overlapping:*) Chill man. Get out my face. Victor I'm not playen.

(*Jim catches Victor with a slap that gets Victor in the eye.*)

VICTOR: Ow!

JIM: Sorry.

VICTOR: Sorry? Never say sorry. Sorry is not an option.

JIM: Alright Yoda, I'll keep that in mind.

VICTOR: Do that. You should be takin notes.

JIM: Maybe you could teach me some more later, but right now I gotta go see a princess.

VICTOR: Don't say anything stupid to Kaila.

JIM: I won't.

VICTOR: I know you will. And read that book. I'll page you up later. *(Quick.)* I gotta go take a power nap.

JIM: Peace.

VICTOR: Damn, Jim.

JIM: What?

VICTOR: Nothing. I'll see you later.

(They exit in opposite directions as lights black out.)

Act 1, Scene 3

(Lights up on Jim at a noisy after school Headstart classroom where he teaches an art class. All the kids are heard and not seen. Jim has just finished a painting activity with the kids and is about to read them a story.)

YOLANDA: Look!

JIM: Thas nice, but it's not done drying Yolanda, could you put it on the table so mommy could take it home later?

ARLENE: Stoppit!

JIM: Kelvis, you listening to Arlene's words, she don't like that.

KELVIS: I'm not your fren!

JIM: Are you comin to the rug? Who wants to hear a story? Come sit at the rug if you wanna hear a story. Alyssa, you wash your hands?

ALYSSA: *(Attitude.)* Yes.

JIM: Then why they purple? Wash'm again. Avery, you puttin out the fire?

AVERY: I'm a...I'm Batman.

JIM: Batman wears a fireman's hat?

AVERY: I'm Batman!

JIM: Hey Batman, you wanna hear a story?

AVERY: No!!

JIM: Well all right you don't have to. I'm startin the story!

(Children are heard rushing to sit down.)

KIDS: Wait! No! I can't see! *(Etc.)*

JIM: I can't start till you're quiet. Bobby could you sit on your bottom so everyone can see? Thank you. Now I told you, today is my *last day.*

KIDS: *(Disappointed reactions.)*

JIM: I'm not gonna to be here next week. Or the week after that. Or the week after that. Or EVEN the week after that. Thas alotta weeks, right?

KIDS: Noo. Your last day? Why? *(Etc.)*

JIM: I'm goin away.

KIDS: Why?

JIM: I'm movin.

ARLENE: Where?

JIM: I'm moving to…a castle.

KELVIS: You rich?

JIM: So this is the last book Ima read to you for a really long time. Maybe even forever. Soooooo who wants to hear it?

KIDS: Me, me, me, me!!

JIM: Ok, then you need to show me how we sit quietly. *(Silence.)* Thank you.

YOLANDA: Jim.

JIM: *(Getting handed a piece of paper.)* What's this?……Thank you.

(A drawing a child made to say goodbye is projected.)

YOLANDA: I wanna live in a castle.

(Blackout.)

Act 1, Scene 4

(Lights up to Jim sitting on a bed in Kaila's apartment. Kaila is preparing for a date. She speaks to Jim from the bathroom.)

KAILA: His set's over at like 12 but I don't know where we goin after that.

JIM: It's for school? You takin pictures? *(Kaila enters.)*

KAILA: I'm *supposed* to be, that's how I'm getting comp'd in.

JIM: How you meet this guy?

KAILA: I told you, my old roommate Leslie—

JIM: Leslie with the yapper dog Leslie?

KAILA: Yeah, it's her brother's friend.

JIM: What's his name?

KAILA: Tamir.

JIM: And Tamir plays the trumpet?

KAILA: Or so he says.

JIM: Didn't your mom tell you bout dating musicians.

KAILA: Yeah and artists.

JIM: I'm a teacher.

KAILA: My mom still talks about you a lot.

JIM: What's she say?

KAILA: That she misses you.

JIM: Does her daughter miss me too?

KAILA: Sometimes.

JIM: Sometimes?

KAILA: She don't miss you when you don't return her pages.

JIM: Will you tell her I'm sorry?

KAILA: I'll pass the word along.

JIM: Thanks.

KAILA: Jim?

JIM: Kaila.

KAILA: Why are you here?

JIM: Did you get a haircut?

KAILA: No.

JIM: You look good.

KAILA: Thank you.

JIM: You look healthy.

KAILA: Healthy?

JIM: Yeah.

KAILA: So I used to look unhealthy?

JIM: No I mean you look well rested.

KAILA: Oh, I don't have those bags under my eyes anymore.

JIM: Sometimes you look tired.

KAILA: Sometimes I am tired.

JIM: Could I see you tonight?

KAILA: I gotta date.

JIM: I'm going painting.

KAILA: Then I don't think we'll see each other.

JIM: I mean later.

KAILA: I won't be here.

JIM: No. Kaila I *need* to see you later.

KAILA: Why?

JIM: I need to talk to you.

KAILA: So talk.

JIM: Later I mean.

KAILA: Tonight?

JIM: Yeah tonight.

KAILA: Why tonight?

JIM: Damn, I'm serious Kaila...Could we talk later?

KAILA: What's wrong?

JIM: Who says something's wrong?

KAILA: So what do you wanna talk about?

JIM: Not now.

KAILA: That's the fuckin worst.

JIM: What.

KAILA: "I got something to tell you. I'll tell you later…." What is that? That's games.

JIM: *(Pleading.)* Can I talk to you later? Please.

KAILA: I should be back by one.

JIM: Could I come by then?

KAILA: Fine.

JIM: I don't like him.

KAILA: Who, Tamir?

JIM: Yeah.

KAILA: You don't know him.

JIM: Would I like him?

KAILA: No.

JIM: Is he your boyfriend?

KAILA: I don't think so. I wouldn't say that.

JIM: Would he?

KAILA: What happened to that girl you was see'n? Alees?

JIM: Alees?

KAILA: Leesda? Something.

JIM: Lisandra?

KAILA: Yeah, whahappened to her?

JIM: What happened was it ended.

KAILA: It ended?

JIM: It got ended. I ended it.

KAILA: Why?

JIM: I had a epiphany.

KAILA: Ooo, an epiphany.

JIM: Yeah.

KAILA: What was it? (*Kaila puts on makeup and does her hair as Jim speaks.*)

JIM: Alright…This one night we were at this party. We were meeting her friend that had just got back from Brazil. It was real crowded. When her friend finally showed up, they ran at each other all hugging and jumping around, "Oh my god, look at your hair, haven't seen you in forever, bla bla bla." Her friend was holding this cigarette. And while they were being all giddy and hopping around, her cigarette connected with this kid's face. It pretty much got put out on his cheek. Party was so crowded he didn't know what the fuck happened. This kid's gonna have a nasty burn and a scar for the rest of his life. I'm lookin at him holding his cheek, and I'm lookin at Lisandra holding her friend holding her cigarette, and they're both still hugging and twirling all oblivious. And it just dawns on me. You're wack. I don't wanna be with you.

KAILA: What did you do?

JIM: Later that night I took her aside. And I tole her…"You wack. I don't wanna be wich you."

KAILA: Jus like that?

JIM: I might have used a few more words.

KAILA: Thas it?

JIM: Thassit. No nasty fight.

KAILA: I miss fighting with you.

JIM: You wanna fight?

KAILA: You have an epiphany about me ever?

JIM: Yeah.

KAILA: What was it?

JIM: *(Making this up as he goes along.)* That we… too young to get married but too old to…—

KAILA: Be good for each other anymore.

JIM: *(Unconvinced.)* I guess that works.

KAILA: Hmmm.

(Jim is sitting on the bed. Kaila is standing in front of him. Jim hugs Kaila still sitting and looks up at her.)

JIM: *(In a deep voice, putting on a funny, romantic accent.)* Joo know I luj you, ri?

KAILA: I love you too...now get the fuck outa here.

JIM: What.

KAILA: C'mon Jim he's gonna be here soon.

JIM: Does he play jazz?

KAILA: Yeah but it's kinda funky.

JIM: Kinda funky huh?

KAILA: Get out.

JIM: *(Puffs lips.)* I bet he got those trumpet player lips, huh? *(Kaila pushes Jim away.)* Yo I c'tell when I'm not wanted.

KAILA: It's about time.

JIM: Have a good night.

KAILA: Be safe.

JIM: *(Looking her up and down.)* Be good.

KAILA: Pshhh.

JIM: I'll see you later?

KAILA: What's up.

JIM: Nothing.

KAILA: What is it? *(Jim shakes his head. Kaila sucks her teeth at him.)* You know this's gonna be botherin me all night.

JIM: If it makes you feel any better, it'll be botherin me too.

KAILA: Alright mysterioso.

JIM: I'll see you in a few hours.

KAILA: OK.

JIM: You gonna be here?

KAILA: I said I was.

JIM: You sure now?

KAILA: Bye.

JIM: Bye. *(Jim exits as lights fade to black.)*

Act 1, Scene 5

(Tape light up to Jim alone speaking into his tape recorder.)

JIM: Entry 2147. Though the teacher acts as dictator and there is no democracy to speak of, the pre-school classroom is a contemporary utopia. A bubble in Babylon for young soldiers. The land of righteousness. *(Taking himself very seriously.)* If you didn't bring enough for the rest of the class, then leave it in your cubby. *(Beat.)* A little revolutionary is born everyday. *(Beat.)* Gato, Marter and myself will secure sixth avenue rooftop at 2300 hours. Kaptn out.

(Jim stops the tape recorder as lights black out.)

Act 1, Scene 6

(Lights up to the words KAPTN, GATO and MARTER colorfully spray painted back to back on the wall. A small UVK is at the end. Lights cross fade to Jim, Victor and Sonny. They have just finished painting. Sonny is pissing on the back wall.)

SONNY: I put it back on the ultra flat, you proly dropped it.

VICTOR: You sure it's not in your pocket?

JIM: Vic—

SONNY: *(Very annoyed.)* It's not in my pocket. I told you I'll get you a Rusto stock.

JIM: You got the—

VICTOR: That was my last German Skinny.

SONNY: Damn, could you whine a little more?

VICTOR: Those are like three for a dollar.

JIM: A Sonny, you got the—

SONNY: Son, I'll get you a Rusto.

VICTOR: I don't want a Rusto.

SONNY: Then shut the fuck up.

VICTOR: *(To Jim:)* You see what I'm sayen?

SONNY: Jim does he ever stop whining?

JIM: Anyone got the time.

SONNY: 12:15. Yo, when NTS sees this shit, they don't got nothin runnin over here.

VICTOR: This's supposed to be their neighborhood right?

SONNY: Son, half the crew lives fuckin like 4, 5 blocks from here. Jim, you
could see your shit good from the train.

JIM: Thanks.

SONNY: Think I went too big?

JIM: Nah.

SONNY: I just can't control myself. After I kicked out my R like that, I was
like, "Fuck it, this shit's gonna be huge, son." Yo who goes bigger than me?
I haven't seen anyone's shit bigger than mine.

VICTOR: Glenn went bigger than you.

SONNY: Son, I'm not talkin about permission walls.

VICTOR: He did.

SONNY: Jim, my shit came off alright though?

JIM: Yeah it's nice.

SONNY: Would be if Victor's fucken O wasn't pissin on my M.

VICTOR: It's my steelo. That's how I style.

SONNY: Fuck your style.

VICTOR: I told you you was starten too close to me.

SONNY: I started too close to you? Jim, you believe this guy?

JIM: You guys ready to get outa here?

VICTOR: You even know what a martyr is?

SONNY: What?

VICTOR: You write "Marter" all over the fuckin world, you even know what
the word means?

SONNY: Fuck you.

VICTOR: You don't do you?

SONNY: I know my own fucken name. Jim, we was just talking about it that
one time.

JIM: That night we hit up—

VICTOR: Don't help him Jim. What's it mean Sonny?

SONNY: Fuck you.

VICTOR: Yo, is it that tough a question?

SONNY: Everyone knows what a martyr is.

VICTOR: Yeah but do you?

SONNY: Jim, Ima hurt this kid.

JIM: Marter's a dope name.

VICTOR: If you know what it means.

SONNY: Alright bitch. Martyr is...To be a martyr is............It's like...It's
like to care about somethin. To care about somethin a whole lot.

VICTOR: To care about somethin a whole lot?

SONNY: Yeah. Right Jim?

JIM: Martyrs care the most.

SONNY: Thank you! I'm the martyr of graffiti. And what the fuck is that "gato" shit? Gato, that's not even a word.

VICTOR: It's Spanish for cat.

SONNY: Oh, so your name's pussy. That suits you.

VICTOR: You don't even spell martyr right.

SONNY: This a fuckin spellin bee? A Jim, how you spell "Kaptn"?

VICTOR: That's Jim's choice, not his lack of spellin ability.

SONNY: Jim, why you even paint with this herb?

JIM: Didn't you call him?

SONNY: Yo I lost your number.

VICTOR: You feelin guilty?

SONNY: The fuck's that supposed to mean?

JIM: You haven't been out in a while.

SONNY: I know. I been wantin to talk to you.

JIM: Should talk soon, got like a day and a half.

SONNY: No shit? You go in that soon?

JIM: Yeah.

SONNY: Man.

VICTOR: What's up with your cousin, Sonny?

SONNY: What cousin?

VICTOR: Leo.

SONNY: Lazy Lee? He been locked up two years now.

JIM: Where at?

SONNY: Raybrook.

VICTOR: You in touch with him?

SONNY: Shit, not really.

VICTOR: You could get in touch?

SONNY: What for?

VICTOR: Tell him Jim's comin.

SONNY: Tell him what?!?

JIM: It's alright.

SONNY: What?

VICTOR: Tell'm to look out for Jim.

SONNY: That's not gonna happen.

VICTOR: Why not?

SONNY: He's my cousin, but not like a cousin cousin. My pops is his god-father. Leo don't give a fuck bout his father, my father, nobody.

VICTOR: You could try.

SONNY: I ain't seen'm in years. You think he owes me favors?

VICTOR: I don't know about that but you owe somebody favors.

SONNY: *(Losing his temper.)* The fuck you tryna say?

JIM: It's cool.

VICTOR: I'm sayen you could at least try.

SONNY: Shut the fuck up, Victor. You think I wouldn't be lookin out for Jim? I went to see Leo. You know that? I went to visit him his third week in. He knew it was me. Had me waitin two hours, wouldn't even see me. An last time I checked Jim, ain't tryna get down with the Aryan Nation.

JIM: Forget it.

SONNY: That's what I'm sayen.

VICTOR: Yo, I didn't know.

SONNY: There's a lot you don't know.

VICTOR: *(Mumble.)* I know how to spell martyr motherfucker.

SONNY: What?

JIM: Yo I gotta break out.

SONNY: Hold up…

JIM: What.

SONNY: I ever tell you bout that shit on TV?

JIM: What shit?

SONNY: Remember that fire on Rivington?

JIM: In April?

SONNY: Yeah. I was watchin the news and they was interviewing a lady across the street from the building…and your shit was in the background…well like half a your shit.

JIM: Where was this?

SONNY: By the Laundromat.

JIM: It was green and white?

SONNY: Yeah, yeah. Your shit was on the news, son.

VICTOR: I heard about that.

SONNY: I tried to record it for you, but my VCR's all fucked up.

JIM: Huh. *(Beat.)* Yo I gotta go.

SONNY: A.

JIM: What.

SONNY: I, I got somethin for you.

JIM: What?

(Sonny hands a small item wrapped in papers to Jim.)

SONNY: Here.

JIM: What is it?

SONNY: It's real, I'll tell you that much.

(Jim discovers a diamond ring.)

VICTOR: You guys gettin married?

SONNY: Just gotta get the stone off.

VICTOR: Where'd you get it?

JIM: This a diamond?

SONNY: It's a fucken big diamond.

VICTOR: *(Mocking Sonny:)* Fucken fucken—

SONNY: I will slap you.

JIM: *(Putting on the ring.)* No one's ever given me a ring.

SONNY: Just before check in and strip search, swallow it.

JIM: And then.

VICTOR: Is this from a movie?

SONNY: I read it.

VICTOR: You read?

SONNY: I c'fucken read.

VICTOR: I didn't ask if you could, I ask if you do.

JIM: Wait, whahappened?

SONNY: You shit it out in jail.

JIM: That works?

SONNY: That's how my cousin got hash inside.

JIM: I want this because…?

SONNY: To make friends.

VICTOR: Yo that c'work.

SONNY: In there you need any advantages you could get. Yo just give it to someone who could get you somethin.

JIM: What would I get?

VICTOR: Protection.

SONNY: Listen B… I was buggin out that night, bein all…That was ill how they just came outa nowhere like that. And I know what they like when they first got you. I know what they say, how they front like, "All your boys pointin the finger at you" an shit—

JIM: What are you—

SONNY: In like movies we all know the rules, keep it in the family, don't say nothin, get some brownie points, you're a hero, go home and it's all caviar and g-strings. In real life, ain't no brownie points or heroes, you be out a lot quicker if you just drop some—

VICTOR: You believe this kid?

SONNY: Son, I know vandal squads lookin for me, before that night even…I don't know what I'd do if—

JIM: I didn't say shit.

SONNY: You didn't say shit?

VICTOR: !Get the fuck outa here, you think Jim would—

SONNY: I'm not talkin a you!!

JIM: What is this, a bribe? You think you gotta pay me off?

SONNY: Nah, I wasn't—

JIM: You really think I'd do you like that?

SONNY: No, but—

JIM: *(Tries to hand it back.)* I don't want this shit.

VICTOR: Dee-vorced.

SONNY: I'm just paranoid, son.

JIM: We all paranoid.

SONNY: Take the ring yo.

JIM: *(Pushing it in Sonny's hand.)* Sonny. I don't want it.

VICTOR: He don't want the ring.

SONNY: Son—

VICTOR: Yo if no one wants the ring—

SONNY: It's just, if I was you, I'da said shit about me.

JIM: Well I'm not you.

SONNY: Yo, I want you to have it.

JIM: Why?

SONNY: Just take it.

JIM: I don't—

SONNY: Would you just take it?

JIM: Would it make you that happy?

SONNY: Yes, it would make me really fucken happy.

JIM: Yeah?

SONNY: Yeah.

JIM: If it makes you happy.

SONNY: It does.

JIM: *(Taking the ring.)* Alright.

SONNY: Thank you.

VICTOR: How fucken romantic.

SONNY: Can I hit him?

JIM: No.

VICTOR: So whas happening with the party man?

SONNY: You haven a party?

JIM: It's not—

SONNY: Yo son, I met these Swedish *au pairs* down by my man Alani's.

JIM: It's gonna be a meeting.

SONNY: A meeting?

JIM: I just wanna talk to the crew.

SONNY: I'm sayen though, like, you want me to bring some girls out?

VICTOR: Do it.

JIM: No. Just the crew.

SONNY: So no girls?

JIM: No girls.

VICTOR: *(Pleading.)* Jim! Swedish *au pairs*!

JIM: No Swedish *au pairs*. Sonny, you'll tell people?

SONNY: No doubt.

JIM: Talk it up. I'm late, I gotta go.

VICTOR: *(Putting his arm on Sonny's shoulders.)* Don't listen to him Sonny.

SONNY: *(Shaking him off.)* The fuck off me.

JIM: Alright then.

SONNY: Yo what time you tryna do this?

JIM: 11:00.

SONNY: Where at?

JIM: Down by the elevated tracks.

VICTOR: Which ones.

SONNY: The one where Glenn…

JIM: Yeah.

SONNY: Tomorrow then.

JIM: Tomorrow.

VICTOR: *(Little smile.)* Tell Kaila I say hi. *(Jim exits.)*

SONNY: Victor, what you bout to do?

VICTOR: I dunno, go home.

SONNY: *(Looking at his watch.)* You wanna come meet these girls?

VICTOR: Do I wanna meet the girls? What are we waiting for? Should I change my clothes? What, at like a party? A bar?

SONNY: Oh wait, I forgot. Sorry man, I gotta go see my spelling tutor. Adios Gato.

(Sonny exits. Victor is alone on stage. Lights fade to black. End of scene.)

Act 1, Scene 7
(Tape Light comes up to Jim alone on stage.)

JIM: Entry 2148. The prison industrial complex is a breeding ground for agents of change. Malcolm X began his self-education behind bars. Nelson Mandela gained international support during imprisonment. The political prisoner will always be far more dangerous than the armchair radical. A caged animal learns patience as it plots in fierce silence. *(Beat.)* Awaiting incarceration, Kaptn out.

(Jim stops the tape recorder as lights black out.)

Act 1, Scene 8

(Lights up to Jim and Kaila in Kaila's room. Kaila is furious.)

KAILA: Stupid! So fuckin stupid!! Thas not even juvenile, thas fuckin infan-
tile!! You not sixteen, you don't getta slap on the wrist! What are you
thinkin?! What goes through your head? Shit's not sexy or mysterious or
whatever you like to think it is! Iss'just straight up fuckin childish! Why?
What's the point? Really. What is it you provin? Does it give you some kind
of street credibility? Does it prove that you down, that you Mr. Hip Hop?

JIM: Kai—

KAILA: I could kill you. How is that you so smart and so...They're gonna eat
you alive. You understand that?

JIM: *(Kinda tough.)* I be alright.

KAILA: You be alright? Don't play tough guy shit with me. I know you.
Tough is the last thing you are. You work with four-year-olds, Jim. Are you
happy about this? You seem so fuckin proud a yourself. Is this all so when
you get out you c'brag about how you served time for some kinda cause?
Thas it isn't it? *(Mocking:)* Huh *Kaptn*? This's all part of your whole fuckin
GI Joe communisto bullshit.

JIM: Are you done?

KAILA: No I'm not fuckin done. We not even at half-way done.

JIM: Jesus.

KAILA: You show up here and tell me this shit. What're you expecting? Pity?

JIM: No. But a little bit would be nice.

KAILA: I'm supposed to feel sorry for you? They caught you breakin a law
you learn in fuckin pre-school. Here's a crayon. See the wall. Don't fuckin
write on it. You teach your kids, that right?

JIM: I don't usually say fuckin when I'm speaking to—

KAILA: I am not in the mood for your sarcasm.

JIM: You don't think this is fucked up?

KAILA: I think you fucked up.

JIM: They lockin me up for bein part of a certain community, for expressing
a culture that they don't—

KAILA: That shit ain't about no fuckin culture. Thas about some *(pretending to write in spray paint)* big dick seven was here. You wanna do some shit
for the community do a mural with some kids.

JIM: I do, I mean I been meaning to but, yo, on a artistic level, you don't see
how my freedom can't be limited by—?

KAILA: No I don't see any of that shit. You c'save that whole argument.

JIM: It's an expression they can't control, so they're threatened by the fact
that we out there—

KAILA: I've heard this before. This is not new to me. I know, I know, you a fuckin rebel.

JIM: Too bad I'm not a rock star, I c'get you on a guest list and you could come take pictures a me.

KAILA: What? What the fuck does that have to do with anything? Oh, I'm sorry I'm doin shit with my life.

JIM: And I do what I do. If one thing, don't question what I believe in.

KAILA: What you believe in. What you believe in?

JIM: What I believe in.

KAILA: The fuck do you believe in?

JIM: What do I believe in?

KAILA: Yeah, what do you believe in?

JIM: I believe...

KAILA: This should be good. *(Beat.)*

JIM: I believe in you.

KAILA: You're a corny motherfucker.

JIM: Thas true. *(Jim hands Kaila the ring package.)* Here.

KAILA: What's this?

JIM: A goin away present.

KAILA: I ain't goin nowhere.

JIM: Shut up, I want you to have it.

KAILA: You're givin me a goin away present?

JIM: It could be a birthday present. I won't be able to see you on your birthday. *(Kaila opens it and discovers the ring.)*

KAILA: Where'd you get this?

JIM: I got it.

KAILA: You got it?

JIM: For you.

KAILA: Where?

JIM: I got it.

KAILA: This is...thank you.

JIM: You're welcome.

KAILA: I hate you.

JIM: I know. So how was the show?

KAILA: What?

JIM: How was the show tonight?

KAILA: It was nice.

JIM: Tell me about it.

KAILA: What.

JIM: Tell me about the show.

KAILA: I was thinking about you the whole time.

JIM: What were you thinkin?

KAILA: That you were gonna tell me some shit like this. *(Kaila begins getting ready for bed, eventually lying down on the bed next to the edge where Jim sits.)*

JIM: You get any pictures?

KAILA: I didn't even remember to take out my camera till the last song.

JIM: So you didn't take anything?

KAILA: I took some a last song.

JIM: What was it?

KAILA: I dunno, but it'd perfect for my portfolio. They had these blue lights on stage. It was nice. Tamir had a mute in and the way he was playing it, it sounded like a voice.

JIM: Like Charlie Brown?

KAILA: Charlie Brown?

JIM: The teacher. *(Jim does imitation.)*

KAILA: Yeah like that. *(Looking at the ring.)* I'll write you letters.

JIM: While I'm in jail?

KAILA: You want me to?

JIM: Every day.

KAILA: You gonna write me back?

JIM: Every hour. You could send me pictures?

KAILA: If you want.

JIM: I do. Like ten a day. I want pictures a everything.

KAILA: Everything?

JIM: Everything. But you don't gotta send ones from tonight.

KAILA: You don't want a picture a Tamir?

JIM: No. Well maybe one. He's cute right?

KAILA: He's cute.

JIM: You goin to sleep?

KAILA: At some point.

JIM: Now?

KAILA: Pretty soon.

JIM: Oh.

KAILA: What are you gonna do?

JIM: Should I go?

KAILA: If you want to.

JIM: Could I stay?

KAILA: *(Indifferent.)* Yeah.

JIM: You want me to stay?

KAILA: I'd like that.

JIM: Why didn't you just say that?

KAILA: That's not how we play the game.

JIM: What game?

KAILA: Where we never say what we feelin. You made the rules.

JIM: I don't wanna play the game anymore.

KAILA: Ok, then what do you want?

JIM: What d'you mean?

KAILA: What do you want?

JIM: Now, or in general?

KAILA: You still playin. What do you want?

JIM: I want...for you to be happy.

(Kaila kicks Jim off the bed. He falls hard onto the floor.)

KAILA: If you're not gonna talk to me I'm goin to sleep.

JIM: I'll talk.

KAILA: So talk.

JIM: I want...I want to skip ahead in time. I wanna be done with jail, and I want to be living and painting and organizing shit and and and workin with kids and makin kids and I want to be wakin up and smellin your breath in the morning and watchin you sleep.

KAILA: When did you decide this?

JIM: Just now.

KAILA: What's gonna happen with your class?

JIM: I told Sandy I won't be able to come in for a while. I said I had to go away cuz of a family emergency.

KAILA: Did you get someone to take over?

JIM: I didn't think a that.

KAILA: You know enough artists.

JIM: I guess I never really told anyone about my job.

KAILA: Why?

JIM: I mean I told people I had to do my community service hours there, but they don't know I kept going back.

KAILA: What, were you afraid people would tease you?

JIM: No, I don't know.

KAILA: Did the people at your trial know? Did you tell them about the work you do?

JIM: They wasn't tryna hear anything I had to say.

KAILA: So what did you tell your kids?

JIM: That I gotta go live in a castle.

KAILA: You mean a dungeon.

JIM: They'll forget about me soon.

KAILA: Their art class is over. They'll be sad.

JIM: For a few days, then they'll get over it. They probably get put in some music class. Find some cute trumpet player.

KAILA: They still miss you.

JIM: How you know?

KAILA: Cuz they love you.

JIM: How you know?

KAILA: They tole me.......Where will they send you?

JIM: Raybrook.

KAILA: Where is that?

JIM: It's upstate. I hope they send me there.

KAILA: Why?

JIM: It's a brand new facility.

KAILA: Yeah?

JIM: Real nice. Isslike Club Med with big gates.

KAILA: Club Med?

JIM: Yeah...I'm just gonna lie out in the sun......lift weights.....catch up on my reading........Yo, time I'm out you won't even recognize me, I'll be so diesel'd my muscles'll have muscles. I'll have so many muscles you won't even know where to begin.....When I get out...we'll run to each other all in slow motion...(*Getting a little too excited about his future muscles.*) My pectorals'll be bobbing, my deltoids'll......

KAILA: Easy tiger. (*Kaila starts to get up to go brush her teeth.*)

JIM: Kaila.

KAILA: Yeah.

JIM: You know if it supposed to rain?

KAILA: When?

JIM: Tomorrow.

KAILA: No idea. (*Kaila starts to get up again.*)

JIM: Wait....I know.......I know things didn't happen right.........with us.......I mean they're still not happening right...but...........

KAILA: What.

JIM: I dunno. I dunno what I'm tryna say........I been searching for the right words since that last time we spoke...but they're not coming. Maybe they don't live in me. You're just...you're too good for me, I know that, you always been too good—

KAILA: Jim—

JIM: No....I.....I should have come by more, but...You don't know how it is......I mean it hurts just to be around you ...an.......just knowin that I won't be able to see you, like physically not able....I......... I need you. I need you. *(Sneaking closer.)* An you may not want me now Kaila Maldero. But I'm exercisin. I'm eatin right. And I'm drinkin milk. So you better watch out... Next thing you know...I'll be so huge that...*(Jim tries to kiss Kaila. He almost has her. She turns away.)*

KAILA: Don't.

JIM: *(Trying again.)* And Ima keep drinking milk, till every last cow is dry...Even after that, even...

KAILA: Stop.

JIM: But I like milk.

KAILA: I know you like milk.

JIM: Do you?

KAILA: What.

JIM: Do you know *how much* I like milk?

KAILA: I do.

JIM: *(Moving in.)* Yeah.

KAILA: Yeah. *(Stopping Jim.)* No.

JIM: Why?

KAILA: Why?

JIM: I just wanna be with you right now.

KAILA: I'm right here.

JIM: Yeah, but—*(Jim moves closer. Kaila stops him.)* Relax.

KAILA: *(No longer playing.)* Jim.

JIM: *(Groans.)* Killin me.

KAILA: *(Not at all sorry.)* Sorry.

JIM: Are you?

KAILA: Not really. Not at all actually.

JIM: Yeah?

KAILA: When was the last time you been over?

JIM: I dunno. A week?

KAILA: I thought you might be dead.

JIM: You was the one talkin bout needing space.

KAILA: *Space*, not miles.

JIM: *(Moving closer.)* Why you so far away?

KAILA: Jim.

JIM: What.

KAILA: Stop.

JIM: OK.

KAILA: Thas not how it works.

JIM: How what works?

KAILA: I haven't heard from you since you had a goatee. You think you could just show up here with a rose in your mouth and we'll dive right into bed.

JIM: Kai—

KAILA: No fuck that. Obviously I wasn't worth the effort.

JIM: What can I do?

KAILA: Get your shit together.

JIM: *(Offended.)* What?

KAILA: You're in trouble and I'm sorry. I don't know what else to say. What do you expect from me?

JIM: I don't *expect* anything.

KAILA: Obviously you do.

JIM: Should I not have come?

KAILA: Depends on why you came.

JIM: I came to say goodbye.

KAILA: You sure?

JIM: Thas how I say goodbye.

KAILA: *(Not at all amused.)* Not to me.

JIM: What the fuck.

KAILA: I need to go to sleep. I'm workin tomorrow.

JIM: How convenient.

KAILA: What?

JIM: Nothin, I'm goin home.

KAILA: Fine.

JIM: I used to hate it when you'd pull this shit.

KAILA: Pull what shit?

JIM: Yo you're right. I shouldn't a come.

KAILA: I didn't say that.

JIM: You didn't have to. I jus…I didn't know you'd act like this.

KAILA: How am I acting?

JIM: Fucken apathetic.

KAILA: Oh, I'm apathetic cuz I'm not suckin your dick right now?

JIM: *(Frustrated.)* Kaila.

(Short silence.)

KAILA: What do you want?

JIM: I dunno. I should go.

KAILA: OK.

(Jim takes Kaila's hand.)

JIM: *(Squeezing her hand softly.)* Have a good year. *(Jim starts to exit.)*

KAILA: Jim.

JIM: What?

KAILA: Goodnight.

JIM: Goodnight.

(Jim exits. Kaila sits motionless. She looks a lot more upset than when she was talking to Jim. She turns out the light. Lights cross fade to the painting Jim, Victor and Sonny just did. The letters NTS have been written over KAPTN, GATO and MARTER. The UVK has been crossed out. As lights fade to black a muted trumpet can be heard playing. End of Act 1.)

Act 2, Scene 1

(Lights up to Jim and Victor. Victor's talking a mile a minute. Jim looks a little lost.)

VICTOR: You're not gonna believe this. O my god yo, I'm lucky to be alive. I'm waitin in Sonny's room lookin at some mags, he's takin his year long shower. Soon as he steps out the bathroom his moms attacks.

JIM: She find some cans or something?

VICTOR: I dunno, but she's all kinds a angry screamin some Italian shit. He walks into the room and starts getting dressed, just ignorin her. I never seen Sonny's mom like this. Yo, she starts beating on him. Hard as she can to the stomach, chest, upside his head, *Fist a the North Star* shit yo.

JIM: Damn.

VICTOR: But you know Sonny's mom. She's a small lady right? So Sonny's like 'whatever' kinda smirken, just standen there taken it. But then she starts *pinchen*. Yo, she got some claws, kid. So now Sonny's payen attention, right? They're both shoutin and he's batt'n at her hands tryna stop the pinches, "Ow...fuckin stop mom. Mom, get the fuck atta here!" Yo I was dyin. She sees me laughin and attacks me.

JIM: What?

VICTOR: (Real quick.) Thas when I ran. (Showing red marks on his arm.) Lookat this shit.

JIM: So what happened to Sonny?

VICTOR: Said he'd meet us here later.

JIM: (Empty.) That's crazy.

VICTOR: What's wrong man?

JIM: Nothin.

VICTOR: (Offering Jim a thermos.) You need some coffee?

JIM: I'm straight.

VICTOR: When you gotta be back in court?

JIM: 7am.

VICTOR: 7 am tomorrow?

JIM: Yeah.

VICTOR: Fuck. *(Beat.)* So what happened with Kaila?

JIM: I dunno.

VICTOR: You stay the night?

JIM: Nah.

VICTOR: So whahappened?

JIM: Drama.

VICTOR: What'd she say?

JIM: Yo I had it all worked out in my head. Everything. Like word for word exactly how the night was gonna go down…but…

VICTOR: But?

JIM: Things fall apart….

VICTOR: Yo, girls like Kaila scare me.

JIM: Kaila likes you.

VICTOR: I know, I'm a likable person, but she's just, do you feel naked around her?

JIM: I *been* naked around her.

VICTOR: No I mean…I was gonna say something deep, but never mind.

JIM: No I know what you're sayen. I know what you mean. *(Beat.)* So who you speak to?

VICTOR: Bout tonight? Everyone. You said 11 right?

JIM: 11 a clock, yeah.

VICTOR: I told Lex, Jeff, Monkey, Greenleaf, the twins, uhh someone told Dante. Sonny said he'd talk to Alani and Cody and those guys.

JIM: Everyone's comin?

VICTOR: They all wanna see you before you leave. I told them we're paintin, we're paintin right?

JIM: I'm not sure.

VICTOR: You still on that meeting shit?

JIM: Why you write?

VICTOR: Shut up man.

JIM: I'm serious, why you write.

VICTOR: Cuz thas my shit.

JIM: But why?

VICTOR: My name…it's my signature, like Ralph Lauren. The name's there so you know it's quality. *(Sonny enters.)*

JIM: What's up?

SONNY: Yo, I just came from a war, son.

JIM: I heard.

SONNY: Son, we need to talk.

JIM: So talk.

SONNY: I feel like a dick.

JIM: What.

SONNY: I hate to ask you like…I dunno what the fuck to do. I need that ring back…

VICTOR: That shit was your mom's?

SONNY: I need it back, Jim.

JIM: Fuck.

SONNY: What?

JIM: I don't have it.

SONNY: Where is it?

JIM: I don't have it.

SONNY: Where is it, Jim?

JIM: It's gone.

SONNY: Well where'd it go?

JIM: Kaila's got it.

SONNY: What!?

JIM: I gave it to Kaila.

SONNY: You what?

VICTOR: Oh shit.

SONNY: You gotta get that shit back.

JIM: Nah man, you take care of it.

SONNY: I will then. Where she live at?

JIM: What are you gonna do?

SONNY: Ima do what I gotta do.

VICTOR: You gonna rob her?

JIM: Yo, I'll get it.

SONNY: My mom already screamed at the building manager, the maintenance man, the *police*.

VICTOR: You fucked up.

SONNY: Victor I'm not in no fuckin mood!

JIM: Damn!

SONNY: I can't believe you.

JIM: You can't believe me? You were expecting it back…?…After I passed it to Don Corleone?

SONNY: I ain't seen my moms cry in years.

VICTOR: She was cryin?

JIM: Yo man.

SONNY: What.

JIM: I'll call Kaila.

SONNY: Good.

JIM: This is fuckin great.

VICTOR: So what's the deal tonight? We paintin or what?

JIM: Maybe.

VICTOR: Maybe?

JIM: Probly.

VICTOR: I'm sayen should I pick up some shit?

JIM: Yeah.

VICTOR: It's your last night. Ima rack you a fuckin rainbow.

SONNY: So you'll talk to her?

JIM: I'll go call her right now.

VICTOR: *(To himself:)* Cherry red, summer-squash yellow, jungle green, true blue.

JIM: Everyone's comin?

SONNY: Everyone's comin.

JIM: Good.

VICTOR: UVK's king'n the city tonight.

SONNY: You'll get it now?

JIM: I said I'll call her.

VICTOR: You goin shoppin wi' me?

SONNY: Yeah. But no summer-squash.

VICTOR: What?

SONNY: You said summer-squash yellow. Son that color's played out.

JIM: 11 then.

SONNY: 11.

VICTOR: Peace and chicken grease. *(Jim exits stage left as Sonny and Victor exit stage right. Blackout.)*

Act 2, Scene 2

(Lights up to reveal Kaila's empty room. Her phone is ringing. Her answering machine picks up and the person hangs up. Lights change as Victor and Sonny run across the stage each hugging many cans of spray paint. A storeowner can be heard shouting at them. Lights cross fade to Tape Light. Jim is alone on stage speaking into his tape recorder.)

JIM: Entry 2149. The movement grows rapidly, while there still lacks any overall solidarity. Current constraints have forced a change in plans. Regardless of reactions, it is time. No one can question my commitment. Not today, not tonight. Meeting convenes in 0700 hours. *(Deep breath.)* This is what it's been building to. *(Long beat.)* Try and make it memorable. Kaptn out. *(Lights black out as Jim stops the tape recorder.)*

Act 2, Scene 3

(In blackout the sounds of many people can be heard. Young men being young men. Someone has a stereo that is playing music. Some Swedish girls are laughing. Lights up on the "meeting." Only Victor and Sonny are seen.)

VICTOR: Thas not what I'm sayen at all.

SONNY: Then what're you sayen?

VICTOR: Like, like look at any new writer. They could have good colors, they could have nice clean letters, but they still missin somethin. What they missin?

SONNY: What?

VICTOR: Flow.

SONNY: I got flow.

VICTOR: I'm not sayen that you don't, but, for example look at Jim's P's, they come up thin then get wider and fatter. Since he's bendin his axis like that, it's gotta lean. Everything's gotta lean, like a heavy table with little ass legs that are about to snap...*thas* fuckin gravity.

SONNY: He does the same shit with his, his K's.

VICTOR: *Thas* keepin it balanced.

SONNY: So my shit's not balanced?

VICTOR: I'm just sayen you could pay a little more attention is all.

(Jim enters holding his tape recorder. He eventually puts it in his pocket.)

SONNY: Where you been, you get the ring?

JIM: She wasn't home.

SONNY: Fuck man.

JIM: She should be in later. I'll stop by.

VICTOR: Jim, you think they really Swedish?

SONNY: I didn't bring'm. They been driven Alani around yo he must brought'm.

VICTOR: Guess who else is here?

JIM: Who?

VICTOR: NTS.

SONNY: Fuck those toys.

VICTOR: How you think they knew to come?

SONNY: I bet Cody told'm, you know Cody used to push NTS?

VICTOR: Really?

JIM: There's a lot a people.

VICTOR: We ain't had everyone like this since at Glenn's—

SONNY: Jim, I'll tell'm to leave right now if—

JIM: Nah. I like the crowd.

SONNY: But they been crossin everybody.

VICTOR: They got no style.

JIM: I thought half these people fell off.

VICTOR: This is like a writers reunion or somethin.

ALANI: Jim, you wanna hit this?

JIM: I don't smoke no more.

VICTOR: Jim's righteous like that.

ALANI: But we drinkin right?

JIM: I dunno.

ALANI: Son, we gotta do it up tonight, it's like your goin away party.

JIM: I don't think this is some shit to celebrate.

ALANI: Jim, this is Wendla.

SWEDISH GIRL #1: Hi.

JIM: How you doin?

SWEDISH GIRL #1: Good thanks.

SWEDISH GIRL #2: Hip hop is cool.

VICTOR: Why you didn't introduce me?

SONNY: You see this kid stare'n?

VICTOR: What kid?

SONNY: *(Pointing.)* That one.

JIM: Should we get started?

SONNY: Get started?

VICTOR: What we startin?

JIM: The meeting.

SONNY: Who we meetin?

JIM: Nah I mean....

SONNY: Should we go some where?

VICTOR: Let's take the girls.

JIM: No...I just I wanna say some shit.

SONNY: Alright.

VICTOR: Nah he means to everyone.

SONNY: You wanna say somethin to everyone?

JIM: Kind of...Yeah.

SONNY: What you mean?

JIM: I wanna speak.

SONNY: What you wanna say?

JIM: I'm not sure.

VICTOR: *(Squinting to see who has the stereo.)* Yo tell'm to turn down the music.

SONNY: You wanna do this now?

JIM: Soon.

SONNY: Fuck it, do it now. A! Dante!

DANTE: What?

SONNY: Kill the music. *(The music is turned off.)* A yo!!! Yo shut up!!! *(There is still noise and interruption.)* Alani man!! Tells those girls to leave!

ALANI: They my ride.

SONNY: Then keep'm quiet.

VOICES: What? Wassup? What's goin on? *(Etc.)*

VICTOR: Jim's got some shit to say.

SONNY: A!! Shut the fuck up!! Jim wants to speak!!! *(Everyone gets quiet.)* There you go Jim.

(Victor and Sonny find places in the audience. Jim speaks to the audience as if it's the crowd.)

JIM: Uh…

ALANI: What the deal Jimmy?

JIM: Is everyone here? This is everyone?

CROWD: *(Overlapping.)* Yeah. Wassup. Whashappenin. *(Etc.)*

JIM: Crew's gotten big. I don't even think I know half a you. *(To someone in the audience:)* Who the fuck are you?

LAZER: Lazer.

JIM: Wassup Lazer. Anyway, uh…Yo thanks for comin out. For real, that means a lot to me.

JIM (cont.)	DAVE
If you hadn't heard,	Swear to god I know
I'll be goin soon.	her. She from Sweden yo.
Tomorrow actually. And uh,	Freak nasty, all them
there's some shit I—	shorty's like that yo—

SONNY: A, y'all need to shut the fuck up'n show some respect!

DAVE: Alright mom.

SONNY: What he say?

JIM: I'll try not to blab for too long, but I'd like say some shit if that's cool.

ALANI: We all wich you.

DANTE: Get open Jim.

JIM: So yeah..uh…It's funny cuz, yo I just been thinkin bout how…How, Ima be in jail….and all I can keep thinkin about is, man Ima miss a lot a walls. That's all I can think about. They're lockin me up an I'm thinkin about all those spots I haven't hit yet and I hope no one hits and part a me's like, "the fuck is wrong with you." I'm a fiend. What the fuck am I doing? What are we doing? Yo, anyone ever get laid for this shit?

DAVE: Not you.

JIM: Anyone? How bout money, anyone ever gotten paid? So what's it all for? Why we doin this?

DANTE: Fame, nigga!

JIM: Fame? The fuck does this for fame? You wanna know where I'm famous, who knows my work? A gang a thirteen-year-olds with pimples and black books, that's who.

ALANI: That's real.

JIM: It's like, the fuck am I doing this for? I dunno…Yo how I see it, it's like this, and I could only speak for myself, but every time I'm out painting. I reach this point where I relax into it just a little. You know when your hand gets fluid and your mind's like in meditation, but still all tense, you know what I mean?

DANTE: Yeah.

JIM: Like I feel, I feel like a ninja.

DAVE: *(Laughing.)* The fuck outta here. *(Makes ninja sounds.)*

JIM: Seriously. And there's this rock in my stomach. This little knot. It's like that tingly feelin when you first sneakin out when you a kid. Like before you even outside when you stuffin your bed to look like someone's sleepin in it. That feelin in your stomach right then. But now it's a feelin more of, that I'm doin something…somethin important. Some shit that NEEDS to be done. Yo, I don't care who you are, why you do what you do, regardless, every time you get up and someone sees that shit, maybe they're like, "Thas some ugly shit," or maybe they're like, "Ooh, those are pretty colors, let's put that shit on a T-shirt…in a museum, whatever." But as long as your shit's up, there's people gonna see it. And deep down they know, it's tellin them someone's not settled, someone's not satisfied with the laws and the order of society. It's a tangible, colorful, mark thas shoutin out a resistance to to to capitalism and greed and all the boojy ass spots that keep poppin up in my neighborhood. What was that hippy shit back in the day all about? Fuck haircuts, fuck soap'n showers, les get high? We on some more prolific shit, we sayen fuck private property. Fuck the ownership a land. If you really break it down, we like the last of the Mohicans. Whether you look at it this way or not, all of us out here, we the most political animals in the jungle today. Where's the Panthers at? Where's Che and the freedom fighters? It's all dead. Yo, they dropped the torch. They dropped it. We pickin it up.

DAVE: Jim for president.

JIM: *(Directed at hecklers:)* I know this's fun and all, and graff's real hip and cool and a big fuckin game… but not really. This is where Glenn died last year. *(Silence for the first time.)* Yeah, remember that? Remember that shit?

R.I.P. Lefty. Wrote that shit everywhere…put that up for months…even writers that didn't know'm. I still put it up…goofy, smiley-ass Glenn. Cop shot'm right here…where we standing. *(Pointing.)* That was the last piece he did.….Now I'm about to go to fuckin jail. We all know vandal squad's huntin. Damn, here I'm up here on some *Braveheart* type shit, "Come and live, stay and die." But for real though, I'm ready to go to war. It's time to start somethin. Somethin. Yo, am I jus talken a lotta shit right now? Are we all just out here fuckin shit up for no reason? I'm not key'n cars, I'm not startin fires. I'm sharin art. I'm riskin my life for…for ….We all risk our lives everyday. It's time to make it worth somethin. Even if it's just us, just us that's out here tonight, thas gonna be the first, that's all it takes. It's real when we make it real. What happens when we step out the shadows, when we stop just scribblin names and start rock'n burners and throw-ups and fill-ins of a revolution!! When we let the world know.

SONNY: UVK ! !

(Everyone begins talking at the same time. There are many voices and lines overlap throughout the rest of the scene.)

CROWD: *(Simultaneous.)* What what! Jim's buggin. Let'm know! A'ight Jimmy! You got another cigarette? *(Etc.)*

DAVE: You know, that dead nigga Glenn was sweet? For real. No? Why'd he always bomb pink then? Yo check his piece over by—

JIM: *(Drowned out by the crowd.)* Yo, we c'do this now. Tonight! We just need to—

DAVE: …talkin bout his dead boyfriend yo.

JIM: *(Realizing he's talking to himself.)* One more thing! A!

ALANI: Jimbo, these girls gotta place uptown, you wanna roll with us an get some drinks?

JIM: I'm not done.

VICTOR: A Jim's not done.

SONNY: Alani, I could get a seat in the car?

ALANI: Yeah, I think we— *(A bottle crashes.)*

SONNY: The fuck was that?!

VICTOR: A bottle.

SONNY: You see who threw that? A!!! *(Looking back into the audience.)* Which one a you bitches threw that shit?

JIM: Sonny—

SONNY: Who the fuck threw that?!!

DAVE: Who you callin a bitch little man?

SONNY: What!! Who the fuck is that?

JIM: Sonny—

DAVE: Who the fuck are you?

SONNY: You NTS?

DAVE: Who wants to know?

JIM: A—

SONNY: You didn't answer my question bitch. You NTS?

DAVE: Yeah I'm fuckin NTS, I'm not with some faggot ass UVK shit.

SONNY: What motherfucker!

DAVE: Yo fuck UVK!!

ALANI: Fuck UVK?

JIM: Sonny—

ALANI: They NTS?

SONNY: You believe this son?

ALANI: Let's handle this shit.

SONNY: Thas what I'm sayen.

JIM: Sonny!

SONNY: What!!

ALANI: Beat his ass, Sonny.

JIM: Yo I'm tryna do somethin here.

SONNY: Then talk to motherfuckers chuckin bottles.

VICTOR: Unity man.

SONNY: What is this, *Warriors*?

DAVE: UVK ain't shit.

JIM: Sonny.

VICTOR: Yo chill, Sonny.

SONNY: Don't tell me to chill!

JIM: Sonny man—

SONNY: He been sayen shit all night. Jim, they NTS.

JIM: It's not about that, cool out.

DAVE: You should listen to your boy!

SONNY: Yo, I'm tellin you right now this kid better leave.

DAVE: I betta leave?

SONNY: You think I'm playen with you?!

ALANI: He's not playen.

VICTOR: Shut up, Alani.

SONNY: You just gonna shout son?!

JIM: Sonny—

DAVE: You don't wanna see me!

SONNY: Let's do this!

JIM: Sonny!

SONNY: You wanna swing at me, swing at me!!

JIM: Sonny, chill!

DAVE: The fuck you gonna do?

ALANI: Yo, he must not know who he's talken to.

SONNY: Come at me, come at me, motherfucker!!

DAVE: *(Standing.)* Bring it on, Pacino. *(Sonny starts towards Dave.)*

JIM: *(Hugging Sonny back.)* Chill, man.

SONNY: The fuck off me, Jim!

JIM: Cool out, man.

DAVE: What then?

SONNY: Get offa me, Jim!

JIM: Sonny, chill. He's not about shit.

SONNY: Alright.

JIM: Fuck this, kid, don't stress it.

SONNY: I'm cool.

JIM: It's not worth it, man.

SONNY: Bro, I said I'm cool.

JIM: Yo, you better than that.

SONNY: Alright man.

JIM: You cool?

SONNY: Motherfucker, I been cool.

JIM: You sure?

SONNY: Live and let live.

JIM: OK. *(Jim lets go of Sonny, still in his face.)*

DAVE: Look at these faggots, yo!

(Pulling a box cutter out of his pocket, Sonny pushes past Jim and charges up into the audience.)

SONNY: *(Enraged.)* Fuck this. Turn around bitch! *(Blackout.)*

DAVE: Yo yo yo yo yo!!

(The sounds of fighting, shouting, girls screaming for people to stop, police sirens and, finally, everyone scattering.)

Act 2, Scene 4

(Lights up to Kaila alone in her apartment. She is wearing the ring. Someone buzzes from downstairs.)

KAILA: Hello?

JIM (O.S.): Kaila, it's me. *(She buzzes him in. Jim stands in the doorway. He is defeated.)*

KAILA: Hey.

JIM: Hey.

KAILA: What's up. *(Silence.)* You OK?

JIM: No.

KAILA: Anything I can do?

JIM: No.

KAILA: You just gonna stand there? *(Jim enters.)*

JIM: *(Beat.)* Sorry about leaving and…I'm sorry.

KAILA: Me too. *(Beat.)* When do you…?

JIM: Tomorrow morning.

KAILA: Am I gonna see you?

JIM: When?

KAILA: Sometime before never?

JIM: I'm not on death row.

KAILA: You want some tea?

JIM: No thanks.

KAILA: I was hopin you'd come back.

JIM: I was hopin you were hopin I'd come back.

KAILA: Yeah?

JIM: Yeah. ….. I had a excuse.

KAILA: What?

JIM: I, I need…Fuck. *(Beat.)* I need the ring back.

KAILA: What?

JIM: I need the ring back.

KAILA: This ring?

JIM: Yeah.

KAILA: You're takin it back?

JIM: I'm not takin it back, it's… it's …

KAILA: What.

JIM: I need it back.

KAILA: You're serious?

JIM: Yeah.

KAILA: If that's how it is then—

JIM: It's not what you think.

KAILA: If you need it, it's yours. *(Kaila drops it into Jim's hand.)*

JIM: I didn't do this………You really wanna know?

KAILA: Yeah.

JIM: It's fuckin stupid. This ring, it's…I didn't know…It was Sonny's mother's ring.

KAILA: Who stole it?

JIM: Sonny. I didn't know.

KAILA: This ring?

JIM: Yeah.

KAILA: The ring you got for me?

JIM: I....

KAILA: Yeah well, that is what it is.

JIM: Fuck...

KAILA: Actually, it makes sense.

JIM: What.

KAILA: You givin me a stolen ring.

JIM: I didn't—

KAILA: That's everything...everything with you's like that....Everything you say you're about, all the shit I know you believe in...*(Holds his hand.)* Even this. *(Beat.)* This. *(Beat.)* There's always gotta be *(as she drops his hand)* some bullshit with you.

JIM: I know, right?

KAILA: Stupid.

JIM: I...uh...*(Starting for the door.)* I need to go.

KAILA: Now?

JIM: Yeah.

KAILA: C'mere.

JIM: What.

KAILA: C'mere!

JIM: You gonna hit me?

KAILA: Get the fuck over here.

(Jim walks over to her. She punches down at his shoulders then pulls him in close and hugs him long and hard.)

JIM: I'm sorry.

KAILA: Shut up. I'm not talken to you.

(The hug is both angry and tender. Jim smells her hair and holds her tight. Silence.)

JIM: Do I take myself too seriously?

KAILA: You take me too seriously.

JIM: I miss you.

KAILA: I miss you too.

JIM: Why's your breath always smell sweet.

KAILA: Cuz Ima princess.

JIM: Oh.

(While hugging, Kaila feels the recorder in Jim's pocket. She removes it.)

KAILA: What's this?

JIM: Hey—

KAILA: What is—

JIM: Yo give it back.

KAILA: What is it?

JIM: It's…..It's my journal.

KAILA: Can I hear it?

JIM: No.

KAILA: Can I say something.

JIM: You wanna record something?

KAILA: Yeah.

JIM: What do you want to say? *(Kaila presses record.)*

KAILA: *(Into the tape recorder:)* I… love… you. *(Kaila presses stop.)* In case you forget. *(Kaila gives Jim a long kiss on the cheek.)*

JIM: Sooooo, make-up sex would be totally out of the question? *(Kaila pushes him away smiling.)*

KAILA: Didn't you say you had to go?

JIM: I do.

KAILA: Bye. *(He turns away. Their fingers are still linked. Kaila pulls him back and they hug.)* You used to come here *soo* late…show up outa nowhere and end up in my bed. You'd be like tryna be quiet, but I'd always wake up. And…there'd be paint all over my body in the morning.

JIM: I wasn't really tryna be quiet.

KAILA: In the shower in the morning. I'd see the colors come off me.

JIM: I shoulda washed my hands before I came to bed.

KAILA: I didn't mind. It was like….like I knew I'd been with you.

JIM: What are you gonna do?

KAILA: When?

JIM: In summer and fall.

KAILA: I don't know.

JIM: *(Mumbles.)* Gonna be with other guys?

KAILA: What?

JIM: Gonna be with other guys.

KAILA: Not as many as you.

JIM: Oh you funny.

KAILA: I try.

JIM: Good bye.

KAILA: Don't go.

JIM: I have to.

KAILA: Wait.

(They hold each other in silence, eyes locked. Kaila leans in real slow. Jim tries to kiss her, but she backs away. Again Kaila leans in and again Jim tries to kiss. Kaila backs away. Kaila leans in and Jim doesn't move. They finally kiss. It is a long sad kiss.)

JIM: Bye.

(Kaila mouths the word "bye" but no sound comes out. Jim exits. Kaila fights back tears as lights fade out.)

Act 2, Scene 5

(Normal light up to Jim alone on stage. Jim rewinds the tape and presses play.)

KAILA (on tape): I... love... you.

(Jim stops the tape and presses record.)

JIM: Entry 2150. *(Long silence. Jim stops the tape. He rewinds it and presses play.)*

KAILA (on tape): I... love... you.

(Jim stops the tape recorder as lights black out.)

Act 2, Scene 6

(Lights up to Victor and Sonny. Victor is scribbling in a notebook while Sonny bites his fingernails.)

SONNY: Can't believe Cody brought that motherfucker. Cody's shady.

VICTOR: Why couldn't you just fight'm?

SONNY: What?

VICTOR: If you're gonna fight, then fight but—

SONNY: Fuck that.

VICTOR: What if he didn't run?

SONNY: Then he gets it.

VICTOR: What's wrong with just fightn'm? *(Silence.)* Why you gotta come like that?

SONNY: That's just how I get down. He thought I was playen son. I'd fucken cut'm from his ear down to his chin so's every time he looks in the mirror he sees that shit and he remembers, "Damn, I should a never fucked with Marter like that." *(Beat.)* That's how I get down.

VICTOR: That's fucked up. *(Jim enters.)*

JIM: *(Tossing Sonny the ring.)* Here.

SONNY: Fuck, thank you. Yo, good lookin.

VICTOR: We still paintin? *(Silence.)*

SONNY: Jim, sorry about...They was bein rude. They need to listen to you.

JIM: You still cuttin people?

SONNY: Nah, but that kid, man, they go over everyone.

JIM: So what?

SONNY: So what?

JIM: So diss his shit.

SONNY: Son, he's a toy, I got a lot more shit to lose.

JIM: You woulda cut him over that?

SONNY: Son, if you wrote on like one a Picasso's canvases, I bet he'd stab you in the eye with a fuckin paint brush.

VICTOR: I was feelin all a that shit you said, Jim. Everyone's so ignorant.

SONNY: You know I had your back though?

JIM: Don't touch me! You did not have my back!

SONNY: I was fighting for you!

JIM: You was fighting against me!

SONNY: I was—

JIM: Don't you get it. You heard one word I said tonight? Do you ever think about what you do? You're so fuckin.......I'm just sayen, shit'll catch up with you.

VICTOR: Karma man.

SONNY: Huh........(*Sonny holds the ring.*) What you think I should do with this?

JIM: Give it back maybe.

SONNY: I know, but, like where should I leave it. Can't just put it where it was.

VICTOR: Teller the truth.

SONNY: What truth?

VICTOR: Sorry Ma, I just needed to smuggle your ring in my friend's rectum.

SONNY: Ima put it in her sock drawer. She'll find it in like a week. We paintin?

JIM: I dunno.

SONNY: You don't got shit else to do.

VICTOR: It's like what you said.

JIM: How's that?

VICTOR: We'll do some shit that needs to be done. So?

JIM: I dunno.

VICTOR: C'mon man.

JIM: I'm not really in the mood.

SONNY: Nah fuck that we paintin.

VICTOR: You down?

JIM: I guess.

SONNY: You got any spots?

JIM: I think so...no I know a spot.

SONNY: Where at?

JIM: The Lower.

VICTOR: Sixth borough.

SONNY: What is it?

JIM: Huh?

SONNY: What's the spot?

JIM: It's a wall. Unprimed. Victor, I could crash at your place tonight?

VICTOR: Yeah. You don't need to go home at all?

JIM: Nah.

SONNY: So this is it?

JIM: That's what it looks like.

VICTOR: Really makes ya realize.

JIM: What's it make you realize?

VICTOR: *(Beat.)* I don't know.

SONNY: Jim, don't take no shit in there. I don't care who it is. Don't let nobody punk you.

VICTOR: We c'have another meetin when you get out?

JIM: We'll see.

SONNY: We got enough cans for a army tonight.

JIM: So let's use it all.

VICTOR: Les do dis.

SONNY: What you have in mind?

JIM: You guys help me do a top to bottom?

SONNY: No doubt.

VICTOR: Course.

SONNY: A' wait here a minute, Ima run home real quick.

VICTOR: That's like fifteen blocks.

SONNY: Could you wait?

JIM: Hurry up.

VICTOR: Don't take a fucken shower. *(Sonny exits.)*

JIM: Victor, you got a bike yet?

VICTOR: No.

JIM: You want one?

VICTOR: I wasn't gonna ask but…yeah.

JIM: *(Handing a key.)* You know where it is?

VICTOR: Yeah.

JIM: Don't let it get rained on.

VICTOR: You really fucked me over, Jim.

JIM: How's that?

VICTOR: Who'm'I gonna paint with now?

JIM: You know people. What about Sonny?

VICTOR: Sonny's cool for a couple seconds, you know I can't stand none a those kids. Ima just be on the dolo.

JIM: That's the best way to go.

VICTOR: I'm really fuckin depressed.

JIM: You be alright.

VICTOR: Kaila was cool about the ring?

JIM: Kaila's cool.

VICTOR: You don't mind if I uh, kick it to her while you're away…I keep her warm for you.

JIM: Thought you was afraid a her?

VICTOR: You said she likes me?

JIM: Kaila's crazy.

VICTOR: I swear you two are gonna get married.

JIM: I wouldn't complain.

VICTOR: At your wedding, I could be the best man?

JIM: Yeah, you could be the best man.

VICTOR: So I'd make a speech? They do that right?

JIM: They do that.

VICTOR: Did you write down that shit you said tonight? I mean did you know what you were gonna say?

JIM: Sort of.

VICTOR: Why you never told me?

JIM: Huh.

VICTOR: Man you never told me nothin. You should have. You shoulda told me. All that shit, what you said tonight, sometimes that type a stuff, that's all I think about, all the fucked up shit thas goin on, rich motherfuckers droppin bombs on the whales or whatever. But, in my head, you know? I wish I could say things like you.

JIM: You don't give yourself enough credit.

VICTOR: No, I know I could say some interestin shit sometimes, but, talkin in front a mad people, fuck that. I'd get a rash.

JIM: A rash?

VICTOR: I can give myself a rash with my mind, the back a my hand, sometimes my feet too. A little Jedi trick I'll teach you sometime. *(Beat.)* A what if they listened tonight?

JIM: What you mean?

VICTOR: What if everyone heard what you said and they was down? No fights, no cops… Everyone's like, "Alright, whas next?"

JIM: We'd have to decide on places and times for meetings, like like other ones.

VICTOR: No, I mean like what would we all do, what comes next?

JIM: Whas next?

VICTOR: What's the action? If you think about, if shit was really gonna go down, like let's say I was gonna die, no I was or like say I'm gonna get murdered. So I need help and it's crucial. So I get all my people together, and since they know shit's crucial, they all get their people, and then all of those people's people's people. You follow me?

JIM: Lotsa people.

VICTOR: Mad fuckin people, like a protest. And we all walking together, fillin the streets *fillin the sidewalks.* And all for this fight or whatever, you know for me, but now it's for everyone. And people got bats and bricks and and Phillips head screwdrivers. This big fuckin mob. And we all running, just all out sprints. And shoutin like, "Aaaaa"!!! *(Beat.)* But who we attack?

JIM: I dunno.

VICTOR: Well lemme know when you know, and then it's on, like "Aaaaaa"!!!

JIM: *(Gives Victor dap.)* Yo it's a deal. *(Beat.)* So what colors you got for tonight?

VICTOR: What colors don't I got. Yo I hate rackin with Sonny man. Clumsy retard, yo. I can't go back to Home Depot for like two years.

JIM: They seen you?

VICTOR: We ran out with the shit. They gettin smarter over there. Don't sleep on Home Depot.

JIM: Yo, how stupid is stealin paint, I mean it's gotta be the bulkiest, cheapest thing to steal. There's expensive ass power tools sittin around an we rackin paint. That's just dumb. Why we do that?

VICTOR: Tradition.

JIM: What tradition?

VICTOR: You gotta steal your paint. Stealin paints different, it's not really like stealin.

JIM: Why do you steal?

VICTOR: Cuz I'm Gato.

JIM: Gato huh?

VICTOR: *(Loud mysteries whisper.)* Gato.

JIM: That's why you write that?

VICTOR: What?

JIM: That's where you got that name from?

VICTOR: I don't know.

JIM: You're Puerto Rican right?

VICTOR: I think.

JIM: *(Chuckle.)* You think?

VICTOR: Cuz I'm not sure, about my father, cuz...

JIM: I forgot about that. Yo, I wasn't really laughing.

VICTOR: I remember when I was like 11 or 12 and I was watchin TV and my cat Mel kept walkin back and forth up on the couch.

JIM: That the one your brother killed? *(Victor is drawing throughout this whole speech and doesn't look up once.)*

VICTOR: No that was Rocky. Mel was the nice one. So she kept steppin on me. And I'm just watchin TV, right? But she's like walkin circles in my lap, like the way they do before they sit down, and she's like steppin on me, you know? And then...like I don't even know what's going on, but I've got a fucken hard on...and then she sits down on me. And I'm like paralyzed. She's lyin in my lap, I could feel her purrin, and I'm lookin at her and I can't move. Then I just get so fucken angry that I just pick Mel up and throw her on the floor. She whimpers and runs away and I feel so disgusting I could cry. *(Looking up.)* So I sat there and cried.

JIM: Damn.

VICTOR: That's disgustin right?

JIM: That's how come you write Gato?

VICTOR: I guess. That's how all my relationships with women have been since. It all started with Mel.

JIM: What women?

VICTOR: Fuck you man, I got women...A, don't tell Sonny, thas personal—

JIM: I know. *(Jim writes something in Victor's book.)*

VICTOR: Who's Sandy?

JIM: Tell her I gave you the number.

VICTOR: What's it for? She needs a boyfriend?

JIM: They need an art teacher. They have a art class for kids...you could teach.

VICTOR: I could teach? Really?

JIM: Yeah.

VICTOR: I'll call it.

JIM: But...I don't think it pays.

VICTOR: That's OK. *(Showing his book.)* You like that A? Does it look like how Restart used to do his A's?

JIM: *(Looking at what Victor's been scribbling.)* A little. *(Sonny is entering. Victor sees him but pretends that he hadn't.)*

VICTOR: Where is this fuckin guido? He stop to make spaghetti or somethin?

(Sonny is in a daze. His words are slow and somewhat monotone.)

SONNY: I gave it to her.

VICTOR: Like in her hand?

SONNY: I put it on her finger.

JIM: Was she awake?

SONNY: Yeah.

VICTOR: What'd she say?

SONNY: She didn't say nothin. She didn't even look at me. She, she wouldn't look at me.

VICTOR: You OK? You look mad shook.

SONNY: I'm good.

VICTOR: I'm prouda you, Sonny.

(Short silence as Sonny regains his train of thought.)

SONNY: We ready to go?

JIM: Yeah.

VICTOR: *(Standing between Sonny and Jim. He puts an arm around each of their shoulders.)* Gentleman. The night is young...*and she's horny.*

SONNY: *(Shaking Victor's arm away.)* The fuck offa me.

JIM: Let's go. *(Blackout.)*

Act 2, Scene 7

(Lights up real dim. Three figures enter and begin spray painting. The figures eventually leave. Voices are heard.)

CLERK: People versus Morgan.

DEFENSE: Ready your honor.

PROSECUTION: Ready your honor.

JUDGE: Mr. Morgan, the court is ready to pronounce a sentence. Do you have anything you wish to say? *(Silence.)* Mr. Morgan, you've been convicted of a violation of section 287, conspiracy to commit acts of vandalism. Since you've been in this courtroom before, I intend to see that you remember this. You are hereby sentenced to six months. You are remanded to custody. Bailiff take him away. *(The gavel pounds.)* Call the next case.

The sounds of inmates heckling Jim are heard. Lights up dim to Jim walking to his cell in jail. He is trying not to look scared. Lights cross fade to Kaila entering with her bag and her camera. She stops at a wall with a huge piece on it. It is large letters that say KAPTN. On one side is a boy in jail. On the other side is a girl with a camera. The letter 'A' is halo'd by a diamond ring, it says "Sorry Mom," over the ring. There is a cat sitting on one of the letters. There is a bent trumpet in one of the letters. There are hands that are just out of reach of each other. Flags are burning and someone's trying to pick up a dropped torch.

The KAPTN lettering incorporates the themes of unrequited love and political uprisings. Under the piece it reads, "IN CASE YOU FORGET." Kaila doesn't know whether to laugh, cry, or take a picture. She touches the wall. Blackout.

Act 2, Scene 8

(Lights up to Jim in his cell with Walter, his cellmate. Walter is much larger and older than Jim. Walter looks out of the cell with a cold and serious gaze. There is a long silence.)

JIM: *(Nervous.)* How you doin? *(Long silence.)* Listen um...I draw, you know, so if you ever need, uh, me to draw anything, I dunno, whatever, let me, just let me know.

(Walter gives Jim a long nasty look. Walter walks at Jim, then turns towards to his belongings and removes a card.)

WALTER: It's my grandson's birthday next week. You could draw somethin in there? *(Walter hands Jim the card.)*

JIM: Yeah, yeah. What's his name?

WALTER: Devonne.

JIM: Devonne, two N's? Like—nne?

WALTER: Yeah two.

JIM: How old? *(Silence.)* He a little guy? *(Walter nods his head. Jim scribbles vigorously with a pencil for a while.)* Alright...let's um...just... Like this is just a outline. Yo, if I had some colors—

WALTER: *(Snatching back the card.)* That's Batman?

JIM: I could erase it. The cape's too long an.... *(Walter retrieves the card. He looks it over sort of smiling.)*

WALTER: That's nice. *(Beat.)* Thanks, captain.

(Tape Light slowly creeps in as Jim is lost in bright-eyed revolutionary scheming. As lights fade to black Jim almost looks optimistic. Blackout. A message is projected:)

> *"Let me say*
> *at the risk*
> *of seeming*
> *ridiculous that*
> *the true revolutionary*
> *is guided by feelings*
> *of love."*
> —Che Guevara

(End of play.)

◆

GLOSSARY

To buff, buffed: To erase, erased.

Burner: A well-done piece that has good bright colors, good style, and seems to "burn" off the wall.

Cap, Fat, or Skinny: Interchangeable spray-can nozzles fitted to the can to vary the width of spray.

Crew: A loosely organized group of writers who also tag the crew initials along with their name.

Fill: The solid interior color of letters on a piece of graffiti.

To front: To hassle, pick a fight, or intentionally mislead someone.

Getting up: To hit up anything, anywhere, with any form of graffiti, from a tag all the way up to a wildstyle burner.

Going over: One writer covering another writer's name with his/her own.

Hip-hop: The culture in the late 1970s and early 1980s that spawned the graffiti culture, break dancing, and hip-hop music.

Hit: To tag up any surface with paint or ink.

Mad: Crazy or lots.

Outline: The drawing done in a piecebook in preparation for doing an actual piece. Can also refer to the outline done on the wall then filled in.

Piece: A graffiti painting, short for masterpiece.

Piecebook: A graffiti writer's sketchbook.

Rack: To steal, usually paint or markers.

Rusto: A generic brand of spray paint.

Tag: The most basic form of graffiti, a writer's signature with a pen or spray paint.

Throwup: Graffiti that is either quickly done bubble letters or a very simple piece.

Top to bottom: A piece that extends from top of the wall to the bottom.

Ultra-flat: A paint preferred by taggers because it sticks to things better than glossy paint.

Wildstyle: A highly complicated construction of interlocking letters.

Writer: A practitioner of the art of graffiti.

by Zakiyyah Alexander

Blurring Shine

CHARACTERS:

LUTHER: Mid thirties business executive. A wearer of many masks.

SPEAKER: He's keeping it real.

SHINE: Eighteen. A true believer in urban gear. Not afraid to represent.

SPOKENFO: Speaks the distorted fragments left from slang.

AVERAGE YOUNG BLACK MAN: Exactly who you think he is.

* *Note on 'Interludes' they should be played straight. The Speaker is a fun-loving television show host. Spokenfo is attempting to legitimately connect with the audience. Average Young Black Man is just what you might expect. Perhaps these characters are masked.*

* */—slash refers to overlap in speech*

Time: Here and now.

Place: L.A. or something like it.

Why: Because there is no choice.

◆

0.

(A spot comes up. LUTHER, clad in business attire walks into the light.)

LUTHER: Good afternoon and welcome. It's good to see so many of you in attendance. We have quite an exciting presentation. To tell the truth I've been so excited that I've barely slept seven hours in the past week, but the sleepless nights were definitely worth it. We are all a part of history today. People, we've made it to the big time. The big time.

As a company, no, as a family we have learned so much about our target audience; we hope to eventually triple our impact. Quadruple our gross revenue. Now, I am not a religious man, but if I were, well, I'd say an amen to that.

What, you may ask, what are we really offering? The answer is: everything. Turn on the television. Go into a store. Open a magazine or a newspaper. Do you know what the common factor is? It's us. We've got a hand in producing the big picture. And this is no small potatoes, people. We. Have. Gone. Global. That's right.

To put it in the most simplistic of terms: what we're offering is contextualization in the most base of terms—and that is no simple task. This MTV generation has no idea what they are, further than their disposable income can afford. That is where we come in. We are hip, fresh, exciting, and hot. People we are hot. Hot. And we will mold our audience (from the inside out) to want, no crave what we've got to offer.

Look to your left. Go on, this is the participation segment. What do you see? *(Waits for response.)* Now, look to your right. You don't see the classification of cool, now do you? No, what you see is the bourgeois class of society that shops at high-end markets and is ruled by an economic stratosphere that dictates a bland fashion sensibility. Let's face it, we are a bland group. Not at all cool—except for maybe Jenny over there in the corner. Ha, ha. No, seriously, I would never consider myself to be a trendsetter. I barely have the five minutes it takes to order my chai tea latté and make it to Pilates. No. We are well-educated consumers with careers. And that is definitely not cool. (How does Jenny do it? Ha, ha. We'll chat after.)

However, we know cool when we see it. And we know how to find the highest market value on it. And where does one find cool? Right under our noses. From our kids. That's right.

The long and the short of it (ladies and gentlemen) is in this twenty first century our corporation is finally prepared to unequivocally corner the market on the authentic version of cool. Hip cool. Urban cool. Ghetto cool. We'll prove to you that with our ten year plan we will single handedly be responsible for (quite possibly) having the greatest impact on branding history since the propaganda of World War II. People, this is big. Bigger than our greatest hopes and dreams. (Can I get an amen now?) So, settle back, hold on to your hats, and get ready...

May I present the construction of a new, advanced technological generation of manufactured...cool cool cool.

(*Blackout. Loud rap music plays.*)

I. 1.

(*LUTHER'S L.A. house. LUTHER is drinking brandy from a snifter and sorting through files in a mechanical way. Easy jazz plays. Doorbell rings. LUTHER looks up in a robotic way. Checks himself, answers door. SHINE enters; he has never been in a dwelling quite this extravagant. It shows despite his best effort.*)

LUTHER: Brother of mine, finally in the flesh.

SHINE: Yo, thought you forgot your blood living the goddamn high life and shit. What the fuck's up?

LUTHER: Wait. Let me get a good look at you. You're grown, man.

SHINE: It's been awhile. Had to get grown. You got old too.

LUTHER: I certainly have. How long has it been?

SHINE: Six years. Since Pop's funeral.

LUTHER: Six years. By god, Stanley—

SHINE: Shine.

LUTHER: I'm sorry—

SHINE: Shine. I go by Shine now.

LUTHER: Oh, I didn't know.

SHINE: S'cool. Would you take a look at this crib. Looks like you ain't no joke. Fuckin upscale and shit. Serious high life, livin like a roller.

LUTHER: I'm doing okay for myself.

SHINE: Sheeit, you finally set yourself up brother man. No wonder you been hiding yourself away. Do the same thing if I was you. Niggas know you got that much dough they be linin outside your door.

LUTHER: Actually I'm hardly ever home. Mostly bi-coastal.

SHINE: ...Oh...Yeah, that's cool.

It's been a long fucking time.

LUTHER: Last image I have of you, you were all limbs, trying to act like a man...Now you are one. Time. How have you been? I mean life. Has it been good? I hope it's been good.

SHINE: 'M chillin like a villain. You know, hanging low and figuring shit out. Maintaining.

LUTHER: Are you in school now?

SHINE: Naw man, I graduated from the school a hard knocks.

LUTHER: But college?

SHINE: I got my own plans. Might not seem like it, cuz I ain't a baller yet, like you. Wait a bit an I'ma blow up; be livin the sweet life witch you, dawg. Just wait.

LUTHER: Well...visualization is one of the best ways to attain your goals. And your mother, how is she?

SHINE: Workin herself to death like always. That's why I got a get a little a what you got and take care a her.

LUTHER: Your mother always was such a great woman. It's too bad our father was...

What are your plans?

SHINE: Sup with the third degree and shit? Baby, I don't hear from your ass in almost seven years and all you got is questions. Didn't come here for no lecture.

LUTHER: Sorry, I'm just a little...eager...Can I offer you a drink?

SHINE: Cool that. You got Hennessey—straight up?

LUTHER: Baby brother done grown up.

SHINE: Baby brother done been grown. I'm eighteen mutha fucka, done made it past the statistics. Way I see it; rest of this trip oughta be some kinda smooth ride an shit.

LUTHER: Let's hope. Cheers to a smooth ride. *(They toast. Freeze for five seconds.)*

SHINE: Don't nobody hear from you in years, and all of a sudden you on the phone talkin bout let's get together and shoot the breeze and shit. Didn't even hear from you when Pops was fightin for his last breath, but here you are—all bedazzled and bling blingin in this crazy crib talking bout let's catch up. We can't catch up, we hardly know each other. What the fuck we got to talk about?

LUTHER: Thing of it is, Stan—uh, Shine. Well, what are you doing for money these days? Do you have a job?

SHINE: What kind a question is—yo, hold the fuck up. Did my mother call you, is that what this shit's all about, cuz I don't need /no bullshit up in my—

LUTHER: That's not it. I'm asking, Shine. Me. Do you have a job?

SHINE: I get by...Got my little hustles here and there, ain't no big deal. Don't look at me like that. We all can't be you, Luther with your white ass Harvard/education and shit.

LUTHER: That's not what I meant.

I've got a proposition for you, Shine. Something that could possibly change both of our lives. For the better. A way to get your mother the break you and I both know she deserves. A way for you to have a little piece of whatever it is you want from the future. It's a way.

But I have to know that you're committed. And you can't fuck this up, little brother. No bullshit. Either you're with me, and paid very well, or not. One way or the other. There's no middle ground.

The choice is yours. (*Pause.*)

SHINE: ...Yo, tell me you ain't runnin up some crazy drug ring or some straight up undercover shit? Is that why you beein all mysterious? Word, that would be so hot.

LUTHER: Sorry to disappoint you, brother, but it's all completely legit.

SHINE: (*Breath.*) What I have to do?

LUTHER: Be yourself.

SHINE: And you gonna pay me for that? My Moms didn't call you?/Don't play with me, man.

LUTHER: It's the real thing. No strings attached.

SHINE: Yo, there ain't no milk left on my breath, knaw wha ah mean, son? I been around long enough to know there's always a string.

LUTHER: We're looking for someone about your age for research purposes. To find out what makes you tick. Look, it pays well, and it's either you or we find someone else. Interested?

SHINE: No bullshit?

LUTHER: I may be a lot of things, but I am never bullshit.

SHINE: What I gotta do?

LUTHER: You'd have to be informally screened to see if you fit.

SHINE: And I get paid?

LUTHER: If you fit the profile. Yes.

SHINE: How much? (*Luther writes figure down, passes it to SHINE.*)

Get the fuck outta here, son. Shit, sign my ass up. See if I fuckin qualify. Fuck that man, I be willin to do a lot a serious shit to roll in bills like that. That's ridiculousness.

LUTHER: (*Takes out a file and a pen.*) I'll ask you a series of questions, keep in mind there are no right or wrong answers. Ready?

SHINE: Shoot.

LUTHER: How old are you?

SHINE: Eighteen.

LUTHER: What terminology suits you best: Afro-American, Negro, Black, or Black-Hispanic?

SHINE: What kinda question is/ that about?

LUTHER: Please. Just answer.

SHINE: Black, baby. Fuck what you heard.

LUTHER: Place of residency?

SHINE: Uh, my Mom's. I mean, I live with my mother up in Downey right now, least till I get a crib of my own.

LUTHER: Annual income—?

SHINE: How the fuck I'm supposed to know that shit?

LUTHER: Over or under fifty-thousand?

SHINE: Under.

LUTHER: Over or under thirty-thousand?

SHINE: Under.

LUTHER: Over or under twenty-thousand?

SHINE: ...(Under).

LUTHER: Sorry, what was that?

SHINE: Under.

LUTHER: On average how much would you say you spend on your apparel?

SHINE: My what?

LUTHER: Clothes, shoes, jewelry. That sort of thing.

SHINE: Oh, um. Well these pants cost like a buck fidy. This jacket was like a gift, but it was at least three huned and change. (But I bet the chick who got it for me caught it hot, but anyway.) This shirt is around seventy. And. Oh, this chain, I dunno, it must be two, three huned, easy, son. I come correct.

LUTHER: That's great.

Okay we're done.

SHINE: That's it? Do I get the job?

LUTHER: The job is yours, if you want it. Each week you'll have to go through a series of questions much like this, and we'll film it. Sometimes you won't be asked anything at all, and you'll have to talk about whatever's on your mind.

SHINE: Yo, I'm ready for my close-up, dawg.

LUTHER: Brother, you should know, at times it might be...difficult.

You could still back out now with no harm done.

SHINE: Luth, for real I been doin some serious thinkin about my life and shit, right? And what I realized is yeah, I need some kind a change or somethin. Cause, well you don't know how it is in my hood. Shit's corrupt and whatnot. And. I look at you and see how you livin. And. Damn. I want some a that.

LUTHER: You give up a little bit of yourself to have something like this.

SHINE: You give up more when you don't got nothing but dreams.

Luther, thanks for giving me this kind a opportunity. I won't let you down. Promise.

LUTHER: I know you won't, brother.

So, I guess this is for you. *(Hands SHINE check.)*

Don't spend it all in one place.

SHINE: My big bro finally came back to get me. Always knew you would, cuz we family, son. We blood. That shit runs deep.

LUTHER: Sometimes I forget how deep it really is.

(Breath.) You've got our father's eyes.

It was good seeing you. And, Shine...we'll be in touch.

SHINE: Gotta get home and let my moms know I'm a be gettin paid like what. Legit and shit. Yo, she might just have a heart attack. It's a god-damn beautiful day. Catch you later, son. *(SHINE exits. LUTHER watches him go.)*

LUTHER: Sold. *(LUTHER picks up a phone. Dials.)*

Andrews? Luther here. We've found what we need...Yes. Start the paper-work. We're in business.

INTERLUDE A

(SPEAKER is on a studio set, campy music plays—a television show. SPEAKER often moves in order to be seen on the different cameras.)

SPEAKER: What's up, yo?

And we're back.

And it's good to be back.

It's time to take another in depth look at what is commonly known as the modern (hip-hop) black man. Who is he? Where does he come from? And how can we appropriate his style without any of that pesky violence that we see on the news?

Let's take a closer look at where the hip-hopper originates from. Surprisingly enough, they are usually found in the rugged urban terrain of large cities; often they live in groups clustered around large building structures known as projects. I should stress, that we are professionals, and that an untrained photographer or journalist or novice fashion maven should never attempt to enter such a climate alone. Do not try this at home.

However, the hip-hopper is known to venture out of its natural habitat occasionally. And you may ask, how would you be able to identify the hip-hopper if you came across one while shopping at the mall, walking down the street, even on the expressway—and what are the proper precautions.

Let's take a look at the hip-hopper in his natural habitat. *(Lights up on SPOKENFO; he is frozen.)*

Note how the hip-hopper of the urban type prefers clothes that do not fit. This is to ensure that his bulbous back-side is hidden from view.

Also, we have found that the hip-hopper prefers to show his inner wear (underwear, that is), and often will prefer to use brand names to mark where he is in a class system.

Let's get closer shall we?

Observe how loud the music, commonly known as hip-hop is played.

Notice that even when I scream very loudly he will have no reaction to this. AHHHHH! Fascinating, isn't it?

If you should come upon one on your own—do not be alarmed. Just like dogs they have a remarkable sense of smell and will be able to sniff out your fear. Rather, the correct line of action should be to make sure that your money and valuables are out of sight. They are drawn to economic pleasures like a carnivore to raw meat. Walk quickly in a determined manner, they are less likely to have a quick reaction this way, and most important—do not make eye contact. If you follow these steps you will out smart the urban male, and have a wonderful story to tell all your friends over brunch: how you survived your encounter with the hip-hopper. And maybe you'll pick up a few fashion trends for your next cocktail party, like this great doo-rag I've been sporting at premieres. Holler. And that's on the real, son. True that.

And now a word from our sponsors.

2.

(Harsh spot hits SHINE. He speaks to unknown source.)

SHINE: So, I'm just supposed to talk about what I'm wearing, right? Till you say stop? You people be wilin', but it's cool. I mean. A'ight, here goes. Um. Well, first off I'm wearin these cargo pants. Yeah. They're army green with big pockets and velcro on em. They're oversized, but not too much, y'know? Cuz that baggy shit went out with VCR's, right.

And. I got this thing about style, right? Like how cool it is to be the baddest one on the block with the hot shit, right. With the new joints.

Everyone see you walkin down the street and they give you like this little chill nod, like "A'ight, dog, we see how you hangin. We see what you got and we know it's sweet." And for like this moment in time you got yourself this little bit of...something big, and you the coolest nigga on the block.

Um, what else? So, all my clothes are oversized, right? I call it urban gear, y'know, with extra room strictly for comfort. Couldn't deal with no tight-ass shit like some pussy muthafucka. It's not me. This is me. It's like my signature, y'know?

Course, it ain't easy to be a black man walkin in these clothes all the time. Somebody in some store gonna be followin my ass around, and yeah,

course cops try to fuck with me, and white ladies be grabbin their pocket-
books and shit, but. Fuck it.

Way I see it, fuck you if you got a problem. Cuz how come it gotta be my
concern that this city is fucked up? Fuck that shit. This is me. You don't like
it. Fuck you. Ya heard? *(Light changes. SHINE freezes. Assumes a pose.
Freeze.)*

Ya heard? *(Assumes another pose. Freeze. Bright light flashes.)*

3.

SHINE: So my Moms baked you this pie. It's stupid, I know. I was all like
Ma, he don't want no baked goods, he probably gets his shit delivered. But
she was just like take it anyway, y'know. He probably don't get no home
cooking and whatnot. She wanted to thank you for everything, and...uh,
guess I do too. I won't let you down brother.

LUTHER: You really don't have anything to thank me for. It's just. It's been
so difficult to maintain a connection with the past and the present. (Sometimes it seems like the future is all I've got the time to consider.)

SHINE: Look, you don't got nothin to explain to me. I'm not a kid, y'know?
Shit happens. S'cool, dawg. We all got choices. But, yeah, it's been good to
catch up with you. *(Notices a picture.)* This your wife?

LUTHER: Oh. Yes. Mirabella. She's actually on holiday in Tuscany. She'll be
back in a few weeks.

SHINE: Yo, check her out. What, you married to a model and shit. Didn't
know you got down like that.

LUTHER: She's a very special person. I hope you get the chance to meet her.
Is there. Anyone in your life right now?

SHINE: I'm just chillin, ain't tryin to get caught up or settlin down no time
soon. Specially now that I'm a have loot comin outta the hiz-ouse, fuck
that. All I need is someone saying I got they baby. Ain't about to be nobody's babydaddy, knaw wha ah mean, son?

LUTHER: I hope you're not wearing yourself too thin.

SHINE: Look, don't hate. Just cuz you figured out where you gonna rest
your head for all time don't mean I have to.

LUTHER: I wasn't suggesting that. Guess I've temporarily forgotten what
it's like to be a young man with the whole world open to him. *(Pause.)*

SHINE: There's been some things on my mind recently. And we ain't never
really had the time to talk, like connect, y'know?

LUTHER: Shine, I know we haven't been very close. But. Well, it's my greatest hope that we learn how to trust each other. I'd like to be your friend.
I'd like to be your brother.

SHINE: Well, this is how it is.

When Pop got sick all he wanted was you. There I was every day holding his hand, changing his goddamn diaper for fuck's sake, but all he could do was call out "Where's Luther, where's Luther" like some broken record.

And, what could I do? Me, the prodigal mutha fuckin fuck-up. Sellin dime bags to get his medicine. Man, I was only twelve. Ma used to cry every night. And you was nowhere to be found.

How come you did him like that?

LUTHER: Let's have a drink.

We. We don't actually know each other so well. And you never had the opportunity, or pleasure (as it were) to meet my mother. She was one hell of a woman. Had this laugh that could make an evil man cry. And I watched her wither away from the inside out, and it was because of your, my father. Because he was unavailable. Emotionally, physically, everything. Watched him drink and smoke his dreams up, one by one. After my mother died (and she was dying for many many years) I left without looking back. I left him in the past, a stale memory I no longer had use for.

SHINE: So, you took off for your big fancy school and was like fuck you all.

LUTHER: No. I took off and became who I am today.

SHINE: Pssh, a success, right? Man, that's cold.

LUTHER: Maybe. But part of the reason I worked so hard was because there was nothing to go back to.

SHINE: And fuck everyone you ever knew who might remind you of who you was and where you came from.

(Even me.)

LUTHER: Shine, how was I going to be there for you when I had nothing, and baby, I had nothing. Didn't even have a reflection. All I knew was I had to keep going.

SHINE: *(Breath.)* Can I ask you something else?

LUTHER: Brother of mine, you can ask me whatever you want.

SHINE: You think. Think shit's different now that you went to that school, and you moved all the way out here? Think shit's better?

LUTHER: Not better. Different. More choices. But I have a secret for you. Go look in the bathroom down the hall.

SHINE: Why you want me to/ do that?

LUTHER: Go on and do it. *(SHINE exits. Pause. Then, he comes back in.)*

SHINE: You educated niggas be buggin the fuck out. Why you got your diploma in the damn bathroom?

LUTHER: Like you said we all have our choices to make. I made mine. But, at the same time I know what they mean, what they're actually worth. And they don't mean shit.

I am so sorry I wasn't there for you when you needed me to be. And I'm sorry that our father was...well, our father. You know I read this statistic once that said black men are eighteen percent more likely to be poor fathers based on the strains of society—but I don't believe that. He was a bad father, because...he was.

This is how it is, brother. You take it or leave it. Understand?

4.

(Harsh spot on SHINE. He speaks to unseen source.)

SHINE: *(Laughing.)* Okay, but man, this is some fucked up shit, but...whatever. Deal is, you be hangin out on a corner or a stoop with your boys, right? Most times it's with your boys. And you see this chick walking down the street, right? And the first one who spots her probably says something, like, "damn, check that shit out," right? And then we all look. And most times if we chillin we feelin nice, y'know, a little high, or whatever. Just feelin nice. So, whoever seen her first probably smile a little, y'know. Just a little smile. Just a little hi, how you doin, but just with the eyes, y'know...

Want me to do it for you?

A'ight...it's kinda like...this. Whatever, it don't seem the same when I just do it without proper inspiration, but. So, this honey walks by and whoever made the eyes steps forward and says, I don't know something. Something his boys will think sounds clever, but also might make this chick stop. And, you don't really expect her to stop. It's not about that. You just clownin, really. But if she do. And sometimes they do (bitches is crazy ghetto in this city too). If they do, well, you look at your boys, wink, lick your lips and walk down the street with her, right? Try'n sweet talk her long enough to get the digits. Once you got em you run back and show your boys. Simple.

(Light change.)

If I'm alone. That's different. You can't plan that shit. In the summer sometimes I fall in love like a huned times a day, no joke. Hunnies got on short shorts with tube tops and shit lookin all sexy, what's a brother supposed to do? So maybe I'm like, hey, miss, s'cuse me you lookin kinda good, you got a man. Or, s'cuse me shorty with the light eyes, you got a minute, I just wanna get to know you better. Let me rap to you a bit.

Sup señorita? You with the thonga, yo, I don't speak spanish, but I flip it so that you know. Smile. What, your man don't know how to make you smile? Bet I could make you smile.

Shorty, you see me lookin at you. Why don't you come over here? Got something I wanna whisper in your ear...

Why you walkin faster, hunh? Baby, I'm talkin to you—not your man. You know you heard me, you fuckin bad weaved witch.

Nappy headed fat lipped two dollar trick. Yo, here's five dollars, get your hair done. Funky assed attitude stank mouthed heifer. Lucky you across the street you fuckin BITCH. *(Flash. SHINE freezes.)*

5.

(Spot on SHINE. Spot on LUTHER. They speak from different worlds.)

LUTHER: It's common to hear that today we have more choices than any generation of civilized human beings. One thousand televison stations. Internet access. Eighty-two ice-cream flavors, if not more. All choices. But don't believe it.

What we have are perceived choices cloaked behind perceived diversity. In truth there are actually a handful of in-tune corporations behind everything. Everything.

SHINE: A'ight, so like if I saw some cat dressed well, I'd be like, yo, he's dipped, right? Or maybe, he's fitted but tryin to floss like he's all that.

LUTHER: Our highly commercialized environment is extremely aggressive. And we've got to do everything in our power to stay on the cutting edge. Language and style are one of our most important assets in this regard.

SHINE: How bout—cats be wilin' all up in this piece, cuz everybody knows that uptown is the shisnet. Shisnet is like "the shit," but flipped pimp style.

LUTHER: We must attack in the heart of the youth culture. Strike at their rebellious sentiment. We must sell the illusion of liberation. This is an enormous sales job. But. We. Are. Up. For. It.

SHINE: This kid was all up in my bumper, and I was like, yo, you better back the fuck up. This is my hood, ya heard? I'd say some shit like that.

LUTHER: There is only one way to ensure longevity.

SHINE: Anyway, this bitch with the stank grill tryin to step to me like some trick hoe. But, you know she jockin you too, right dawg? No doubt. That'd be a ghetto situation.

LUTHER: We must listen to what is being said, and say it back. What we need to sell is: the *illusion* of choice. This is a totalitarian system—that is, when it works.

SHINE: Yo, let's chill at the party and be bling-blingin all up over it. I gotta friend who always be sayin shit like that.

LUTHER: What we're selling is anxiety. So they'll keep coming back for more.

SHINE: Let's get blazed and shit, ya heard? Like it's four twenty on the real.

LUTHER: We have broken the code of authenticity.

SHINE: I'ma dip outta here.

LUTHER: Decoded the hieroglyphs of their reality.

SHINE: No, I gotta bounce. I'm ghost.

LUTHER: Unearthed the secrets of their originality.

SHINE: That's what's really good.

LUTHER: Times are changing, people. Together, we can brand the world.

SHINE: Man, can we stop for a minute? Yo, I don't. I don't know what else you want me to say.

6.

SHINE: Yo, Luth this is amazing. It's beautiful. I don't know what to say.

LUTHER: You like it then?

SHINE: It's off the hook. Straight up. I ain't never seen no car like that. You serious? It's mine f'real?

LUTHER: Consider it an incentive, and, well. A thank-you.

SHINE: No one at home's gonna believe this shit. It's like a video.

LUTHER: Drive them around and check out the horsepower. The surround sound speakers. The customized rims. They'll believe you.

SHINE: I wish...Don't you ever wish Pops could see us now? Fuckin chillin like this.

LUTHER: Shine.

SHINE: Look. I know you two never saw eye to eye, but. Don't you think he'd be proud?

LUTHER: The old man's in the ground. Let's leave him there.

SHINE: But, don't you think we—

LUTHER: Look at the time. I've got to pick Mirabella up from the airport.

SHINE: Finally I'ma meet wifey, hunh?

LUTHER: Absolutely. She's an exquisite woman. I've never met someone as refreshing as her. I'm a lucky man.

So, Shine, if you'll excuse me—

SHINE: I'm a bounce. Get outta your way.

And yo, thanks, for the wheels, son.

LUTHER: You deserve it. You're doing one hell of a good job.

SHINE: Give my love to wifey.

LUTHER: Will do. (*SHINE exits. Alone, LUTHER dresses methodically in front of a mirror.*)

Brush hair back to front seven times on the right side. Seven on left.

Check skin. Moisturize ashyness away.

Clean glasses. Not a spot.

Run pants with lint brush. Run jacket. Missed a spot.

Buttons buttoned. Even this one here.

Creases creased. Yes.

Fingernails clean. No long nails. No hang nails. Soft skin. Yes.

Shoes spotless.

Add lip balm. Teeth clean. Breath fresh.

Perfect. Perfect. Perfect.

Pronounce all the end-ings. I am speak-ing clearly to you.

Practice small smile: Yes, just park it in the lot, thanks—this is for you.

Can I see a wine list with that, yes, of course.

Excuse me, which way are the restrooms?

Thank you, thanks very much. Yes.

Medium smile: James, good to see you. How's the wife? Great.

Linden, next time we tee off let's do mimosas. That's right.

Congratulations on that hefty merger. Go team.

No, no, no, I've got the bill. You got it last time, hahahahaha.

Hey Babs, could you take this message for me, and let Bert know I'm in.

Thanks. Thank-you. No, really, thanks. Good to see you. Take care. Bye-bye now.

Drinks are on me.

Large smile: Darling, you look wonderful. How was your trip?

A vacation in Spain would be fabulous.

Baby, you are the greatest. Of course I mean that. I do.

I. Love. You. I really do...Really. (*Mechanically, LUTHER switches off, prepares to leave. Checks himself one more time.*)

Wear the mask. Own the mask. Become the mask.

(*Breath.*) Perfect. (*LUTHER exits.*)

INTERLUDE B

(SPEAKER reading a letter. Campy music plays.)

SPEAKER: What's up, yo?

And we're back.

And it's good to be back. That's what's good. Word. Keep it locked right here, you heard?

Today we have a letter all the way from a woman in Minneapolis. She writes:

Dear Speaker,

First let me say, I have always been a big fan of your show, and whenever I can't catch it on TV, I make sure to Tivo it and watch it after Oprah.

(Isn't that sweet? Well, flattery will get you everywhere, and that's on the real, Boo.)

Recently at a tupperware party my girlfriends and I were talking about the invasion of the hip hop culture, and what part (if any) we should play in it. We consider ourselves to be very progressive. We turn a blind eye to inter-racial dating, are big fans of motown, and love soul food. But, we do real-ize that there is always a threat of danger when dealing with this particular group of society.

My question is: what should I do if I come across an angry black man? Are there any ways to protect myself and my well-being? I am a strong believer in non-violence, and hopefully will not have to ever use the shotgun my husband keeps behind the kitchen cabinet. As a woman, however, I feel an inherent sexual threat. Are there any precautions I could take?

Signed, Desperately trying to do the right thing.

Well, Ms. D.T.T.D.T.R.T., you've raised a very important issue, and one that I'm sure many have thought about, and that's for sheezy. What to do if the urban male crosses your path. Let's take another look at the hip-hop-per. *(Lights up on frozen SPOKENFO.)*

Notice how easily the slang falls from his lips.

The anger and frustration in his eyes.

Oh, yes, and how he uses his sex as an instrument of character. This is an animal that does not mate for life, oh, no.

He is always ready for copulation, and so the inherent threat is (of course) obvious.

So, what do you do if you suddenly find yourself confronted alone with this ghetto of situations? Well, don't overreact. We've found that certain words only threaten the hip-hopper. For instance we've found the biggest no-no's to be: the word "boy," as in "Come heah, bwoy." *(At the mention of these words SPOKENFO moves, slightly.)*

As well as that controversial "n" word, "nigger."

However, if you feel bold enough simply leave off the "er" sound and re-place it with an "a" as in "nigga," or perhaps "niggaz" and the hip-hopper will know that you're down, and mean no harm at all. (*SPEAKER speaks to SPOKENFO.*)

Relax, my nigga you know I feel you. (*SPOKENFO relaxes. SPEAKER has proved his point.*)

There are also many remedies that you might find in your own home that will calm even the most threatening of the ghetto male.

We have found that a mixture of kool-aid, gin and juice with equal parts of Alizé can put even the most wildest of species down.

If that doesn't work play a blend of "old-skool" beats (which we're offering for the low, low price of nine-ninety-nine), while showing him the back-side of a woman grinding (preferably in a thong th-thong thong thong). This can easily be found on any popular video network (like that of our sponsor).

Offer him a puff of cannibis, commonly known as weed. (If you don't have any, your children certainly do.) This should subdue even the largest and most angry of the hip-hoppers.

Most important, do not threaten him with incarceration. Rather, while he is drinking, or distracted by the music video, politely excuse yourself to call the proper authorities. This being done, sit back, relax and enjoy some Alizé yourself.

And, if that doesn't give you enough comfort, you may want to purchase this on-line edition of *Rappers Spread*. Published by the L.A. 5-0, it comes with hundreds of full color profiles and mug shots of the hottest thugs around. That's what's really good on the 411.

Well, I hope this answers your question, and feel free to hit me with a follow up email if you have the chance. This week you may notice I've been sport-ing arm bands from the couture street collection of Tanisha Tischman and, yes, I've also got a little bling thanks to the peeps from Tenement Chic. Make some noise like what. And remember to always, always keep it real.

And now a word from our sponsors.

7.

(*SHINE enters LUTHER'S office.*)

SHINE: Yo, Luth, I wanted to show you this new watch I got. It's so dope, fo real. I could check the time all over the world, like in Japan an shit. It's the hotness. Luth, you home? (*SHINE realizes that he is alone. He sits at LUTHER'S desk, puts his feet up. Picks up the phone, pretends.*)

Wassup it's Shine, in the mutha fuckin hiz-ouse. Betta act like ya know. (*Pause.*)

This is Shine, I mean...This is Stanley, that's right.

Put Martin on the line, have him book the jet, let's take off for Paris, whaddya say? Ha, ha, hahaha.

How hot would that shit be...?

Yes, this is Stanley. I'd like to arrange to have four supermodels come for a private shoot with me in the Bahamas, yeah, very private. Word.

Send my car around, would you, and put some Cristal on ice for me.

This is Stanley, yes, I'm running things now. Luther? Oh, Luther got all fucked—I mean detained. Yes, so you'll want to run everything by me. That's right. (*Phone rings. SHINE backs away, then looks around and answers it.*)

Yo—I mean hello. Um, no, this is his...business associate, yeah. The report? Uh. It's urgent?

Let me look for it. Hold on. (SHINE hesitates then looks through files on the desk.)

Case number seventy-three?

It says...It says that the data is in. Yeah. I'll have him fax it out.

...No doubt, I mean, definitely. Well alright...Thanks.

Good chatting with you too.

Bye. (*SHINE hangs up, and reads the file. LUTHER enters.*)

LUTHER: Enjoying yourself, little brother?

SHINE: Yo, Luth, I—

LUTHER: No, don't get up. You look comfortable.

SHINE: I just dropped by for a minute, and you was out, and I was just chillin, and the phone rang, and this dude said you needed to fax him the latest report. And. That's it.

LUTHER: Was that everything?

SHINE: Case study number seventy-three? What the fuck's that? What is alla this?

LUTHER: Research. I told you.

SHINE: Feels mad suspect.

All these questions I'm supposed to be answering. No matter what I say it's never enough.

LUTHER: I told you this could get difficult.

SHINE: Lately I been feelin like I'm spinning round on a turn-table. What's the shit really about?

LUTHER: It's good to ask questions, an inquisitive mind is a healthy one. But, there's no point in going over all the boring logistics, is there?

Let me try to simply explain. My company, the one we both work for, is one of the top five corporations in the world.

SHINE: True.

LUTHER: And we've got a piece of everything. Like, that watch. Why did you buy it?

SHINE: Yo, cuz it's crazy souped. It's got ridiculous functions. Internet access, digitally programmed, a camera.

LUTHER: You already had a watch. You don't need the extra functions, yet somehow you had to have it no matter what the price.

That's what we do. We make you want.

SHINE: *(Breath.)* That's crazy, kid.

LUTHER: It's an important role we're playing.

SHINE: Never knew it was that deep.

You wouldn't ever lie to me, would you Luth?

LUTHER: This is business, Shine. Don't take it personal.

I've got your best interests in mind.

Trust me.

SHINE: Yeah. We blood, right?

Guess I should bounce, unless. Man, you wanna visit the old hood? See what it looks like now. Could introduce you to my peoples, /an we could just—

LUTHER: Maybe another time, Shine. I've got a lot of work to get back to.

But say hello to your mother for me.

SHINE: No doubt.

But…maybe later, when you got free time, right?

LUTHER: That sounds great. I'll make a note of it…

SHINE: Cool that. Um. Catch you later, a'ight?

LUTHER: You bet.

Oh, and Shine, thanks for the message. You're doing great work.

SHINE: Yo, thanks, f'real. I mean it. Peace. *(SHINE exits.)*

LUTHER: Peace indeed.

8.

(Harsh light on SHINE.)

SHINE: Sometime it's like I don't got no answer for the shit ya'll be axin. You all be catchin me off guard an shit.

Course I respect myself. What kinda question is that? Like last week this nigga wanna step to me talkin all a this salty nonsense, an I was like, son, you don't know me, right? Betta step back, kid, don't play yourself. Had to

set him straight, right? Cuz that shit matters. Your street cred is like a re-
sumé. Sets up who you are. Can't let nobody take that shit away from you.
Lose that and you ain't got nothing left.

(Light change.)

Course I done shit that I ain't proud of. But. Everybody done some shit
they don't like to talk about.

There was this kid. Yo, I ain't thought about this in years. But.

Grew up round my hood, y'know? Like I went to school with him, and
knew who his parents was, but it wasn't really like I knew him for real,
right?

Anyway. He always had on pants that was too short, like flood pants.

High waters, dig? That was round the time when all your shits had to be
logo-ed out, right? But, his moms must a been buyin his shit at the five n
dime, cuz he always looked mad busted. A bunch of us was smoking in the
bathroom when this kid came in. And, yo, I don't know what happened, or
who started it, but we started sayin it was time he flooded his pants. Time
some high water actually dripped outta his pants. Finally, he must a been
real scared cuz he peed himself. And we just laughed. Kid spent the rest a
the day smelling like piss in his high water pants.

Thing of it was. It wasn't his fault for real. But when you a kid all you
see is what you see.

And.

That shit was years ago.

...Walter. That kid's name was Walter. *(Flash. SHINE freezes.)*

9.

(LUTHER on the phone.)

LUTHER: So, he picks up this sneaker, this prototype of this women's
trainer, from LAST season that wasn't selling. You get me so far? Yeah. He
looks at it, and get this, he says, "This is bug!" Yes, Anderson, like an insect.
Bug. He says, "This is bug. Oh, shit. This company is starting to get so
much butter!" Not better. Butter. He's a genius. The real fucking deal. Pay
dirt. No question. Bug. Butter. Genius.

(SHINE enters.)

SHINE: Yo, L, we need to talk.

LUTHER: Andrews, hold for a sec...Yup, our star player has just entered the
field.

How are you doing today, Shine?

SHINE: Bro, this shit's getting crazy.

LUTHER: Call you back. Right. Ten minutes.

What's going on?

SHINE: Look, in the beginning the shit was cool right? Sit down answer a few questions, leave. Easy. But lately—

LUTHER: Lately?

SHINE: It's getting outta control, man...

LUTHER: Shine, I think you're getting ahead of yourself.

SHINE: Sometimes they don't ask nothing at all. Just want me to talk. And. I don't know how to explain. But. Yo, something don't feel kosher. It's like they want everything I got so there's nothin left. They lock the door, and don't tell me how long I gotta stay. Sometimes it's like for fifteen minutes, but yesterday they had me on lock for the whole day. The whole fucking day. And. I ain't been sleepin well at night. Wakin up in sweats. Feel like people watchin me no matter where I go. Mad paranoia, on the real, son. Man, you gotta do something. *(Pause.)*

LUTHER: I know what this is all about.

SHINE: Good lookin out. I was like, yo, Luth don't even know what's goin on up here. I was tempted to be like, ya'll don't even know who my brother is. Betta show some respect. Recognize.

LUTHER: You're a shrewd, shrewd business man, *player*, just what I like to see. Runs in the blood.

SHINE: Man, I don't know what—

LUTHER: And you do deserve a raise for all your time. You are absolutely right.

SHINE: Luther, this ain't about no—

LUTHER: How's this figure sound to you? Can you work with this? *(LUTHER writes down a figure.)*

SHINE: Seriously, Luth, this really ain't got nothing—

LUTHER: Alright, alright, you've got me by the balls. How about this? But I warn you, we really can't go any higher. *(LUTHER writes down another figure.)*

SHINE: Yo, is you serious?

LUTHER: You deserve it, brother.

SHINE: Get the fuck outta here. For this kind a cash you could strip me naked, son. Fuck what you heard.

LUTHER: Way I see it, every man's got his price. Just got to make sure it's named.

SHINE: Word.

LUTHER: Well, Shine, I hate to be pushy. But, I really have to take this. You understand.

SHINE: *(Breath.)* I see.

Yo, cool that.

I'm a bounce. *(SHINE exits. LUTHER picks up the phone.)*

LUTHER: Nope. We're good. Right on schedule. Yes, Andrews. The word is bug.

10.

(Harsh spot on SHINE.)

SHINE: A'ight check it. Today, I'ma talk about love and life and values. Ready? Course you are. Let's see...I don't believe in marriage, or monagany or none a that shit. Cuz it don't work. It's not natural. On the real I ain't never seen that kinda white wedding bullshit work. Specially not with my parents. Fuck that.

Either you playin like you what she needs, or she playin you. But, truth is you both know that the whole thing ain't gonna last much more'n a minute. You just usin each other so you ain't gotta sleep alone.

And the shit just goes on and on and on.

Once I figured that shit out didn't matter who I fucked long as I was fucking. No reason to get all sentimental, ain't no ring involved. Just a moment in time.

So, yesterday I was downtown, right? Was gonna meet one a my boys later, so I went and had this drink in this shitty bar, right? Minute I walked in all these white girls was trippin. A bunch a them was drinking together, lookin like they was nice. Anyway. I sit down and order. One a them comes over, and offers to buy my drink, light my cigarette, whatever just so she could talk to me. *(Breath.)*

White girls is crazy, man. They be fucking trippin you up. Don't get me wrong, I been around. Had all types a girls on my shit, no doubt. And on the real pussy is pussy. It act the same. It taste the same. But with white girls. It's like from the get they wanna know what your dick's all about, right. See if the heavy and dark a my shit'll make em do tricks, make em cum for days. And they a little afraid, but that's what gets them wet. Then they can run home and tell their girls they made it with a black dude.

They wanna touch my hair—they always be sayin what beautiful hair I got. Wanna touch the kinks, feel the naps. Sheeit.

And the ones that stick around. They think they all advanced cause they could see past color and whatnot. And, yo, I'm a playa by heart. Used to thrive on it. Cuz you could fuck a bitch like that, fuck her like you can't usually fuck somebody; like you was angry. And not call her later. Cuz it's momentary. Just a story to tell.

Anyway, this chick, she steps to me. And, I'm tired, and she ain't all that pretty. But she wants me. And, for like a second, for this moment in time I thought I should just fuck her to fuck her. Fuck the shit outta this little white bitch the same way she done rehearsed it in her fantasies. But I didn't, cuz I don't do that type a shit no more. I'm serious, man. I don't. I don't hate like I used to.

11.

(LUTHER stumbles around in the dark, looking for the light.)

LUTHER: Fuck. Fuckfuckfuckfuckn. Shit. *(LUTHER finds light switch, turns it on. He is dishevled and drunk. He pours himself a stiff drink. Mumbling.)* Hm, yes sir Mr. Nathan.

Hmmph.

What can I get for you. Shit. The fuck. ThefuckyouthinkIam.

Shit. Hmmph.

Tell me. Tell me. Should tell you. Tell you. Who you think you talking to. Hmmph. Hhhh. Ha hah hah haha ha.

Next time it ain't gonna be like that. Fuck. Who the fuck you think I am? You think. Mutha fucka?

Shit. I am the player. The player. You heard? Playin alla your asses. Shit.

Can I get you a martini, sir?

Can I light your cigarette, sir?

Can I wipe your ass, sir?

Can I bend down so you can fuck me...sir?

Shhhh. I'm grown damnit. I'ma grown. See, see seeseeseee theythey they don't know. Don't even know who I am. Hmmph.

Tell me the proposal needs work. Tell me that I I don't know my clientele. Muthafucka I INVENTED the clientele. Shit. Who you think started the mother fucking Don't Hate campaign? This is my world, man, my shit. Who the FUCK you think makin this shit work? Howard? Ha, he works for me. They all work for me.

Wear the mask, Luther. Play the part, Luther. You ain't that kid from the hood nickel and diming on the streets no more.

Fuck.

Mr. Nathan, I'll be sure to get your approval. Yeah, you the one with your fucking ear to the floor, fucking selling your SOUL. Right. Shhh. See, seeseesee they don't know. *(LUTHER finds a hat of SHINE'S, puts it on. Looks at his image in the mirror.)*

Sup, muthafuckas. The baller is in the micky fickin hiz-ouse. What? Yo, what you say to me? Step close cuz I don' think I heard you correctly, boy.

I called you boy. What? You wanna step? Then step muthafucka or back off my grill. Cuz I'm comin correct, y'heard. This mah house. Betta act like you know. Yo, say my name. Say my mother fucking name. *(LUTHER takes off hat, assumes new posture.)*

See, the thing of it Nathan, you don't mind if I call you Nathan, do you boy? I thought not. That's Mr. Luther to you. Actually, just call me Mister. It'll be easier on both our ears. Ahahahahaha. Oh, Princeton was it? Oh, just undergrad? Never could stand Jersey. Not a fan of slumming it. Boston all the way for me. Yes, I rowed crew, slept with the President's daughter, graduated with honors. And it's been up up up since then. Straight to the top. Too bad affirmative action doesn't work the other way. We better black you up a bit, hunh? That was a joke. That means laugh. Ahahahahaha. Nathan, one more thing—get on your knees and stuff my black cock in your mouth. And Nathan, I want to see you smile when you swallow. *(LUTHER puts hat on.)*

What? Am I makin you unfuckincomfortable? Shit. Wouldn't wanna do that, baby. Naw, cuz you my nigga. Yeah, you my white nigga Nathan, and yo, that's a good thing. You my boy, y'heard? Say it with me, y'heard? Betta act like y'heard. Wasn't my ass that made the rules a the game, but you be damn sure I'ma play em. And I roll to win. *(LUTHER takes hat off.)*

Nathan, maybe you don't understand, but I am the mastermind of this deal. What, you think white boys found rap alone? You think it's all a co-incidence that we got kids talking the same talk, walking the same walk. Got white girls looking and singing like black girls. Got black girls think-ing they're white girls. Got the consumer audience so confused they're ready to buy anything just to have something sweet to eat. Honestly. Do you think that happens naturally? That there is no master plan. *(LUTHER puts hat on.)*

Betta reckognize that it's me, son. And I ain't goin nowhere. Ya heard? I'm runnin this town like what. I'ma change yo ass from the outside in.

Gonna make you do shit you ain't even know was possible. Gonna bleed yo identity so slow you won't even know it's happening, so slow you gonna think you enjoyin it. And by the end you gonna walk like me, talk like me, dress like me. Gonna be callin me god wishin you was me. Gonna be snif-fin my shit lookin for diamonds. And you gonna like it. You gonna love it. You gonna thank me. And you gonna mean it. Ain't no two ways about it. You gonna be kissin. my. black. ass.

I'm runnin this joint now like what. What? What?

(Blackout. End of Act.)

II. 1.

(SHINE in a spot. He stares out for a full fifteen second count.)

SHINE: Ya'll just gonna stare at me and not say shit?

(Light change. SHINE in a spot.) First thing is to buy yourself a cigar. My choice is a Wide Owl, but a lot a cats dig Philly's, or Dutchies. Your choice. Make sure the shit is fresh, though. Could fuck yourself up with a stale one. Right? You take it, and make an even cut straight through to the end. Now, you gotta get rid a the tobacco an shit. We don't need that. Okay, so cool, next thing is to take out the inside skin. Look how perfect I did it. Careful not to rip it. Takes practice and time. A'ight, next we need the herb. Make sure it's broken up proper, no seeds, no stems. Next comes the smooth part. Take the skin and lick that shit till it's wet. Give it attention like you do your lady. Just. Like. That. Now, we take the herb and spread it evenly. Cool. Then you gotta seal it closed. Best way to do it is lick that shit again, right? Now I know you thinkin, how you gonna smoke that soggy shit, but we ain' done yet. You need a flame, like this, and you heat that shit dry. Like that...See? A perfect el. Ready to be sparked. Yo, don't sweat if you can't get the shit right the first time. It's a skill.

(Light change.)...Fuck.

How much longer we got? And why the doors always gotta be locked? This ain't prison. I don't gotta say shit if I don't want to.

Hello?

(Light change.) A-yo, can we shut the camera off for just a fuckin minute an talk fo real?

Man. I don't know what you want me to say.

Ain't no words left. *(Breath.)*

It don't matter what I say, do it? Do it?

How come everything gotta wind up being corrupt and shit?

Can you turn off the fucking camera for one fucking minute?

You ain't gonna let me out till you hear what you want.

Tell me what you want to hear.

A'ight, word, you wanna know who I am? Fuck it then. I'm whoever you think I am. I'm a baller like what, a player, a fuckin pimp, shit. I'm that thing that happens in the blackest a night when you think you sleep but realize you ain't and wake up with a chill. I'm your fucking nightmares.

I'ma fuck yo shit up. I'ma get all into your crevices and steal what you didn't even know you had, an I'ma be high when I do it, y'heard?

Fuck, turn off the camera. Turn off the fucking camera!

(Light change. Shine raps Public Enemy's "Black Steel in the Hour of Chaos"

from the first line, "I got a letter from the government," to the end of the first verse, "I got a raw deal, so I'm goin' for the steel.")

(Light change.) Yo, I gotta pee. No, f'real. I'm not playin. Can we stop for just a second? I be right back. A-yo, I said I gotta use the toilet. We gotta stop. I ain't playin with you. Five minutes. I gotta piss. I said I be right back. We gotta stop. Turn the shit off, man. *(Breath.)*

Please. *(SHINE pisses his pants.)*

(Light change.) When I was a kid everybody used to say they knew I was meant for somethin big cuz I used to smile all the time. Said I used to enter a room and just light up the place or some shit. Said I used to just shine. So, they started callin me Shine. Don't remember when it happened. One day it just did. That's what happens with a name sometime. People just decide what you should be called. And they call you it. They call me Shine.

(Light change.) A'ight, look, I ain't playin no more. Tell me what you want me to say, and I'll say it. F'real. Tell me who you want me to be, and I'll be it f'real. Just. Let me. Go.

(Breath.)

(Breath.)

(Breath.)

(Light change. SHINE looks out, count fifteen seconds.)

(Light change. Tight spot on SHINE'S face.)

A. A. B. C. D. E. F. G. H. H. H. *(Breath.)*

I. J. K. L. M. M. M. M. *(Breath.)*

N. O. P. Q. R. S. T. U. V. W. X. Y. Z...*(Breath.)*

A. B. C. D. E. F. G. K. L. M. M. M. M... *(Flash. SHINE freezes.)*

INTERLUDE C

(SPEAKER in light.)

SPEAKER: What's up, yo?

And we're back.

And it's good to be back, on the real, yo. Keep it locked right here. On a personal note thanks for continuing to make this show number one.

Today we'll be taking yet another look at the urban man. Where does the hip-hopper originate from? Homies, the answer might in fact surprise you.

If you ask an average black man on the street about the history of hip-hop and urban 'gear' his answer probably won't shock you.

There's one now, let's ask. Excuse me, Average Young Black Man?

AVERAGE YOUNG BLACK MAN: Sup?

SPEAKER: Can I ask you a question?

AVERAGE YOUNG BLACK MAN: Shoot.

SPEAKER: Where does hip-hop come from?

AVERAGE YOUNG BLACK MAN: Well, it originated in part as a reaction to the economic bracket that black people lived in. There was a development of culture that could be insular, negotiated for and by the people. Clothing like baggy clothes grew from the concept of wearing hand-me-downs, extended from a copying of the clothing worn in the prisons and chain gangs, and represented a newer voice in society. Music and a language sprung from this as did dance until finally a new culture had surfaced in mainstream America.

SPEAKER: Thank you for your time, Average Young Black Man.

AVERAGE YOUNG BLACK MAN: No doubt. A-yo, could I give a shout-out to my peeps?

SPEAKER: Certainly.

AVERAGE YOUNG BLACK MAN: Yo, I wanna give a shout out to all my peeps in Sunset, sup dawgs we livin like what. South-side. Wanna give a holla to all my boys—and you know who you is. Make some noise like what!

SPEAKER: Give me some love.

Now, that seems like a perfectly rational answer, doesn't it? Hip-hop was born because a culture needed a voice of its own. Reasonable.

Reasonable but wrong. Hip-hop was actually the brainchild of a certain Ludwig Van Heis of Eastern Germany. Due to his ethnographic research he discovered that there was a market gap in urban cities. According to his research an entire percentage of the market was being overlooked leaving out many of the underpriviliged and under-represented communities especially those found in black and latino neighborhoods. He was so excited when he realized this that he made a call to America shouting, "I have found an idea that will make the tip-top of the economic stratosphere crumble." But, due to his heavy accent and bad connection, all the person on the other end heard was "hip-hop" and thus a culture was born, true that. In honor of the crazy ghetto economy of today I'm wearing a gold cap straight from the mouths of the hippest hip-hoppers around. Now this is a smile with flavor. Don't forget to keep it real. Say what.

And now a message from our sponsors.

2.

(SHINE at LUTHER'S desk. He is blasting music, and his feet are up. He has a black eye. LUTHER enters.)

SHINE: Sup brother?

LUTHER: Shine. What are you doing here?

SHINE: Moving in. Uh, uh, uh, don't say shit. It wasn't a question. My ass is already moved in. Gonna live like a king, son. Don't act like you ain't got room. I been through this place before, could live here a month, an you wouldn't even know.

LUTHER: This is a bad idea. Trust me.

SHINE: No, you trust me. You. Need. Me. Take a good look. Notice anything?

LUTHER: Oh god, what happened? Are you alright?

SHINE: Got jumped in the hood. Six cats tried to take my ass down in front of my own crib. Know what they said? Said I'm a sellout.

LUTHER: We should get you to a doctor.

SHINE: Am I a sellout Luther? Am I? Cuz here's the thing: I swear to god, last year at this time I would a gone back and taken somebody down, busted a cap. But you know what I did? I left in my four hundred dollar shoes. Waved goodbye wit' manicured fingers. Like a fucking punk. I was like, fuck all you ghetto ass niggas hustlin' for some cheese. I'm out. I grew up on those streets, son.

Who the fuck do I think I am?

When the fuck did I get soft?

LUTHER: You're a man with some sense. Good thing you got out before something worse happened.

SHINE: Something worse done already happened.

I'm tired, Luth. Tired of this treacherous shit. I'm supplyin you with important information, right? Goes both ways, you need my case study ass, and I ain't givin you shit less you put me up. No, brother, I ain't drivin back and forth no more bein caught in traffic and stopped by the 5-o. I want what you got.

Don't turn that shit down. I like it loud.

LUTHER: Understand me, Shine, if you move in here...well, let's just say I'm not sure how long my company will have use for you.

SHINE: Hell, you pay me and I'll sing as much bullshit you wanna hear. Ain't stupid, son. I see what's goin on: I'm the real mutha fuckin' deal. Ghetto superstar number seventy-three, right? Roll tape.

LUTHER: You've really got to weigh this situation carefully.

SHINE: Situation is weighed. It's carefully weighed, brother.

LUTHER: All actions have consequences.

SHINE: Word.

Don't start acting like all of a sudden you give a shit about me. Ready to sell your own flesh down the goddamn market for a buck, so fuck that. Least I still know who I am. You sold your ass to the man a long time ago. Fuck, you became the man. Cuz see, nigga I see right through you.

LUTHER: Shine, this is as a good a time as any to learn that this, life, is actually a game. It is. If it's my grammar that offends you, my clothes, my refusal to let my world be dictated for me, well all I can say is—they are my game pieces. And I. Will not be. Trumped. Ask yourself, what is your part in the game? Take a good look at yourself and ask the question—am I that fucking original? *(Pause.)*

SHINE: See, there you go tryin to intimidate me and shit. But, check it—this is my game too. And you gonna give me everything I want. It's what you call a quid pro quo relationship, right dawg? Tit for mutha fuckin tat. Learned that shit from watchin you, bro. Don't hate.

What you all got to eat in this piece? *(SHINE exits. Pause. LUTHER picks up phone, dials a number.)*

LUTHER: Andrews? I think we have a problem.

3.

(SHINE in a harsh spot.)

SHINE: Never thought I'd get so tired a hearing my own voice.

But, if ya'll don't care, then...whatever.

...So, I bumped into my old girl from high school a couple days ago. She was like my first love an shit, right? Charlane. Beautiful girl. Had these eyes the color a copper pennies dropped in the rain.

She told me once my biggest problem was that all I saw I saw through my own eyes. At the time, for real, I didn't understand her. I was like, yo, whose eyes you think I'm a look with. But she was serious.

Once she told me I was beautiful, and dig it nobody ever said nothing like that to me before. I was all like, no, baby, you the one who's beautiful. Cuz she was. But she looked at me, stared at me real hard. Then she came over and held my hand. And kissed it. She said this hand is big, and it is rough, and it is beautiful. She put her hands on my face and traced it with her fingers and said. This face is hard and it is soft and it is angry and it is beautiful. For the whole night she went over each and every part a me and let me know what she thought. Funny thing of it was I was crying, and I don't know why. She kept saying, I know you hard but you beautiful, and baby you dark and you beautiful, and you a fighter, but baby you got to know you beautiful too. Somebody has got to tell you so you know. So you always know.

I never told nobody that before.

...That's all I got to say about that.

(Light change.) Ain't no more words left. *(Flash. SHINE freezes.)*

4.

(SHINE and LUTHER: confrontation.)

LUTHER: Have a seat, Shine.

SHINE: Met Mirabella yesterday. How come you never introduced me to your wife before, hunh? Me. Your brother. Had to run into her in the hallway.

LUTHER: We've got something very important to discuss.

SHINE: Light skinned. Color a butter. Figures that you marry someone who look white.

LUTHER: I'm sure this really can't come as a complete surprise.

SHINE: Long straight hair. Smooth, smooth skin.

LUTHER: Up to this point your work has been exceptional.

SHINE: But she told me, bro, she told me you ain't been taking care a business.

LUTHER: Your work has been greatly appreciated.

SHINE: You wasn't laying down the pipe. Turns out you ain't never laid it down proper.

LUTHER: You've been a highly valued employee.

SHINE: So, I had to take care a business. And she thanked me for it several times.

LUTHER: I'm glad we had the opportunity to work together.

SHINE: And I thought, why, with such a fine wife would brother-man, not be hittin the shit every night.

LUTHER: It's been a very satisfying arrangement up to this point.

SHINE: And then I realized. Click. Just like that.

LUTHER: I hope that everything has been satisfactory for you as well.

SHINE: Big brother business man is a faggot. A straight up pussyfied punk.

(Long pause.)

LUTHER: Right on schedule.

(Breath.) Your services are no longer required at this company.

SHINE: Well, damn, ain't that a point for brotherly love.

LUTHER: Termination effective immediately.

SHINE: Ain't that a trip?

Well, I just gave your proposition some serious mutha fuckin consideration. And I decline your offer.

LUTHER: I'm afraid you don't understand.

SHINE: You need what I got. And I ain't done giving it. Y'heard?

LUTHER: Shine, Shine, Shine. I never knew that you had such an aptitude for business. Must be a family trait. But, I'm afraid that you have gotten the wrong idea.

Why do you think we hired you?

SHINE: Cuz you needed a pawn. Someone to clue you in to what's on the streets, right? And me. I'm perfect for that shit. Ain't no one like me.

LUTHER: No, Shine, we picked you to make sure that our research has been correct.

Let me be clear. Nice outfit, Stanley. Very cool. Pick that out yourself?

SHINE: Nobody got this shit yet.

LUTHER: We picked what you're wearing. Down to that little fro you're sporting with confidence. Nappy is officially in style. We picked it, we planned it, including all those little slang expressions you think you own. Take a look at this. *(Hands SHINE a picture.)*

SHINE: It's a picture of me.

LUTHER: Look closely, at the face. It's not you. It's the marketable modern black man in the age range of seventeen to twenty-four. It's a mock-up. This image was digitally constructed five years ago. Amazing isn't it? Dressed just. Like. You.

Take a look at this. It's not set to hit the market for another two years, but I trust you'll keep it under your hat. Cool, isn't it? Or should I say phat, butter, off the heez-ow, off the bracket—oh, wait that idiom doesn't come out until next year, but you know what I mean.

You fit the perfect marketable profile: income, residence in a low-income neighborhood, music, style, profanity, drug use, sexual activity.

And we were right, even down to the sort of woman that would turn you on.

SHINE: Mirabella—

LUTHER: Is an excellent actress, isn't she? Straight from grad school, don't worry she was very well compensated. Oh, and use of the word "faggot"— to tell the truth I didn't actually think we'd be on the nose about that, but well done, Shine. Looks like we've done our job very well.

The thing is you are a dime a dozen, my brother.

SHINE: You saying everything I known, everything I believed in was created in an office? That's crazy. Yo, I don't—

LUTHER: We took over hip-hop seventeen years ago. It's not an identity, it's a market. It was a job, Stanley. I chose you because you needed the employment, and I wanted to ensure that you could open your eyes to the big picture. It's big. Bigger than the two of us.

Don't look so crestfallen...Listen, the same game was played on me. And look, I survived.

SHINE: But, you ain't nothin but a shell. You ain't even real no more. This shit's crazy. I'm about to bounce.

LUTHER: I'm sorry. I can't let you do that.

Do you really think you can go back to living your life with the informa-tion I just exposed you to? We're talking about a billion dollar company, and knowledge that could severely set us back several years /and one kid from Downey isn't gonna bring this company down.

SHINE: Naw, hell no, muthafucka this shit is my life, and I ain't no sell out.

LUTHER: You think that you, a little snot nosed, uneducated kid from the hood is going to change a plan that has been in progress for longer then you've been alive?

You're playing my game now, Stanley. Fuck what you heard. And you know what the shit is? It's code-shifting, brother. It's being who we need you to be when we need you to be it. If I say you're from the hood, that's where you're from. See, I'm a chameleon, son. Ever muther fuckin changing. I didn't invent the game, but I damn sure know how to play it.

This is the auction block, son. Your interest has just risen. Better thank me for it. Without me you'd just be another nobody wanna-be thug from the hood with nothing. Cause you don't know how to be a man. And the only model you got didn't give you shit but a name, baby.

Go. Show me how you can change the future... (*SHINE goes to leave. He can't. He tries again, something holds him back.*)

SHINE: I came here cuz my big brother was gonna offer me this new thing called opportunity.

LUTHER: This is what opportunity looks like.

You walk out this door and you got nothing.

SHINE: Fuck that, son. I got something. I know I got something. Don't tell me I'm nothing.

LUTHER: Simple economics and bad luck. Not your fault you were born a poor black man. I'm offering you the world.

All you have to do is work for us.

SHINE: But you fired my ass.

LUTHER: Actually I terminated you from your previous position, but you, my brother, you have been promoted. (*LUTHER tosses a bag to SHINE.*) These are yours. Not to worry, it's the coolest shit around. The hottest sneakers, CDs, video games, keys to another new car parked outside. You'll have it before anyone else.

SHINE: What I'm supposed to do with this?

LUTHER: Just wear it. Live your life. That's enough.

SHINE: I could take this shit and never come back.

LUTHER: Due to some computer flub, you've got a small record of incarceration.

SHINE: Yo, I never been to jail.

LUTHER: Not according to our records.

Plus, I'm sure you'll want your mother to continue to live in the fashion she has grown accustomed to. We can make sure that she is always taken care of.

SHINE: My Moms?

LUTHER: It's what you've always wanted.

SHINE: I wanted respect. I wanted a brother.

LUTHER: No. You wanted fantasy. And you got that. You got that and more.

SHINE: *(Breath.)* You done disappeared me, Luth. Fuckin evaporated my whole world. There ain't nothing left.

No one'll have to know, right?

LUTHER: Discretion is of the upmost importance.

We have a deal then.

SHINE: ...It's all a game, right?

It's not like I can hate...right?

A'ight...

LUTHER: Welcome aboard.

Your first job will be to find number seventy four.

And, by the way, you'll be called Stanley from now on.

INTERLUDE D

SPEAKER: What's up, yo?

And we're back.

And it's good to be back. Hope you're keeping it locked.

I'm glad you could join us on our last day of a very special segment. Today, you're in for a treat, no doubt about it. Today, we have actual footage of the hip-hopper attempting to communicate in his own language. This is very sensitive material, and for mature audiences only, and not the faint of heart. May I give you the hip-hopper.

(SPEAKER pulls duct tape off of SPOKENFO'S mouth. Bright light hits him.)

SPOKENFO: Man, Ah ain' tryin to come up all in dis piece an spk some blazed out crzy shit. Man fuckin true what you heard. Word. Cuz on da real alls Ah gotta say is peep dis shit and holla. No doubt. Holla! Truf is dis piece got some crazy shit n cats be ballin on da real an yo, an ya'll best come correct. Yo, ya'll best ta listen, ya heard. Ah'm comin correct. Like what. Ah ain't tryin ta peep like what, cuz shit is rough—act like ya know mo fo's be sayin sheeit tryin ta act like we da ones fuckin ballin like we dipped fa sheezy ya heard. But it ain't true. Fuck. Yo, dis ain't how da shis-net spozed ta be comin out, 's twisted. What the fuck yo, yo, fuck, man Ah got some shit ta spk on da crzy dwn low, but ya'll gotta peep it, dis ain't no joke, yo what the fuck, man? Shit. Yo, mah shit ain't comin correct. Fuck. Yo, ya'll gets the shisnet fo sheezy, right? SHIT. On da real Ah ain't frontin we jes tryin ta keep it real but—yo, what da fuck's goin on? Da shisnet's crazy in dis hiz-ouse, ya heard? Ah ain't buggin. Yo, ya'll cd peep this shit, right? Say what! Ah ain't tryin to be fitted like a playa—yo what the fuck! Get outta my bumper an peep dis cuz it's serious on the real, yo. Yo, Ah got some shit ta spk on da real. Dis shizzle gots ta be represented on da flava dealy. Nigga, what da fuck. Fa sheezy, yo, Ah ain't gots no mo words on da real, yo. A-yo, yo, I got sm shit to spk on. Ah got sm shit ta say. Ah gots words. Plz, lemme spk mah words. Word, yo. Ah got some shit to flip ya heard? Some seriousness fa real. Gimme mah wrds. Yo! Yo, peep this. Fa real! A'ight? A'ight? A'ight?

(SPEAKER reapplies duct tape—and steps back. SPOKENFO struggles in attempts to communicate.)

SPEAKER: Fascinating, isn't it?

Now that's keeping it real.

Maybe there will one day be a time when we are able to communicate with the urban black man. If we can teach a gorilla to sign then by god, we may one day be able to decode the modern hip-hopper.

But until then, pick up the CD, *Still Ghetto* a compilation of all those popular tracks re-recorded re-mastered and re-digitized by the hottest hipsters around. Just blaze.

And now a word from our sponsors.

5.

(House lights are on. SHINE stands center stage, lit from behind. LUTHER circles him.)

LUTHER: People, we are selling a mirror, and that mirror is the market. If constructed correctly that mirror will tell our target audience what to think and feel. It will tell them who to be—if they buy what we have to sell. Is there an inherent responsibility in this? Of course, we are well aware of it. But, our research assures us that with the perfect strategic foresight our future impact on this culture will be positive. Imagine, if you will, a generation that has grown up saturated with the view points that we have outlined. Spirituality is in. Family values are *en vogue*. Violence is becoming less of a threat, social conformity is on the up up up. Thanks to our "don't hate" and "strive to be a baller" campaigns, well, progress has already been made. People, we may just be responsible for creating a new utopia.

In ten years, if we are as successful (as I believe we will be)—well, advertising will be all that's left. And each and every one of you in this room have played a part in making this our future reality.

Give yourselves a hand. I mean it. Applaud this achievement, we couldn't have done it without your continued support. I told you we were making history here. Together.

This brings us to a wrap—no pun intended. I hope it was informative. There will be a question and answer session over brunch and chai in the green room. I'd like to leave you with a few images that will hopefully tie up any loose ends you might have. Sit back and appreciate the hard work we are all doing for you, while you invest invest invest.

And people remember—don't hate. Ahahahahaha.

(LUTHER exits. Lights lower. Rap music plays. A slide show full of relevant fashion, music, and urban stars from rap to pop to actors and actresses. These images are reflected on SHINE, who stands impassive.

At the end of the barrage of images there should be images of audience members—perhaps walking into the lobby, perhaps while they watched the show and were unknowingly captured as consumers.

Blackout. Music swells. End of play.)

PART III

Solo Performance

The plays in this part, all featuring a solo performer, reveal Hip Hop Theater's important connection to *Djelia* and the role of the storyteller as communal history-keeper and cultural critic. One-person performance, however, can also reflect the current economics of commercial theater in the
United States. It is easier to mount a solo show than a larger performance
piece. It is also less risky, especially for mainstream theaters who may not
know if their subscriber base will support a genre like Hip Hop Theater.
Solo shows can tour more easily, especially internationally, and can be an
easy access point to the genre for a non–Hip Hop audience, as the solo performer will often make a direct connection with the audience. These pieces
are also often flexible enough to play at conferences, festivals, and alternative venues like art galleries, community halls, churches, synagogues, museums, and even living rooms.

Like other plays in this anthology, *You Wanna Piece of Me?* by Joe Hernandez-Kolski reveals the complex world in which Hip Hoppers live. Of
mixed heritage and part of a generation transitioning between economic
classes and educational opportunities, either for reasons of immigrant parents or grandparents and/or class mobility, Hernandez-Kolski weaves his
own life experiences into a performance that is part poetry-slam, part
stand-up comedy, and part autobiographical exposé. The format of his performance follows that of a distinguished line of solo performance artists
such as Tim Miller, Marga Gomez, and Dan Kwong. The uniqueness of this
piece, however, lies in the ways the piece is specifically Hip Hop. Hernandez-
Kolski doesn't just have a DJ on stage—he interacts with the DJ throughout,
being pushed and pulled by the music spinning and frequent interjections

from behind the 1s and 2s. Hernandez-Kolski self-locates by means of a chronology of musical tastes and narrates his shifting identities through a period in which Hip Hop itself was negotiating its own identity. Thus he suggests that the specificity of his own mixed heritage parallels Hip Hop's own hybridity—that Hip Hop is, perhaps, the Aztlan for this global generation of mixed heritage youth.[1] Hip Hop is a space that welcomes and appreciates mixed heritage as its own identity—not two halves of anything.

Rha Goddess is a well-established rap, poetry, and music artist who is highly respected not only for her creative work, but for turning down major-label contracts and self-producing in order to maintain the creative and ethical integrity of her own material. With *Low*, Rha Goddess brings together all these skills in a solo theatrical performance. The play's protagonist, Lowquesha, speaks in several voices, and the scenes or episodes move from straight narrative to internal dialogues, rapped fantasies, and epic tragedy, ending with a poetic tribute to all people in Hip Hop communities affected by the ways in which marginalized people, especially people of color, are often pathologized.

Rha Goddess is an example of the modern Hip Hop entrepreneurial activist. We Got Issues, one of several organizations she founded, is committed to training a generation of young women leaders, using the arts as a vehicle for self-expression. She also created the Hip Hop Mental Health Project to provide information and dialogue at performances of *Low* around the country. Rha Goddess reminds and informs her audiences about the humanity and struggles of individuals like Lowquesha, whom education and parenting have left behind, caught in a downward spiral of trauma with no adequate support services. *Low's* rapid descent suggests that "crazy" may be, in some cases, a condition of marginalization and the post-traumatic stress resulting from the way that certain lives are delimited and structured by mainstream society (see Leary 2005). The scenes with authority figures—here teachers and doctors—reveal the "colonization" of the mind that young people, and specifically youth of color, often suffer. *Low* follows the important tradition of "edu-tainment" and works to change people's attitudes and lives wherever it plays.

A third play, *From Tel Aviv to Ramallah*, by Rachel Havrelock with Yuri Lane and Sharif Ezzat, is a full-length beatbox theater piece. Because of its media content, it does not appear in the print version of this book but can be found online at http://www.press.umich.edu/special/hiphop/. The piece is

---

1. Another early example of Hip Hop Theater is *Mixed Babies* (1991), a short play by Oni Faida Lampley.

performed entirely by Lane and Ezzat—Lane speaking, singing text, and creating vocal ostinatos simultaneously while beatboxing (a virtuosic act that gives the impression of overdubbed recorded music) with visual artist Ezzat VJing hundreds of images behind Lane to help tell the story of two young men on either side of the wall separating Israel/Palestine. This groundbreaking piece is included for several reasons. First, as Hip Hop is about plurality, this play suggests its breadth. Human beatboxing is not only a fundamental element of Hip Hop performance, but perhaps one of the most useful skills for creating a mobile theater that does not need to rely on heavy technology, sets, or lights. The beat emanating from the body clearly connects Hip Hop Theater to its ancestral origins.

Second, how Hip Hop functions in conflict zones across the world is a crucial point of connection for people whose affiliation with Hip Hop is motivated by a concern for social justice and being part of a global culture of activism. A growing number of documentary films demonstrate the vital role that Hip Hop plays in youth activism internationally. For example, *Masizakhe: Building Each Other* relates how young people in South Africa connect Hip Hop to the rebuilding of the supposedly new, but ailing postapartheid South Africa. *From Tel Aviv to Ramallah* demonstrates how Hip Hop engenders survival—how it gives young people in traumatic and violent settings a sense of purpose and self.

Finally, *From Tel Aviv to Ramallah* embodies the interrelation of all the elements of Hip Hop and the power of bringing them together in a theatrical context. Lane's performance text relies heavily on sampling and mixing—his voice and body become turntables. Crucial to analyzing the complexity of his performance is understanding the aesthetic and technical language of DJing. Ezzat also participates in a form of DJing, but visually. This performance speaks to the multiple intelligences of the Hip Hop audience and connects to this culture's aesthetic context. In other words, together Lane and Ezzat speak their audience's language in three dimensions—auditory, visual, and textual—exploring form as much as content as the means of communication. The cross-cultural collaboration is also deeply Hip Hop and shows what is possible in Hip Hop's democratizing new world order—Lane is Jewish-American of European heritage, grew up in San Francisco, and lives in Chicago; Ezzat is the son of Egyptian immigrants, was born in Utah, grew up in Chicago, and now lives in San Francisco. This is Generation Hip Hop.

By Joe Hernandez-Kolski

You Wanna Piece of Me?

◆

<u>PRE-SHOW:</u>
(As the audience walks in, there are slides projected on the back scrim—Boon-docks comics, LA Cucaracha comics, etc. Lights fade. DJ Jedi enters and fades pre-show music.)
[DJ JEDI SCRATCHES "THE JEFFERSONS" THEME SONG WITH BDP'S "DUCK DOWN."]
> *We finally got a piece*
> *We finally got a piece*
> *We finally got a piece of the pieeeeee.*

<u>I. INTRO.</u>
(Center light comes up onstage. JOE enters.)
JOE: Waddup, y'all! Give it up for DJ Jedi on the ones and twos!
> I'm really excited that you're all here, thank you so much for coming.
> I've been writing a lot...
> Normally I don't preface my poems but this seems like the place and time
> I just wrote this in one sitting and it's very raw so if I lose my place...

It's a work in progress
It's a real rough draft but I've gotta bust it
You guys don't mind if I read from the page, do you?
I don't have it memorized yet
I'm sort of a slacker
So forgive me
It's kinda messy I might trip
Can you guys hear me?
I'm not sure if...
This poem's brand new
I'm gonna try and pull somethin' different off
Alright, I'm just gonna jump into it...

Actually, no, I'll do this one I have memorized
(Joe puts away paper.)
Yeah, my heart's telling me to do this one
I'm sorry I wanted to try something new
But this is the start and I wanna kick it off right so let me do this...
Ok, y'all
It's been a while
Since I've performed
This one
So bear with me
Hopefully I can
Remember
What I've done
When I wrote this I was never sure about
The middle part
So just go easy
I'm gonna let my work speak for itself...

I have to say that I was half asleep when I wrote this
So it's definitely grammatically incorrect
You can listen to it but I'm not
Responsible for the third line in the 2nd stanza
Where it doesn't quite rhyme
And there are four syllables where there should be
Five but my girlfriend at the time
Called and she was totally freakin' out and
Broke my rhythm
So don't hold it against me

It's not my fault
That's what I'm tryin' to say...

So I'm gonna do some poetry unless, Jedi, you wanna drop a beat and I'll freestyle
No, that's okay
I'm just gonna throw this at you.

This poem is entitled: "No Disclaimers."
(*Blackout*)

II. WHY HIP-HOP?
[DJ CUE—"IT'S JUST BEGUN" BY THE JIMMY CASTOR BUNCH]
(*Lights fade up slowly. Joe is moving in the center as the lights are fading up slowly. He's creating shapes that dance with the lights. He begins a dance routine and it's moving. He's flying. At some point, DJ Jedi switches to Lil Jon's "Get Low." Joe is startled, not sure what to do. He looks at Jedi like "What are you doing?" Jedi pays him no attention. The music switches to Chubb Rock's "Treat 'Em Right." Joe starts moving again. The music switches back to "Get Low." Back and forth, Jedi is controlling Joe's movements and mood. Back and forth, back and forth, faster and faster. Somewhere in there, Outkast's "Bombs Over Baghdad" makes it and Joe does his booty-poppin' best.*)
[DJ MUSIC GETS LOUDER.]
JOE: Top rock
  Pop 'n' lock
  Body rock
  Don't let it stop, Mr. DJ
  As I lace my sneakers
  Gettin' ready to battle this b-boy
  While the graf artists're playin' with their toys
  Sendin' visual stimulation
  To play with MC communication
  Don't let it stop!
  Don't let it stop!
  Don't let it stop!
[DJ MUSIC CUTS OUT]
  Hip-Hop!
  Hip-Hop's about
  Taking a punch
  In the center of/ your stomach
  Bending over/ Brushing yourself off/ And getting back up from it.

Hip-Hop is/Taking your dad's dusty ol' 45
Puttin' it on your/ Superfriends Mattel record player and
Makin' your basement come alive.
Hip-Hop is/ abandoned mattresses
When other kids were taking/ gymnastic classes.
Hip-Hop is challengin' the/ Status quo
Not flexin' in Benzes/ Tryin' to steal the show.
Hip-Hop's / A book, a thought/ A state of mind
Not "It's a business, yo/ I got ta get mine."
But
Hip-Hop's not/ Talkin' smack 'bout our/ Brothers, either
Just bring him in/ Make him feel he's in/ Help him let go of his fear.
Inclusion/ Treat a brother to the conclusion
That life begins again/ When he's ready to make amends.
Cuz when Hip-Hop's used/ In the right way
You can't say nothin'/ You're just blown away
A man or woman droppin' words for/ All who want to listen
They're tellin' you what's wrong/ What's missin' from the kitchen
How ya gonna eat/ When all you got is bread?
Don't you need somethin' in between/ To keep your bellies fed?
Ain't there somethin' wrong/ When the corporate roaches eat more/ Than
the kids
Somebody stand up reach out/ And feed these kids!
And I'm not talkin' Mickey D's
I don't mean Frito Lay
Give 'em that shit
They won't have energy to play.

Give 'em food they can chew on
Give 'em food that's tough
The Mighty Mos Def and Kweli ain't enough!
Well yeah, it's the first step in a/ Well balanced meal
But c'mon y'all/ It ain't enough to heal
The stomach pains/ of 10 million children sayin'
FEED ME MORE/ GIVE ME MORE/ KEEP THE ROOTS PLAYIN'

While I change my shoes/ And change my socks
Who needs Nike when/ I've got thoughts?

Hip-Hop/ You're the love of my life
Hip-Hop/ Help me change their sights

Hip-Hop/ You help me relax

Hip-Hop/ With you every day's a class.

[DJ CUE—"MOVE SOMETHING" (INSTRUMENTAL) BY TALIB KWELI & DJ HI-TEK]

Waddup, y'all! Yo, it's a pleasure to be here. Representin' Hip-Hop! Where are all of my Hip-Hop headz at?? Yo, let's get something started here.

When I say "Hip," you say "Hop." C'mon—HIP!

ALL: HOP!

JOE: HIP!

ALL: HOP!

JOE: When I say "Hip-Hop," you say "Rules"—Hip-Hop!

ALL: RULES!

JOE: Hip-Hop

ALL: RULES!

JOE: When I say "Hip-Hop Rules" you say "The World"—Hip-Hop Rules!

ALL: THE WORLD!

JOE: Hip-Hop Rules!

ALL: THE WORLD!

JOE: When I say "Hip-Hop Rules The World" you say "And It Won't Stop"—Hip-Hop Rules The World!

ALL: AND IT WON'T STOP!

JOE: Hip-Hop Rules The World!

ALL: AND IT WON'T STOP!

JOE: When I say "Hip-Hop Rules The World And It Won't Stop," you say "Word." C'mon, Hip-Hop Rules The World And It Won't Stop—

ALL: Word.

JOE: Hip-Hop Rules The World And It Won't Stop—

ALL: Word.

JOE: When I say "Hip-Hop Rules The World And It Won't Stop—Word," you say "Based on its globalization as a mass-marketed commodity that used to be simply a community-based form of self-empowerment until it was stripped of its authenticity for profit but WE'LL TAKE IT BACK!" Okay, here comes the beat. C'mon—Hip-Hop Rules The World And It Won't Stop—Word...

What? C'mon! What? Cut it Jedi. *(Jedi cuts music.)* Based on its globalization as a mass-marketed commodity that used to be simply a community-based form of self-empowerment until it was stripped of its authenticity for profit but WE'LL TAKE IT BACK! Cuz Hip-Hop's my life. Like KRS-ONE, one of the forefathers of Hip-Hop said—I don't listen to Hip-Hop, I AM HIP-HOP! Livin' it, breathin' it, eatin' it!

Cuz I believe that Hip-Hop can be an incredibly motivating force. Not this crap that you see on MTV. That's about 1/10 of a culture that's so much richer than that.

Hip-Hop today ain't like when we were kids, right? Back in the day the shit was raw, it was real. NWA wasn't a joke, they were talking about what was really happening! Where are the KRS-ONEs of the world? The Public Enemys? The X-Clans? Like back in the day!

JEDI: *(Cuts out the record.)* Um, Joe. What are you talkin' about?

JOE: Huh?

JEDI: Back in the Day?

JOE: Yeah, you know, back in the day, high school, when WE were kids, when Hip-Hop was real. New. FRESH.

JEDI: Yeah, but if I'm not mistaken, wasn't THIS your favorite band in high school…

[DJ CUE—"HOT FOR TEACHER" BY VAN HALEN]

JOE: Van Halen, yeah. But that song's from "1984," probably my least favorite of their albums, not counting the Gary Cherone ye—

JEDI: Or what about…

[DJ CUE—"REVOLUTION CALLING" BY QUEENSRYCHE]

JOE: Queensryche's "Revolution Calling," a CLASSIC.

JEDI: Or what about…

[DJ CUE—"CULT OF PERSONALITY" BY LIVING COLOUR]

(Joe and Jedi thrash to the music.)

JOE: Living Colour, YEAH, so?

JEDI: So why don't you tell them…*(With echo fade:)* THE WHOLE STORY.

(Slide shows Joe as a teenager standing with Vince Neil. Mullet and all.)

III. MY MUSIC

JOE: Yeaaaah, I had a mullet.

From little boy
To young man
It's my music that keeps me breathing
Help me do what I can
Now if you have a minute
I'll tell you my story
It begins in Chicago
On a northwestside 2-story

Classical's what I conduct
At the early age of three
Sundays mornings in the living room
I wave my hands to feel free.

At the age of six
Grease is the word
Olivia Newton John
Is all that I've heard
I hold the record sleeve
And stare into her eyes
Her pretty airbrushed face
Leaves me mesmerized.

At my tenth birthday
Good music doesn't exist
I want Huey Lewis
And I'm given…
[DJ CUE—"WHEN DOVES CRY" BY PRINCE]
…Prince
Purple Rain's in my walkman
For maybe 'bout a minute
But I haven't matured
So I put *Footloose* in it.

The teen years arrive
Jean jackets rule the streets
Hangin' out on Chi-town corners
To guitar riffs and heavy metal beats
Van Halen rules my world
A close second's Living Colour
Ozzy, Anthrax, the Crue
I listen with my surrogate brothers.

Now during the day
I walk the halls of Whitney Young
Studyin' on the westside
With the theatre crowd I've always hung
I'm crushed by rap and house
Music I don't understand
They take my rock and metal
Sample it leave it for dead
I'm a heavy metal headbanger
In a Black high school
Although I'm open-minded
I don't have a clue

When I throw my parties
There is no Run DMC
No Slick Rick
Only C & C Music Factory
Snap, that type of shit
But I do dig the club scene
Medusa's goin' late into the night
I still remember my exact spot on the dance floor
When I first hear…
[DJ CUE—"GROOVE IS IN THE HEART" BY DEEE-LITE]
…Deee-Lite.

Then college begins and
I arrive at Princeton University
Talk about culture shock
With minimal diversity
I grab onto that
Which to me is most familiar
I'm either on the theatre stage
Or in the multi-cultural center
And in a matter of moments
In a matter of seconds
Hip Hop and House rule
Leavin' all else past legends
Digable Planets, Todd Terry
New legends all around
Jumpin' in battles in New York City
There is no slowin' down.

I desire more
I'm growin' up fast
I enroll in Afro-Am 201
Introduction to Jazz
I learn more about Miles and
The beauty of Charlie Mingus
I listen to "Haitian Fight Song"
A mix of passion and bruised fingers
Powell and Monk
Takin' me to the highest heavens
I learn it was Mary Lou Williams
Who gave 'em their lessons.

And then comes…

[DJ CUE—"GET UP" BY JAMES BROWN]
I need not say more
The original funk the original groove
B-boys and b-girls to the dance floor!
[DJ CUE—"SUCKER MCS" BY RUN DMC]
Cuz now, for me, today, it's Hip Hop
The next movement of change
The Civil Rights Movement had Dylan
We've got many names
Kweli
Mos Def
The Roots, preferably live
Lauryn & my man, Common
And Tupac will never die.

Our music taste can't be stereotyped or generalized
Commercial radio pushin' falsely constructed lies
Keepin' our children separated and compartmentalized

I listen to everything from De la Soul to Rubber Soul
Bauhaus to Eek-a-Mouse to Deep House
Li'l Louie Vega and Mark Grant
To KD Lang and Robert Plant
Earth Wind and Fire to the Rolling Stones
John Mayer to the Commodores
Cecilia Bartoli to the Zero of 7 and Remy
To Stevie Wonder, Coltrane and Gorecki

I'm inspired by Kuti and Mellencamp's stories of struggle and survival
Their passion and perseverance is undeniable

And when it comes to dedication?
You've gotta clap
For U2 and old skool rap
KRS
P.E.
Rakim
EPMD
Simple Minds reminds us
[DJ CUE—"DON'T YOU FORGET ABOUT ME" BY SIMPLE MINDS]
Don't you forget about me
Don't Don't Don't...

[MUSIC CUTS OUT]
<u>Don't</u> let me be boxed inside
Reflections from a TV screen
The trickle down theory of a marketing scheme
I simply want
My Dave Matthews
My Cee-Lo
My Smashing Pumpkins
My Me'Shell NdegeOcello

As I continue to grow
My freedom is clear
Channels might try to profit
But beats, rhymes and my life are all I hear

My music allows me to breathe
I put it on when I wake
If it's gonna be another rough day, Lord,
I pray my boom box don't break!

(Blackout)
[DJ CUE—"THE MESSAGE" BY GRAND MASTER FLASH & THE FURI-
OUS FIVE]

<u>IV. MY LIFE, PT. 1</u>
(Lights up.)
JOE: "Why'd you do that, mom?
   Now I'm not gonna get any work!"
I am 12-years-old
And I am being a complete jerk to
My mom who tries to remain calm
As we sit in my agent's office

I just got my first headshot
And my mom put my name on it
"Joe Hernandez Kolski" *(Slide of headshot.)*

Now I was born Joseph Edwin Kolski
Joseph my Mexican grandfather
Edwin my Polish grandfather
The Hernandez added by my mother
Mexican pride the intended goal of adding
It to the other name but I complain

"I sincerely believe it will affect
My ability to get acting gigs"
Now the question is…where did this idea begin?
Imagine a young brown boy
Named Joey with Grandma Charlotte
Making pierogies
Her friends arrive and Charlotte says to them
"This is Joey, my Mexican grandson"
Which immediately for some reason reminds me of
"Francis the talking mule"
Now although only 3 years of age
The seeds of confusion
Have been unintentionally planted
By one of the most selfless women
Ever to live on this planet
Giving love was my Grandma's only bad habit
My Polish Uncle Edmund took my name and ran with it
"Hi, José"
"But my name is Joey"
"Your name is José" he would always repeat
And I'd just give him a hug & a kiss on his cheek
But it always stayed with me
Appearing every so often
This self-hate now revealed
Here in front of my mom in my agent's office
My mom decides that the Hernandez will remain as part of my name
And she comes up with a plan to help me embrace it

Even though being Mexican is an issue for me
Speaking Spanish is so cool to me
The way my grandmother converses in secrecy
With my aunts in the kitchen
Which I witness as a child hiding under the table
Thinking I am able to turn invisible
Listening in on their conversations
"If only I understood what they're saying"

"Mom, I wanna learn Spanish"
"Mijo, you wanna know the best way?
Visit your Tía in Mexico City
Where you'll speak it from sunrise to sundown
Every single day."

So for three months I lived in el Distrito Federal
Mexico City
Con mi tía y mis primos

I am on my first trip ever
Without my family!
Yes!

Señores y señoras
Damas y caballeros
Bienvenidos al primer "landmark"
En la vida de Joe Hernández-Kolski

I return with stories of
Los pyramides de Teotihuacan
The sun and the moon pyramids
Filled with history
Or the coast of Mexico in Zihuatenejo
Where I witness the most beautiful sunset ever and pray to God to
Please let me fly over the ocean at this moment
And I will go to church every Sunday for the rest of my...
Well, for a really long time.
Or la barbacoa
The barbecue!
Where I witness the unearthing of a dead goat
Buried
Cooking over hot coals underground
The blood dripping off the body and made into soup...
Are there any hamburgers?

I also return
Not only with incredible stories
And my first case of homesickness
But I just so happen to be twelve years old
Going through puberty
Three inches taller
With facial hair
And a much deeper voice

YES!
8th grade girls
LOOK OUT!

JOE HERNANDEZ-KOLSKI
IS HERE TO STAY!

Yeah
I wish it was like that
But my cultural identity
Can't be wrapped up that easy
What
Three months in Mexico
And I know who I am?
My identity
As I believe all of ours are
Is...a bit more complicated than that.
[DJ CUE—"KNOWLEDGE OF SELF" BY BLACK STAR]

V. JUSTIFIED
I
I hate
I hate the
I hate the fact
I hate the fact that
I hate the fact that I
I hate the fact that I really
I hate the fact that I really love the Justin Timberlake CD
[DJ CUE—"ROCK YOUR BODY" BY JUSTIN TIMBERLAKE]
(Joe dances as if he's alone in his bedroom doing his best Justin moves. Music
cuts out. Joe is busted.)
I feel like such a sucker
A trained capitalism monkey
"Oh, this is the flavor of the month?
Two scoops, please"
Ice cream all over my mouth
As I enjoy the ridiculously expensive
Production value of every track
Thank the Gods of pop music for The Neptunes!
Pharrell says
"Ladies and gentlemen
It's my pleasure to introduce to you
He's a friend of mine
All the way from Memphis, Tennes—"
Let me guess...

He grew up singing in his poppa's church choir
Making money by dancing on street corners
Listening to his momma's R&B records
Influenced by Stevie Wonder, Smokey Robinson and
Michael Jackson (no shit)
It's good to be white in America!
Whether you're Justin
Eminem
Britney
Beck or Beyoncé!
Now, Joe, you might say
That is a strong statement to make
JEDI: Are you sure you're not just bitter that they got a break?
You need to take a look at yourself
JOE: I'm not exactly a Nubian prince
JEDI: Are you sure there ain't some self-hatred going on?
JOE: Yes, I agree there's some of that happening
Anger at the way that I'm viewed
But my name is not what you call me but what I answer to
Soy Chicano y Polanco de Chicago
Half-Polish half-Mexican
Born in Chicago uniquely American
Still not sure if I should grasp onto my whiteness
Attempt to re-define it change its perception
Or criticize it say it was ill upon conception

White to me brings to mind…Moby Dick
Chapter 42
"The Whiteness of the Whale" where
Melville explains how white as an image of purity is
Merely a false creation of beauty

White to me brings to mind
The insincerity and plasticity of television

White to me brings to mind
All of the blond women
Supposedly only 15% of whom are natural?

White to me brings to mind
The arrogant, privileged asshole at the restaurant
Talking down to the employee serving him his food

White to me brings to mind 1961
Freedom Rides
Bus riders of all ethnicities
Being treated so viciously
By white southerners fearful of change
One woman describes seeing a man dragged
From the bus his eyeballs pulled out
Of their sockets reaching all the way to the side of his head
Fueled by hatred of skin

But that was 1961, yo
Over 40 years ago
The connotation of white has changed
Sting will tell you
It's a Brand New Day
Color doesn't kill people
People kill people
JEDI: Pay no attention to Raynard Johnson. *(Joe and Jedi look at each other.)*
JOE: 17 years old
In the year 2000
In the year 2000
Raynard dated a white girl in Mississippi
45 years after Till whistled
Raynard's found hanging from a tree
The veil continues to separate and divide
When the community screams lynching
And the coroner calls it suicide

There's such a chasm between the societies
Misunderstanding of true cultural value
It feels like mainstream media's singing
"Red Rover Red Rover send Shakira right over"
Mass produced stars for the
Mass consumed minds
Brown kids spendin'
Green bones on
White images from a
Stolen Black background

Or am I doing that which I oppose?
Am I closing instead of opening doors?

Do not judge by color of skin
Soul is deeper than color

Brown kids spendin'
Green bones on
White images from a
Stolen Black background

White to me also brings to mind many of my mentors
A white woman in Los Angeles dedicated to afterschool programs for all of
our youth
A wealthy white man in DC dedicated to health care for all Americans
A wealthy white college professor who taught me about the civil rights
movement
Two wealthy white men who helped make college a possibility for me
My grandfather who taught me to speak up for the disenfranchised
My father who created me
Dammit, I can not condemn myself
But I can't deny corporate wealth
Mere talent doesn't determine contracts when I see
Li'l Latinas with bright blue contacts

And I'm not saying that these are not talented people
Britney, Justin and the rest of the Mickey Mouse crew
On the boards at an early age
Being groomed by Disney
For the World Stage

And Eminem's "Lose Yourself"
An instant classic inspiring me
Like Bob Marley reminding *me*
"Don't give up the fight"
But don't act like you've never heard
Nas and how all he needs is
ONE MIC

All I want is our kids to be told they're right
You're right
You are special
You're right
You are talented
You're right

You are beautiful
You're right
You deserve a chance
You're right
The white kid at the open mic
Does sound "Black"
But that's fine
As long as he is himself *he is Justified. (Blackout)*
[DJ CUE—"ROCK YOUR BODY" BY JUSTIN TIMBERLAKE]

VI. MY LIFE, PT. 2
(Lights up.)
JOE: I arrive at Princeton and consider myself more a Chicagoan than anything else. I'm very headstrong when it comes to my Chicago heritage. I wish that I can say, however, that I'm just as headstrong about my Chicano heritage. See, I told you it's not as easy as one trip to Mexico when you're twelve and you're fine. I'm a freshman at my first Chicano Caucus meeting. I walk in the door—

and it seems to be mostly a bunch of students from Texas, excuse me, Te-jas, and I'm excited cuz this is the first time—
[DJ CUE—"POR TU MALDITO AMOR" BY VICENTE FERNANDEZ]
(Joe does his best to sing along with the ranchera, not knowing any of the words.)
And the worst, the WORST, is when I show up to a Chicano birthday party and everyone's happy, having a good time, the cake comes out...

Happy Birthday to—
[DJ CUE—"LAS MAÑANITAS"]
"Las mañanitas..." *(Joe does his best to sing the words. He backs out of the room.)*

So the layers are being added...Chicagoan, actor, headbanger, ivy-leaguer, dancer, Chicano...who doesn't know the lyrics to Las Mañanitas.

But none of it matters once my Junior year hits. It's some October morning and my phone rings.

(Groggy.) Hello? No, of course not, it's... it's 6:30 mom, c'mon.

Why, what happened?

Okay. Let me know as soon as you find out.

Walter, this kid that's been living with us…just shot a kid up in Minnesota. He was a part of a gang intervention program that my mom ran and he started living with us, living with me in my room when he was sent up to Minnesota to be a part of…I'm sorry. Hold on.

(Answers phone again.) Hello? Of course I'm awake. Uh huh. My mom says, as far as she can tell, "you know Walter. He was being a smart ass, teased some kid about his tattoo, the kid told him let's take it outside, they did, the kid pulled a gun, they struggled for it, it fell, and Walter got to it first."

Okay…Really…Look, I've gotta go. I've gotta get to class. I love you too. Bye.

I walk out of my door room and I feel like…My mom said, "Joey, pray hard, this is gonna be a tough one." Walter not only shot this kid but he unloaded the entire clip into his chest. *(Joe holds the gun as if firing it sideways.)*

1-2-3-4-5-6-7-8-9 bullets piercing this kid's skin.

The campus looks so different now. I feel like… I look at people and the place that surrounds me and I feel guilty, ashamed, pissed off. I stop caring about anything. I just start throwing papers together and turning them in. Nothing matters. I wanna scream at the world, "Do you know what's happening outside of our li'l ivy-covered utopia? And do you even give a shit?" And I'm screaming this in my own head, more to myself than the rest of the world. Why am I here? I feel like…I feel like it's my first day again and I'm standing next to my parent's car outside of freshman orientation.

[DJ CUE—"THE STUDIO CITY STOMP" BY JOHN LEITHAM]

(Joe performs an "interpretive dance" telling the story of his Princeton adventures)

1. *Slowly sits down into car seat*
2. *Gets out of car*
3. *Says goodbye to parents*
4. *Happy! Walking through campus*
5. *Enters dorm and falls asleep.*
6. *Wakes up!*
7. *Eating all the Frosted Flakes I want!*
8. *Taking notes in class*
9. *Gym work out*
10. *Performing in play*
11. *Cafeteria job. Dirty but loving it!*
12. *Reading*
13. *Typing paper*
14. *Staples paper but the staple gets stuck. Throws out staple and restaples.*

15. *Turns in paper!*
16. *Goes back to sleep*
17. *Repeat all steps but faster!*
18. *Repeat all steps again (except for "gym work out") even faster!*
19. *Exhausted. Finally going to sleep*
20. *Woken up by phone*
21. *Gets news of Walter*
22. *Hangs up phone & spins until center stage*
23. *Walking through campus in slow motion*
24. *Looks at watch*
25. *Sits down prepared to write*
26. *Types paper*
27. *Stapler gets jammed again. Keeps stapling until in tears.*
28. *Walks paper to turn it in, thinks for a moment*
29. *Sees each room disappear (classroom, dorm room, cafeteria, etc.)*
30. *Decides to turn in paper anyway*
31. *Begins to walk downstage and gets stopped*
32. *Asked to sit down*

(Blackout. We hear Joe breathing heavily in the dark.)

VII. SEVEN WORDS

December
Damn, it's too cold to be running
I haven't eaten all day I can hear my stomach grumbling
Merely 20 years old a Junior in college
Where I gain the knowledge
That spark on the side of the lake that night
A light that would forever change my life
The New Jersey clouds are pourin' down rain
My headphones can't drown out the pain
My running clothes are all soaking wet
I cannot cry there are no tears left
I keep thinkin' 'bout the hours before
I keep thinkin', "How will I survive this storm?"

I run so fast I'm losing my mind
I run so fast breath is hard to find

The Dean who's like a mother to me
Entered her office and said lovingly
"Joe, you've been suspended"

I sat there, I couldn't comprehend it
The golden boy was asked to leave
But I'd worked so hard at this university
From the theater stage to the school newspaper
From the dance studio to the international center
Running discussion groups directing plays
A volunteer Big Brother like a mouse in a maze
I kept running around took no precautions
Searching for food found only exhaustion
It came down to one big paper
Afro-Am History thank God my major
Started at midnight finished by nine
Printed it up
Turned it in on time
Not my best work but I figured I was fine
But my mind had come up with a different design
My body could no longer tolerate this arduous path
So my mind helped and found an escape hatch
I pushed eject and for a sec I believe I can fly
Then gravity arrived I had to leave for a year's time
Plagiarism would forever be in my file
A devastating thought as I run that last mile

I run so fast I'm losing my mind
I run so fast breath is hard to find

I arrive at the lake
My heart pounding headphones blasting
I've let my parents down shame everlasting
What am I to do?
I am no longer the shining prince of the family
My direction if I only knew
People make mistakes, but can that be me?
People make mistakes, but can that be me?
I approach the thought ever so gradually
I ask for guidance and direction
Is it possible that I'm human with imperfections?

And at that moment my life changes forever
The pieces of the puzzle have finally come together
At that moment my fears take flight

The doors in my mind open to a great new light
This is the chance I've been waiting for
The word "suspension" is nothing more
Than cartoonish implausibilities
I have one year with limitless possibilities
Ahead of me a wide open ocean
Behind me in my wake only false notions
Of punishment pitched at a speed blazing hot
I'm gonna catch it and say "Is that the best you've got?"
Suspend?
You can't suspend me
That's like trying to stop Inertia multiplied by Chi

Seven Words come to my mind
Seven Words I scream so loud breath is hard to find

I no longer live for my family I live for me
Within this crisis I will find opportunity

Seven Words come to my mind
Seven Words I scream so loud breath is hard to find

There will be no more guilt no more shame
No more martyrdom no more blame
I create the world in which I want to live
I create the life that I want to live
I am human standing here with no armor
I can finally live my own life with dignity and honor

Seven Words come to my mind
Seven Words I scream so loud breath is hard to find

I look up at the corner traffic light
It brightly shines red
I tell myself when that light turns green
Life begins again

I think I'll walk back
I'm tired of running
As I repeat seven words to myself:
"Bring on your warriors
I fear nothing." *(Lights transition.)*
[DJ CUE—"SPIRIT IN THE DARK" BY ARETHA FRANKLIN]

VIII. FEMINISTS ANONYMOUS

(Joe enters as a timid, shy "feminist.")

Hi, my name is Joe and I am a feminist

I guess I've always been a feminist. At least, I've always respected women.

And as I've gotten older, it's gotten worse.

It all started with Kathy Restis

We were both 3 years old

Naked and bathing together

Outside playing together

We were inseparable

She was my very first best friend

Until I left Chicago for South Bend

Indiana from the age of four to seven

Where I fell in love with Ms. Simmons

My teacher in kindergarten

My problem was getting worse

Enamored with Ms. Simmons by day

Playing catch with my neighbors Wendy and Jill by night

Well, at least until sundown then we had to be inside

And as a kid I always had close friendships with boys

From Dusty to Gary to my cousin Joe

But they were never enough, ya know?

I've always been addicted

Addicted to that female spirit

And I just wish I could do something about it

Why did my mother have to be such a beautiful woman?!

Why did my parents raise me to be such a responsible older brother to my
sister?!

Why were lessons on being a gentleman so important?

Opening doors

Standing on the outside of the sidewalk

Walking with a woman and not in front of her

Why can't I just cross that thin line

Between chivalry and chauvinism

Why did the girls have to write in my 8th grade year book

"Stay sweet and cute"?

WHY?

Why can't I just be an asshole?

Why can't I be the guy who gets the woman
In the one night stand with no strings attached?
Why can't I be the *Bad Boy*
Who's dark and mysterious
Leave women wondering "What did I do wrong?"
As I exit their life forever?

But...
I must take responsibility
That's the first step towards recovery, isn't it?
I am a feminist
I must first accept that before I can start my life anew
Dating the jiggy women
Pimp-slapping hos within an inch of their life
Degrading woman's natural beauty
Passing legislation attempting to control their bodies
But...
Before I enter this misogynistic utopia
I'm unable to understand how it's possible
That those who gave birth to us
All of us
Are forced to deal with
The catcalls and whistles on a daily basis
Let alone the glass ceilings and lower wages
Women constitute half the world's population
Perform nearly two-thirds of its daily working operations
Receive one-tenth of the world's income and
Own less than one-hundredth of the world's property?
Dear God, have we sacrificed our greatest gift
To this planet
For spokemodels?
In today's society
Is it really the less a woman has in her head
The lighter she is for climbing?

I challenge all men to think
Would you wanna change places
For one day?
(Joe returns to his "normal" self, acting a li'l self-righteous)
We wouldn't have the strength

So for
Sojourner Truth
Olive Schreiner
Rosa Parks
Indira Gandhi
Gloria Steinem
Jill Scott
And the girl from the Corona ad who's really hot
I take one more step towards recovery
By declaring I am a feminist
What are you? *(Blackout)*
(Joe is sitting in the audience. Applauding wildly.)

IX. THE RESPONSE

JOE: YEAH! Yo, man, I was really feeling that piece. That shit was tight…

Are you fuckin' kidding me? Do you really expect these women to fall for that shit? Feminist, do you even know who Gloria Steinbrenner is? Feminist my ass, you're just trying to get laid like the rest of us. Alright, let's say you're picking up your boy and he gets in the car and tells you about this great date he had the night before. The first question that you're gonna ask him is…Guys, help me out here. What's the first question he's gonna ask him? C'mon. The first thing that you're gonna ask your boy is—"Did ya hit it?" Cuz that's what you're thinking about all day. Okay, maybe not *all* day, cuz you're also thinking about what poem can I perform tonight to seduce a girl so I can hit it and do I have any condoms at home after I seduce the girl when I do hit it. What, you've got a problem with catcalls and whistles on a daily basis? When I honk my horn at a woman, that's just my way of saying "I appreciate you." Oh, but we don't wanna change places for one day, guys, we wouldn't have the strength—I've got all the strength I need right here *(grabs his package)*. Like you can intimidate me into feminism? "What are you?" the way you make your voice go really deep telegraphing to the women in the audience, "I'm really serious about this part of the piece. I'm sensitive yet very masculine." They're all techniques, son. Performance techniques 101. Lights! *(Joe exits theater. Blackout.)*

JEDI: Ladies and gentlemen, next on the open-mic, give it up for Poncho Joe.
JOE: *Pocho* Joe.
JEDI: Sorry. Poko Joe.

JOE: *Pocho* Joe.

JEDI: Punchy Joe, that's what I said. (*Joe gives Jedi a look. Before performing CLICHÉS, Joe puts the mic to the side.*)

JOE: (*Pretending to be barely audible.*) So this piece was co-written by me and my boy Stricke-9. It's entitled *CLICHÉS*. Can you hear me?

(*Feigning disgust, Joe brings the mic back out front. In a regular voice.*)
This piece was co-written by me and my boy Stricke-9.

X. CLICHÉS
I sometimes cry alone at night
About my light
My light at night
Like my nightlight
Plugged next to my bed
I dread Donny Hathaway
Can't keep away my NIGHTMAAAAARES
My fears got me sinking
These thoughts got me thinking
My third eye needs to blink-ing
Inking words
Words like herbs
Growing in my vocabulary garden
And the clarity is free of pesticides and vulgarity
Who fucking harvested my sincerity?!
My grandfather published Langston Hughes
I've been ohming since I was two
And if we're talking yoga moves?
I will levitate on you!
"Girl you know it's true
Ooh ooh ooh I love you"
You said your words
And what I heard
Words like
FIRM and
SILICONE and
LESBIAN KISS
Sent a tremor down there to my "magic place"
The heat coming off me like an open-faced reuben
I slid my fingers to my corned beef

Hoping no one would see my hand going back and forth
Like spreading mayonnaise
I wanna slide my hands where no one will see me
Tug my manhood
Up and down
Up and down
Up and down
Work the balls
Work the balls
Up and down
Up and down
Up and down

My environment made me the poet that I am
But this is not a poem about poets or poetry
I'm about romance
Never about performance
I'm about keepin' it real
I'm not about record deals
I'm about late-night cravings
Fuck daylight savings!
Time is on my mind
But I'm losing my mind
Due to time on my mind
Which I'm losing
You make me wanna jump in the shower
Where is the hour?
I should be spending it with you at a Starfucks counter
You're my chai latte and I need an ice cube
You're too hot for me
Too hot for me *(hand gestures 2-HOT-4-ME)*
2 HOT 4 ME but
I'm 2 HOT 4 YOU!
(Joe drops the mic. Arms wide open waiting for the applause.)
(Black out)

XI. DJ JEDI SOLO
JOE: ALL THE WAY FROM CULVER CITY, CALIFORNIA, GIVE IT UP
  FOR DJ JEDI!
[DJ JEDI'S SOLO.]
(Black out)

XII. WALTER

(Joe is seated center stage. In the dark we hear…)

WALTER: 4-5-6…*(Lights up slowly. Walter is holding the gun sideways like Joe was earlier.)*

7-8-9

You think that's cool, huh? Cuz it's not. I held the gun like this. *(Walter turns the gun right side up.)*

Fuckin' Joe. Li'l Joey Kolski! I'm touched that you've included li'l ol' me in your production. I hardly deserve such an honor.

Now, if I may, I'd like to give my own humble opinion on certain things. First of all, the fight broke out because a kid teased *me* about *my* tattoo, not the other way around. And just between the two of us…and I guess all of you…I killed the kid more over a bad business deal than a smart-ass comment. Of course the smart-ass comment didn't help the situation one bit.

The crazy thing is…the kid I killed was the adopted brother of the only friend I had in Minnesota. And he was Colombian too. I had no clue about this until it was all said and done. If I'd known he was my friend's bro, it might not have gone down the way it did. It was bad enough me killing another Colombian in Minnesota, what are the odds, but the bro of my close friend?

Oh, and I didn't unload the entire clip into the kid's chest. I did unload the clip, but it was sorta all over his body; there were holes everywhere.

"Stay sweet and cute." That shit really bothers you, huh? I wonder what was written in my eighth grade yearbook? It's amazing how being away from women for as long as I have has really taught me to appreciate them. Shit, the prettiest girl we've got in here is toothless and benches 350…and has a dick. But seriously, when it comes to women, I don't give a shit if they've got dreadlocks, fake titties, blond hair or hairy legs. My only problem is that I fall in love with a different woman every time I get a different letter. You know I'm a big fan of the señoritas.

Fuckin' Joe. Damn, kid, you were pretty hard on yourself back in the day. Your people had high hopes for you and apparently you felt it. You felt the pressure to succeed that bad, huh? I guess you can say this about someone who ends up in prison. The fact that I don't wake up and stab someone to death is about all that is expected of me. That's an accomplishment. When you become a part of all this *(gestures around him)* any and everything you do is deemed quite the accomplishment just as long as you don't end up in the hole. People are sometimes like, "Wow, Walter, you made your bed today. That's great! That's really really great." It's insulting how more often than not my peers and I are treated like retards…Oh, my bad. "Mental" retards.

But regardless, I wouldn't trade my life, my experiences, who I am or where I am with anyone else. Even though I killed that kid, I am a good person with good intentions. We are who we are and we deal with what is in front of us, good or bad, and that's my reality. You know, you and me both have been presented with opportunities to do good and we've done just that. We've touched other people's lives and that's all that matters. In or out of prison, ex-felon or not, young or old, that's just superficial crap. About the only difference is that your work has the potential to be noticed on a larger scale while mine, well, it goes noticed by the people who know me best and I'm just fine with that.

It's good to be here. I hope that I haven't complicated anything, what with all this rambling on and all but, shit, I saw you doing it so I figured…(*Walter looks offstage left. His mood changes.*)

I've gotta go. Feel free to bring me back anytime. My schedule's pretty free right now. Oh, except I begin tutoring this month. You wanna know something that is cool? Tutoring is cool. Cuz let me tell you, Joe, the respect of a real convict is worth more to me than that of any dignitary I could ever think of. (*Walter lowers his head. Lights fade. In the dark we hear…*)

XIII. COOL

JOE: Rick Schroder in his black leather pants/ Is not cool
George W. Bush speaking in Spanish/ Is not cool
Calling a burrito a wrap/ Is not cool
Calling a woman a bitch/ Is not cool
Hummers in parking spots labeled "COMPACT"/ Are not cool
Cell phones that ring in the middle of a movie theater/ Are not cool
Then the dude who answers it and is like "I'm at the movies, what you up to?"/ Is extremely not cool
Parking Enforcement Officers/ Are not cool
Forwarded e-mails that say things like
"Please forward this to ten of your friends or bad stuff will happen to you"/ Are not cool
The peroxide bottle that attacked Shakira and Beyoncé/ Is STILL not cool
Leaving a voice mail message and giving the phone number really fast/ Is not cool
Those mornings when it feels like your goals are completely out of reach/ Are not cool

A 21-year-old b-boy of mine
Being shot and paralyzed
For being at the wrong place at the wrong time
Is not only not cool
It is a painful reminder of the realities of living in our world today
And Neo-Cons using federal money like it's their own private piggy bank
Is not cool

I'll tell you what I think is cool
Smog free LA the day after a rainstorm/ Is cool
Quiet vibrating cell phones/ Are cool
Telling our children how special they are and how much we love them/ Is cool
Making eye contact and saying hello to a stranger on the street/ Is cool
Treating our women like the Goddesses that they are/ Is cool
The United Farm Worker's relentless pursuit of justice/ Is cool
Free Food/ Is cool
Cornel West's lectures/ Are cool
Any Toni Morrison book/ Is cool
Any John Mellencamp CD/ Is cool
A father walking with his son at the zoo/ Is cool and beautiful
Cute chicks in ugly cars/ Are cool
Voting/ Is cool
Enjoying what you do/ Is cool
Being alive in the present/ Is cool
Working to create change/ Is cool
Never giving up/ Is cool
(Taking a deep breath)/ Is cool
My producer Justin Yoffe/ Is cool
My director/ Benjamin Byron Davis/ Is cool
People who visit pochojoe.com/ Are cool
The one and only DJ Jedi/ Is cool
The audience tonight/ Is cool
Walking down into a dark, sweaty reggae club and hearing…
[DJ CUE—"YOU DON'T LOVE ME" BY DAWN PENN (STEALY AND
CLEVIE REMIX)]
…Is cool!

So, as we leave tonight and I thank you so much for listening
Please remember as I continue to remind myself:
Living your life by Rousseau's philosophy that

"All men are inherently good"/ Is cool
Treating all people as you wish to be treated/ Is cool
Giving your own life the respect that it deserves
That's the coolest of them all.
[DJ CUE—"IT'S THE REAL THING" BY THE IVOR RAYMONDE ORCHESTRA]
(Lights fade.)

by Rha Goddess

Low: Meditations Trilogy Pt. I

SETTING:

The present, Brooklyn, NY

CHARACTERS:

LOWQUESHA GODDESS: 25 year old Blacktina, round the way–Hip Hop B-Girl/MC from Brooklyn. Born and raised on tru skool and new skool Hip Hop. High energy, intelligent, street smart quick tongued & tempered, courageous, vulnerable, strong spirited, confrontational …a survivor.

Note: some character voices are recorded. They are specified in the following manner (Name-VO)

◆

1. Saying Grace

LOW: It is Sunday, I am 8
  And I am sitting at the table
  I have been left here with my sister Anna
  because I did not clean my plate
  I smell half eaten turkey bones
  with dry cranberry sauce,
  mashed potatoes and cold gravy

  But mostly, I smell cinnamon
  and the cold soggy, wrinkly
  skin that holds mushy orange flesh

  I will not eat it, no matter
  how long I have to sit here
  I like school, but I will be absent
  tomorrow—I will be right here
  Still refusing to eat it.

  "Hurry up and get it over with"
  says Anna, raising the left side of her
  lip—I can see her fangs,
  she's such a bitch sometimes

  "I ain't eatin it!"
  "Yes you are" She says
  "Eat it now before I come over there and make you"
  "No!" I say "you ain't the boss of me….."

  And she scoops the pumpkin colored mush
  into her hands and splats it onto my face.
  I gag for air as the disgusting slop goes
  up my nose.

  Anna is laughing hysterically

  "I hate you!" I scream
  scooping my own glop to sling
  I grab another and another
  as Anna runs around the
  new dining room table
  cackling like a witch

Then I grab yam guts in
both hands and sling them
at the same time, at last
I hit my target
The orange sludge slides down the side of Anna's
head and lands right on top of her Sunday blouse

"Look what you did stupid!"
All of a sudden we look
around the room, there is
sweet potato everywhere

Oh shit! Says Anna,
We better hurry up and clean this
up before Mommie gets back.

That night,
I am in the room I share with Anna coloring

The first time I hear it
I think it's coming from the TV

"Ay! Ay! Ay!
ANNA! Come here right now!"

Even before Anna can reach the
front room I hear my name
"Low did it Mommie—remember how
you told her to clean her plate…"

I am off my bed and out the
the door, I come in at the top
of my lungs, "No Mommie!
Anna started it, she threw
yams in my face."

Neither one of us can
finish because Mommie
has left the room—

We stare at the walls and the carpet
with the light on
They look disgusting

We stare at one another knowing
what will come next,
Run!

Mommie's footsteps are
already back on the
hall, she grabs Anna first
thank god, I see the extension
cord whip through the air and come
down on her legs and back

When you are being hit
with an extension cord,
it feels as if you are
being lit on fire
The cord leaves large red whelps
and Mommie
hits hard enough even to mark
my chocolate flesh

The storm is over and Anna and
I are on our knees with a
bucket of Mr. Clean and water
trying to get the dried
yam out of the rug

I will not touch another sweet potato
as long as I live.

2. Fifth Grade Assignment

(TEACHER-VO:) *Children, today I have the most exciting assignment for you
in honor of Independence Day each of you will create a family tree
All of us have immigrated to this country from somewhere else
so go back across the ocean and tell us where you are originally from...
and remember to have fun with it!*

LOW: Dwight who sits in front of me, we call him BlackWatch because he's
always wearing Dashikis and raising his fist like this *(gestures)*, is about to
go off—he says when his dad finds out about this he's gonna come to
school and shut the teacher down for giving such a racist assignment—
"Black people were sold in bondage that's how we got here! To subject me
to such humiliation as to make me admit to the entire class that I don't
know where I come from is cruel and unusual punishment."

Whatever! I'm still trying to figure out how to get more branches….Mommie swears she was an orphan. So that means it's just me, Mommie, Anna, and maybe Rosa her best friend.

Wait, I know! I'll do a whole section on my uncles, you know, Mommie's men friends? Let's see, first there was Juan, the mortician who smelled funny and always picked his nose, then Arthur with the really thick glasses who studied the Bible while on the toilet, then Hector who cried, any time Mommie asked for money, and Willie and his 10 dirty ass kids who always had they hand out, and um Luis who bought Mommie a red spandex dress and usta sing "the blacker the berry," then Danny, then Harold, then Melvin, no wait I think it was Harold, Melvin, Bobby, then Danny, then Charles, then Rudy, then Paul, hmmm, no, wait, then Jimmy, then Paul, and then Victor who wore panties and changed his name to Jasmine when they broke up, and my most favoritest of them all; Jonnie B. Jonnie B was the shit! I could tell Mommie really loved him too. He usta make the best barbeque chicken and fried plantanos, we ate real good when he was around. Always bringing me candy, and teaching me funny songs, he even knew how to argue, which was most important because Mommie is a professional. He'd just tell her, "Look a here, anytime you don't want my lovin' just let me know, I'm sure I can find somebody'll help me eat these pork chops." Next thing I know she'd be laughing and he'd be in the kitchen cooking up a storm…Mommie could never stay mad at him. But then one day he just stopped, no big scene, no last supper, he just disappeared. After he left, Mommie got real quiet, and there were no more uncles for a long time. I think she's hoping he'll come back, but I don't think he will.

Wow, look at my tree now!

3. Higher Learning

LOW: I am 16 and I am in Ms. Murphy's class
    Ms. Murphy teaches English. English is my favorite
    subject—except I don't like her. She's always
    talkin' about how Black and Latino authors were
    influenced by White ones, like White people
    where the first and only people on the planet to ever
    do anything right.

So most days I just ignore her lectures, but
I always read the books.

Jonnie B told me that lots of Blacks and Latinos
have done great things for America, but he says
they'll never teach you that in school. So when
Ms. Murphy announced that we were going
To study the Harlem Renaissance, I asked if I could
Read a poem by Langston Hughes and she said
Of course I could.

Jonnie B told me all about him, he was this really
great poet who wrote about the struggles
of being Black in America during the '30s and '40s and '50s.
He gave me a book of his poetry that I still keep under my pillow.
We haven't heard from Jonnie B in a very long time
and I've been re-reading the book because I miss him.

When Ms. Murphy starts to talk about Langston
I raise my hand. But she ignores me,
and goes on and on about how Langston
got his inspiration from Walt Whitman

I got so pissed off . . .
I took my hand down
took out my book
and started reading to
myself.

(starts reading aloud:) "What happens to a dream deferred?"

(MURPHY-VO:) *"Lowquesha, did you want*
To say something?"

"Forget it"

(MURPHY-VO:) *"Why don't you tell us*
How you learned about Langston Hughes?"

I keep reading my poem aloud, like I don't hear her
"Does it dry up like a raisin in the sun?"

(MURPHY-VO:) *"What's that you're reading?*
Give it to me...you can pick it
up at the end of class, but right now
you're supposed to be paying attention."

I go to put the book away cause
there is no way in hell I'm letting
her have this book.
She tries to snatch it out of my hand
and it rips.

I jumped up and smacked her in her face.
"You fuckin bitch! Look what you did!"

Now she's telling one of the White students
to run down to the office and get the
Principal.

"Don't you tell me what to do, it's your fuckin
fault you got smacked in the first place."
You not supposed to put your hands on me!
You not supposed to put your hands on my stuff either
you racist bitch!"

The principal who has just walked in
motions for Ms. Murphy to come into the hallway
She looks like she's about to cry

After a few minutes he swings open the door

I grab my stuff and storm out....
They gonna call Mommie,
I don't care
she'll take my side,
I know she will

4. No Type a Remedy

(DR. LONG-VO:) *Hi Lowquesha, my name is Dr. Long.*
LOW: He is big and hairy with curly hair, a beard and mustache,
   His smile is warm and friendly
   I almost forget whose side he's on.
(DOCTOR-VO:) *So I hear that you haven't been sleeping.*
LOW: *(Gently shakes head.)*
(DOCTOR-VO:) *What about your appetite—are you eating?*
LOW: *(Shrugs—opens palms.)*
(DOCTOR-VO:) *How are you feeling right now?*
LOW: *(Big shrug—pause.)*
(DOCTOR-VO:) *Happy, sad, angry, nervous, anxious, irritable?*

LOW: *(Pause—thinks—begins to look around the room and touch things.)*

(DOCTOR-VO:) *Lowquesha, do you have difficulty remembering or keeping track of your thoughts?—Oh, please be careful with that.*

LOW: *(Shrugs—gently puts object down.)*

(DOCTOR-VO:) *How are things at home?*

LOW: *(Starts to walk around—arm moving.)* Okay…

(DOCTOR-VO:) *Okay like how?*

LOW: I don't know, some days it's okay, like okay and some days it's like really bad my mother can be a real bitch sometimes so can my sister Anna.

(DOCTOR-VO:) *Lowquesha, do you ever feel depressed or lethargic? Lethargic means you have very little energy….*

LOW: *(Turns and rolls eyes.)* Sometimes …

(DOCTOR-VO:) *I understand you are having problems in English right now…*

LOW: No, it's just I don't like my teacher *(Looking at picture on shelf.)* oh, is that your wife? *(Smiles.)*

(DOCTOR-VO:) *Yes, that's my wife—so why don't you like your teacher?*

LOW: Cause she don't respect me, she always be trying to put me down in front of the class, fuckin bitch.

(DOCTOR-VO:) *So yelling at your teacher makes you feel good?*

LOW: *(Quiet.)* Can I tell you the truth? It felt really good to smack her!

(DOCTOR-VO:) *What else makes you feel good?*

LOW: Rappin, you know, spitting lyrics over a beat.

(DOCTOR-VO:) *Hmm, can you give me an example?*

LOW: Public Enemy? *(Sucks teeth.)* Will Smith?

(DOCTOR-VO:) *Oh! Rapping, I got it…What else makes you feel good?*

LOW: Huh? Um, being with my boyfriend…

(DOCTOR-VO:) *Do you see him often?*

LOW: Sometimes I cut class to be with him, we…you know….

(DOCTOR-VO:) *Really?*

LOW: *(Nods.)*

(DOCTOR-VO:) *Lowquesha, I want to do some tests just to make sure, but I think I have a sense of what is going on with you and I believe that we can help you feel better.*

LOW: So I'm not in trouble?

5. Meeting Darnell

LOW: I was at my girl Shawna's
She was having a little celebration
for Junior who just got outa jail

Everybody always liked Jun from when he was little
Shawna been in love with him since the 2nd grade.

Me and Jun had a little thing
kept it on the down low tho'cause
Niggas talk too much
I wasn't in love with him or anything
I was just in a bind and he
helped me out—so I had to show my gratitude.

The house is packed, cause all his boys came through
Some from around the way, some from being on lock and some other
dudes he met when he was doing that music
thing.

The Ole E is flowing, and Jun is holding court, reminiscing.
Eventually, memory lane leads back to me.

Jun ain't crazy, Shawna would kill us both
So he ain't saying shit out loud....but I can
tell he's talking because as soon as he's done gesturing
Niggas is looking at me like, "What's up shorty?"
"And that's my word," was all you heard him say.

Now, one of the music ballers is giving me the extra eye
He's rocking a cobalt blue leather baseball jacket with a
mini afro and those sculpted sideburns that I love
Thick juicy lips, that blush red in the middle with a natural
brown outline—he licks for my benefit.
Eyes dark, lashes long, jawbone strong—just the way I like 'um
Yea, he's definitely clocking, and yea, he's definitely cute.

I find a reason to walk past, I can tell exactly when
he's gonna put his hand on my arm too,
it will be just before I get totally out of reach
Done so as not to be obvious to the other brothers
who by that time are through looking at my ass.

He doesn't say anything, just grabs on like he knows me
Then quietly releases before I blow up his spot....
I move deeper into the kitchen
then turn and give him a fly girl smile

All dem Niggas start laughing, and I hear his
name, "Yo, Darnell, pass that libation." He obliges
pretending not to feel me looking—but the deal has already been
inked, as my man Dinero would say..........

Three hours later we in the back of his whip
and he is handling his business
No small talk, no profiling, no pretending
just straight up—"let's do this"
I'm feeling good, cause it's nice to be
wit a guy who knows what he's doing
Things are getting freakier by the minute
But that's all right with me...cause I know
just how to play it....

I let him start to feel it
Let it start to get good
And then I pull away and
say—"Hold up"—he looks
like he's about to explode
"You feelin me special—or is this
just some everyday shit?
I wanna know before I let
this go any farther."

He's caught and we both
know it—cause ain't no way
he turning this down
I slowly start to pull my pants up
"Whhhoaaa Shorty, slow down
Allright, let's talk"...I smile in the dark.

6. Taking my Medicine:

LOW: You see these labels? I know them in my sleep!
And there is no fuckin way I can take all of this
shit and be normal.......

Warning! Do not take on an empty stomach. Warning! Do not take
while operating heavy machinery or driving an automobile. Warning!
Do not mix with alcohol. Warning! Do not exceed the recommended
dosage. Warning! Do not refill this prescription unless you call this
number first.

The blue ones make me dizzy, and give me tunnel vision like I've been running around with my neck up my ass. If I combine them with the round ones I get the head bobbles and really bad gas, which the square ones turn to full blown diarrhea.

If I take the round ones with the pink ones, and the squares, I get the hiccups, every thing becomes gray and fuzzy, my face twitches, and I can't get out of bed.

The green ones, make my tongue thick, make my speech slur, make my mouth overflow with saliva, when combined with the blues make me blind and jittery and I don't want any food or sex.

I take the blue ones every other day because they are really expensive and a half of pink one gives me the same effect.
I take one green a day which I cut it in half to give me two treatments.

I won't take the green ones when I see Darnell
I will take an extra blue when I deal with my mother
And I will only take a half of the round one when I go to work
I wish there was a pill that made me pretty.

7. You think you look good?

LOW: Today, is a good day
   I am staring at my reflection
   in the mirror
   I can see the mystery in my eyes
   and a subtle glow in my skin
   My breasts, my hair and my smile
   are all pleasing to me
   Today, I fully accept who I am
(LOW MEAN-VO:) *Bitch please, wasn't you just on your knees*
   Wit a knife at ya life, cause the nigga
   Didn't leave you a message, Low, you don't get it!
   He don't give a shit about you—why you stressing?
LOW: Hey! Don't start all right! Nobody's talking to you
   so shut up!
(LOW MEAN-VO:) *Low, I'm doing you a favor*
   Even though he talk a good game
   He a playa—freak what he said, I 'un care
   You betta watch what he do—is he good to you?
   Down for you? Real wit you? True?

LOW: I'm not listening to you
   I'm not listening to you
   I'm not listening to you
(LOW MEAN-VO:) *Yea, okay whatever,*
   but you ain't clever you don't even
   make him pay when he treat you like
   scum—how you let him dis you,
   lie—then dismiss you. Yo Low,
   come on! Why you actin' so dumb?
LOW: Shut up!
   You don't know what you're talking about
   Darnell does care about me
   He's just busy
(LOW MEAN-VO:) *Pretend all ya want*
   But I deal in the real
   And the real deal—is you ain't never been
   The one, beg and plead
   All you wanna, call and chase
   If you gonna—but the truth is the truth
   So, girl you can't front—
LOW: *(On cell phone:)* John—You see Darnell?
   You told him to call me right?
   Yo, Monifa dis Lowquesha
   Darnell come to class last night?
   Yo Jamal, where ya man at?
   Hey Sal, he come to work today?
   Biz, what the deal? D ain't come around your way?
(LOW MEAN-VO:) *Low, why you wasting the pretty?*
   You don't need that nigga's
   Pity, you too fly to be sittin'
   By the phone. Fuck him! Keep um guessin
   That's when he'll start sweatin, when
   He realizes you gotta life
   Of your own!

LOW: *(cell phone, continued:)* Hey Misha, seen your brother?
   Yo, bitch this is WIFEY! Betta not be runnin' wit my man!
   Darnell? Why you ain't call me? Busy?
   Doin what? And you couldn't take two seconds and call me back?
   You fuckin' up!
(LOW MEAN-VO:) *(Starts laughing.) Um Hmmmmmm*

8. High and Dry (song)

LOW: **Oooo Watch that glare! Watch that glare! Watch that glare!
Whaaat?! Peep that shine! Peep that shine! Peep that shine!
Oooo Watch that glare! Watch that glare! Watch that glare!
Whaaat?! Peep that shine! Peep that shine! Peep that shine!**

Standin in the Waldorf Astoria
In my red leather looking mighty Blaouh!
Limo pick me up at a quarter to three
Take me to the studios of MTV

Gotta interview wit Carson on TLC
Gonna talk about what? Hit number 3

Beyoncé betta watch her back
Climbing up the charts movin mighty fast
Waving to the haters—how you like me now?
Rollin wit the majors' in a drop DL
Busta Rhymes, Method Man, Nasty Nas
LL, Jay Z, Linkin Park
All want me to come lace 'dey tracks
Cause they hooked on this lyrical acrobat

**Oooo Watch that glare! Watch that glare! Watch that glare!
Whaaat?! Peep that shine! Peep that shine! Peep that shine!
Oooo Watch that glare! Watch that glare! Watch that glare!
Whaaat?! Peep that shine! Peep that shine! Peep that shine!**

Breakin all kinda records
Imma rising star
Wit' my hot butta flow
I'm raising the bar
Got a fly hook to put me on top
Crossing over to R&B and POP
Buzz so loud you can barely hear
Taking over the Grammy's this year
(kissing at her adoring fans)

(RECEPTIONIST-VO:) *Lowquesha, there you are, Dr. Green will see you now.*

9. Can I Help You?

LOW: Hi, can I take your order?

(calls over shoulder:) Yo, let me get a Grande double shot expresso wit a
shot a vanilla

(calls over other shoulder:) Mira, I need a Caramello, Frappachino extra thick wit chocolate sprinkles
No scratch that, make it an iced Grande Moca Nut Frap, extra thick wit caramel sauce

Yea, can I get a Grande Soy Chai Latte, extra hot no foam
And a Venti Vanilla Hazel Nut Roast, wit a shot a Cinnamon Dolce?

Yea, I need a Tazo Calm and a Expresso Con Panna and, make um stand tall please!

When people ask me what I do, I tell um I talk to addicts all day

Suits and ties
Wigged out college heads
Hip Hop wannabees
Constructionites
Ghetto Bougie Paris Hiltons in waiting
Thug Mugs hooked on the summer drinks
The whole rainbow.

And all of them are anxious
Stressed out-hyper excitable-high octane-withdrawal-
having-Fuckin' Fiends!

I know they never talk about this shit,
But coffee is DEEP

Yea, let me get a Marble Mocha Macchiato, Grande, wit a shot of expresso, and whip it high!

I love being on the register
and calling out the orders
I use um to practice my fast diction
Any MC worth her salt has got to be
able to spit fast and clear

When I am on the mic—I mean the register and it's really busy
I gotta represent!

Especially for them stick-up-the-ass Wall Street types

This is how I do them,

Hi, can I take your order?

"Yea, I'll have a Venezuela Sunrise, with a hint of soy, easy on the foam"

What size sir?

"Make it a Grande"

Ay yo, Felippe, lemme get a Venus Sun, smack it with a fake cow and wipe its mouth!
Oh yea, and make it a stepchild.

He's shakin' his head now cause he's sure I fucked up his order!

He's like "No, I asked for a blazzzy blah blay-blah blah blah……"

I say, "Sir, I got you…"

He's back five minutes later,

"This is not what I ordered!"

Are you sure you didn't take someone else's drink, sir?

"Get me the manager!"

My shift manager, Don, is some young up-and-coming
from Connecticut who's studying Poly Sci at NYU

He takes one look at the guy and knows exactly what happened.

Of course my man walks out with free coffee.

Hi, can I take your order?

Felippe, I need a Venti White Chocolate Mocha Latte—scratch, it's a Grande Cinnamon Dolce and a Venti Gingerbread Latte with extra foam—scratch, no foam

Don is on my ass now, cause I'm fuckin up….I promised to work a double shift today…and we're in the middle of a noon day rush.

I can hear him correcting me in the background with each order

Yo, can I get a Cinnamon Gingerbread shit! Scratch a Grande, Vanilla Latte, no, a tall Vanilla Latte and a Grande Peppermint Mocha with a shot of Java chip, sorry, with a shot of Java Chip Light and chocolate sprinkles.

It's mad busy, the line is damn near out the door, and I can see people looking at their watches, anxious, high octane withdrawal, don't wanna hear my sob story about why I can't get it right, Fiends who need their fix so they can make it through the rest of the day.

Hi, can I take your order?

"I'm sorry, so you want a Tall black coffee, a Grande Tazo Refresh, and a
Venti Soy Latte w/ extra foam?"

At the end of my first shift, Don pulls me aside.
I try to focus on the words but, after a while, I don't have to,
Something about because I can't make the coffee,
Him needing people who are versatile …..

It ain't til I'm on the train that I realize what I did.
I look in my case and the other half of my round pill is missing.

10. Have Mercy

LOW: His dick is in my mouth but I don't feel it
Feel him cause he don't give a shit about me
My head bangs against the door with every thrust
Which is every "fuck you" spelled backwards

This is why I blew up his phone
Got my hair done, put on lipstick
This is why I made Shawna lend
Me her gold blouse this is why
I made small talk with
His mother, this is just how bad
I want to go out, but we never
Made it to the restaurant, so I'm settling for drive
thru instead. He got the Big Mac,
and I am left with the Happy Meal

This is why I hound
His boys call his job befriend his sister
This is how bad I want to be
Down, in love with him lust with him
Feel more than used by him
And here he comes, spewing
Guilt, pity and relief all over
My face, rubbing in just how dirty
And desperate I am, just how fucked
Up and crazy I've been because he and I both
Know I'll be at it again tomorrow

This is why I threatened that Bitch
Told her to call me Wifey
Cause I get quality time
Yea, I got a front row seat
And he be doing me,
Just like this.

11. Slay Me

LOW: I am a piece of shit!
  A good for nothing
  Dirty cunt-butt fuck ugly
  Stupid, screwed up
  Crazy desperate bitch

  I can't keep a job
  I can keep a man
  I can't do anything

  I ain't no real MC
  I sound like shit—I can't even
  keep a menial ass job slinging coffee at
  Starbucks how the hell do I think
  I'm ever gonna be a rap star?

  Fuck it! *(Pulls knife, holds to her wrist)*

  He promised me I could have dessert
  I really wanted the crème brulé
  Why would he say he was gonna take me?
  All we did was fuck in the back of his car....
  Why would he lie like that?

12. I Don't Feel Well Today

LOW: I don't feel well today.
  And I'm just letting you know. Okay?
  Some people get offended when I say that,
  like it's about them.......
  Why some people always think it's about them?

  It's just that some days, I don't feel so good.
  And I'm trying to be considerate and let you
  know.... so that you could stay away

So that you had some warning so that you'd know, that
now might not be a good time to start no shit!

I would appreciate it if you said it to me,
cause I know what it's like not to
feel so good.........no, I do, really.

But this bitch here? Been told, but
She don't listen I be telling her

MA, I'm not feeling very well today,

I'm not feeling well, and I'm not feeling you
So can we talk about this another time?
She's still talking—running her mouth—like I didn't say anything,
following me around the house, like she don't know I'm liable
to.....MAAAA! I don't give a fuck about your bag a cheese doodles
I can't remember if I ate them or not, I might have, I'm sorry, I'll buy you
a new bag tomorrow, but right now, what I really need is for me to lay
down and for you to shut the fuck up!!!!!!

She still talking, only now she's
diggin in the crates of past bullshit
like more ammunition's gonna help her cause
I always do this...blah blah, blah blah
I'm so inconsiderate, blah blah, blah blah
I swear I hate that shit, even when I'm feelin' well.
If you mad at me about something...
stick to what you mad about don't be tryin' to
build no federal case......over a fuckin' bag
a cheese doodles? Naw, for real, over a fuckin'
bag a cheese doodles!!
(Lunges at Mother, arms swinging:) UM! AK! RAT! SHT! FUTG!
(Choking her:) YOU FUCKIN BITCH! YOU FUCKIN BITCH! YOU
FUCKIN BITCH!
Now her eye is swole and her lips is bleeding
and I can hear them banging on the door....

And here I go, back in the hospital, all
because, a stupid bag of cheese doodles was
missing.......

13. Slow Motion
LOW: Ummmmmmmmmmmmmmmmmmmmmmmmmmmmm
What

Was
I
Saying?
This is drugs
This is my brain on drugs
Do you
Ever wonder
Who
Was the first
Person to ever pick
Their nose?
Everybody does it now
But who
Was
The
First?

I bet
It was
A man

Cause they
Are always
Digging
And
Fiddling
With
Themselves
At the
Most
Inappropriate
Times

He must
Have
Done
It
In
Public

So
That
Everyone

Could
See
And
Would
Know
Exactly
How
It
Was
Done

Either
Way
I'm
Just
Happy
That
In times
Like
This
I
Can
Have
Something
To
Do.

14. Hail Mary

LOW: *(On cell phone:)* Hello Mommie...
   I'm coming home
   They just released me
   I don't have my keys so I just want
   to make sure you'll be there
   And I'm really hungry ...can you make
   me some chicken with rice and beans?
(MOMMIE-VO:) *I just get off the phone with Dr. Green*
   He say you getting worse,
   You always been strong willed Low
   You do what you please
   It's just too much
LOW: What are you saying to me Ma?

(MOMMIE-VO:) *I don't know all about this what he's saying*
   All of the time we fighting
   I don't know where I go wrong with you
   Look at your sister, she doing good
   Even though she don't call me
   Or sometime say mean things that
   Hurt my feelings, she got her own life.
LOW: Mommie, what are you saying to me?
MOMMIE: *Do you know how long it take my eye to heal?*
   2 weeks I was shamed to go to work,
   3 days I stay home
   But I need the money so I go in
   You hurt me very bad Low on the inside
   I don't feel to trust you
   I'm not sure I can take care of you
LOW: Stop talking crazy....you're scaring me!
(MOMMIE-VO:) *(Silence.)*
LOW: Mommie, I'm hanging up the phone
   right now, and I'm coming home!
(MOMMIE-VO:) *I pack up your things and*
   Give them to your friend Shawna down the hall
   I won't be here so don't ring the bell
   And don't ask Hector because I tell
   Him not to let you in.
   I can't take care of you anymore
LOW: Mommie, where am I supposed to go?! Listen, I'm sorry I hit you
   but you wouldn't leave me alone. And I'm sorry I just yelled at you.
   Mommie, please don't do this...I promise I won't argue with you anymore
(MOMMIE-VO:) *I hang up now*

15. Low Freestyle-Battle Song
LOW: *Battle song*
   I'm getting my battle on
   When things go wrong
   I get my battle on.....

(Verse:)
   High steppers
   Come on get ya weapons
   We 'bout to do this shit
   For go-getters

We 'bout to catch wreck
From trend setters
I'm getting
The fuck outta dodge
Before I wet her
You got hell real quick
For killing ya moms
Word to the Bible
It's all about survival

How you gonna dis me
Over cheese doodles?
How you gone dismiss me
After all we been through?
Just goes to show
That blood ain't thicker
Nothing
Curb ya own daughter
Now she gots to rough it

These streets is mean
So I gots to be tougher
I usta love her now
Fuck my mother!!

Kicked me out
To fend for- my- self
Kicked me out
Even though I need help

She broke my heart
But I can't fall apart
Word to the Bible
It's all about survival

Battle song
I'm getting my Battle on
When things go wrong
I get my Battle on
Battle on:

16. On the Down Low

LOW: I am dreaming of
  A beautiful bathroom
  It has a Jacuzzi

And lots of Hollywood
Star lights around the mirrors
The porcelain belly of each sink gleams
and my image is reflected in the chrome fixtures

I am sitting on the toilet
I have had a full night
Of wine and food and people
My belly is full and all it
Wants to do is release.....ssssssssssssssssss

My first night on the street
I had this dream
And peed all over myself
I didn't even realize it
Until the morning
Buried beneath the cardboard
Wooden crates and tarmac
The dumpster's charity
Made me invisible
And I took my very last pink pill
So I could sleep.....

The pavement's chill
Seeped into my bones
And I woke up
Wet and frozen

I need to change
I ain't got a lotta shit with me,
Just another pair of pants
A shirt and two panties
I figured that wherever I wound
Up, I'd be able to rinse out my bra and socks.

McDonalds doesn't open til 7am
And their public bathroom is disgusting
I stay crouched beneath the dumpster
Cause I don't want no trouble
Try not to think about
How foul this is
How nasty my skin feels
How badly I smell

Trying to imagine myself
Back in that bathroom
I peel off my clothes
And step into the Jacuzzi
The water is warm and smells
Of rose and lavender
I am washing my hair
And it feels soo good
WHITE GUY: *Hey, get the fuck outta there!*
LOW: Some white guy's yellin' at me
  in a dingy burgundy shirt
WHITE GUY: *Oh shit, goddamnit—you fuckin' smell like piss*
  Get your skanky ass out of here…
LOW: I am trying to figure out how to ask him
  Um can I please use the bathroom….?
WHITE GUY: *Bitch, if you don't get the hell away from me,*
  I'm gonna fuck you up!
LOW: Please sir….I really need to.
WHITE GUY: *If I let you use the bathroom I'm gonna have to clean up after*
  you.
LOW: I shake my head, no, I'll clean, both bathrooms if you let me wash and
  get some breakfast

  He's looking around—contemplating
  if he's getting a good deal
WHITE GUY: *Tell you what, I'll let you wash and eat*
  if you clean both of the bathrooms—and suck me off.

  I step out of the Jacuzzi
  And wipe the steam from the mirror
  I look into my eyes
  I look so peaceful….

17. **Gutter**
LOW: On my fifth day in the street
  I got desperate
  I was so anxious
  My face began twitching
  Like crazy and I knew
  That the medicine was
  Almost out of my system

I had to move from the
Alley behind McDonalds
Because the manager
Told all the guys
What happened
And they would be out back
Lined up offering me
Cheese burgers and French fries to
Do it to them.

I got tired of eating
McDonalds though
I kept seeing posters
For that movie
Super Size Me
And one day
I snuck into
The theater
And watched it

Now, I'm near a vegetarian
Restaurant, but they don't
Throw as much away
Cause of all that recycling
Bullshit.

Trying to keep my mind
Off the drama I be writing
Rhymes on paper bags, pretty
Soon I'll have enough for an album
The days out here pass so slow
I had to move from out my
Neighborhood so that
People wouldn't recognize me
Funny, but when I can get into
A bathroom and stare at myself
In the mirror
I don't barely recognize me either

Mommie still hangs up
When I call her
I don't even bother with Anna

I know Shawna would take me
In if Junior wasn't there.

I can't let Darnell
See me like this
I keep trying him
But he don't never pick up
Or call me back
Pretty soon they gonna cut my phone off
And then he won't have no
way to get at me.

I been finding so many
Pennies on the ground
And the old timers, like John
Sometimes let me help
Them with the bottles

I buy soap mostly
Cause I just can't stand to stink

I try not to look
Too dirty which is
A sure fire way to get
The cops on your ass

One of them is already trackin'
I think he knows about my
Mickey D's hustle
But I ain't fuckin' with 5-0 like that

I been thinking about checking
Myself in—but I gotta wait till
Shit gets really bad, cause
Otherwise they put you
In the dungeon at county and make you wait
For a bed.

I had a friend who got put there
And woke up with some dude
On top of her—she spent the next
3 days runnin' from his ass

I don't know if I can fuck wit
County.

I'll just have to wait
Til I feel the shit coming on and fall through
The door
This way they gotta take
Me……...

18. Red Dragon

LOW: I am sitting on the train on my way to see Anna
I am sitting across from this well dressed man
who is eyeing me

He is probably a very nice man
who is really concerned

But I don't like the look on his face

You think you know me?!

You make assumptions about my life
And go, "Wow, isn't that
interesting?"

You think your pity
is something I need
to be normal, okay, acceptable

While you watch me
while I sit here
with my guts hanging out

While you watch me
while I sit here
pointing to all the sore spots

Don't feel bad for me
don't feel shame for me
do not even remotely
think you understand

Because while you are nursing
your bleeding heart, motherfucker

I'm going flying!

On the back of a red dragon
Whipping through the flames

Of this cruel world
Laughing my ass off

I am above all of this
Lifted out of
My misery instantly
And on a daily

All I gotta do is
Say the word
And I got a ticket to
Ride

I am moving
Way too fast for
Any of this shit to matter

Feel the tough scales between my legs
Hear the snarl and grunt of this beast
Edging on the galaxy with a Ya! Ya! Ya!

I go faster, faster, and faster
Until I am a blur to you
Something you can't even
Make out in the distance

Whizzing past purple planets
And indigo people burning
Medicinal herbs to help
Me remember
Who I am
Who I was
Before all of this

My soul fills the air
My conviction rises to
The roof of my mouth
Fantasies surround me in
Technicolor screaming
Pick Me! Pick Me!
I will make you Happy!

I am soaring so high
Looping, diving, swerving

Spinning so fast
My path is invincible
My mouth is open
Wide and I am catching
Stars between my teeth

Then spitting them back
Into the sky like Pu-Pow! Pu-Pow!
And I am making
My original sound
Orchestrated by
The Tango of heart and lungs
Brewed in the fire of my belly

My spirit marinates
In the swirl of it all

Oh I wish you could see what
I see when I get way up high

You wouldn't be so quick
To judge me with your sorrow.

Cause I can leave this place
Like that *(snaps fingers)*
Anytime I please.

19. Small Talk

LOW: I don't do Manhattan
   unless I'm clocking paper.
   And since my money and circumstances
   is really strange right now
   I am definitely not trying to be here
   I walk past tinted windows
   eyeing knuckleheads behind velvet
   ropes that draw color lines
   on their own people
   (Enters restaurant and sits down.)

You've come a long way Sis
from extension cords and
sweet potatoes
You rockin' a full length leather
got your hair straightened

pulled back and wound up tight
I can tell you been fucking a White boy
you don't even need to say it
Did he teach you how to hold your nose like that—in the air?
I am clearly riding your coattails tonight.

Mommie would lay down and die
if she knew, but she ain't seen you either
Maybe that's why she's trippin'
ANNA: *Order anything you want...it's on me*
LOW: I wanna say "fuck you" as
    I sit there trying not to look homeless
    I want to show some form of dignity
    While you wave your perfectly manicured
    hand in the air golden bangles dance
    and I think of our childhood playgrounds
    and hoola hoops.

What the fuck happened to me?
Yo, what the fuck happened to you?
I will sit here for the next hour and try not
to wolf this meal down, the most I have had in
over three days. I will excuse myself now and go to
the bathroom so I can wash my ass surrounded by
ceramic tile and scented candles...I will pretend that
all this shit is mine until I return to the table
and see your pity being served then you will
open your mouth to get your conscience out of
the way.
ANNA: *Listen, it's just not a good time for me,*
    things are hectic at work, I'm up for a promotion,
    and I'm really tryin' to focus right now, you know?
    I'm sorry Mommie kicked you out, I know she can be
    A real bitch sometimes, can't you stay with Shawna
    till she calms down?
    (Whispering:) *Listen, don't look at me*
    like that! Nobody told you to hit her,
    you promised all of us you'd take your
    medicine.
LOW: I watch her lip curl
    Peep those fangs

and realize ain't a damn
thing changed.

I will not cry in this
stuck up-fucked up restaurant
Where everybody smiles and
rattles off reasons why the world
should suck their dick

And they have no idea
how dumb they really
look to people like me.

I will not be a homeless
crazy bitch who's been
dissed by her sister
At least not until I get back to Brooklyn
Where I can be assed out on my own
terms.

This chicken is cooked just how
I like it: extra-crispy on the outside
but real tender on the in
And the potatoes are whipped
with garlic and butter
it all tastes so good
and right now all I wanna do
is forget about how bad
I feel and just pretend
that we are sisters
catching up

ANNA: *Low, your face is twitching.*

LOW: Yea, it's from the stress *(touches cheek)*

ANNA: *What are you gonna do?*

LOW: I don't know *(shrug)*, I been thinking about checking myself in.

ANNA: *Will they take care of you?*

LOW: Depends, if I can get transferred out of County to a better place
    It will bide me some time, at least until I can figure out my next move

ANNA: *Here*

LOW: She reaches into her purse, leans over and shoves a $100 bill into my
    palm. I sit there, and for the first time in seven days I feel safe enough to
    cry.

20. Somebody Fuck Wit You

PETEY: *SOMEBODY FUCK WIT YOU…*
Somebody fuck with you act like you Crazy!
Somebody fuck with you act like you Crazy!
Crazy! Crazy! Crazy!

LOW: That's Petey he's originally from Chicago.
He was let out of some hospital upstate when
the budget cuts happened.

He's yellin at the passing cars
because he thinks they are ghosts
trying to swoop in and take his
soul.

Out here, there are generally
three kinds of people
1. The Druggies
2. The Crazies
3. And The Really Unfortunate

The Druggies are strung out, mad desperate, and can't be trusted.
I don't mess with them—unless I need weed.

The Crazies are crazy, like Petey, but they can't help it; most of um need
medicine, but can't get it. They ain't dangerous really.

The really unfortunate are good people in fucked up situations, divorce,
fire, lay-offs, evictees, that would be me.

Most of the old timers are in this last category. They may have started out
in the others, but it takes a lotta smarts to survive all those years on the
streets. You can't be living foul and expect to make it. Everybody knows
how bad the shelters can be, so we all take their chances out here.

PETEY: *Somebody Fuck With me!*

LOW: Now Petey's taking off his clothes and throwing them at the cars

PETEY: *And I went CRAZZZZZZZZZZZYYY!!!*

LOW: And there he goes running up the street—buck naked!

21. Pride

LOW: On my 21st day in the street
I stopped sleeping
The left side of my face became numb
and I had this constant sinking feeling

in the pit of my stomach
My legs and back felt like
they were on pins and needles
And somebody wouldn't stop whispering in my ear
I knew I was fucked up, but I was trying
to hold on.

Petey got beat down
a couple of nights ago.
There's a crew a kids going around
attacking homeless people
Somebody told me they
even been throwing gasoline
and setting them on fire.

John and the rest of the old timers have
gone underground until things cool down.

I didn't go with John because I knew that
once I crossed that line and entered
that world, I would be saying to myself
this is who I am now.

So it's just me and a couple a prostitute
drug fiends still up here in the alley.

I don't think I can do this anymore…..
I try to stand up but there is this racing pain
that keeps shooting up and down my legs..
I grab onto the dumpster and pull myself up.

Fuck it! I'm going in!

When you get locked up
or brought in by the police
they automatically take you to the County Hospital
and assign you a counselor
Problem is most of um,
if they really trying to do their job
don't stay long
The conditions at County is so fucked up
you got to be in really bad shape
to the point where you don't even care
So I go to the free clinic instead

The line for Psych is damn near out the door
and half of the people I can tell are out
here just like me they been drying out hoping to get rushed
into a bed, hoping and praying that the demons will swoop in
just in time so they can cut the line...

If I am belligerent they will make me wait longer
even if they think I'm symptomatic
People's personal shit is always in the mix

I am falling, slipping, sinking
Something blaring between my ears
10 fingers not enough to grip safety
But willing fingers to hold on
I'm going DOWN
Heart beat inside the soles of feet
Black gapolyghouls slither past my
Periphery they are the ghosts of foul
Shit—revisiting bad circumstances
Bearing my name
Quick shutter images, fast frame
My bullshit flies before me
Sinking dips lower, turns
Somebody's breath
Hot sa-liva mixes
Molten tones and phrases in my ear
And I can't tell if they're really here
Or in my head....just don't cut the line,
Don't cut the line, don't cut the line
Ooooooooooooaooooaoaooaoaoaaa
Aoooooooooooooooooaoooooooooaaaaa
(motions as if brushing off the demons)

All of a sudden SILENCE
I can't hear anything
Then my skin on fire being pricked
with a thousand needles—AAARAAAAAAGRH....

22. Get the Fuck Out My Face (song)
(Full scale brawl with self.)
LOW: *Hard rock enough to put a knot on your dome single-handed*
    When I go toe to toe—you know even the most masculine can't stand it

Papi Chulo think he a gansta, now you know he got slanted
And all that macho shit he was talking before
Now what? Yo, it's stranded......

ILLL—whenever I flip the lyric
ILLL—when it comes to this
"Hands on" business
ILLL—motherfucker don't you
Even try it

I'll leave you devastated, emaciated, annihilated,
Intoxicated, toxic wasted, hella frustrated,
Eat down from the beat down
To the street down
Violated.

Blaw! Rock your spot
Welcome to the school of
Hard knocks and thick plots
Fuck wit me and I'll
Help that ass to the concrete
With a big fat red dot—X marks the spot

Guess how many dogs
I drop in a week
But they too weak
To speak anymore
Blasphemy
Popped shit got smacked up nastily

If you know what's good for you
Betta stop askin me...
Stop askin me...
Stop askin me...
(Swinging wildly, falls onto the floor.)

22a. Pride (con't)

LOW: My teeth start to chatter
Arms and legs sensing beef involuntarily thrust back

Thrashing, thrashing, "back the fuck up off me, I don't care
ghosts, demons, and orderlies........"

Convulsing convulsing, convulsing, convulsing "I am being
held against my will, they are invading my house"

"GET THE FUCK OFF MY PROPERTY!!!"

Holding, holding, "get the fuck!"
spitting-spitting, buzzing buzzing

(STRETCHED-STRETCHED-STRETCHED)

I fly up into the air, soaring towards the sun
Turned blazing shimmering magnet
Lifted-way up-high-back into the SILENCE
Suspended in ……..
DROPPED falling, spinning, swirling
Down, full momentum whoosh
Turning-SLAMMED back into my body

Incredible pain
Heads blurred, faces contorted with concern
Moving in around me

I am sitting in a wheelchair in the hallway
My hands and legs are tied up.

What was I saying?

23. On Lock

LOW: I feel myself being wheeled out, put into a van and transported,
I hear them say that the other hospital is full so they're taking me to
County

I hate County

I wake up the next morning
in a room with white bare walls
on a hard-ass twin bed
My wrists are killing me
and my tongue is swollen
I feel like I have been hit by a truck

I slowly get up, moving slowly
slowly moving towards the small closet
where they have
stored the rest of my bullshit
Even my cell phone which is off now
is still in my bag.

There is a small desk with a couple
of towels neatly folded
and a tiny bar of soap *(Reaches for towel and soap.)*

I go down the hall, moving slowly
to find the bathroom
and showers
I can't wait to feel the warm
ORDERLY: *Hey! Get Back in your Room!*
LOW: Eyes flicker, try to focus on
   this massive wall moving

hands take liberties
strong arming me
back to my room

Something small inside
screams "get the fuck….."
But I can't find it.
ORDERLY: *Hey, ya not supposed to be going to the bathroom*
   by yourself—if you crack ya head—I could lose my job
   And I ain't losing my job on account of you—
   Stay right here and I'll get the nurse.
LOW: Suddenly, staying in bed seems like a much
   better idea.
   Hands, pulling on sheets
   soft Jamaican accents float
   through the air…..
NURSE: *Lowquesha, why ya pee all over yaself?!*
   Why didn' ya call me?
   Come, I have to change the bed
LOW: Lifted, coaxed gently onto the floor
   I smell ammonia
   Shuffling, shuffling
NURSE: *Hold onto the rail chile—*
   Stay along the wall
LOW: The rush of the water,
   feels so good on my skin.
   I am handed another pill.

24. Paranoia

LOW: You can't touch me can't hold me
   Don't own me, control me—never!
   Keeps my eye on the sparrow, stone cold thug
   In da marrow, beyond chemically impaired
   And I'm still spittin' arrows—
   Climbing Jacob's ladder wit rhymes badder than
   An angel, who be doped up on some ole straight and narrow
   Save the forty libation for your own situation
   Cause even in the hardest times
   I still draw power.
   Dis is about elevation to the next
   Level, combatin the demons and devils who anticipate my arrival
   I keeps it moving through the darkness, jagged edges and marshes
   Cause at the heart of the matter is always survival.

   My soul transcends the fragmented flesh of me
   And I'm ill to the nth degree but where my
   Spirit lies these earthly curses are shamanic gifts to me
   Crafty with the verbals, lyrical herbals I got the remedy
   But it's rooted in rhymes I gotta wait a few more lifetimes till humanity's
   Understanding can catch up to me.

   In the meantime, I pace padded cells dousing hells towering infernos
   With poetry. My shits episodic stronger than any narcotic
   (Struggles to stand.)
   And you best believe you ain't heard the last a me.

25. How Do You Spell Relief

RHA: This is my sister, she was diagnosed in 1998
   She's been suffering since 1972….
   It is like the plague,
   Highly contagious, and rapidly moving
   To an individual near you.

   What used to be an oddball rare occurrence
   Precipitated by blue moons and "not supposed to be
   Kissing cousins" dysfunctional family inbreeding
   Has become more common than place.
   Has the whole world gone mad?

   The modern culture has declared that
   There is no such thing as a down day, and certainly

Not more than two in a row......
So, if your ass is feeling blue, look out!

Prozac's gettin' popped like Tic Tacs
And Chicklets have had to give it up to Ritalin...
"Johnnie's got to curb his enthusiasm"
And you just laid 5 Xeroxed chapters of
"Driven to Distraction" in my lap.
As I flip through the pages I am told
That I will find you there when you are
Very clearly standing right in front of me.
"You don't understand," you say
Maybe this will help you...

Help me understand,
How to love you and remain sane.

What a funny ass word, I still ain't clear about the definition...

In more innocent times I would say they was buggin', you know trippin'
Actin' ill whatever wildin', now they are
Bi-polar, manic depressive, psychotic, schizophrenic,
Attention deficit with pathological features,
Psychopathic with borderline features,
Pre, post and currently traumatically stressed.

No longer the dusty trench-coated
Piss smelling man on the train that continues to shout
"Hallelujah" to no motherfuckin body in particular ....

My phone rings with the urgency and desperation of your situation
when most times it is all I can do not to freak....
You just "need to talk it out" you say....it is 3am in the morning.
Has the whole world gone mad?

I just want my people back...
From this modern day slave,
This spook whose been sitting by the door
Of societal protocol waiting to be served

How dare we ignore the signs,
You know the writing on the wall?
The words spelled in blood of victims

Unfortunate enough to be in the proximity of
Tightly wound rubber bands that have snapped!!

Carrying postal bags, carrying executive pink slips,
Carrying Jansport backpacks, brand new babies, freshly worn heartbreaks
And I don't love you anymores…
Pretty soon the random is not the random but
The pattern—of a patchwork society that would rather
Drug and confine…..
Than love.

Far worse than Small Pox
Tuberculosis, or Scarlet Fever this is the mental HIV
Of the new millennium, and we are surrounded
Nobody move, nobody drink the water….
Until they can assure any of us…..
That at least one of us…..
Is sane.
THE END

with Eisa Davis, Danny Hoch, Sarah Jones, and Will Power

Hip Hop Theater Wiki: a conversation
moderated by Holly Bass

It's rare that an artist realizes at the time of creation that she or he is pioneering new ground. Eisa Davis, Danny Hoch, Sarah Jones, and Will Power—four artists at the vanguard of what is called "Hip Hop Theater"—certainly didn't consider that they were spawning a new genre of performance. In fact, many of the artists who fall under this umbrella question the validity of the genre itself, while others are outspoken in their tacit rejection of it. But all of these artists share something in common: they have all given voice to the stories and truths of our lives and our generation, often working outside of established arenas. They have all maintained integrity in their field, creating works of such compelling power and grace that eventually the old-guard stages—that initially rejected their work—had no choice but to open up the gates. Necessity has always been the mother of invention. And the birth of the NYC Hip Hop Theater Festival and other similar-minded venues, festivals, and theater companies is no exception.

Now, a decade later, as the contributions of Hip Hop Theater artists in the areas of literature, drama, and pedagogy are recognized and celebrated, it's worth having a conversation about how it came to be and where it might go from here.

Holly Bass: Even now, ten years after "Hip Hop Theater" emerged as recognizable entity, folks are still obsessed with defining what is or is not Hip Hop Theater. What's the obsession with definitions? Is this necessary, fruitful, useful, harmful?

Eisa Davis: I think Hip Hop Theater has entered so many artists' aesthetics in such varying degrees that we don't need the term except when describing a

369

community we're part of or an impulse in a work that's outside of that community or a set of tools that an artist can apply experimentally. It feels like a historical marker now, just as there is/was a jazz theater or a rock and roll theater or a theater of the absurd. People still use these tactics, and our history is our present.

Sarah Jones: I think Hip Hop Theater as a label has benefits for many artists for different reasons. I have tremendous respect for my peers who self-identify as practitioners of Hip Hop Theater. I've said before that as a black woman whose work already runs the risk of being perceived, and even dismissed through a nonprogressive lens, as part of a hyphenate subgenre of "legitimate" theater (female/ethnic/urban/theater of color/spoken word theater), I'm leery of labels imposed from without. My love of Hip Hop culture notwithstanding, I'm not eager in general to affix to my work any one modifier that might restrict its fluidity and may not fully reflect the nature and varied facets of what I do.

Of course, as a member of the Hip Hop generation, I can appreciate the motivation to designate one's work as Hip Hop Theater, especially if it includes any of the four elements, or is intended to reach members of a young or "Hip Hop oriented" audience or to make theatrical use of the diversity and tradition of excellence within Hip Hop that is all but nonexistent on mainstream airwaves nowadays.

Will Power: I agree with Sarah and Eisa: who knows what the future holds? I have things in my mind that excite me and I love that feeling I get when I see something on stage that opens me up to things I didn't know could be. I look forward to continuing this process of learning and teaching—on we go!

Danny Hoch: I agree with everyone here 100 percent. I also think that one of the things we must remember is that most people (even inside Hip Hop) have a poor definition of what Hip Hop is to begin with. The mainstream sees Hip Hop in its own dictated narrow way because corporate culture defines it as narrowly as possible, and academia has its own convenient definitions. Therefore you say the word *Hip Hop* and a myriad of images come up for folks, most of which are inaccurate or incorrect. This is why I consistently try to distinguish that Hip Hop Culture, Hip Hop Generation, and Hip Hop Theater are three different things, and we can't begin to define the third if we haven't fairly explored the first two. At the same time, I'm not gonna front and deny the fact that many of us use the term "Hip Hop Theater"—knowing that many people have no idea of the spectrum or canon of Hip Hop Arts, yet we know they will come to the performances precisely because of their narrow definition of the term Hip Hop.

We will get both the people who know and the people who don't know into the theatre to see this work. That's important.

Holly: When you began this genre of work, did you have any inkling it would blow up to this extent?

Eisa: I just wanted to make something that I wanted to see, something that represented my experience, something I hadn't seen before. I didn't know anyone else was thinking in these same ways, until I wrote about Will and Sarah and Jonzi and Universes and Danny in *The Source* article. I'd seen Will (Power) and Mohammed (Bilal) with Midnight Voices, but, at the time, I considered that an experiment in music, not theater. Until I discovered what the community was doing, the concept of using Hip Hop as dramatic form was just an idea to me. I was working with Hip Hop as content, not form, and then these artists revealed to me what else could be done. As for it blowing up, who knew? I don't think Grandmaster Flash or Kool Herc ever imagined they'd be drinking Hip Hop water in 2008.

Sarah: I honestly don't know if my work really qualifies as Hip Hop Theater, or ever has. But I think the passionate commitment of the community has contributed mightily to the success of "mainstream" work, including Broadway shows from *Def Poetry Jam* to *Bridge & Tunnel* to *Passing Strange* to *In the Heights*, whether those shows fit an exact definition of Hip Hop Theater or not.

Will: No, I had no idea what this could be or what it would become. For me, my part in pioneering this whole thing, it was really a way to express myself as a young artist. My group Midnight Voices, we were trying to make it as a traditional Hip Hop group, but we were not traditional. Like Eisa said, you could see the strands of Hip Hop Theater in our live shows which featured actors, dancers, a light designer, etc. But she's right in the sense that we were (or were trying to be) a music group. At the time we didn't think of it as Hip Hop Theater or a new theatrical aesthetic until later. It's funny because we had the best live show in town, but our records on a production level couldn't match those of our peers in the area. We would burn them on the stage and they would crush us on record. We were frustrated because we wanted to be a part of the "record business." Little did we know what we were doing was supposed to be about the live, it was supposed to be about the theater.

Danny: This question lends itself to all the beef around definitions again because of the word *genre*. Agreeing with Sarah on some level, I don't think Hip Hop Theater is a genre. I think that we are all creating theater that reflects and responds to what is happening in our culture and generation. This generation is the Hip Hop Generation. There are new forms in Hip

Hop culture and in the generation, and some of them have spawned new genres. But when we talk of Hip Hop Theater as a whole, I believe that we are really talking about contemporary theater that happens to be happening during the time of one of the most influential generations of the last century (Hip Hop). Did I think it would blow up like it did? Yes, because I knew folks were hungry to hear their stories and language on stage. Theater can be a powerful affirmation of place, time, experience, and living history. The Hip Hop Generation's living history was absent from the American stage when we all started rockin our shit. So we were welcomed like water in the desert (by our audiences) and with careful intrigue (by mainstream theaters).

Holly: What do you foresee as the future of this form/genre/industry? Where would you like to see it go, if different?

Eisa: I can't see the future, thank goodness, but I know that it will bring unbelievable new talent and stories and ideas to the table. That's what young people, what artists do. I'd like to see more action art—we are in a time when we need to make some big changes to sustain life on this planet, so whatever can help us do that, and think about that, is welcome. That's a challenge I have to hold myself to as well . . .

Sarah: I'm with Eisa, I'm no Miss Cleo, but I hope Hip Hop Theater (unlike Hip Hop music in its current lyrically anemic, ringtone-centric state) will offer new insight and fresh (in the old-school sense and otherwise), intellectually and aesthetically stimulating approaches to theater.

Will: I feel the term *Hip Hop Theater* is a bit dated at this point. There was a time when it was important to define work in this way. I know when we were starting to innovate the form back in the early 1990s, several mentors of mine, such as Baraka Sele, advised us to claim and define what we were doing so that others outside the culture would not define it for us. Sister Baraka was coming from the reality of the 1960s and 1970s when many so-called jazz critics who were white and from upper-middle-class backgrounds began to be the official voice in claiming what was or was not jazz music. I took their advice. And, like Eisa said, as a tool to unite communities of color, to that extent the term is still important, I suppose. Also, it's a good way to give folks historical and cultural context for the work. I'm doing quite a bit of public speaking these days where I'll go to a university outside of urban areas, or perhaps a city in another country, places where they've never heard the term and know nothing or very little about the things that have taken place theatrically over the last ten to fifteen years. In that context, I use the time to pass along an understanding. What is happening now is that a tremendous amount of exciting new work is being produced by young and young spirited artists and finding its audience. Shows like *Passing Strange, In the Heights,* Sarah's work—it's just incredible what's going on right now. Even my own pieces—we just did *The Seven* at the La Jolla Playhouse and the amount of young people that came out, as opposed to when we did it at New York Theatre Workshop just two years ago, was astounding. The genre is finally beginning to find its audience and it is not just about a Hip Hop sensibility; but that it can be and is part of the larger picture, which is, like I said, new theatermakers creating some incredible theater.

Danny: I think that we are already seeing mainstream theater co-opt the idea of Hip Hop Theater to suit its marketing and social responsibility needs and, of course, it does a disservice to us as a generation when this co-optation prohibits our stories from being told. On one level, I see the future of Hip Hop Theater in a similar way to what happened to Hip Hop music and Hip Hop literature. Commercial and large nonprofit entities quickly recognize the depth, attraction, and marketability of Hip Hop Art. But none of these institutions have an understanding of the work, or any relationships with the community that it serves. So they either by mistake (or on purpose) begin to support artists that identify themselves as "Hip Hop" but who are either (*a*) not Hip Hop; (*b*) Hip Hop but not theater artists; (*c*) artists who serve a non-Hip Hop audience with Hip Hop Gen work; or (*d*) bad artists. Thus begins the destruction and dilution of the "form," and history repeats itself. On another level, I think that, as Hip Hop Gen Theater artists mature, those of us that can make a living creating new work and those of us that are afforded the luxury of being able to develop new work are going to continue blowing people's wigs back. But the Hip Hop commercial world has to step up and support this work if it's going to endure. We can't depend on historically whites-only-run, whites-only-subscriber theaters to support the future of Hip Hop Theater, the same way we can't look to whites-only-run record conglomerates to support the future of Hip Hop Culture. That would be absurd.

Holly Bass: I still remember the first time I heard a Hip Hop song. A schoolmate had spent the summer in New York with his older brother and he brought the vinyl record of "Rapper's Delight" back to California. It had actually already been out for close to a year, but I had never heard it (this was pre-Internet, pre-YouTube, pre–*Yo! MTV Raps*). We sat in his room and listened to it over and over. We laughed and danced, memorized each line. It was the beginning of something beautiful and new.

But the new can't stay new. What's cutting edge eventually becomes canon, or simply fades away. First-generation Hip Hop arts creators recognize that there is a fine line between preservation and ossification. Just as there is a danger in not self-defining and allowing one's work to be classified by outsiders, there is an equal danger in insisting on a fixed, unchanging codified form. Part of the beauty of Hip Hop culture—and Hip Hop Theater, in particular—has always been its fluidity, its ability to change and adapt, to grow. Personally, I've always defined Hip Hop as an organic form of urban postmodernism. Urban in that it was born out of cities and slums. Organic in that it arose naturally from young people looking for ways to express themselves and have fun. And postmodern in its approach and methods: making something out of nothing (b-boys and girls creating dance floors out of cardboard and scavenged vinyl), the belief that nothing is sacred or off-limits (i.e., DJs sampling everything from Beethoven to the Beatles), and using traditional mechanisms in nontraditional or even antithetical ways (scratching a record? turning machines into musical instruments?). Hip Hop breaks rules and blurs boundaries. And Hip Hop Theater employs all of the aesthetic possibilities of Hip Hop culture, live and direct on stage.

Growing up in multiculti, middle-class California, the concept of blurring boundaries and crossing genres was perfectly natural to me. Where I lived, the rappers danced and the dancers tagged and the DJ made the music with his (or her) mouth like Biz. We were making something from nothing, often subverting the status quo just by virtue of staying alive, let alone making ourselves heard. And, as a dancer and self-described theater geek, it was only natural that this aesthetic would find its way into my work and the work of my peers.

Who knows what the next beautiful and new thing will be? Sure, there have been new musical and performative styles since Hip Hop, but nothing has so revolutionized global culture the way Hip Hop has (and rock and roll before it). Perhaps the new youth movement won't be sound-based at all, so much as technology driven. Like my peers, I only hope that my mind and ears will still be open to receive the fresh outpourings of the next generations. And we can only hope that, in some way, our own experiments and innovations have helped further the continuum of theater arts and laid ground for what is to come.

with Fabian "Farbeon" Saucedo

Say Word! Glossary

As stated in the "Introduction," there are many Hip Hops. A few sentences cannot do justice to a 35-year history of artistic and cultural production. Please treat these introductory explanations as a way to introduce this history to readers who are encountering the work for the first time. This glossary is by no means meant to be definitive or authoritative. It is just a beginning . . .

B-Boy or **B-Girl:** Originally referring to Hip Hop dancers who may have also practiced other forms like **Rapping** or **Writing**. Now the term typically refers to breakdancers. Developed during the 1970s among African and Latin heritage youth in the West and South Bronx, "breaking" borrowed elements from such influences as Salsa, Mambo, Capoeira, tumbling, Kung-Fu and the dance moves of James Brown. Besides "breakdancing," there are other Hip Hop dance styles such as Popping, Locking or Electric Boogaloo that originated on the West Coast. Each dance form has a different history and set of aesthetics and techniques.

Break-beat: An instrumental or percussive interlude of a song that energizes the listener. Often called the "boogie down" part of the song.

Cipher: The collective circle of self-expression and, often, competition in which **B-boys, B-Girls, Emcees, Human Beatboxers**, poets, and other **Hip Hop heads** gather to create sound and movement improvisation and practice their craft.

DJ, or a disc jockey: An individual who plays recorded music in a club, on the radio, at a party, etc. In 1973, DJ Kool Herc developed a technique that would allow him to extend the break-beat (see above) by mixing back and forth between two records on two separate turntables. Today, the Hip Hop DJ must develop an arsenal of techniques that allow her or him not only to play music, but to manipulate sounds and create original soundtracks. Such skills include scratching, back-spinning, beatmatching, and beat juggling.

Emcee, aka MC: The Emcee started out as a helper to the DJ to "move the crowd" and then attained her/his own prominence. Whether hosting or rapping, Emcees engage their audiences through their use of spoken word. Emcees must master rhythm, rhyme, and delivery. Raps can be both written and/or **freestyled**.

Freestyle: The art of improvisation, creating in the moment a.k.a. "off the dome" or "off the top of the head." Practiced in all of Hip Hop arts, but most frequently referred to in **Emceeing** and **B-Boying/Girling**.

Hip Hop Head: A member of the culture; a person who participates in the performance elements of Hip Hop or engages as committed audience.

Human Beatboxing (sometimes called "Beatboxing"): The art of vocal percussion. The term "beat box" was first used to refer to electronic drum machines. Human Beatboxers create beats, rhythms and musical sounds with their lips, tongue, and voice. Though beatboxing is strongly related to Hip Hop culture, it is not limited to it and has been practiced in many cultures prior to Hip Hop. Hip Hop Beatbox artists have expanded their techniques to include other musical instruments like the didgeridoo and the harmonica.

1s and 2s: The DJ's turntables.

Rapping: The art of speaking rhythmically in time to a beat. Today, the term Rap often refers to the music that the commercial record industry labels as Hip Hop. But the technique has existed for centuries, dating back to the bards and *Griots/Djelis* (West African artists of Orature) of ancient times. Rapping can occur *a cappella* or with musical accompaniment, including human beatboxing. The term within Hip Hop culture is most frequently **Emceeing**.

Remix: The artistic process of directly citing and borrowing pre-existing materials and reworking these "samples" into new work. **Remix** is generally thought of in terms of music; but today the term **remix** can be applied to many aspects of culture. Musical remixers use audio mixing to create alternative versions of master recordings. Adding to, subtracting, or altering elements of a piece of music can make it seem as if a musical track is new, yet still connected to the past.

VJ: Video Jockey. An artist who mixes and performs visual images similar to what a DJ does with audio material.

Writing (a.k.a. Grafitti, Graf Art, Graff or Graf, Aerosol Art): The application of a writing material on a surface. Wall art has existed since pre-historic times in the forms of cave paintings. The roots of Hip Hop styled graf pre-date the birth of Hip Hop in the public art and demonstrations of both political activists and gangs of the 1960s. **Writing** specifically refers to Hip Hop's aerosol art form. The pioneers of this Hip Hop styled public visual art began with the writing of their own tags (i.e., their name in calligraphic/hieroglyphic/cursive form) and evolved to the development of entire "top-to-bottoms" (i.e., large murals that took up entire subway cars or walls of other public spaces), among many other terms and practices. Today, Hip Hop styled **Writing** can be found on public surfaces as well as celebrated in museums, art galleries, and private collections throughout the world.

Bibliography

Ankeny, Jason. 2008. *The Last Poets.* http://allmusic.com/cg/amg.dll?p=amg&sql=11:07d2vwpva92k~T1 (accessed July 1, 2008).

Baker, Houston A., Jr. 1991. "Hybridity, the Rap Race, and Pedagogy for the 1990s." *Black Music Research Journal* 11 (2): 217–28.

Bambaataa, Afrika. 1996. "Interview w/ Afrika Bambaataa: Hip Hop's Ambassador." Interview by Davey D, September. http://www.daveyd.com/interviewbambaataa96.html (accessed June 10, 2008).

Banks, Daniel. 2008. "The Agenda of Hip Hop Theatre?" Panel discussion at Tisch School of the Arts, New York University. March 12, 2008. Unpublished manuscript.

Bass, Holly. 1999. "Blowing Up the Set: What Happens When the Pulse of Hip-hop Shakes Up the Traditional Stage?" *American Theatre,* November.

Benston, Kimberley. 2000. *Performing Blackness: Enactments of African-American Modernism.* London: Routledge.

Boyd, Todd. 2003. *The New H.N.I.C.: The Death of Civil Rights and the Reign of Hip Hop.* New York: New York University Press.

Burnham, Linda Frye. 2005. "A Place in the Sun: Report on the 2005 Ensemble Theater Festival." *American Theatre,* September.

Byrne, Rhonda. 2006. *The Secret.* DVD. Directed by D. Heriot. Produced by P. T. Productions and N. N. Australia. Warner Bros. Digital Distribution.

Chalfant, Henry. 2006. *From Mambo to Hip Hop.* DVD. Directed by H. Chalfant. Produced by E. Martinez and S. Zeitlin. City Lore.

Chang, Jeff. 2005. *Can't Stop, Won't Stop: A History of the Hip Hop Generation.* New York: St. Martin's.

Chang, Jeff, ed. 2006. *Total Chaos: The Art and Aesthetics of Hip Hop.* New York: Basic Civitas.

Davidson, Tamara. 2008. Email communication with the author. July 21.

Davis, Eisa. 2000. "Hip Hop Theater: The New Underground." *The Source,* March, 172–76.

Decker, Jeffrey Louis. 1993. "The State of Rap: Time and Place in Hip Hop National-ism." *Social Text* 34: 53–84.

Du Bois, W. E. B. 1926. "Krigwa Players Little Negro Theatre." *Crisis,* July, 134–36.

Flores, Juan. 2000. *From Bomba to Hip-Hop: Puerto Rican Culture and Latino Iden-tity.* New York: Columbia University Press.

Forman, Murray, and Mark Anthony Neal, eds. 2004. *That's the Joint: The Hip Hop Studies Reader.* New York: Routledge.

Fricke, Jim, and Charlie Ahearn, eds. 2002. *Yes Yes Y'All: The Experience Music Project Oral History of Hip-Hop's First Decade.* New York: De Capo.

Geertz, Clifford. 2000. *The Interpretation of Cultures.* New York: Basic Books.

George, Nelson. 1998. *Hip Hop America.* New York: Penguin.

Glissant, Edouard. 1989. *Caribbean Discourse: Selected Essays.* Charlottesville: Uni-versity Press of Virginia.

Hale, Thomas. 1998. *Griots and Griottes: Masters of Words and Music.* Bloomington: Indiana University Press.

Harrison, Paul Carter. 1972. *The Drama of Nommo: Black Theater in the African Con-tinuum.* New York: Grove.

Harrison, Paul Carter, Victor Leo Walker, and Gus Edwards, eds. 2002. *Black Theatre: Ritual Performance in the African Diaspora.* Philadelphia: Temple University Press.

Hebdige, Dick. 1987. *Cut 'N' Mix.* London: Methuen.

Hoch, Danny. 2004. American Theatre. "Here We Go, Yo . . ." http://tcg.org/publications/at/Dec04/go.cfm (accessed February 27, 2007).

Hurt, Byron. 2006. *Hip-Hop: Beyond Beats & Rhymes.* Directed by B. Hurt. Media Education Foundation.

Jeffries, Eden. 2008. Email communication with the author. July 22.

Kelley, Robin D. G. 1997. *Yo' Mama's Disfunktional!* Boston: Beacon Press.

KRS-One. 2003. *Ruminations.* New York: Welcome Rain.

KRS-One. 2008. Temple of Hip Hop. "The Refinitions." http://www.templeofhiphop.org/index.php?option=com_content&task=category&sectionid=4&id=13&Itemid=28 (accessed June 10, 2008).

Leary, Joy DeGruy. 2005. *Post Traumatic Slave Syndrome: America's Legacy of Endur-ing Injury and Healing.* Portland, OR: Uptone Press.

New Federal Theatre. 2004. *NFT News.* http://www.newfederaltheatre.org/images/NFTNewsletter2004.pdf (accessed July 28, 2008).

Parks, Suzan-Lori. 1995. *The America Play and Other Works.* New York: Theatre Communications Group.

Perkins, William Eric, ed. 1996. *Science: Critical Essays on Rap Music and Hip Hop Culture.* Philadelphia: Temple University.

Powell, Catherine Tabb. 1991. "Rap Music: An Education with a Beat from the Street." *Journal of Negro Education* 60 (3): 245–59.

Power, Will. 2008. Telephone call with the editor. July 28.

Rha Goddess. 2004. "Hip Hop Theatre: Routes and Branches." Session co-led with Daniel Banks at the Black Theatre Network conference at Kent State University.

Rivera, Raquel Z. 2003. *New York Ricans from the Hip Hop Zone.* New York: Palgrave Macmillan.

Roberts, Sam. 2008. "In a Generation, Minorities May Be the U.S. Majority." *New York Times,* August 14, A1.

Ruiz, Don Miguel. 1997. *The Four Agreements.* San Rafael, CA: Amber-Allen.

Wallace, Rodrick. 1988. "A Synergism of Plagues: 'Planned Shrinkage,' Contagious Housing Destruction, and AIDS in the Bronx." *Environmental Research* 47 (1): 1–33.

Woodgett, Wanita. 2005. "Carriers of Culture: The Hip Hop Artist as Griot." Colloquium Rationale, Gallatin School of Individualized Study, New York University.

Contributors

DANIEL BANKS (volume editor) is a theater director, choreographer, educator, and dialogue facilitator who has worked internationally at such institutions as National Theatre of Uganda, the Belarussian National Drama Theatre, The Market Theatre (South Africa), La Monnaie/De Munt (Brussels), and New York Shakespeare Festival. He taught in the Department of Undergraduate Drama, Tisch School of the Arts, New York University, for thirteen years, where he founded the Hip Hop Theatre Initiative. HHTI uses Hip Hop Theater for youth empowerment and leadership training and has worked on campuses and in communities across the United States and in Ghana, South Africa, Hungary, and Mexico. In 2006, accompanied by ten NYU/HHTI students and alums, he taught at the University of Ghana–Legon under the auspices of the NYU-in-Ghana program, where, along with Ghanaian students, they led Hip Hop Theater workshops at Buduburam, the then UNHCR Liberian refugee camp, and at the Children's Christian Storehouse, an after-school arts program in Accra.

He is the recipient of the National Endowment for the Arts / Theatre Communications Group Career Development Program for Directors and holds a Ph.D. in Performance Studies from NYU. He is on the Steering Committee of Theatre Without Borders, on the Editorial Board of No Passport Press, and on the Advisory Board of the Hip Hop Education Center (NYU). Publications include "Unperforming 'Race': Strategies for Re-imagining Identity," in *A Boal Companion: Dialogues on Theatre and Cultural Politics*

(Routledge, 2006), "How Hiplife Theatre Was Born in Ghana," *American Theatre,* November 2008, and "Youth Leading Youth: Hip Hop and Hiplife Theatre in Ghana and South Africa," in *Acting Together: Performance and the Creative Transformation of Conflict,* vol. 2 (forthcoming, New Village Press). He is Co-director of DNAWORKS, an arts and service organization committed to using the arts as a catalyst for dialogue and healing, and on the faculty of the M.A. in Applied Theatre, City University of New York.

PHOTO BY ABIOLA ABRAMS.

ABIOLA ABRAMS is a writer, filmmaker, and TV personality. Abiola's debut novel *Dare* is a Hip Hop retelling of the classic German fable of *Faust.* She has hosted shows for BET, HBO, and NBC, among others. As a director, Abiola's movies investigate the themes of gender, race, and empowerment. Her plays and films have screened and been performed in theaters, museums, galleries, and festivals worldwide. The goal of all of Abiola's work is to use pop culture entertainment to create inspiration. Abiola has a BA from Sarah Lawrence and an MFA from Vermont College of Fine Arts. Her writing is also featured in anthologies by Eve Ensler, Paula Derrow, and Ellen Sussman. Please read more on her interactive site www.thegoddessfactory.com.

PHOTO COURTESY D'AMBROSE BOYD.

ZAKIYYAH ALEXANDER is a writer and actor whose plays include *Sick, The Etymology of Bird, Blurring Shine, Sweet Maladies, After the Show: A Play in Mask, Pralya, Elected, ghost,* and *(900).* She has received developmental support from the Bay Area Playwrights Festival, Rattlestick Theater, Hartford Stage, Penumbra Theatre, Providence Black Repertory Company, 24/7 Theater Company, Hip Hop Theater Festival, Vineyard Theater, Women's Project, GAle GAtes et. al, La Mama Theatre, Greenwich Street Theater, and others. Current commissions include the Humana Festival (2008 Anthology), the Philadelphia Theater Company, Second Stage Theater, and the Children's Theater Company. A graduate of the Yale School of Drama (MFA in playwriting) Zakiyyah is a native New Yorker and was raised in Brooklyn.

HOLLY BASS is a writer and multidisciplinary performance artist. She has presented her solo work at respected regional theaters and performance spaces such as the Kennedy Center (DC), the Whitney Museum (New York), and the Experience Music Project (Seattle). A Cave Canem fellow, her poems have appeared in numerous anthologies including *Callaloo*, *nocturnes (re)view*, *Role Call*, and *The Ringing Ear*. She was the first journalist to put the term *Hip Hop Theater* into print in *American Theatre* in her article "Blowing Up the Set: What Happens When the Pulse of Hip-Hop Shakes Up the Traditional Stage?" (1999). She is one of twenty artists nationwide to receive the 2008 Future Aesthetics grant from the Ford Foundation/Hip Hop Theater Festival.

CHADWICK BOSEMAN received a Jeff nomination for *Deep Azure*. Other stage writing credits include *Hieroglyphic Graffiti* and *Rhyme Deferred* (coauthor). He is the winner of the *Creative Screenwriting Magazine*'s feature-length competition for *The End Zone*, and winner in the short film competition at the Hollywood Black Film Festival for writing and directing *Blood Over a Broken Pawn*. He is a Drama League Directing Fellow and was awarded an AUDELCO Award for Best Supporting Actor in a Drama. He has guest starred and recurred in *Law & Order*, *Third Watch*, *CSI New York*, *Lincoln Heights*, *ER*, and *Cold Case* and is a series regular on the FOX-produced sci-fi thriller *Persons Unknown*. Chad starred in the Universal Pictures film *The Express*.

Plays by **EISA DAVIS** include *Bulrusher*, which was a finalist for the Pulitzer Prize in 2007 (published in *New Playwrights: The Best Plays of 2006*), *Warriors Don't Cry*, *Hip Hop Anansi*, *Angela's Mixtape*, *Secretary of Shake*, *Paper*

Armor, Six Minutes, Umkovu, and *The History of Light.* She is the winner of the Helen Merrill Award, the Whitfield Cook Award, and the John Lippmann New Frontier Award. As an actress, Eisa appeared in the Broadway rock musical *Passing Strange* as well as the Spike Lee film version, the film *Robot Stories,* and numerous television appearances. Eisa's article "Hip Hop Theatre: The New Underground" for *The Source* (2000) was one of the first mentions in print of the genre.

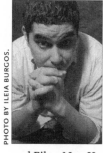

PHOTO BY ILEIA BURGOS.

KRISTOFFER DIAZ is a playwright and educator. His plays (including *The Elaborate Entrance of Chad Deity* and *Welcome To Arroyo's*) have been developed and performed at Second Stage, The Old Globe, Mixed Blood, Interact, Center Theatre Group, Victory Gardens, American Theatre Company, the Humana Festival, the Hip-Hop Theater Festival, The Lark, the Summer Play Festival, Ars Nova, South Coast Repertory, New York Stage and Film, New York University, and New Dramatists. Kristoffer is a recipient of the Jerome and Van Lier Fellowships and residencies at London's Donmar Warehouse and Chicago's Teatro Vista. He holds MFAs from New York University's Department of Dramatic Writing and Brooklyn College's Performing Arts Management program. His play, *The Elaborate Entrance of Chad Diety,* was a finalist for the 2010 Pulitzer Prize in Drama.

PHOTO BY ELI CEBELLOS.

RHA GODDESS is a performing artist, activist, and social entrepreneur. Rha's debut project, *Soulah Vibe,* received rave industry reviews. As founder and CEO of Divine Dime Entertainment, Ltd., Rha was one of the first women in Hip Hop to create, independently market, and commercially distribute her music worldwide. Her activist work includes cofounding of the Sista II Sista Freedom School for Young Women of Color, serving as the first International Spokeswoman for the Universal Zulu Nation, and creating and serving as Executive Producer of the performance movement We Got Issues! and the Hip Hop Mental Health Project. Rha is a 2008 recipient of the National Museum for Voting Rights Freedom Flame Award for her work in the field of arts and civic engagement (www.rhaworld.com).

ANTOY GRANT is a beautiful, sexy, Caribbean chameleon that can flip the script to fit the theme of any scene. Originally from Jamaica and a graduate of Texas Southern University, Antoy embraces all aspects of the entertainment business. Television and film production credits include *General Hospital, King of Queens, Law and Order, Devil's Advocate, Deconstructing Harry, Eraser, Gloria, One True Thing,* and *The Substitute 2.* Music videos include work by Wyclef Jean, Jay-Z, Super Cat, Freddy McGregor, and Ini Kamose. Antoy is also featured in magazines: *Today's Black Woman, Sister 2 Sister, Black Haircare, Scholastic,* and *Black Romance.* In 2007, Antoy created Mangoseed Productions, a full-service production company and online network based in Beverly Hills, California (www.antoygrant.com and www.mangoseedproductions.com).

JOE HERNANDEZ-KOLSKI is a Chicago-born actor / spoken word poet. A graduate of Princeton University, he has appeared twice on HBO's *Russell Simmons Presents Def Poetry.* He currently tours around the country with his performance entitled, *Refried Latino Pride.* His blend of comedy, social commentary, and personal stories attracts fans from all different backgrounds. He has opened for one of his childhood idols, John Mellencamp, and can be seen in *Hancock,* starring Will Smith. Joe's short film *Afterschool'd,* which he wrote, produced, and acted in, was one of seven finalists in NBC's Comedy Short Cuts Festival. He is proud to be one of the cofounders of Downbeat 720, the premier open stage for high school performers in Los Angeles (www.pochojoe.com).

RICKERBY HINDS is one of the most influential individuals to enter the theater world in a generation. He has the unique ability to challenge conventional notions of the stage while remaining respectful of its history and traditions. Rickerby immigrated to South Central Los Angeles at age thirteen from Honduras. He has an MFA in playwriting from UCLA's School of Theater, Film and Television, where he was twice awarded the Audrey Skirball-Kenis (ASK) Award for best play. He strives to create visionary works, including *Blackballin', One Size Fits All, Straight From Tha Underground, Keep Hedz Ringin, Dreamscape,* and *Buckworld One.* Hinds is currently Associate Professor in the Department of Theater at the University of California, Riverside.

PHOTO BY SHIRLEY MIRANDA-RODRIGUEZ.

DANNY HOCH is a world-renowned actor, playwright, and director whose plays *Pot Melting, Some People, Jails Hospitals Hip-Hop, Till The Break Of Dawn,* and *Taking Over* have garnered many awards, including two Obies, an NEA Solo Theatre Fellowship, Sundance Writers Fellowship, CalArts/Alpert Award In Theatre, and a Tennessee Williams Fellowship. His writings on Hip Hop, race, and class have appeared in *The Village Voice, New York Times, Harper's, The Nation, American Theatre,* and various books. His theater work has toured to fifty U.S. cities and fifteen countries. Danny Hoch founded the Hip-Hop Theater Festival in 2000, which has since presented scores of Hip Hop generation plays from all over the world and now appears annually in New York, Chicago, DC, and San Francisco / Oakland.

PHOTO BY DEBORAH MARCANO.

SARAH JONES is a Tony Award–winning playwright and performer. Her multicharacter, one-person show *Bridge & Tunnel* was originally produced by Meryl Streep and became a critically acclaimed, long-running hit on Broadway. Educated at Bryn Mawr College and the United Nations International School, Sarah recently returned to her UN School roots by becoming a UNICEF Goodwill Ambassador, traveling as a spokesperson on violence against children, and performing for audiences from Indonesia to Ethiopia, the Middle East, and Japan. Most recently, she was invited by First Lady Michelle Obama to perform at the White House in celebration of Women's History Month. Sarah is currently at work on a commission for Lincoln Center Theater and a television project based on her characters.

WILL POWER, an award-winning actor, rapper, play-wright, and educator, is a pioneer of Hip Hop Theater. *The Seven*, his adaptation of Aeschylus's tragedy *Seven Against Thebes*, ran off-Broadway at New York Theatre Workshop in 2006 and La Jolla Playhouse in 2008. His solo show *Flow* was featured in the 2003 Hip-Hop The-ater Festival before touring nationally and interna-tionally. Power's numerous awards include the TCG Peter Zeisler Memorial Award, a Joyce Award, a NYFA Fellowship, and two AUDELCO nominations for his solo shows, including *the Gathering: a hip hop theatre journey to the meeting places of Black men*. Power was the 2007–2008 Playwright-in-residence at the McCarter Theatre in Princeton, which resulted in *Fetch Clay, Make Man*, directed by Des McAnuff, featuring the legendary Ben Vereen. Will Power now lives in New York with his wife Maria Teyolia and their two children.

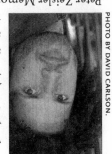

PHOTO BY DAVID CARLSON.

FABIAN "FARBEON" SAUCEDO is a community artist based out of Brooklyn, New York. Whether in the recording studio, on stage, behind the lens of a camera, or in a classroom, FARBEON is dedicated to supporting and documenting Global Hip Hop his-tory and culture in order to bring about dialogue and understanding, to fight injustice and oppression through activism and advocacy, and to pave the way for the next generation of Hip Hop ARTivists. You can find out more about his work at www.farbeon.com.

PHOTO BY JARED RODRIGUEZ.

A Bay Area native, BEN SNYDER has worked consistently as a playwright for the past several years with the Hip-Hop Theater Festival and Center Stage New York, where he also serves as Director of the Literary Department. Among his credits are *In Case You Forget* (New York Stage and Film), *You Can Clap Now* (HBO Comedy Arts Festival), and *History of the Word* (Vineyard Theater). Ben was awarded the Lucome du Nouy Playwriting Prize in 2005. Most recently he was a guest playwright with the New Africa Theatre Association (NATA) in Cape Town, South Africa. Ben currently lives and teaches in Brooklyn.

PHOTO BY ARI ISSLER.